EVERYDAY ETHICS

Making Wise Choices

in a

Complex World

2nd Edition

Everyday Ethics

Making Wise Choices
in a
Complex World

2nd Edition

Catharyn A. Baird

EthicsGamePress
Denver, Colorado
2nd Edition
2012

ETHICSGAME, PUBLISHER
6 Inverness Court East, Suite 220
Englewood, Colorado 80112
USA

TORAGAMI EAST, DESIGNER
100 S. 12th Street
Richmond, Indiana 47374

Printed & bound in the United States

EVERYDAY ETHICS:
Making Wise Choices in a Complex World

ISBN: 978-0-9831106-0-6 Softback

For educational and individual sales information,
contact EthicsGame:

888-248-6974
www.ethicsgame.com

TO MY PARENTS

who helped me frame the original question:

IS IT POSSIBLE TO BE COMPASSIONATE AND SPIRITUAL
WHILE BEING EFFECTIVE AND ETHICAL?

TO MY STUDENTS

who journeyed with me through the
thickets of learning to make
good ethical decisions.

TO *the memory of*
PRINCESS JUANA, S.J.,

the first and only woman Jesuit.

The EthicsGame Family of Learning Tools

This text is designed to be used with the EthicsGame Core Values or Hot Topics simulations, web-based ethics simulations that allow participants to assume leadership roles in a fictitious organization or company. Participants have the opportunity to solve ethical dilemmas that are typical of those facing people in management structures in the United States and around the world. These choices have both intended and unintended financial and social consequences, mirroring the sometime randomness of our lives.

The thesis of this book and the EthicsGame simulations is that the vast majority of people want to become effective ethical decision makers, but they are rarely given either the opportunity to examine their beliefs or training in how to develop their ethical skills. The pedagogy of the simulations is based on educational research that demonstrates that with imagination, thought, training, and practice, we can avoid ethical pitfalls and learn to make better decisions.

Research indicates that in order to become ethically mature, we have to integrate both ethical theory and ongoing practice in decision making. This text provides a theoretical base for a learner-focused approach to ethics and assists in practical mastery of concrete problems. The simulations are designed to imitate life by allowing participants to try unfamiliar decision making models and receive feedback—while having a bit of fun. As learners work through a series of dilemmas, they increase both their self-knowledge and their understanding of their community. In the process, each may even acquire a tad more wisdom and a carefully honed sense of what behavior is appropriate in a given situation.

The book and simulations may be used as part of a traditional undergraduate or graduate ethics class or to facilitate a company's leadership or ethics training. The Ethical Lens Inventory. can also be used to assist learners in identifying their own preferred ethical lens. This foundation helps them better understand the world of ethical plurality, where different value priorities may result in varying—and sometimes contested—courses of action.

For more information about the EthicsGame family of learning tools, please visit our website, www.ethicsgame.com.

TABLE OF CONTENTS

TABLE OF CHARTS

A Parable

A little girl was watching her mother prepare a ham for Easter dinner. As she looked on, the mother sliced both ends off of the ham before placing it in the roasting pan. "Why are you doing that?" asked the little girl.

Her mother thought for a moment and admitted, "I don't know. It's what my mother always did. Maybe you should go and ask Grandma."

The little girl found her grandma and asked, "Grammy, why did you cut the ends off of hams?"

Her grandma thought for a moment and confessed, "I don't know. It's what my mother always did. You should ask Great-Grandma."

Off went the little girl to Great-Grandma, to whom she posed the question. Great-grandma smiled and with a twinkle in her eye said, "Well, I can't speak for your mother or grandmother, but I always cut the ends off the ham so it would fit into the pan."

Preface

People have fussed over the relationship of ethics and business for as long as organizations have existed. The first person who cheated his neighbor or lied about a product triggered a conversation designed to resolve questions such as "How does our community define what is fair?" and "What is the right way to do business?" Over many years, stakeholders in for-profit and nonprofit business enterprises — owners, employees, customers, suppliers, and the community — have asked perennial questions such as:

- ❖ What is a fair price for this particular product or service?
- ❖ What is a fair wage?
- ❖ What is the proper way to treat people?
- ❖ What are the customers' responsibilities when they purchase goods or services?
- ❖ Who should bear the risk for the failure of a company or the safety of a product?
- ❖ What responsibility does this company have to the larger community and the environment?

Depending on the time, place, and society, the specific answers to the perennial questions differ. But we are often like the mother with the ham — we use the tools and understandings of the past to solve the problems of the present, sometimes without understanding why we do what we do. As technology advances and distances between our global neighbors shrink, the answers of the past are frequently inadequate. Further, because professional ethics is applied ethics, each situation has subtle nuances that require thoughtfulness. Culture and our understanding of ourselves are always in flux. Relating individual and community norms to specific business issues requires thought and discretion, because what a community or an individual accepts as an ethical result is often peculiar to that culture and time.

The upshot is that over the centuries, our understanding of what is considered fair, just, and ethical behavior in business has changed. In developed Western countries, the methods used to assure compliance with ethical norms have evolved from shunning or marginalizing someone, to an ever-changing legal system that now not only includes the opportunity for redress after injury but also seeks to prevent harm through a regulatory system. Nevertheless, whatever the system, the core questions remain the same.

On the threshold of the technological age, members of the industrialized world community ponder the implications of a global economy while confronted with the economic fallout caused by corrupt behavior at the very top of highly respected corporations. The stories that punctuate the business pages of the press as our community transitions between the 20th and 21st centuries rock the confidence of the whole community—investors, employees, and consumers. Overwhelmed by business shenanigans, people are demanding new solutions for a new era.

Participants in the American and global economies are not satisfied with "cutting off the ends of the ham" just because that is how business has made things fit for centuries. Rather, we want better ways to articulate and practice traditional values. Lacking confidence in historic approaches to business ethics, leaders are searching for new methods and constructs for evaluating problems, reasoning about appropriate solutions, and fashioning behaviors that will bring out the best in each person and organization that participate in building a thriving economy.

DISTINCTIVE FEATURES OF THIS TEXT

This text, which is designed to be used with an accompanying ethics simulation or other learner-centered approach to business ethics, provides a refreshing method for solving today's questions while accomplishing the following:

GIVES READERS THE TOOLS TO SHARPEN THEIR ETHICAL DECISION MAKING SKILLS

Children learn the fundamentals of ethics in their family and immediate community. As adults, our responsibilities increase and we need more than the rudiments of ethical decision making to be successful. We need to acquire finely-honed skills to assist us in resolving hard problems in a complex world.

This text walks through four specific approaches to evaluating ethical questions: what are our rights and responsibilities; what results do we want; what relationships are important; and what is our reputation and character. The learner-focused approach also gives us an opportunity to practice decision making using a variety of templates. As we learn to analyze issues using these four ethical frameworks, situations that were fuzzy and unintelligible will come into focus and decision making will be easier.

Addresses the emerging issues of a postmodern world

Over the past several decades, scientists and philosophers have articulated new theories about the formation of knowledge. Realizing that trying to identify core ethical principles that meet the rigors of modern scientific analysis is futile, philosophers (particularly those who study applied ethics) are coming to terms with what it means to live in a contingent world. Each person has limited knowledge; none of us can ever know all there is to know. Further, our ideas and values are personal and cultural. These individual differences are magnified in a diverse community where people embrace the beliefs of different cultures and religious teachings. Thus, universal agreement about what particular action is ethical becomes impossible.

The study and pedagogy of applied ethics, the discipline that addresses the question of how a particular person is to live in a particular community, must change its course. The search for timeless philosophical or theological foundations that promise to ground specific ethical decisions in universal principles and values is problematic. Rather, in community, people are given the opportunity to ask questions, find the best answers given limited knowledge, and act in a way that moves the community toward the greater good and the individual towards ethical maturity.

Embraces values-based management and corporate social responsibility

A key lesson learned from the scandals of the past two decades is that individuals alone cannot be responsible for the ethics of an organization. The culture of the organization itself mediates the values that are held by individuals, expected by the community, and practiced by an organization. A newly-emerging conversation considers the scope of corporate social responsibility as companies decide how best to be members of their communities. The emerging consensus is that organizations must not only meet the best interests of their shareholders, but also must consider other stakeholders (employees, consumers, suppliers) and the community as a whole as decisions are made. Today's leaders need a new set of tools to meet the expected triple bottom line—economic growth, ethical behavior, and environmental sustainability.

Explores leadership opportunities to pace progress towards ethical excellence

Organizations cannot develop and sustain an ethical culture without ethical leaders. As leaders face their personal psychological shadows, acknowledge individual weaknesses, and explore their own mixed motives for acting, they will see the problems in their company more clearly. As managers contemplate the implications of people having a mixture of honorable and suspect motives and behaviors, they will need creative strategies for encouraging organizations to be more ethical while managing the bottom line. Leaders who are able to meet both economic and ethical objectives will be able to pace the ethical development of their organization's culture and their personal quest for excellence.

As we are each part of the ongoing conversation, we have the privilege and responsibility to determine for ourselves what essential ideas of past traditions need to be brought forward and reappropriated. As we use experience and imagination to explore rights and responsibilities, choose preferred results, nurture relationships, and protect our reputation, we each can determine how best to be an individual in community while fashioning a world where all—our own and future generations—can live and thrive.

ACKNOWLEDGMENTS

This work could not have been done without the wonderful students at Regis University in Denver, Colorado. Exploring Jesuit pedagogy, with its commitment to participatory learning and justice for those without power, has informed my understanding of the obligation and opportunity for those who work in a variety of organizations to model ethical behavior in a fiscally and socially responsible manner. My students constantly challenged me to "walk the talk" and thus profoundly shaped my thinking.

I am also indebted to my friends at Regis, especially my writing partner Aimee Wheaton, who was relentless in her encouragement. My compatriots in the Colleagues in Jesuit Business Education, a consortium of faculty members from the business schools of Jesuit universities, and my colleagues in the Academy of Legal Studies in Business, buoyed me when I was floundering.

The second edition was greatly improved by conversations with those who used the first edition in their classrooms and for their research projects. Taum Dell'Armo, the copy editor, as well as Jeannine Niacaris, wielded their red pencils to make the writing crisp and intelligible. The graphic designer, Genevieve Baird, provided an exquisite layout, assuring that the complex charts are accessible to the readers. All errors are my responsibility alone.

The idea for the simulation came from my son, Thor Nelson, who remains an ardent gamer. Embracing the family vocation of teaching as an affiliate faculty member in the MBA program at Regis University, he invited me to consider how to engage today's generation of students into strategies of ethical decision making. The structure evolved in conversations with Jeannine Niacaris, a human resources expert extraordinaire who assured that the project reflected real life. As the simulation evolved over several years, I am grateful for students who provided valuable insight and critique.

My husband, Bob Russell, has been unwavering in his support—even when he scowled and told me to get my fingers flying on the computer keyboard. My daughter, Jeanne Peterson, and her husband, Lee Peterson, provided invaluable legal and financial advice, as well as research support. And finally the financial supporters, David Lincoln, Jeannine Niacaris, Erwin Trautmann, Connie Talmage, and the rest of the EthicsGame investment family, assured that the Ethics-Game project moved from a tiny seed of an idea to a company that provides ethics education to more than 200,000 learners per year.

I have been blessed in my vocation. This book is my offering to the community to further the conversation about how we all can be more effective in our work, which is an essential part of being human. As we endeavor to live out our heart's desires and provide quality goods and services at an appropriate price that enhances the world community—in short as we learn to be effective and ethical—we can provide another link in the chain of civilization.

And, perhaps, together we can make this astonishing world a little bit better.

Peace,

Catharyn A. Baird, J.D.

PART 1

THE PERENNIAL QUESTION — *How Should We Live?*

THE FOUR ETHICAL LENSES*

RATIONALITY
(reason/head)

RESPONSIBILITIES-BASED THEORIES
(DEONTOLOGICAL THEORIES)

*An ethical action is
doing one's duty and following
ethical standards of action.*

RELATIONSHIP-BASED THEORIES
(JUSTICE/SYSTEMS THEORIES)

*An ethical action is
one that will sustain integrity-
building environments.*

AUTONOMY
(individual)

EQUALITY
(community)

RESULTS-BASED THEORIES
(TELEOLOGICAL THEORIES)

*An ethical action is
one where the act creates the greatest
good for the greatest number.*

REPUTATION-BASED THEORIES
(VIRTUE THEORIES)

*An ethical action is
one that is consistent with
good character.*

SENSIBILITY
(intuition/heart)

* Adapted from Petrick and Quinn, *Management Ethics: Integrity at Work*
and Ken Wilber, *Sex Ecology, and Spirituality.*

... the world we live in,
our view of it and the values we attach to it,
is shaped by what we know.
And when what we know changes,
the world changes and with it, everything.

James Burke[1]

CHAPTER 1

Exploring Ethical Decision Making

THICS IS THE STUDY OF HOW humans are in relationship with themselves and others. With a focus on the way that our core values are translated into behaviors, the study of ethics invites us to consider both what kind of people we want to be and in what kind of community we want to live.

Ethics can be studied from various perspectives. This book falls in the category of applied ethics: how can we learn specific tools that help us as human beings make better decisions about how to be a person-in-community, one who is both an individual as well as a member of multiple groups.[2] This book is also written from what is known as a contextual worldview. This worldview invites us to look at a specific situation and determine the best way to behave in that setting.[3]

We begin our study of ethics by exploring our core values, those values that provide the rationale and the energy for our life choices. Our core values are formed from two sources: what we consider to be true about ourselves and others and what human qualities are intrinsically good or valuable. Because individual and community ideas about what is "true" and "good" vary, throughout history, people have had spirited conversations about what specific kinds of behaviors count as living out universal, or at least shared, core values—what behaviors are ethical. The conversation often has three facets.

First, what behaviors are grounded in values that are so unacceptable that one who does that act will no longer be able to be a free member of the community? For what behavior will a person be literally or symbolically "thrown off the island"? These conversations lead to sets of rules, or norms, which all members of the community are expected to follow. These rules determine whether a person can be part of a community as well as the rights and responsibilities of people, both as individuals and as members of a community.

The laws of a community tell us what behaviors are unacceptable and will result in punishment. The laws of the community provide the outside boundaries of acceptable actions; they define the sandbox in which we get to play. Sometimes we deliberately choose to violate the laws of the community in order to show that they are unjust or no longer useful. That action is called civil disobedience and should be taken thoughtfully, with full awareness of the consequences. Other times we play the edges and hope not to get caught or that the rules won't change. The study of law and compliance with the law helps us both know the rules as well as how to respond to those rules.

Second, what behaviors are exhibited by someone who is well respected in the community, a leader or ethical role model? These conversations focus on aspirational goals, directing someone to consider what values and behaviors people of high moral convictions exhibit. The expectation is that people will consider the gap between their own values and behaviors and the ones expected of well respected members of the community, and model their own behavior in light of the example of the role models.

Third, what values and behaviors do I as a member of this community expect of myself and others? This conversation forms the personal code of ethics that emerges from our own values and commitments. The degree to which this personal code, often referred to as morality, is congruent with the community ethics will determine the ease with which we fit into that particular community.

Over history, diverse communities have had widely disparate notions about what constitutes ethical or unethical behavior — what specific behavior "counts" as meeting the requirements of the community values. However, even though the specific content (what behavior is considered ethical) of the ethical standards may change, the conversation and the foundational vocabulary remains relatively constant because all communities must come to terms with how to balance the rights of individuals against the claims of the community.

When one takes a bird's eye view of the ethical landscape, a pattern emerges. Over the course of history, four different perspectives have vied for predominance based on which *values* the ethical advocate believes are the most important and which *process* is more trustworthy for prioritizing those values.

As seen by the chart on the first page of this chapter, one thread of the conversation focuses on the rights of individuals (*autonomy*) in opposition to the demands of the

EVERYDAY ETHICS: *Making Wise Choices in a Complex World*

community *(equality)*. This dialogue explores when individuals should be able to assert their prerogative to live their lives as they see fit, and when they should modify their behavior to meet the expectations and constraints of community norms.

A second thread focuses on when individual reflection and community expectations will provide the lodestar for what is right and wrong by setting predictable criteria for behavior *(rationality)*, and when our actions are appropriately guided by changing circumstances and emerging goals *(sensibility)*.[4] This conversation is heard as one school of thought advocates for consistent principles applied by all people while another school of thought focuses on developing "emotional intelligence" in order to effectively choose behaviors to build community.[5]

Each of the core ethical frameworks approaches the question about how to rightly prioritize our values differently.

- ❖ **RESPONSIBILITIES LENS** (deontological tradition with a focus on duty: emphasizes the right of individuals as sovereign agents to determine the principles that govern how they should best live.

- ❖ **RESULTS LENS** (teleological tradition with a goals focus): encourages individuals to choose goals that will make them happy in light of changing needs and desires.

- ❖ **RELATIONSHIP LENS** (deontological tradition with a justice/systems focus): determines when and how community interests should take priority over individual interests in the name of justice.

- ❖ **REPUTATION LENS** (teleological tradition with a virtue/character focus): explores how character is shaped as individuals respond to community expectations.

A HISTORICAL PERSPECTIVE

A glance at the history of ethics in the Western world shows that, from Plato forward, various ethical frameworks have come in and out of prominence in a relatively predictable sequence. Given that each of the approaches balances the excess of another, the pendulum swings as intemperate behavior in the name of one particular theory is corrected by the opposite theory coming into vogue. Current theorists advocate tempering the seeming over-emphasis of the two individual frameworks which have held sway for some two hundred years as they highlight community concerns.[6]

During the past forty years, we have seen correction within the teleological tradition. The guiding principle of utilitarianism, finding the act that will provide the greatest good for the greatest number, is being moderated as virtue ethics has moved to center stage. The current emphasis on character *(Reputation Lens)* seeks to correct the excesses of the utilitarian *(Results Lens)* frame that put the goals of the individual above the needs of the community. During the same time frame, the deontological tradition *(Responsibilities Lens)* has also been calibrated as justice theories *(Relationship Lens)* are offered to offset the perceived selfishness and isolation that comes from overemphasizing individual rights.

From the Modern to the Postmodern Era

But we're getting ahead of the story. Let's go back to the beginning of what is called the Age of Enlightenment and see how we created this kaleidoscope of opportunities and challenges that defines the 21st century. While change happens gradually, the watershed years, which moved us from what is known as the Medieval Age to the Modern Age (the Age of Reason), are the 1500s, with the growing acceptance of the scientific method as the path to knowledge and the Protestant Reformation.

The notion that emerged from the monastic laboratories was that through reason and research we could find out how the physical world worked. The scientific method was then applied to what came to be known as the social sciences. Theorists asserted that the underlying principles and rules for ethics, economics, and politics could be discovered through reason and research rather than through revelation in scripture or the precepts of tradition.

This approach to knowledge has been named The Enlightenment Project. The underlying faith in the power of science and reason led to the expectation that people and civilizations will continue to progress to perfection.[7] With the goal of human perfection in mind, philosophers and theologians set themselves to the task of identifying the universal principles that undergird all moral action. Using the tools of the Age of Reason—a scientific, rational approach—the question was whether universal ethical principles could be identified and then made the basis of human action. Put another way, the question was whether individuals, through their use of reason, could determine what was "true."

The spokesman for the deontological tradition, Immanuel Kant [1724-1804], offered what he called the categorical imperatives, which could be used to determine the universal principles to guide ethical decision making. Kant believed that after determining the principles that determined our rights and responsibilities, we would be able to choose appropriate goals for our lives.

The spokesman for the teleological tradition, John Stuart Mill [1806-1873], asserted that the goal of an excellent life was to find what course of action would result in the greatest happiness for the greatest number of people. Put another way, the question was whether individuals, through following their individual sensibilities, their hearts, could determine what was "good." Mill believed that as individuals chose what goals or ultimate ends would make them happy, we would be able to identify the core principles of ethical behavior that could guide individuals and policy makers. Conversations about which of these approaches was correct (and variations on the themes) dominated the discourse about ethics until the middle of the 20th century.

Mid-twentieth century scholars began to suspect that the project to find universal principles was going to fail. The implications of the new physics—in particular Albert Einstein's theory of relativity and Werner Heisenberg's uncertainty principle—shook the certain foundations of science. As Einstein demonstrated that everything, even time, is relative to the observer, the belief that science could provide facts that were independent of the observer faltered.

Then Heisenberg demonstrated that the very process of science was subject to bias. For example, when one conducts experiments to determine the nature of light, if one asks questions about light particles, one sees particles. However, if one asks questions about light waves, one sees waves. In other words, one sees what one seeks. Thus, everything we believe that we know is limited by the very questions we ask and the methods we use in seeking and validating the knowledge.[8]

Sociologist Peter Berger continued the conversation in the social sciences by demonstrating that every person's knowledge of reality, our convictions about what is real in our world, is constructed from our beliefs. As we walk through life, our worldview is shaped by an elegant intersection of the authorities we find persuasive, the traditions we consider important, how we learn and what we know, as well as our personal experience.[9]

At the same time that the worldview of science was shifting, the ethical limits of the Enlightenment Project were also being reached in commerce. In a pre-industrial economy, individual workers were able to negotiate prices and conditions of work, and so the ethical foundations of Kant and Mill worked relatively well. With the emergence of the industrial revolution and the creation of large corporations, the power of the individual was diluted. Many philosophers wrote about the evils of the new economic system; the name that immediately comes to mind is Karl Marx, who vilified the new captains of industry.[10]

The limits of the modern age were also seen in the political arena with the advent of Nazism and the atrocities that were committed in German WWII. Nazism was denigrated, the world turmoil resulted in the mirror of racism being held up to the people in the United States, revealing its own issues with those who were not White Anglo-Saxon Protestants. The discrimination against African-Americans, members of the Jewish community, and Catholics came into focus.

A new way of determining the "good" and the "true" needed to be articulated. Within the deontological tradition, John Rawls [1921-2002] put forward *A Theory of Justice*, which invited us to consider those without power and structure our systems to consider ways of reallocation of resources to help those who were left out of the economic mainstream. Drawing upon a broad history of a call to justice, Rawls provided a balance to the radical individualism that had emerged since the acceptance of the theories of Kant, Mill, and other Enlightenment thinkers.

The teleological response was not far behind as Alasdair MacIntyre [1929 -] reminded us of the tradition of Aristotle and virtue ethics. MacIntyre also responded to the emerging postmodern conversation by discussing how determining what was ethical begins with the belief system of the individual. He asserted, however, that the conversation about what was good and true needed to be a continuing, robust dialogue among individuals and members of the community as we continually recalibrated our living into the core virtues of justice, integrity, and courage.[11]

EMERGENCE OF POSTMODERN THOUGHT

By the mid-1900s, in response to Berger's work (and that of many other sociologists, philosophers, and linguists), a broad category of concepts named postmodernism challenged the underlying premise of the modern era: if we sought objective knowledge, we could with certainty find and verify "the truth" and determine what was "good." The promise was that by using the tools of science and rationality, what was true and good could be identified, giving people universal, and thus certain, foundations for ethical actions that would withstand the test of time.

The expectation was that these ethical truths would be obvious to people who used the same analytical processes that were based on the scientific method. What was forgotten in the search for absolute ethical principles was the difficulty of moving from the abstract to the particular, the challenges of what is called applied ethics — what one should do in a particular situation. The tools of postmodern inquiry were useful in answering this more important and practical question.

As noted by the postmodern thinkers, the understanding that individual and community questions, assumptions, and resulting beliefs shape a person and a culture posed an interesting conundrum for those who were part of the classical school of thought. If the theorists were right that the matrix from which ethical decisions arise is personal and communal, rather than universal, the Enlightenment Project of finding timeless rational foundations for all ethical action was doomed for failure.

The insight of the postmodernists was that the worldview of individuals and the community (the sum total of their beliefs) provides the foundation for understanding how to live in community, not abstract rules grounded in universal ideals. Postmodernism also provided a way out of the dead end of dualism, where every act is either "right" or "wrong," by providing a more holistic approach to life, one which legitimizes the grey shades of both/and as we seek the true and the good in the "better" and the "best."

The postmodern conversation requires that philosophers, theologians, and ethicists redefine their task. If, in fact, the rational foundations for the universal truths do not hold, the question becomes whether the appropriate quest is to seek what is ultimately true and good. The other option for ethicists (and persons-in-community who want to act ethically) is to attend to the perennial questions as they seek better answers to today's problems.

These questions have no pretense of giving us absolute answers for determining "right" or "wrong" behavior. However, carefully crafted questions can guide the discussion as well as help us clarify our beliefs and prioritize our core values while keeping us off the slippery slope of ethical relativity as we move to ethical purity.

While the broad ideas of postmodernism have been accepted, the concern is that if everyone is able to define what is ethical for one's self, all efforts at shared understanding of accepted behavior will dissipate like a wisp of cloud burned off by the sun. The question is how to acknowledge that all truth, everything that we as humans know, is contingent and always changing at the same time that we find shared understandings of how we can best live together in community. It turns out that if we continually test what we know against what we experience, we can find what is true and good.

As we live, we note that our definitions are the best that we know today and may be subject to change as we are called to higher understandings of what is ethical. As we blend the truth revealed through rationality with the good experienced in sensibility, we can find an ethical path. As we seek to act with wisdom and with love, we take the pieces of our experience that don't make sense, given what we believe, and seek more complete answers to our questions about life and the meaning of our experiences.

Postmodernism actually makes intuitive sense for those in the trenches who have to apply ethical theory to the practice of everyday life. Rather than straining to find agreed upon universal principles by which to live our lives, we can ask what particular behavior is the most ethical action in this specific situation. By using the analytical frameworks which have informed ethical thought throughout history, we can find the best possible solutions to difficult situations. The task of ethics thus changes from a preoccupation with correctly identifying the right rules to using a thoughtful iterative process for choosing the most ethical course of action.

In the process of working through a problem, we may find that two solutions are both ethical as the different frameworks emphasize different values. The traditional approach is to say that one value must take priority over the other, an either/or approach. But now we have the opportunity to harmonize the conflicting values by using a both/and approach.

For example, we believe that employers should provide a safe workplace for employees. We also believe that employees should be responsible and work to avoid injury on the job. Traditionally, when deciding whether enhanced requirements for safety should be made law, such as requiring that employers provide their employees state-of-the-art ergonomic equipment, we have tried to decide whether the value of a safe workplace (even if it will increase the cost of goods and services to the community) should be given priority over that of employees assuming the risk of injury. In that case, the value we (either as an individual or as a community) believe is most important will determine both what we do and what we will require others to do. A holistic approach would determine where employer and employee responsibility converge and from there implement a nuanced policy.

As we take responsibility for creatively solving today's problems, we are encouraged to help fashion a world that provides greater dignity to all humans and allows communities to thrive. The ethical decision-maker gets to ask, "What is the best way to approach ethical decision-making if I want to make sense of my life and continue in my quest to 'be all that [I] can be' while building a healthy community?"[12] In the process of asking questions, we can each take responsibility for the decisions we make rather than being content with having our choices validated by other people or beliefs.

As we engage in this new quest, contemporary philosophers and ethicists remind us that we construct our own lives by the way we tell our stories, contextualize our experience, and determine what is meaningful.[13] We can embrace the privilege of becoming fully functioning adults as we use our mind and imagination to make sense of our place in this world and take responsibility for our choices and actions. In the process, we develop the skills needed to become mature ethical decision makers in an emerging technological age — the ability to be effective while assuring that in the future we have a planet and community for our children.[14]

BECOMING A RESPONSIBLE ETHICAL DECISION MAKER

While the implications in theory and practice for this new way of looking at our world are not all known, the immediate question is whether all ethics boils down to radical relativity — we all get to do what we want — or whether we can identify some constraints for unrestrained individualism. A responsible inquiry-based method of resolving ethical issues does not allow us to rely only on our own unreflective personal preferences but demands that we also ask what will serve the community as a whole. History teaches that when either the community ignores the legitimate needs of individuals or when individuals abuse their prerogatives, both suffer.

The study of ethics invites us to balance the claims of individuals and the community as well as seek balance between the personal and work aspects of our own lives. In the process, we learn when to act in our own enlightened self interest and when to overcome our biases and fears to act for the good of the community. We also learn when we need to take a stand against community expectations that seemingly require us to violate our own sense of what is right. In short, we can learn how to be an ethical and effective person-in-community.[15]

The thesis of this book is that whether we call it being ethical or moral, the vast majority of us want to be good individuals and citizens. Researchers in ethics find that all of us seem to have a desire to be ethical and/or to be perceived as ethical.[16] As we look for patterns in the stories of those who have breached the ethical norms of the community, often the problem is that they may not have had either the knowledge or the skill to make effective ethical decisions. Thus, to restore confidence in our individual ability to make good decisions and to create an ethical culture, we need opportunities to stretch and move beyond our childhood understandings of ethics and become ethically mature.

One of the difficulties in an ethics text is that theorists have not agreed on the definitions of ethics and morality. One conversation flows along the autonomy-equality continuum. In common usage, an *ethical person* is one who acts from a set of ethical principles and a *moral person* is one who follows the standards of conduct expected in the community.[17]

Another interesting distinction is that *morality* defines how we as humans use our freedom and *ethics* is how we think about and reflect on the appropriate use of freedom. The conversations also distinguish between individual acts that can be considered ethical and the formation of a moral character.[18]

A second conversation flows along the rationality-sensibility continuum. As highlighted by Kant, the project for ethics was to use one's reason to determine the principles by which one should live. In the process, over two centuries the role of emotions was diminished. During the last half of the twentieth century, theorists who wished to reclaim the role of emotions in ethical decision making tended to use the term morality as distinguished from ethics. Conversations about morality highlighted factors such as caring for the other person (e.g., Nel Noddings[19]), developing our conscience (e.g. Charles Shelton[20]), or enhancing our emotional maturity (e.g. Daniel Goleman[21]).

In reality, the distinction between ethics and morality is not as tidy as portrayed in this book. However, highlighting the difference in an intentional way allows us to explore the tangle of reason and emotion that forms the matrix for our decisions, whether labeled ethical or moral.

So, while definitions of ethics and morals may be contested, for purposes of this book a distinction is made between *ethics*, which are the shared expectations for behavior in particular circumstances, and *morality*, which is our individual moral compass that lets us know what behavior we expect of ourselves and others in a particular situation.

BAIRD DECISION MODEL

One contemporary philosopher who carefully engaged the question of how to find better answers in a contingent world was Bernard Lonergan [1904-1984], a 20th century Jesuit philosopher who asked how we could be responsible agents in light of our incomplete knowledge and the uncertainty of life. Using scientific inquiry as his starting point, Lonergan noted that given everything we know is contingent, our most complete knowledge is still based on our best, current information.

Lonergan observed that as we continue to live and work in this world, we see that pieces of our knowledge and experience don't fit our existing notions about the world, leaving us with unanswered questions. Lonergan asserted that every person's core desire is to make sense of the world, to make the pieces fit, which he called our unrestricted desire to know. While his work (like that of all good philosophers) is dense, requiring much study to begin to understand all of the implications, he articulated a four-step decision-making process.

His clear method provides an excellent concept map for those seeking to be responsible while making hard choices in a complex world.[22] Drawing upon a growing body of research highlighting the importance of conscious action, I added the fifth step in the decision model to highlight the importance of reflection in the decision process. The five step process is called the *Baird Decision Model*.

Step 1: Be Attentive

The hardest part of being fully present in the world is paying attention to what is happening around us, attending to human affairs as we live in our fragile world. This is the same process as taught in Buddhist philosophy and meditation techniques called mindfulness — noticing what is happening without judgment.[23]

As we are mindful, we gain knowledge about the context of the dilemma — what is really going on this situation. Part of evaluating the context is finding out what we do not know. When we see a fact or hear an assertion, we need to check whether we can attest to that piece of data or whether we need more information. We also need to ask what information is missing, what details have been ignored, and what is not being said.

The next step of being mindful is to pay attention to the perspective of the ethical decision maker. The attention that Lonergan envisions involves not only attending to the facts and situations outside of us, but also the process of knowing ourselves, our motives and nature, inclinations and foibles—our very identity. Further, each of the four ethical lenses anticipates that the ethical decision maker will view the context from different vantage points. One might take an omniscient, bird's-eye view or focus on the very personal goals and desires of the person making the decision or view the situation through the lens of virtues required for a particular role.

Finally, being attentive requires that we carefully articulate the issue before us. This task demands that the ethical decision maker have well-developed moral sensibilities and be able to see ethical issues, even though flashing neon lights do not boldly announce their presence. Once the issue is clarified, the ethical decision maker begins to use the tools of critical thinking to resolve the problem.

Step 2: Be Intelligent

The first step of being intelligent is to identify the stakeholders present in the situation who have varying interests and expectations. Some of the stakeholders will be directly affected by the decision, so their perspectives and preferences will impact the decision. Other stakeholders will not be impacted and will become interested bystanders.

As the interests of the ethical decision maker and stakeholders are articulated, the values in tension will become evident. Ethical issues are always about competing good solutions. The crux of decision making is identifying the competing individual community values that underlie the ethical conflict.

Finally, as we choose options for action, we need to evaluate the situation carefully. The process of being intelligent requires that we use our skills of critical inquiry to determine what is accurate and trustworthy in what we see. What is the true state of affairs? What is happening around us? What is the most reliable data that we have?

In this stage of inquiry, we seek to learn the best available information about how to live well in this world. As we work through this phase, we do not refuse to see what is about us, even if the information is disquieting. From a careful read of the situation, the ethical decision maker can craft possible options for action.

Step 3: Be Reasonable

As human beings, we must judge among many good things and multiple goals. We must choose among competing values. We have the opportunity to assess the truth or falsity of another's statements as we discern for ourselves what is *true* as well as determine what we prefer, that which is *good*.

Those who do not learn to discern truth are at the mercy of the last book they read or the last polemic they heard. Being reasonable includes analyzing what will or will not work, what is or is not feasible. For this step, Lonergan invites us to move towards the greater good, to find the best result given what we know about the world and the humans who inhabit it.

Being reasonable requires that the ethical decision maker work to evaluate multiple courses of action against varying criteria for excellence, the different standards for ethical action as reflected in the four major ethical traditions. We must look carefully at all facets of the problem. Then we can explore the ramifications of action by synthesizing two or more of the ethical and moral frameworks as we determine which value(s) should be emphasized in this particular situation. The more complex the problem, the more valuable a multi-faceted and synergistic approach becomes.

STEP 4: BE RESPONSIBLE

A telling critique of many ethics classes is that we discuss endlessly without helping people learn to come to resolution. Yet, every day each of us makes a multitude of small ethical decisions. We decide among competing rights and responsibilities. We choose one set of goals over another. We decide to give up our own prerogatives (or not) in order to maintain relationships with those who are important in our lives. We consider our reputations and what is essential to us. All of these choices are ethical choices. Lonergan challenges us not to wander mindlessly through life but to be intentional and responsible as we decide what to believe and what to do.

Therefore, as we choose to act, we have the ongoing opportunity to correct for personal bias and attend to the common good, a holistic worldview that considers and balances the needs and privileges of both the one and the many. Because each of us has blind spots and tends to be selfish, the notion of ethics carries with it the expectation that we will become self-reflective and self-regulating persons who can temper our choices to correct for personal preference and cultural bias.

Being self-reflective requires that we pay attention to our motives and our actions. Each of us has the capacity to be ethical — to have our best self show up and act on our most important values. We also have the capacity to have our worst self show up, the self that can be petty and mean. As we regulate our behavior, we choose not to act from the values of our worst self, but rather have the self-discipline to do that which is right even when we don't particularly want to.

As we act responsibly, we can seek answers to our ethical conundrums that most elegantly balance the competing values in the community. For instance, the lessons of the 20th century teach emphatically that we are all connected both economically and ecologically. The phenomenon known as the butterfly effect, which states that the flutter of a butterfly's wing changes wind patterns across the globe, reminds us that the business decisions of leadership as well as ordinary people in organizations impact an entire economy, as seen by the economic implosion of 2008.

The decisions we make also affect the physical well being of our planet. Forgetting to check a battery in a detection system or choosing to use a less expensive precaution for safety can result in ecological disaster, as seen with the 2010 explosion of the BP deep water drilling platform in the Gulf of Mexico and resultant oil spill.[24] We attend to the common good by finding the decision that will benefit not only ourselves but also those around us.

STEP 5: RETURNING TO AWARENESS—A REPRISE

After going through the first four decision steps, I invite us to pause and reflect. After we act, we have an opportunity to notice again the intended and unintended results. We also get to learn about ourselves, our strengths and weaknesses. The process of continual self-awareness and self-regulation lets us see where our actions fail to match our expectations for ourselves and thus demand change. Self-discipline requires noting where we need to restrain our desires and inclinations to reach the goals we have set.

Thus, our world views intersect with each other in a lacework of fractals—seemingly random events that create exquisite patterns of life. As we move in the world, others decide what our actions mean and the context in which they want to hold the event. We need to attend to their interpretation of the event as well.

FORMATION OF BELIEF SYSTEMS

The *Baird Decision Model* also mirrors the process by which we each create our belief system, the worldview we form in childhood and modify as adults. This outlook becomes the lens through which we look at the world—our belief window. Thus, a belief system is the totality of a person's ideas.

We go through life and things happen—neutral events from which we get knowledge and experiences, the building blocks of our worldview. As we name these neutral events, we come to hold certain truths about ourselves, our community, and our work. We then interpret these events based on what we believe and know to be true. From our "truth" we make fresh choices, which give new results and additional explanations about life.

Some would argue that no event is truly neutral. Even the very act of noticing something requires judgment and evaluation. However, the mental discipline of stripping away as much as possible of our preconceived notions, which come from bias embedded in our culture and from our personal history, helps us open possibilities for recontextualizing an event and giving it a different meaning. As we see an event with fresh eyes, we can then respond differently than we may have originally anticipated.

For example, those of us who were born and raised in the United States tend to see everything first through an individualistic, free-market lens. Thus, the arrangements that Europeans make for caring for the sick and elderly do not make sense to us. Europeans, who tend to see through a communitarian, social-democratic economic lens, find our arrangements for health care similarly mystifying. If we try seeing with another lens, we as Americans may find ourselves becoming more generous than we originally thought as we distribute health care resources.

Knowing how we remember, retell, and contextualize the experiences of life (the Heisenberg principle of "when we look for light waves, we see light waves" in action) makes understanding the dynamics of the workplace much easier. If we believe that most people are out to cheat the system, what we see in the vast majority of cases is people cheating the system. If we believe that most people are basically honest, what we see as we look around are people being honest. How each of us decides what to believe is a perplexing question. What, exactly, is truth? What, exactly, is good?

PROCESS OF FORMING BELIEF SYSTEMS

The process of observation, decision, action, and reflection informs the structure of our belief system. From the moment of our birth we collect information about how we fit in the world. While our first information comes before we learn how to reason, through trial and error we learn how to see and evaluate our surroundings.

We first notice something. Then we make a decision about whether that something really exists, in the sense of whether it has an anticipated particular structure, value, or meaning. From that decision we choose a course of action. That action results in intended and unintended, anticipated and unanticipated, events. As the cycle is repeated, we form a set of beliefs about ourselves, others and our world. Our total set of beliefs is our worldview.[25]

A poignant example of the first step of the process of deciding what truly exists comes from the popular movie *A Beautiful Mind*. The main character, John Nash, suffers from paranoid-schizophrenia. At a critical point in the movie he has to determine whether his companions are real or not. He determines that they do not really exist because over the years the little girl who has been an important part of his life has never gotten older—she is perennially ten years old. Nash has to rework his belief system to reflect that his companions—both good and evil—are not real. We may not have hallucinations, but we all have beliefs that may not be grounded in truth.

Interestingly, biologists tell us that the action of the brain mirrors the philosophers' teaching about how belief systems are formed. According to Andrew Newberg, M.D., who has exhaustively studied the way the brain processes information, the first step of perception occurs when the primary receptive areas, which are dedicated to the five sensory systems, receive unprocessed data. Then the perceptions move to the association area where the data are matched with the memory and emotional centers as the brain organizes the information. The finished image only becomes accessible to the conscious mind when the image combines with memory and emotion. These steps give the image context and meaning. The final stage comes as the image is assimilated and processed through the visual association area where it is then correlated with information from other parts of the brain.[26]

Daniel Goleman's research indicates that sometimes information gets to the emotional circuitry before it goes through either the long-term or short-term memory centers. Because of variations in processing information, sometimes information is scrambled on the way to the memory centers. This scrambling may result in a person responding inappropriately to the data, such as the tragic circumstances where a father kills his child who is wandering around the house at night. The emotional center registers "unknown noise ➤ intruder ➤ danger" before the parent can note that the wanderer is a child.[27] Goleman's research reminds us that we need to pay attention to both rational and emotional data to assure that we respond properly to environmental cues.

NOTICING NEUTRAL EVENTS

The choreography is fascinating. The dance begins when we notice something happening in our world. Through our senses we apprehend a flower, a sunset, a tone of voice. Many philosophers assert that these events have no meaning in themselves: they are neutral events. Nothing that we see, hear, or feel has by itself any intrinsic meaning. All events are interpreted either through our cultural and/or personal context.

For example, the exact same event in a divergent time or an alternate place may take on a different meaning. When I survey my lawn, a dandelion is a pest to be eradicated. When my five-year old grandson brings a dandelion to his Grammy, the dandelion becomes an act of love. Same flower/weed, different context—totally new interpretation.

Because so much information is available, we only see (hear, feel, touch) that which we have named or expect to see. During the late 1800s, when publishing his seminal work on bacteria and disease, Louis Pasteur was ridiculed by the medical establishment for asserting that disease was transmitted by contaminated hands and instruments. Given that a status symbol in the medical community was how much blood was on an apron, his colleagues contended that because the microbes could not be seen they did not exist.

By demonstrating that microbes caused infection, Pasteur changed "the way we frame disease and what we can do about illness. From this point forward, disease would be framed in terms of specific living causes, an idea that was called the *germ theory of disease*." [28] The practice of medicine changed because Pasteur asked different research questions than his peers. The belief system of the medical profession was shown again to be critical "because what is done about the sick person depends on the conception of what is wrong with him or her." [29]

Those in every other profession have experienced the shift in worldview that heralded the birth of scientific medicine. Some embrace the reframing of their professions while others are skeptical. Thus, the human tendency to see only what we expect to see gets replayed in the business world as we make decisions based on what we have previously named. As one pundit says, we drive with our eyes on the rearview mirror. That is, we look for what we have seen previously; then we respond to new events based on information stored in our personal historical archives.

Task 1: See what is not expected or not named

One of the primary tasks of an attentive person is to be willing to see what is not expected or what is not named. While we may never be able to be free from our cultural understanding of the world, the act of trying to see every event as clearly as possible helps us lessen the dangers of myopia.

For example, when women began naming their experience of being treated as sexual objects in the workplace as harassment, because the culture didn't have a category called "sexual harassment on the job," their experiences were initially trivialized. However, once we knew what to see and decided that the behavior was not acceptable, people noticed occurrences of sexual harassment everywhere and began pressing for behavioral change.

The difficulty with newly named unethical behavior is that actions that are not sexual harassment may be labeled as such. The challenge is to notice what others don't see and to evaluate that particular event in light of itself and not be quick to judge in light of past labels or choices — either positive or negative.

EVERYDAY ETHICS: *Making Wise Choices in a Complex World*

Task 2: Learn to see without judgment

The second task is learning to see without judgment, with no value added. This developed ability to see events as neutral allows us to see what doesn't seem to fit or make sense, to change context quickly, and to respond to change. Newspapers are filled with tragic results that come from people not being able to change behavior when they receive new information or are confronted with a unique problem. A stark example of this pattern was seen in Virginia Tech where a gunman shot two people at a dormitory and then two and a half hours later killed 31 more, including himself, in a classroom building.[30]

The administrators were criticized for not giving the students an earlier warning of the danger. According to Charles Steger, the university's president, "administrators and police initially believed the first shooting was an isolated incident and did not see a need to close the university. He said they believed the gunman had fled the campus.'We can only make decisions based on the information you had at the time. You don't have hours to reflect on it,' he said."[31]

The President of Virginia Tech and the police had to decide whether to treat the situation as a classic domestic violence situation, where the gunman would probably flee the scene after the first incident, or escalate the warning and close down the campus, perhaps unnecessarily alarming people. As they met, the second incident exploded. Choosing a moderate path resulted in 31 extra lives lost. Sending out a bulletin warning more than two hours after the initial event was too little, too late. Should the leadership team be faulted for following conservative, established procedure? Should they have been trained to respond to the crisis at hand rather than acting from a script?

Everyone who has put in place processes and protocols for action knows the difficulty of those choices. On one hand, fidelity, faithfully following the processes and rules, is essential for uniform action and results. On the other hand, we want employees and others in our community to respond creatively to an emerging, new situation. Being trained to see an event as neutral—without inherent meaning or value—and to respond from a rich repertoire of actions tends to get better results than acting from prejudged bias or habit.

Task 3: Notice rational and emotional components

The final step in evaluating neutral events is to notice we apprehend all events in two ways: with our emotions and with our mind. The emotional response is our first indicator of danger or safety—to fight, flee, or stay for dinner. For much of modern business history, we have been told to ignore our emotions and pay attention only to our minds. The popular wisdom is that emotions are unpredictable and unstable, even though people talk about following their gut instincts.

At the end of the 20th century, psychologists began exploring the realm of the emotions, especially as they affected ethical behavior. Daniel Goleman, who coined the phrase "emotional intelligence," says that impulse is the "medium of emotion and those who are at the mercy of their impulses, who lack self-control, are morally deficient." [32]

Emerging research indicates that the ability to notice and manage our emotional response to an event is a critical skill. Those who cannot manage themselves are often unable to be ethical in their business dealings. To be ethical, one needs both the skill of self-awareness as well as self-regulation, also known as self-management: doing the right thing even when no one is watching and no one will ever notice the difference.

❖ *Noticing a neutral event*

Be Attentive: *Brian Smith had just picked up his mail, which included his fifth rejection letter. As he walked across campus he found himself wondering why he hadn't found a job. He studied hard, mastered the material, and had all the required credentials for a great job. Brian was sure that being unemployed is not his fault. There must be another problem.*

❖ *Does this event exist?*

Be Intelligent: *On his way to class, Brian stopped to talk with friends. Mike Gonzales was excited because he had just received a job offer from his first choice employer. Brian learned that Heather Black was going to start work right after graduation with the company where she interned. John was still hoping to hear from the company where he interviewed last week. Brian knew that he was as qualified as his friends, so now he knows that something is wrong with the system. After all, he is the only white male in this group and the only one without a job prospect. Being treated differently as a white male than his women and minority friends had happened before when he was waitlisted for admission to the university. Is reverse discrimination to blame for no job?*

Naming the Neutral Event

The mind, the intellect, knows and names the event and gives it being. *The Baird Decision Model*, a five step process based on a decision model advocated by Bernard Lonergan to determine how to appropriately respond to a situation, helps in the process of evaluating our belief systems.

As stated earlier, the first step is to be attentive. As we find ourselves in new situations we are given the responsibility of naming what is going on in that situation. The naming includes both the activities of the event as well as our own response to the stimuli. The gift of naming is one of the most important processes that we as humans have.

It is no mistake that in Genesis, the first book in the Jewish/Christian canon, after God created the world, Adam was instructed to name all the plants and animals. Through the gift of naming, humans were given power over all creation—and themselves. [33] Because of the power of naming, some cultures give every person a secret name so strangers do not have power over them. [34]

The second step in the decision model is to be intelligent, to use tools of critical thinking to determine what is really going on. Naming an event involves three questions: A) does this event exist; B) what are the values that are present in this event; and C) what is the meaning of this event.

The first choice is to give the event life, to determine whether or not what we see really exists. The naming is arbitrary, based on the intersection of our mind and physical being. From the moment of birth we continuously compile a personal directory of experience with corresponding judgments about those experiences. These judgments form a data bank for all we know.

Each new event becomes a version of the game "one of these things is not like the other." As we compare and contrast our current experience with previous data, we put the new experience into an existing pigeon hole, sometimes jamming it into the conceptual box to make it fit. Then we decide how to value the emerging event.

Putting a value on events is also highly personal. Based on the context in which we place the event, we evaluate an event as good or bad, useful or not useful. We also evaluate the behavior associated with the event as ethical or not ethical based on personal expectations and roles.

❖ *How should this be valued?*

Be Intelligent: As Brian mulled over his increasing anger and disappointment, he found himself wondering if his feelings of frustration were the same as those other times when he was rejected? Was this feeling good or bad? What to make of his job rejections? Should he do something? Talk with someone?

Some thrive on the adrenaline rush of excitement and chaos and so find highly challenging events good. Others prefer a much more ordered life with little risk and so embrace much more tempered events. Some also tend to see the world through the proverbial "glass half full" lens while others take a darker view of what is going on around them. Because what we seek out and how we name what happens to us depends on how we contextualize the information we have received about our world, we need to attend to our own personal biases.

The way we value events also depends on our temperament and native abilities, characteristics we have had since birth, as well as the accumulation of our life experiences. Current research indicates that who we are, both our inherited traits and our learned behaviors, is a mix of both genes and our choices and responses to life.[35]

What we call instinct is often those gifts with which we were born. Our beginning palette of skills, whether they are mental acuity, empathy, or spiritual awareness, provides the oils and pigments with which we start to paint the picture called our life.

Interestingly, research indicates that "nature can only act via nurture."[36] Our genetic inheritance can only be activated as the gifts are nurtured through the choices we make and the opportunities we have growing up. The most malleable time is when we are children. Goleman asserts that by the time we are adults where our inherited genes have predisposed us to experience our environment in certain ways, our "intelligence is like personality: mostly inherited, partly influenced by factors unique to the individual and very little affected by the family" into which we were born.[37]

Thus, a person who is born cautious with a skeptical approach to life will, without working to overcome the tendency, tend to be risk-averse and so avoid risky ventures as well as evaluate events as more intimidating than one who is born adventurous and thus embraces challenges. Because who we are is a combination of "aptitude and appetite," what we prefer influences what we choose to do and believe, which then reinforces what we prefer.[38]

We can learn to change our response to life through making a conscious choice to become more aware and walk new paths as we intentionally change our belief system and actions. We can examine the beliefs that we inherited and absorbed from our family and our community of origin and choose to retain those beliefs or substitute another set of beliefs.

The choices offered to young women born into Hispanic families provide a striking example of this dilemma. The culture and often the family teach that taking care of the family is more important than education. Young women in college who are given responsibilities for the siblings often must choose between continuing their own education (and perhaps being called selfish) or dropping out of school to care for family members (and thus sacrificing their own dreams and desires).[39]

This cycle of becoming aware of our beliefs, tracing their origins, and then choosing to retain the original belief or substitute the belief with another one continues over an entire life, not just during the first few years. If we are not aware, we mindlessly reinforce existing community and family beliefs and learned bias. If instead we discipline ourselves to see with fresh eyes, we can evaluate our world more carefully. Through mindfulness, education, and practice, change is always possible.

❖ *What is the meaning of this event?*

Be Reasonable: Brian thought about his job rejections. His parents had made it clear that he had to start supporting himself—and moving home was not an option. Then he had those student loans to pay. Brian knew that he was qualified for the job. He also knows that when he gets his foot in the door, he interviews well. He found himself wondering if the rejections were coming because he is a white male and companies are still stressing racial and gender diversity. Maybe he really doesn't have a chance!

The next decision involves giving the event meaning. What are the cause and effect relationships that are alive and well in this situation? How does this event fit within the fabric of our own lives? We all want to make sense out of our life and experience. We are often tempted to ignore events that do not seem to fit within our belief system. However, if we are attentive, we can evaluate the event and clarify our own world view, thus giving the data new meaning and enriching our belief system.

At this point, the strong tendency (which needs to be resisted) is to place the information in a context that makes our own previously developed, established, and preferred world view correct. The most important lesson to learn from this section is that without being attentive and intelligent, *we choose meanings that make us right, to validate our own preferred worldview—even when*

Everyday Ethics: *Making Wise Choices in a Complex World*

we may be wrong. Thus when we see an event — something that could be interpreted two different ways — we interpret the event to fit what we already believe to be true about the world even though a different, competing interpretation of the event would be more useful and, in the situation at hand, give us a better result.

This bias towards making our worldview correct even in the face of inconsistent data has caused untold misery in our community. One might be a Galileo who had the temerity to suggest that the world revolved around the sun and so found himself in the middle of the Inquisition or a scientist who notes that the O ring on a space shuttle needs attention and finds himself battling a culture of cutting costs rather than attending to the science — and then testifying before a Senate sub-committee.

In all of those situations, those in positions of power do not like to admit that they may be wrong — often with disastrous results.[40] We replicate that error in smaller ways in our everyday life. For example, when we have a conflict at work that could be either attributed to our misunderstanding of the situation or someone setting us up for failure, we tend to believe that someone else is responsible and we are blameless.

A person needs a great deal of integrity and discipline to interpret a problem as a flawed personal belief system. Given that the stakes are very high if we interpret the world around us incorrectly, having a worldview that is as accurate as possible is critical. Every situation, every neutral event, emerges from the intersection of at least two sets of beliefs and actions. To both acquire wisdom and be effective in our community, we must be willing to admit errors of interpretation and continually modify our beliefs.

❖ *What are earlier, similar events?*

Be Reasonable: Brian remembered being wait-listed for the university and that Mike Gonzales received the internship he had really wanted. This data confirmed the nagging thought that he continued to have: that companies were discriminating against white males — and no one really cares. Maybe he should just become a truck driver.

❖ *Deciding about the event*

Be Reasonable: Deeply discouraged, Brian almost didn't see Professor Steele walking toward him in the quad. Professor Steele stopped Brian and asked how his job search was going. After listening to Brian's tale, Professor Steele asked how many résumés Brian had submitted. Brian proudly answered twenty-five. Professor Steele explained that he worked with Mike, who sent out over one hundred résumés. Brian suddenly realized that while Mike had a job, he also had more rejections than Brian.

RESPONDING TO THE NEUTRAL EVENT

After we name the experience, we formulate a series of possible responses to the event. The options range from ignoring the stimulus to the full engagement of our mind and body. When children are little, parents quickly learn the difference between naming unidentified noise as a problem to be solved or children at play. Some parents agree the first person who notices that something is amiss with the kids has to address the situation. As intervention requires work that cannot be passed off to the other, parents become skilled in differentiating between sibling

Be Responsible: *Brian decided that he needed to end the pity party. He sent out many more résumés and found himself going on several interviews, knowing that he could choose a job that was best for him rather than worrying about not having employment. He also realized that his belief about being overlookd as a white male was only limiting him. He had always gotten ahead by working hard; finding employment required the same diligence.*

❖ A new, neutral event

Be Reflective: *As Brian worked his way through the job search process he realized that he did not have to be or play the victim role. This understanding changed his perspective both about the job hunt as well as what would be required in his new job. Now, he no longer sees himself as a victim, works hard, and is on his way to becoming a successful employee.*

bickering and emergencies that require parental involvement. In the process, children learn to become responsible for themselves and play with others.

In choosing among the options, our ideas and beliefs about ourselves as well as our dreams for the future play important roles in the selection of a preferred mode of being and acting. By using our imagination, we can begin to explore different potential choices. We can think about which results, which naturally flowing consequences from our actions, will be the best for us and fulfill our own dreams. In evaluating our action, if we are thoughtful, we will also include the possible reaction and reasons for action of the others who are involved. The final step is to consider what options will benefit those who will be affected by the choice.

The cycle begins again. Each action results in a response and another action. The results will be both anticipated and unanticipated. Because those who react to our actions will make their own choices based on their belief systems, we can never really predict what someone will do. In any event, we have new information for our belief system, information that will either confirm our worldview or require us to adjust it. The next time we act, we will make new choices about what to believe and what to do through the filter of our current belief system and the lens of our core beliefs.

SOURCES OF INFORMATION FOR BELIEF SYSTEMS

We have four sources of information for our belief systems that correspond to the four principal contextual questions that provide the foundations for the inquiry-based method of ethical decision making: reason, experience, authority, and tradition.

- ❖ Reason allows us to look within ourselves to determine whether the information we receive is accurate.

- ❖ Experience allows us to use personal action and life events as a test case for our ideas.

- ❖ Authority helps us choose whether or not to accept the ideas of others.

- ❖ Tradition helps us evaluate what others have taught as truth, both in the theory of what is true and the practice of how to be in community.

COMPONENT 1: REASON

The primary source of information about our belief system is our own personal capacity for reasoning—for evaluating and choosing what we will believe, what values are important, and then how we will act on those values and beliefs.[41] Reason is a primary source of information because we all make choices regarding what we see and how to interpret the data.

Why this choice? REASON	*How do I fit?* AUTHORITY
EXPERIENCE *What should I choose?*	TRADITION *Who am I?*

As children, we get information first through our emotions. As adults, we use complex emotional information to interpret events, what is happening to us, while using our reason to interpret the data collected from our experience.

We use reason in two ways. First, we have the *process* of reasoning itself. Learning the tools of critical thinking helps us reason more effectively. As we practice the skill of critical analysis we make better ethical decisions. Second, we have the *content* of reason, what we know and believe to be true. As we learn more about our world through study and research, we have more information available with which to make decisions.

People who did not know that the Black Plague was caused by rats carrying the disease blamed the deaths on so-called sinful people who brought down the wrath of God. Today, faced with an epidemic, science tells us the causes of the illness. We can then change behavior (such as by washing our hands) to stop the spread of disease.

Effectively using our reason is central to being a self-aware person. The gift and curse of being human is the ability to think, with the attendant responsibility of free will. To responsibly exercise our prerogatives of freedom and action, we must assess rational and emotional information. While we use authority, tradition, and experience, at the end of the day our minds determine what information we consider persuasive and what we will decide to do.

COMPONENT 2: EXPERIENCE

Wending our way through this world, we create a database of experience from which to evaluate life. As our primary goal is survival, we look at past experiences to let us know whether a particular course of action will keep us alive. This practice is useful as we learn that fire is hot and driving recklessly may endanger our lives. This tendency may be detrimental if the conditions have changed that make past action no longer valid or if we have additional skills with which to navigate the danger.

Experience helps us expand our worldview. After developing relationships with people from different religious or ethnic backgrounds, those who were previously biased may find their prejudices dissolving. People who have never been poor have a very different view of poverty after spending a day or two with someone trying to raise a family on minimum wage. People who have always been healthy have a whole new perspective after becoming sick or sitting with someone during a critical illness. Abstract concepts such as sick leave, health insurance, and co-payments become concrete when faced with a medical bill from an industrial accident.

In using our experience as a touchstone, we must be careful not to generalize all situations based on our interpretation of a prior series of events. Because of the limitations of our own experience, we may interpret an event incorrectly. For example, we may see someone making what we think is an absolutely incorrect business decision. However, with more experience or more data, we may see that the decision is, in fact, correct.

We must also be careful not to discount the experience of others. Those who came of age during the Civil Rights Movement of the 1960s have a very different experience of discrimination than those who entered the job market in a time of more equality. A pundit once said that one knows that progress is made when instead of hitting the glass ceiling at 25, women don't hit it until 35 or 40. Those who are older have to understand that the generations who follow them experience a world of equal opportunity in school and athletics, and thus may not be as passionate about "the movement" as their parents or grandparents. This experience of equal opportunity in their teens translates to an expectation of equal opportunity in employment in their twenties and thirties.

Finally, we must continuously evaluate the naming of our experience. This process can be easier if we are careful about our use of emotion-laden words. One way we socialize children is by telling them that certain actions are bad and wrong while others are good. Hitting other children is bad; sharing toys is good. Often the words come with a disapproving tone of voice or punishment, which makes us feel shame or guilt. As we become adults, we carry the emotional imprint of that early conditioning. Thus, as we decide that certain actions are "good" or "bad," we may also have an emotional response to the naming.

While this socialization is essential if children are to learn how to fit into society, as adults we have the opportunity to review our upbringing and choose for ourselves what is "good" or "bad." Sometimes evaluating a course of action without the emotional baggage of our childhood becomes easier if we name the events as "useful" or "not useful." So, deciding to always keep our promises is not only "good" because that is what we were taught, but it is also "useful" in building relationships and trust. A belief that self-assertion is "bad" because we need to be seen as modest and gentle may be "not useful" if we want to be an effective advocate for justice. Thus, we may choose to change our beliefs through experiencing ourselves as brave and strong.

If we are to become effective ethical leaders, we must be willing to see ourselves as responsible adults who use personal and corporate power wisely. If a decision we made about ourselves and our abilities is no longer useful, then we must discard it. Sometimes we have a set of failures that we attribute to our own shortcomings. Sometimes those events have nothing to do with us. In those circumstances, labeling ourselves as failures is not appropriate. Sometimes we think we are being effective using a strategy that worked for us before, even though we are no longer getting desired results. Through the continuous mindful evaluation and reevaluation of our experiences, we can set ourselves on a course for greater ethical maturity.

COMPONENT 3: AUTHORITY

Our first source of information about life comes from our parents in the first five to seven years of life. They teach us their truths of the world, including religious and political views. Their understandings of work shape what we believe is possible for us. Early on we learn what tasks are appropriate for men and women, for people of different races, and for people in "our family."

One particular family may relish eccentricities and value those who are neither pretentious nor evaluate people based on appearances. Thus, each generation of that family may recount with pride stories of their grandfather, dressed in his overalls, ready to pay cash for a car: if a person wouldn't serve him based on how he was dressed, that person didn't get the sale.

Another family may highly value living into the expectations of the community for dress and manners. Thus, one who did not dress appropriately for the situation would be chastised—and perhaps shunned—until they met the community standards. Many a parent has fought with their child over length and color of hair, kind of dress, body piercings and art. Ironically, sometimes those who were chastised by their parents for the length and unruliness of their hair some twenty years later get agitated by their child's eyebrow piercing.

As we progress through school, we are exposed to other sources of information that we might find persuasive. One of the tasks of becoming an adult is to critically consider the information we received about the world from our parents and our birth community. Over the years, we gather knowledge and consider ideas that are very different than those of our families or the communities in which we were raised.

At some point we have to evaluate whether to accept these new worldviews into our own belief system. The difficulty is that we all tend not to evaluate authorities carefully when we agree with them and to be super-critical if we disagree with the premises. Learning to listen to authorities in terms of the soundness of their information, care of reasoning, and implications for the ideas is difficult.

One strategy is to "try on" the new information and see what difference the new information or way of looking at the world would make. A colleague described his journey from a closed, Protestant community to being comfortable in a predominately Catholic environment. He found his childhood notions of the world comforting but not useful for being an aware adult in a complex world.

The old biases against Catholics that he had growing up in a blue-collar, prejudiced neighborhood were not going to be useful if he was going to teach at a Catholic university. He had to critically evaluate his belief that all Catholics needed to convert "to true Christianity" and "to be born again." He also had to decide whether what he was taught about other religions, their ethical structure and their legitimacy in the community, was true.

After study and soul searching, he "tried on" the idea that tolerance of other faith traditions made sense because none of us can really claim to have a corner on the truth. He found that the new idea supported his sense of himself and helped him be an effective teacher. That decision also opened the door to exploring the possibility of celebrating the gifts of other religious traditions. Although the full shift in understanding took time, each new instance of experiencing the value of other traditions strengthened his new worldview. After a while, the new way of thinking was habitual and he couldn't remember thinking any other way.

The change also had a bittersweet result. His children adopted his new way of thinking, taking for granted the value of religious plurality and tolerance and not placing the same value on organized religion as he did. That which was important to him was not valued by his children. Every change in beliefs results in multi-layered changes, some of which are neither foreseen nor intended.

We have three primary sources of authority that inform our belief systems and that give us plenty of new ideas to try on:

Philosophical and religious sources

For many, religion and philosophy are the most important sources of information about the world and form the foundations of "right" and "wrong." Because the United States was formed in religious diversity, we embraced the notion of separation of church and state.

From the beginning, many of the communities were tightly homogenous, and so we did not have to learn to live effectively with diversity. To honor the right of each person to choose which ideas to believe, because our ideas are precious and because we think of religion as private and business and government as public, we are reluctant to tell people about the religious views we cherish and that deeply inform our sense of self, others, and the world.[42]

Our awareness of the differences among people grows as the population of United States becomes more ethnically and religiously diverse. As the people of the West explore and increasingly embrace the religions and philosophies of the East, the illusion of agreement continues to dissolve. At the same time tensions increase as people want to reclaim some sense of grounding their personal and professional life in their religious beliefs.

A new area of study, spirituality in the workplace, has seen an explosion of books and research as people are searching for ways to integrate their deepest values with their work. Research in this area of management explores what difference our faith and longing for wholeness makes in how we do our work as well as how we treat other people. The research indicates that as we attend to our spirits, minds, and bodies, we tend to be more effective in our work as well as more content. As people increasingly demand that their work be meaningful and fulfilling, conversations about faith and religion crop up around water coolers and employee lunchrooms.

A corresponding concern about giving religion or philosophy too much preeminence in the workplace is that our faith or philosophical ideologies will impel us to a particular action that we might then force on others. Sometimes the choice has good results, such as the owners of Chick-fil-A deciding to keep their restaurants closed on Sunday to honor the Christian first day.

Other policies come from a desire to honor the sacred dignity of each human person, such as making sure privacy policies concerning Internet and computer use are the same for all employees. Other times the decisions are more problematic. We scowl when those in authority prominently display a sacred text, not so subtly implying that the successful employee is one who embraces that text, or leaders demand that all participate in specific religious services. Wisdom and discretion are needed to discern between using our beliefs appropriately to inform actions and using personal or corporate power inappropriately to impose those beliefs or requirements for action on others.

The study of ethics explores the conversation among people of different beliefs and experience to see how they come to a shared understanding about how best to live in community. The study of ethics also provides the basis for individuals and groups to assert that certain actions are appropriate or inappropriate. To fully appreciate the interplay between conversation and convention, we must remember that our faith (whether in the Absolute, the Sacred, or in humans[43]) and our philosophy provide the strongest grounding for our actions. Being aware of our own beliefs and those of others helps us negotiate the dialogue.

For example, if we disagree with someone on the authority of a particular scripture, we know that the text will not be persuasive for us in informing our belief or action. This truism is often lost. I experienced the narrowness that can come with righteous ideological purity while standing in line in the San Francisco Airport. I struck up a conversation with the gentleman in front of me and we talked of our work. When I said that I was a lawyer who taught ethics, he burst out laughing. Then he said that people didn't need to be taught ethics, they just needed to follow the Ten Commandments as written in Exodus.

When I asked about those who were neither Christian nor Jewish, his retort was that they just needed to convert. Those who hold their own faith or philosophical commitment dear would just as strongly contend that conversion to Christianity or any other belief system should not be a requirement for living in any community. And so many communities—and the United States in particular—live into the value for religious tolerance that allows people to worship and believe as they deem best.[44]

In attending to our world, we can certainly find those who share our beliefs. If we are courageous, we will also listen to those with different beliefs without demanding that they convert to our worldview. The saving grace is that often the same behavior is recommended and expected by different religious and philosophical convictions. So in the everyday world we can often agree on what to do even when we may not agree on why we are doing it.

The Enlightenment Project, the quest to ground ethical beliefs in reason rather than revelation, was envisioned as a way around the contested authority and meaning of religious texts. As Protestants and Catholics disagreed to the death about the meaning of the Bible and whose authority and interpretation was binding, the notion was that if people could use their reason to find the rules of life, we could reach a common understanding about what we should do.

In the intervening 200 or more years since Immanuel Kant wrote *A Critique of Practical Reason*,[45] which asserted through reason we can find universal foundations for ethical action, we have become more comfortable with the idea that philosophical traditions are just as contested as the religious ones.

Our philosophical beliefs are also shaped by what we understand about the nature of humans, the purpose of property, and the proper use of power. As inheritors of Cartesian dualism, the Western community has two competing notions of human beings: one is that we are all deeply flawed and thus need to be tightly managed to avoid making mistakes; the other is that we are basically good and thus as we are guided and inspired by friends and colleagues with whom we are in relationship, we can be directed to do that which is right.

We also have competing notions of property: one is that it is to be used for the good of humans; the other is that it is to be conserved for future generations. Finally we have competing notions of power: one is that people need external constraints to keep from abusing power; the other is that as we are in relationship we will learn how to use power appropriately. Each of these positions has a corresponding set of desired ethical actions that rise from differing value priorities.[46]

After centuries of debate and contemplation, no agreement on these three seminal understandings of the world is on the horizon. Philosophers have different understandings of the core questions, which often mirror the view of the theologians. So the two primary strands of dualistic ethics, deontology and teleology, contain representatives from both philosophy and theology. The postmodern twist works to move from dualism to a holistic ethical monism, sometimes named meta-ethics, or "beyond" ethics.[47] No matter which approach we find persuasive, as an individual in community, our knowledge, beliefs, and dreams continue to set the trajectory for our actions.

Social sciences

The second source of authority comes from the social sciences like economics, psychology, history, sociology, anthropology, and political theory. Through use of the scientific method borrowed from the so-called hard sciences, these disciplines explore the nature of being human, how we use property, and the use and abuse of power. Based on their underlying beliefs about the nature of humans and society (informed by theology and philosophy), scholars have put forward theories about how we behave and offered norms, or rules, for how we should live.

Each school of thought offers a description of the human condition based on its observations and experience and predicts how people will behave in the future. As with any study, the questions we ask and the emphasis we place on the data drives the conclusions. In economics, if we focus on how people who are in charge of their own destiny seem to be more proactive and productive in their work, an argument can be made for an unrestricted free market.

If we focus on how people abuse power or how those without access to financial resources may not be able to take charge of their destiny, an argument can be made for an economic system which provides resources to those without. Different ways of organizing our political life will have corresponding strengths and weaknesses. Just like theology and philosophy, the social sciences have not been able to provide any certain answers for how we should live that will satisfy all persons in varying circumstances.

Natural sciences

The natural sciences provide two important sources of information. The first is data about what "is." Medical science made tremendous gains when microscopes revealed a teeming world of microbes that profoundly affected our ideas about health. Technology put copper cabling out of business as we discovered that fiber optics were much more effective at transmitting data than copper wires. The experiments and insights of our scientists provide the building blocks of our enterprises. As we get new information about our physical world, we dream about what can be.

The hard sciences also let us know what we can know. The modern quest, informed by a Newtonian worldview, sought to understand the nature of things, to find the quintessential qualities that would be the same for all people. Scientists worked to find the physical properties of matter that were not dependent on the observer but on the nature of matter itself. However, that quest would not end satisfactorily.

As scientists began working with smaller and smaller particles, they noticed at the quantum level that the results of an experiment changed based on whether a person was watching the test as well as the conditions of observation. With inconsistent results for identical tests, scientists put forth the idea that we could never with certainty identify physical properties of matter. All of our knowledge about our world is dependent in some small way upon the observer. The promise of Newtonian physics, that we could have certainty about our physical universe, could not be kept. Rather, quantum physics must be satisfied with probabilities. Thus, the work of scientists subtly shifted.

While scientists still seek to find universal truth, they know that the structure of the world also involves uncertainty. Our understanding of the world is now colored by the fact that knowledge is contingent. As scientists are always bringing forth new information and data, we cannot definitively know the unchanging *nature* of the world. We can only know its current *state*—our best understanding of its condition right now.[48]

COMPONENT 4: TRADITION

Culture is transmitted from generation to generation as we adopt the traditions of the community into which we are born or that we join. The earliest traditions come from our families and our national community. Cultural traditions are also part of every business and profession, as well as any type of group or organization. We can recognize tradition when we hear someone say, "we have always … ." An interesting exercise is to ask ten people what makes "Thanksgiving" for them. Many will begin by saying, "We have a traditional meal of … " and then the differences begin.

Starting with varying methods of preparing the turkey or goose to selecting all the side dishes and continuing on to acceptable dress, family activities (exactly how much football?), and the guest list, tradition is multifaceted indeed. The links to the past that are established through tradition provide continuity not only for families but also for professions, businesses, and communities as a whole. As humans we yearn to belong to a group and to know our place in that community. As we adopt the traditions of our chosen peer groups, we know that we belong.

The difficulty with tradition is knowing when the customs need to be kept for cultural continuity, or changed to adapt to new needs and situations, or when the habits are destructive and impede progress. Often tension emerges between tradition and knowledge: what can be changed as the culture evolves and what practices are essential to the identity and maintenance of the community. Sorting through the questions provides communities an opportunity to continually redefine themselves.

Who belongs?

Controlling membership is a key method for maintaining a community. Whether the criteria is ethnic (Sons of Norway), economic (being able to pay the initiation fee), or testing (passing the bar to become an attorney), those who are part of the group determine the requirements for membership. Particularly for professional and business membership, a certain threshold of knowledge and experience is required to do the job.

However, because we like to do business with those we know and with whom we are comfortable, businesses are challenged to assure that belonging is somehow tied to competence rather than whom we know because of our social circles. A current conversation about belonging centers on whether universities should admit "legacies," the children of graduates, even if they have lower test scores or grades than others who are not admitted.

The question is poignant as programs of affirmative action to assure that people of color, an under-represented gender, or those of lesser economic means can be well represented in académe have been rejected. The difference between accepting someone because they are knowledgeable or because they networked effectively and packaged themselves well is subtle.

What behavior is acceptable?

While secret handshakes are parodied, every business and profession has a set of acceptable behaviors that may or may not be shared with the newly admitted member. In academics, each discipline has a carefully nuanced set of protocols for writing papers, presenting at conferences, and critiquing each other's work.

Professions and businesses have their own barriers to entry. A former student recounts that on his first day on the job he cheerfully greeted everyone and introduced himself. He didn't know that the unspoken (but disliked) rule was that the newbie didn't speak until spoken to. The CEO was so impressed that he took the new hire under his wing and showed him the ropes, much to the chagrin of his colleagues.

If we are lucky, when we take a new position, an established member of the group will help us sort through the protocols and we will be able to understand and implement the suggested course of action. If we don't have a mentor, we must be very attentive to the unspoken traditions of an organization and make judicious choices about when to push the edges of acceptable behavior.

What protocols must be maintained?

Many of the judicial systems in countries who were part of the British Empire maintain the protocol of lawyers and judges wearing wigs. Each different style of wig signifies appointment to a different level of court with the more ornate wigs signaling increasing levels of respect being due.

American judges and lawyers don't wear wigs, but no-one ever calls a judge by his or her first name unless one is either also a judge or related to a judge. In universities, an interesting protocol is how long a class must wait for a tardy professor. Traditionally, the higher the rank of the professor, the longer the student must wait. With an emerging sense of egalitarianism between students and professors, that protocol is slipping.

Many lament the emerging informality, seeing the practice as a loss of respect; others find the changing protocols refreshing. Again, discerning between essential and non-essential (but sometimes wonderful) protocols to maintain the integrity of the practice requires gentle wisdom.

The same wisdom is needed in deciding how to begin new traditions or translate old ones. One of my cousins delivered the first dollar from the tooth fairy to his daughter, complete with a personalized certificate of achievement. A few days later, he didn't have time to do the same thing with the second tooth. The following morning, he had to scurry to placate a distraught seven-year-old who wanted to know why the tooth fairy hadn't left the certificate. The next night, the certificate appeared, complete with an apology.

In the business world, attention must be given to traditions such as welcome and farewell events, award ceremonies, and other community-building activities. If someone anticipates a certain ritual upon a rite of passage and the ritual is skipped, that employee will be upset, defeating the purpose of the traditions.

What beliefs and knowledge must be adopted?

Traditions also have a set of accepted beliefs and knowledge. For example, in order to be part of a religious group, one must attest to a certain set of beliefs about that faith. In order to be an art conservator rather than a repair-person, one must not only be technically competent but also agree to certain beliefs about how to best preserve the historical past.

Art conservators have lively conversations about whether a patron should be able to see where a piece of art has been treated. For some, the integrity of the art demands that the difference between the original art and the intervention be clear. Others believe that good conservation requires as little distinction between the original art and the treatment as possible. Those in the latter school believe that with good conservation the patron cannot immediately tell where the repair has been made.

The general rule is that we must be accepted into the tradition before we can change that tradition. Sometimes meeting this requirement is difficult if we are a member of a group that cannot gain access to a tradition. A solution may be to appeal to reason and experience to get people to change their attachments.

As the Civil Rights Movement took hold, many who were part of the white-male establishment were persuaded that people of color and women should be granted access to all of the schools and professions (and we rose up and called these white-male pioneers blessed). Thus, they worked within the system to help those outside gain access to economic and political power in the United States.

Sometimes those who are excluded start their own traditions. Thus, women and minorities who were not welcomed into the existing power structures started their own businesses, social clubs, and networking opportunities to find occasions to excel. These groups also made the argument that as they struggled to survive in a hostile environment, they should be given certain considerations to be able to get contracts and other employment. Their lack of inclusion gave rise to affirmative action and minority set-aside programs, which have always been resisted and are now under increasing scrutiny.

Another impetus for changing tradition is slow death or irrelevance. As young people refuse to participate in a group or tradition, those who are part of that tradition find that they must change or become increasingly irrelevant. For example, we currently see a trend where young men as well as young women are changing professional traditions as they demand that their work include flexibility to be part of their children's lives.

The story is told of a partner in a New York law firm who was arguing against making a young attorney a partner. Even though the requirements of partnership had been met, the partner asserted that the young man wasn't committed enough. The partner continued by saying, "I gave this firm three marriages. I'm not sure that he will do the same." Others in the room gently asked whether the criteria for partnership should include a willingness to get one divorce, let alone three. The young man was accepted for partner.

CONCLUSION

Learning how to make ethical decisions in a contingent world requires a slight but very significant shift of perspective and a willingness to engage in the task of shaping ourselves and our community. The recursive design of the decision-making templates allows us to engage in the process of reflective action, learning to identify the best knowledge we have about both the nature of the world and its current state.

We have an occasion to look at our personal beliefs as well as the beliefs and values of the community in which we work. We have the opportunity to examine the world of organizational ethics to see what works and doesn't work, what fits and doesn't fit. We also have an opening to explore a variety of problems using different ethical lenses and asking different questions, to see how the vantage point changes with a new focus. Then, we get to act again and see what happens.

Because we make these decisions in relationship with others, we also learn to negotiate among competing values and visions. As we practice, we not only learn to attend to the formation of our belief system, but also the belief systems of others and the whole community. With practice, we also learn to make better decisions and more effectively communicate our values and commitments to others. As we dance the minuet of life together, the community's culture—its underlying beliefs and assumptions—change as well, for good or ill.

This chapter began with a quote from Burke, who asserts that "when what we know changes, the world changes and with it, everything."[49] If the physicists who study rocks and light are right that what they know is shaped by the questions, experience, and context of the observer, then our world has changed.

The implications for those who study ethics is profound: given our understanding of the contingency of knowledge, the focus of ethics must shift. Rather than searching for the absolute truth that determines the rules that guide our actions, we must turn to the study of the individual ethical decision maker.

How can we, both individually and as groups, better decide the best course of action given our contingent world, which is subject to uncertainty. The process of knowing becomes as important —if not more important—than what is known. Given that each of us is shaped by what we notice, how we name that event and then how we respond, learning to become skilled knowers will help us become mature, ethical persons-in-community.

CONTINUING THE CONVERSATION

1. Find an article in your local paper or a news magazine that deals with a current ethical situation. Read the article using the four steps of Lonergan: 1) *Be attentive:* What assertions are made by the author? What information is missing? What viewpoints are not present? 2) *Be intelligent:* How trustworthy is the data? How does what the article asserts fit with your own knowledge and experience? 3) *Be reasonable:* How do these assertions fit with your value systems? What are the implications of the options that are presented? 4) *Be responsible:* If you had to make a decision in that situation, what would it be and why? Compare notes with colleagues to find similarities and differences.

2. Find a neutral event in your life—something as simple as a flat tire on the freeway. See how many meanings you can give the event: how can you change the context to make the event good, bad, the best thing that happened that day, an absolute tragedy.

3. Interview someone you respect and ask them how they formed their beliefs about business ethics. How did they use the four building blocks of a belief system to shape their ideas about ethics? 1) What values are important? 2) What experiences have they had? 3) What authorities are important to them in deciding what is right and wrong? 4) What traditions are essential?

4. Write a brief description of your own beliefs about business ethics using the four building blocks. Especially attend to how your family and birth community have shaped your ethical belief system.

PERENNIAL ORGANIZING QUESTIONS

WHAT IS TRUE?

DEONTOLOGY

What would an ideal person be, do, and have?

What would an ideal community be like?

SCIENCE

What do we know about how the world works?

What do we know about how best to do our work?

TELEOLOGY

What would a person living out a particular role be, do, and have in this community?

What are the realities of living in this time and place?

GOVERNMENT

What is the best form of government?

How should we create and distribute our resources?

WHAT IS GOOD?

So it is the process of learning that breaks the vicious circle.
Judgment on the correctness of insights…
occur[s] within a self-correcting process in which
the shortcomings of insight provoke further questions
to yield complementary insights.

Bernard Lonergan[1]

CHAPTER 2

The Person-in-Community

IMAGINE A COMMUNITY WHERE ALL PERSONS with an education are killed. Every accountant, artisan, doctor, entrepreneur, judge, teacher, nurse—anyone who has any skill or knowledge is murdered. A leader has come into power who believes that those with education and professional skills are the cause of all the problems of the community. This leader believes—and convinces others—that by having a society comprised of people who are neither corrupted by education nor blinded by initiative, the innocence of an earlier agricultural age, a seemingly more pure and simpler time can be regained. Because of his ruthless personal power and charisma, within four years, two generations of wisdom and knowledge evaporate as approximately 1.7 million people lose their lives, 21% of the country's population.[2]

During the bloody years, the people learn to trust no one. With the deaths of the skilled and educated adults, the history of the community is gone. All of the cultural knowledge and wisdom that is held and transmitted by an educated population and the elders is buried. All of the memory of how the infrastructure of the community operates is missing. All of the information about how to establish a business and conduct commerce with the wider community is forgotten. Now, the people only know terror and fear—and that they no longer want to live this way.

Now, imagine that you are part of a project to reestablish the community. Your job is to help the people determine how they are to live together, how to find and balance their very human needs for autonomy and equality as well as fidelity and charity. Where will you begin? Because you know about the needs of persons-in-community, you have perplexing questions.

- How will you reweave the fabric of a community that doesn't know how to articulate or inculcate the values necessary to establish a culture that supports persons-in-community?[3]

- How will you interact with others to replace the reality of fear and violence with beliefs and experiences that will allow them to live together and rebuild a safe community and stable economy?

- How will you teach people to create, maintain, and be faithful to the ethical and legal systems required for individuals and communities to flourish?

- How will you convince them to follow shared ethical norms and rules, the law, so the community has a measure of fidelity and safety, rather than the radical individualism that leads to anarchy and chaos?

- How will you describe the beliefs that are foundational for a respect for the human person?

- How will you talk about the value of private property and balance that against the needs of the community?

- What principles of ethics will you teach? What goals will be valued? What virtues will be extolled?

- How will you convince people that the foundations for those ethics are secure enough that the norms should be embraced?

- How will you help people trust each other and the institutions of their community while being aware that they also need to protect themselves?

Judge Juanita Rice, a former District Court Judge in Centennial, Colorado, tells of working in such a community—Cambodia. From 1975 to 1979, the Khmer Rouge regime, headed by Pol Pot, "combined extremist ideology with ethnic animosity and a diabolical disregard for human life to produce repression, misery, and murder on a massive scale."[4] After Pol Pot was deposed and exiled, the people struggled to rebuild their community but lacked the essential building blocks of a civilization—the knowledge transmitted from person to person and institution to institution through education and continuity of community.

Many members of the global community went to Cambodia to help. One such project was the Cambodian Court Training Project. Judge Rice spent two years, from 1995 to 1997, working in Cambodia as part of a team tasked with rebuilding the judicial system. The team was not only trying to recreate an infrastructure (processes for filing papers and keeping records) but also dealing with corruption (judges were paid by the party who won the lawsuit because state resources were not sufficient to guarantee salaries) and ignorance, as the rationale for the values and ethics of a legal system were not part of the shared memory.

As Judge Rice experienced the difficulty of rebuilding a community, she began to have a deep appreciation for a vibrant culture and a healthy country that provides a matrix in which individuals can thrive. At the conclusion of her presentations about Cambodia, Judge Rice emphasizes that each person, no matter how insignificant their life and work may seem, is a link to the past, a foundation for the present, and a trajectory toward the future. As each individual chooses how to work and be in a community that is a part of a greater whole, that person helps or hinders everyone else from reaching their goals and dreams. The task seems doable when we focus on our small community; as we focus on larger diverse segments of our country, the problems often seem intractable.

The lesson of Cambodia is that each of us contributes to the embodiment or destruction of society's shared ideals and values. The task is to not only be a responsible adult but also live so that we support the institutions that provide the fabric of our civilization. Accomplishing the goal of balancing the prerogatives of individualism with the demands of community requires rethinking the very assumptions that have governed both the Eastern and Western communities for some four hundred years.

As we examine the core values that shape our community and the resulting public policies and economic structure that come from those core values, we can begin to make some sense of the problems that face us. At the threshold of a technological age that is marked by a global economy, we need new strategies for answering complex questions in our very complex, pluralistic world.

THE BUILDING BLOCKS OF THE COMMON GOOD

From the first moment that more than one person inhabited the planet, communities evolved and participants debated about how to treat people, the right use of property, and the proper use of power. The book of Genesis in the Judeo-Christian tradition recounts the creation of social systems in light of the core values of the community. The first hierarchy (or partnership, depending on how one reads the text) emerged when Eve was created. Further, Adam and Eve were given responsibility for the animals and the land. In fact, many current environmental debates turn on what exactly is meant by God giving "dominion over the land" to the new inhabitants of the Garden of Eden.[5]

That story is followed closely by the first murder, when Cain killed Abel. Cain's rejection of personal responsibility is articulated in the haunting phrase "Am I my brother's keeper?"[6] The writer recounts that God was not impressed with Cain's dissembling and imposed the sentence of exile without death.[7] Other cultures have similar creation stories that articulate the relationships and responsibilities among individuals in community. These stories were followed closely by narratives that taught people to respect and follow the teachings of those in authority and schooled them on the rules and responsibilities, goals and dreams of the community.[8]

The narratives that embody the expectations and rules of a community are transmitted through the family anecdotes, religious teachings, ethical norms, and legal structures of the society.[9] These stories provide a context for technological developments that energize the creation and distribution of resources and legitimize governments. While the oral and written traditions that shape people's expectations differ across communities, the task remains the same: to assure that societal institutions, such as family, church, business, and government, are both constrained and agile enough so that individuals and the community as a whole can thrive. Over the history of civilization, societies perennially tinkered with their ethics and laws to find and maintain the proper balance between autonomy and equality, as well as between sensibility and rationality, so that individuals can effectively function in a strong and healthy community.

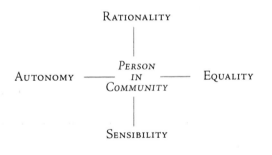

BUILDING BLOCKS OF THE COMMON GOOD

As we look for the patterns of ethics (expectations about how people should treat themselves and others) and public policy (expectations about the proper relationship of the government to its citizens) across the sweep of history, we notice that each community must determine the balance to be struck between protecting individual freedom—*autonomy*—and assuring that all members of the community receive comparable treatment—*equality*. Communities must also decide how to let people know what to do. By identifying universal rules that apply to all people, we use the tools of *rationality* to create the structures we need to make sure that people are treated fairly and are faithful to the community norms. By noticing that particular people have specific needs, we use the tools of *sensibility* to allow for flexibility and generosity.

The arrangement of these core values in a community provides the building blocks for the common good. Just as varying configurations of brick and stone create different buildings, public policies and ethical norms that tilt the balance toward one core value over another will result in divergent cultures and different communities.

EVERYDAY ETHICS: *Making Wise Choices in a Complex World*

The four core values are overarching concepts. In our lives, we approach our ethical decisions through a set of principles (rules) and/or goals that we hold as persons-in-community. As we choose which actions to take in a particular situation, we give priority to seeking justice and/or embodying different virtues, specific moral qualities regarded as good or meritorious by individuals and their community, associated with each core value. After considering the values inherent in the four approaches to ethics, we choose to act.

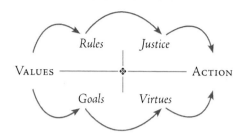

FROM VALUES TO ACTION

As the conversation about which values are the most important—what specific action counts as being ethical—has continued over the course of history, two broad positions emerged. The deontological tradition is home to those who believe that the ethical path is best walked by finding and following universal principles (rules). The teleological tradition is home to those who believe that the ethical path is best walked through seeking specific goals that will lead to the good life and embodying the virtues that are appropriate for one's role in the community.

As people work together to determine the restrictions and opportunities of their society, they consciously or unconsciously determine the appropriate tradeoffs and balance among the competing core values. The goal of the balancing act is to provide an environment where, given the realities of the community in a particular time and place in history, an individual living in association with other individuals, a person-in-community, can thrive.[10] Given that community is created as people come together to share a common set of narratives, traditions, and values, each person and each generation has the task of understanding the history of the community, mending the breaches that have resulted, imagining a better way to live together, and then building their society.[11]

Each person also participates with others of his or her generation to weave a new segment of the civic fabric. People begin by picking up the threads of the environment into which they are born. They then creatively integrate their individual and shared experience as well as their dreams for the future as they create the next portion of the tapestry for their children and grandchildren.

Despite frequent failure, the task of a person-in-community is to strive for what may be called the common good, a community where people can live, work, raise families, and be whole persons.[12] In the process of community building, people experiment with new societal forms and negotiate with each other while engaging in the perennial question: How do we assure that the building blocks of the common good, the four core value sets—autonomy, equality, rationality, and sensibility—are balanced and harmonized so that the foundations of the community are strong? Thus personal and organizational ethics, as well as public policy decisions, require a continuous calibration to find that perfect tension that creates balance. Let's look at each foundational block in detail.

SECONDARY VALUES ASSOCIATED WITH *AUTONOMY*

Free	❖ ❖	*Diligent*
Authoritative	❖ ❖	*Meritorious*
Self-Controlled	❖ ❖	*Dutiful*
Independent	❖ ❖	*Accountable*
	❖	*Responsible*

A cluster of secondary values associated with the core value *autonomy* gives people incentives to become resourceful and skilled as they embrace their rights and corresponding responsibilities.[13] The gift of freedom, which is bestowed on adults, carries the expectation that individuals will not become unduly dependent on others to care for them. The value of liberty, the privilege of each person to choose how best he or she is to live, emanates from autonomy. Conversations about ethics explore the privileges people can claim against others because they are human. What rights of ownership can we demand from our labor, from our property, and our bodies to give us the tools of equality and resources for safety? The values related to autonomy also carry with them the notion of self-control and accountability. As we embrace our individual rights, we also agree to take on personal responsibility for ourselves as well as our community.

BUILDING BLOCKS OF THE COMMON GOOD

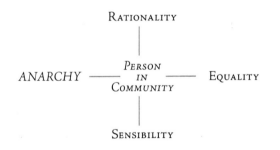

Abuse of Autonomy ➤ ANARCHY

If either the community allows or an individual demands too much autonomy, the result is *anarchy*, where each person does only what is right in his or her own eyes without regard for others. If people do not have enough autonomy, they either do not or cannot become fully functioning adults. The tension is to recognize the uniqueness of each human person while also acknowledging real differences in need or ability.[14]

A society may limit autonomy by not treating a member as a full person with a mind and free will. For instance, some communities have not considered women or certain minorities capable of becoming fully adult and thus have limited their opportunities. Loss of autonomy may result from the strictures of the society that limit individual choices, such as denying access to certain jobs or schools based on criteria other than whether one can do the required tasks. Individuals can also choose to restrict their autonomy through believing they are powerless, refusing to embrace the responsibilities of adulthood, or choosing to give up personal rights for the good of the community.

EVERYDAY ETHICS: *Making Wise Choices in a Complex World*

The cluster of values associated with the core value of *equality*, which is always in tension with autonomy, allows individuals to thrive as people take responsibility for themselves and their own well-being. Equality reminds us to provide some measure of fairness in distribution of resources along with assistance for those who are not always able to care for themselves. These values help to assure that all in the community have sufficient resources to survive. For a person to thrive in community, society must provide both access to economic resources and the opportunity for meaningful participation in the political structure. Solidarity, individuals banding together to share communal burdens and benefits, emerges in communities that value equality.

Fair	❖ ❖	Proper
Equitable	❖ ❖	Impartial
Evenhanded	❖ ❖	Balanced
Unselfish	❖ ❖	Restrained
Just	❖	

Conversations about ethics explore the two ways that the community can choose to limit the autonomy of individuals while expanding opportunities for those who are not privileged. The first approach focuses on redistribution of resources. Through taxation or charity we can help those without access to money or opportunity thus assuring that all members share in the basic goods of the community—food, shelter, education, and health care. This strategy emphasizes equality of result. The second approach provides people with access to the institutions and resources of the community like education, employment, and capital. This strategy emphasizes equality of opportunity as members of the community need certain resources to move safely towards self-sufficiency.

BUILDING BLOCKS OF THE
COMMON GOOD

Abuse of Equality ➤ APATHY

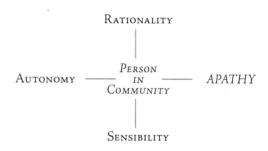

If a community demands too much equality, the result is *apathy*. If people believe that the incentives for working or consequences for not working are insufficient, they may despair and not exert themselves. If people expect too much equality, they may not take enough initiative to assure that all members of the community have the resources they need.

One source of unevenness is the difference in ability of each of us to provide for our own needs. This inequality may come because of physical restrictions, illness, or disability. Persons with physical or mental limitations may not be fully employable and thus not be capable of earning sufficient money to provide for themselves. A second source of unevenness may result from inadequate access to resources such as education, information, capital, or power. If a person does not get a basic education or information, that person will not have the tools to function effectively in a community.

Inequality may also result from systems that prohibit people from fully participating in the community. Racism and sexism have often limited people from access to good jobs and resources. If people in power believe that certain categories of people are not qualified for particular jobs or positions, a society constructs implicit or explicit institutional barriers. People who see those barriers may give up and not even try to become part of the community or may choose to go "underground" and create a separate society of their own.

Many experiments in communal living (as well as group projects) fail because people do not take personal responsibility for assuring the tasks are completed. On the other hand, without equality of opportunity or resources, people may not have the tools to become independent adults. The conundrum of equality emerges as we seek fair treatment while we remember that each person is unique and not a "fused self with others in a single totality."[15] Even though we have similar needs, we are not all alike. Each person has different dreams and goals, different abilities, strengths, and weaknesses. We all need sufficient breathing room to be individuals at the same time that we make sure that everyone in the community has a sufficient supply of basic resources to thrive.

SECONDARY VALUES ASSOCIATED WITH *RATIONALITY*

Loyal ❖	❖ *Faithful*
High principled ❖	❖ *Pure*
Inviolate ❖	❖ *Predictable*
Honorable ❖	❖ *Scrupulous*
Upright ❖	❖ *Trustworthy*
Incorruptible ❖	❖ *Consistent*
	❖ *Entitled*

The cluster of values associated with the core value *rationality* lets us plan for the future and live with a modicum of safety because we know that the moral conditions that are necessary for individuals to thrive will be met, even if they do not live in the same physical or economic community. Rather than treating people differently based on their particular circumstances or giving favorable consideration to those whom we know, we can use our reason to determine the universal rules that all should follow. By "sharing a commitment to the same rules," we can have a community that has some sense of ethical obligations to each other even though we might be strangers.[16]

Because our global community is diverse and we are not bound together by family or even national obligations, we need to have some sense of the expected community norms and rules, so that we know what behavior is required. When we are able to connect with those whom we have never seen in a chat room with the click of a mouse, and have friends across the globe tracking our joys and sorrows in Facebook™, the relationships that both define and guide us are certainly more dispersed than when our best friends lived right around the corner.

The discipline of rationality allows us to faithfully follow norms and laws of the community. The image I use to hold the concept of rationality and fidelity comes from Dr. Seuss' children's story *Horton Hatches the Egg*. Horton promised Maize, the flighty mom, that he would sit on her egg until she returned. As the weather turned bad and the days turned into months,

Horton's refrain was "I meant what said, and I said what I meant! An elephant's faithful, one-hundred percent!"[17]

Using our minds to rationally determine which rules we will scrupulously embrace regardless of the nature of our relationship to others in the community is critical for a well-functioning society. In legal language, because of his promise, Horton had a fiduciary duty to Maize that transcended his personal preferences or family obligations. Once having promised, his duty was to honor the promise and be true to his word regardless of the personal cost. As rationality is valued in a community and we adopt the norm of "the rule of law," we know what behavior is accepted, what behavior will not be tolerated, and what actions will result in punishment.[18] The more consistent the punishment for breaking the rules, the more effective the norm will be for modifying behavior of the individuals in that community.

The second gift of rationality is security. Those who emphasize reason as the road to ethical behavior claim that if we as members of a community are faithful to one another, regardless of our blood, cultural, or geographic ties, we will also put appropriate safety nets in place that protect individuals who are not part of our group from the financial uncertainty of disasters such as a flood or unemployment as well as from the violence of those who would destroy the community. Thus, each person gives up some degree of autonomy and flexibility in order to have a community with physical as well as economic safety.

To provide a safe community, people must give up some personal liberty and share some resources to create the infrastructures of sanctuary. These infrastructures include police and military protection, the legal system, and pension and health care plans. Conversations about ethics explore the claims individuals and the community make on each other to assure essential military, police, and fire protection as well as to protect us from the greed of others in the community. An ongoing question is what individual freedoms should be relinquished and what resources should be shared to preserve autonomy and assure equality of opportunity.

If a society or its people rely too heavily on rationality, the result is *immobility*, as people become restricted and cannot innovate or respond to changing conditions. By demanding too much security, the richness of intermingling cultures and people is lost, which diminishes our ability to meet their physical and economic needs. If people cannot get to their work because of physical barriers, their ability to provide for

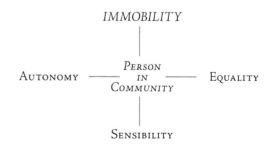

BUILDING BLOCKS OF THE
COMMON GOOD

Abuse of Rationality ➔ IMMOBILITY

themselves is limited. With limited security or unpredictability because people cannot depend on others to honor the rules, members of the community may choose not to be responsible for themselves or others because of fear or because they know that whatever they do today might be destroyed.

This conundrum is seen in the continuing tension between the Palestinian and Israeli communities on the West Bank of Israel. The Palestinian community finds its economic health decaying as people cannot go to work on the West Bank because the Israelis deny the Palestinians access to their places of employment in the attempt to preserve or at least maximize the security of the Israeli community. However, the greater the physical barriers and the more the economic health of the Palestinian community deteriorates, the more likely the Palestinians are to risk everything, including resorting to terrorism. Their desperation contributes to a devolving spiral of physical and economic insecurity.[19]

Individuals and communities have always vied for resources, most commonly land, labor, and capital. Through war and violence, people seize for themselves power and assets. The history of civilization is strewn with the bloody and broken remnants of communities waging war on each other to garner for themselves more resources.

A black strand of history embroiders the tales of those who embrace violence and war for the sake of power, greed, or a belief that their way of life demands that others either embrace the conqueror's culture or suffer the penalty of annihilation. Another dark thread traces the shenanigans of business leaders who betrayed the trust of their constituents and caused loss of money and the demise of companies. A key task of ethics and law is to restrain greed and abuse of power so that individuals and the community as a whole can survive.

SECONDARY VALUES ASSOCIATED WITH *SENSIBILITY*

Charitable	❖ ❖	Prudent
Courteous	❖ ❖	Respectful
Moderate	❖ ❖	Temperate
Measured	❖ ❖	Benevolent
Beneficent	❖ ❖	Kind
Generous	❖ ❖	Merciful
Compassionate	❖ ❖	Grateful
	❖	Flexible

The cluster of values associated with the core value *sensibility* is held in tension with rationality. Because the value of moral sensibility is contextual (depending on the situation) rather than universal (applying to all people at all times), we can embrace kindness and tolerance as needed, which allows people to change in response to emerging events as well as new opportunities and challenges. Gracious flexibility allows us to adjust to the changes in our community. We explore new concepts about the nature of the person-in-community (philosophy), and accept innovative ways to build community (technology). Compassion allows us to respond appropriately to the specific misfortunes of life such as floods, famine, and other natural or human-caused events, whether in our backyard or abroad.

One of the historical strengths of the United States is that it embraces the core value of charity, both in terms of financial generosity and the liberal acceptance of diversity and quirky individualism. Ironically, charity was bifurcated by role: men were expected to respond rationally to impersonal needs (poor-houses and orphanages) while women were responsible for meeting particular needs as a corollary to the running of the households.

Even though the theorists of the Scottish Enlightenment (David Hume, Adam Smith, and Francis Hutcheson) extolled the value of moral sensibilities that responded to particular contextual needs and circumstances, that value was marginalized as people tried to make sense of the emerging philosophical and political notions of individual freedom and social contract. In light of the challenges of the increased mobility of humans and resulting loosening of the community connections, rationality became the norm and province of men while sensibility was tolerated and became the province of women.[20] The consequences of this split, with a corresponding call for unity that is nourished by self-reflection and is not role-dependant, are seen in the novels of Jane Austen such as *Sense and Sensibility*. According to Alasdair MacIntyre, Austen underscores that

> … just as patience necessarily involved a recognition of the character of the world, of a kind which courage does not necessarily require, so constancy requires a recognition of a particular kind of threat to the integrity of the personality in the peculiarly modern social world, a recognition which patience does not necessarily require.[21]

As the roots of dualism grew deeper into our culture, we denigrated sensibility as mere emotivism that is an ethical theory that stating all moral judgments are "nothing but expressions of preference, expressions of attitude or feeling, insofar as they are moral or evaluative in character."[22] Many fretted that relying on emotions to make the hard decisions at best makes us soft or at worst leads to no foundations for a moral community.

However, charity of spirit is always in conflict with fundamentalism—whether it be political, religious, or corporate. Thus, many advocate holding tightly to the "fundamentals" of our beliefs to assure that we are not being contaminated by the new-fangled ideas planted by those who advocate for tolerance and flexibility. The tension becomes, as Austen noted, knowing when constancy is required to counteract the corrupting tendencies of our society and when charity is useful as we explore new ways of living together and honoring the uniqueness of each person.

In the business sphere, this tension becomes evident as conflicts arise about how much risk-taking is appropriate, which is a key feature of flexibility and tolerance. Different persons and cultures have varying threshold tolerances for risk-taking, or in management terms "uncertainty avoidance." Those persons with a high risk threshold find themselves in sales or entrepreneurship. Those cultures who embrace risk tend to value equality of *opportunity* over equality of *result* in allocating rewards. However, those who are risk averse or don't have as many resources to hedge against losing (either opportunity or money) may prefer a system that favors equality of result or a helping hand in the face of failure.

The United States has as its central narrative a celebration of those who embrace the risk of taming the wilderness. Unsurprisingly, the United States also has policy and financial structures that reward risk-taking and innovation—equality of opportunity. Europeans, whose central narrative celebrates national identity and continuity of community, have policy and financial structures that result in much more equality of result. Thus a core question for ethics becomes what minimum safety nets—what resources—should be in place for community members and businesses so they are protected against the vagaries of life at the same time that initiative is encouraged and nourished through well placed stepping-stones to success.

BUILDING BLOCKS OF THE COMMON GOOD

Abuse of Sensibility ➤ CHAOS

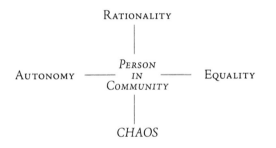

RATIONALITY

AUTONOMY — PERSON IN COMMUNITY — EQUALITY

CHAOS

If a community or its people rely too much on sensibility with its resulting flexibility, the result is *chaos*. A key critique of situational ethics is that people can rationalize any activity based on the fact that in this time and in this place, that decision seems the best. The restraints provided by the value of rationality help us gauge the risks for any venture. Without the structure of accepted norms or a legal system, subtle forms of favoritism, which at the extreme result in discrimination and bribery, creep into the system.

Also, if people demand unrestricted permission to do whatever they want, fraud and charlatans are tolerated and the common good is shredded. In a macro-sense, with too much sensibility the social tapestry becomes moth-eaten from environmental degradation as businesses demand the right to pump anything into the air or dump anything into the water they want. In a micro-sense, the cloth becomes frayed when people, either individually or collectively, use personal and political power to demand unfair bargains from workers (low wages and no benefits) or consumers (shoddy goods and no service).

This drama is played out every year when Congress determines who will get tax dollars for local transportation projects. One such project, a two million dollar bridge to connect a handful of citizens on an island off of the mainland of Alaska, was justified by the Representative by stating that his job was to "bring home the bacon" for his constituents. Thus, the restraint that is provided by rationality as the needs of the whole are considered in light of limited resources falls to the Siren call of sensibility where local benefits translate into votes for reelection.[23] Intentionally weaving sensibility through the warp of rationality assures a strong social fabric that holds individual desires and preferences in perfect tension with the needs of the community of as a whole.

CORE VALUES AND ECONOMICS

All conversations about business ethics explore the dynamic between ethics (doing good) and economics (doing well). According to the dictionary, economics is "the science that deals with the production, distribution, and consumption of wealth and with the various related problems of labor, finance, taxation, etc."[24] Thus, the continual conversation about the relationship between doing good and doing well depends on whether economics and ethics are seen as being in competition or partnership. For most of our history, economics and ethics were seen as partners. In fact, each of the core values has a role to play in the creation of an effective economic system.

People who are careful about the use of their resources value *rationality*, since the security of the individual and the community depends on having sufficient resources to sustain them during difficult times. One of the prairie farmers' key lessons was that in times of scarcity, they never ate the seed. Without seeds, no crop could be planted the following year, a recipe for community extinction.

Embracing *sensibility* allows dreamers to develop new products, services, and processes to capitalize on emerging scientific and technological developments. The notion is that people will develop their own personal capabilities in order to adjust to emerging societal situations. Immanuel Kant asserted, for example, that we each have a duty of self-improvement. Thus, our community well-being depends on each of us becoming more effective ethical decision makers.[25] Further, an open market guarantees tolerance and freedom where people choose how they will spend their time and money with minimal regulatory constraints from the government. Thus, if people want to choose from among fifty varieties of cereal, the market provides a multitude of opportunities.

As *autonomy* for individuals increased in importance during the waning days of a feudal economy, the right to private property was extended to more people than the feudal landowners. Enlightenment philosophers provided a rationale for claiming individual rights, so people began to assert their prerogative to use their property as they liked and to exercise their legitimate personal power to gain more wealth. The full understanding of private property that operates in the Western world today is relatively new. For most of our history, people were expected to restrict the personal appropriation of property in favor of community use and need.

The values of personal effort and ingenuity took hold in the imagination of the common folk as the individualism of the Protestant Reformation moved from the church to the marketplace. In addition to being able to have freedom to choose their religious practices, people asserted that they should receive in salary and lands that which they personally earned based on their effort. The claim that people have a right to use their resources any way they choose as they make their way through this world reached full bloom in the unregulated market economy that formed the economic foundation for the United States in the 1700s.

Equality is advanced by the notion that all members of a community have the right to share in some of the basic goods and services provided by the community. Whether through the voices of the Old Testament prophets calling Israel to accountability for proper use of wealth and caring for the widows or orphans, or Karl Marx championing a radical reorganization of wealth, the claims of the community compel us to look at fairness in distribution of resources. We all have some sense that all people who are part of the community need certain threshold goods to survive—food, shelter, education, and health care. One thread of ethics explores what claim members of the community can have on the wealth of others based on their very presence.

History tells us that a strong community is one in which all members have a chance to share in the opportunities and wealth. This belief is played out in the Western commitment to a strong fluid middle class that allows people to move into positions of wealth based on merit and effort rather than pedigree. Equality of opportunity provides this movement. What we also know is that when the discrepancy between the "haves" and the "have-nots" gets too great, the community fractures into lawlessness or revolution. Equality of result reduces the disparity between those who began with many gifts and resources and those who were thrust into this world with many fewer choices.[26]

ECONOMIC JUSTICE: A CONSUMER WORLDVIEW

Current research shows that we are born with the tendency to share and reciprocate.[27] Thus, people seem to have an innate sense of fairness and define the economic balance as ethical if the act and result are deemed "fair." However, as Michael Walzer in *Spheres of Justice* notes, we have different criteria for determining whether an allocation of resources is fair.

The criterion that embraces both rationality and sensibility is the market: we can get what we can purchase with our personal resources.[28] Economics gurus are fond of saying that as people make decisions based on enlightened self-interest, the market will stabilize as people will restrain their tendency for greed in order to assure that the free market system works. The question, which parallels the rationality/sensibility axis, centers on the amount of regulation that is appropriate for a properly functioning market.

EVERYDAY ETHICS: *Making Wise Choices in a Complex World*

Fair play embodies the notion that each person and group is entitled to having the market follow the same rules, including being treated as fully human and assuring that the bargains they make (sanctity of contract) are honored. Like any other human activity, rules are needed to assure that everyone is treated the same. Thus, a properly functioning free market tolerates some regulation to provide rationality and safety. From moving from a barter system to coinage, which gave rise to a strong middle class, to ongoing conversations about how much government regulation a community needs to assure that all people have the same chance at creating and maintaining wealth, the expectation of fair play levels the playing field for consumers and producers alike.[29]

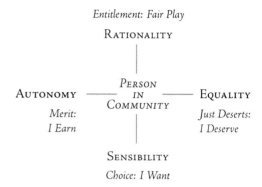

CRITERIA FOR
ECONOMIC JUSTICE
CONSUMER WORLD VIEW

Entitlement: Fair Play
RATIONALITY

AUTONOMY — *PERSON IN COMMUNITY* — EQUALITY
*Merit:
I Earn* — *Just Deserts:
I Deserve*

SENSIBILITY
Choice: I Want

The notion of *choice* is that each of us gets to determine how we will use our core resources, our time, our talents, and our money, parallels the core value of sensibility. Thus, those for whom time is valuable may choose to be in a job that doesn't pay top dollar but allows a great deal of flexibility and reduced hours. Freedom of contract provides charity and tolerance as we make choices that then, in the words of Adam Smith, provide the invisible hand of the market.

This value system masks the role of inheritance, where the original position of all members of the community is not the same. Thus, some inherit wealth or ability, which by definition results in inequality of opportunity. Since we do not all begin at the same place on the racetrack of life, whether the rules governing the distribution of goods is seen as acceptable depends on the core values one advances and whether the members of the community believe the results are fundamentally fair.

This tension between rationality and sensibility can also mask an unjustified sense of entitlement as people struggle to differentiate between their needs and their wants. Part of this conversation requires determining what kinds of resources individuals in a community need. For example, if we all need water to live, the community must find ways to provide that essential good to which all members of the community are entitled. However, the water can also be considered a public resource to be sold. These kinds of questions underlie the conversation where Coca-Cola purchased water rights in Kerala, India. One could praise Coca-Cola for providing clean water and products for the citizens or vilify them for quickly depleting the aquifer and selling what was previously a free resource.[30]

Finally, as we balance between rationality and sensibility, we must determine to what degree the community is going to protect individuals and organizations from taking ill-advised risks. During the economic meltdown of 2008, Bernie Madoff became a household name after bilking many people and institutions out of millions of dollars in a classic Ponzi scheme. Those who lost money wanted protection— either from the law or the government. However, the flip side of the question was how people, including sophisticated investors, honestly thought that the return was justifiable. As Stephen Mihm noted in *The New York Times*,

> Many of us bought into the ethic of "something for nothing" that ruled the economy in the last decade. The homeowner who counted the soaring value of his decrepit tract home as money in the bank, the financial wizards on Wall Street who turned bum mortgages into AAA securities, and the many investors in those securities who took at face value the idea that they could get a risk-free double-digit annual return—they all were willing participants in scams that, while not technically illegal in the way that Mr. Madoff's exploits were, nonetheless skirted the boundaries of what was reasonable, if not ethical. [31]

Is it unreasonable to expect those who want to live by an unregulated free market should also take the hits that come from predatory firms that take advantage of their customers? Reams of paper have been devoted to the government bailouts of 2009, each author exploring how deregulation of various financial industries led to the economic meltdown as people took more financial risks than were prudent. Thus, as Yves Smith notes in *Econned*, maintaining the balance between rationality and sensibility in the world of economic regulation becomes critical if one is to have an ethical economic system. [32]

The economic criterion that parallels autonomy is *merit*: we are entitled to that which we have earned through our own efforts. Merit is the notion that each person and/or group can purchase whatever they have earned in the marketplace for whatever price they are willing to pay. Thus, if a company can only get the CEO that it wants for $4.5 million dollars a year but can get a cashier for $14,000 per year, using the criterion of merit, those wages and allocation of a firm's resources are perfectly acceptable.

The criterion that parallels equality is the concept of *just deserts*, those goods and services that we deserve because we are a part of a community. The underlying assumption is that members of a community deserve certain threshold goods and services simply by being part of the community. Of course, core to the conversation is defining *who* is in the community (e.g., citizens, resident non-citizens, or undocumented workers) and *how much* of the basic resources they can claim.

For example, if a company provides health care for the members of its community, the question arises how many hours a person must work in that community to be considered a member.

For some employers, the magic number is 32, which is why so many people are offered part-time employment. For others, who have strong feelings about making benefits available to part-time workers regardless of what the law requires, the threshold number is 10. In making an ethical evaluation of a company, we might say that the company who cuts off benefits at 32 hours is meeting the requirements of the law but is not being ethical (e.g., assuring equal access to the resources provided to all members of the community).

In fact, William Greider asserts that the willingness of employers to pay a higher cost for temporary workers because they are expendable not only demoralizes workers but leads to the weakening of democracy. When participants in the market economy have unequal power, our economic structures teach both passivity and powerlessness while restricting "human dignity, equity, and self-worth" because the ability to actually make effective economic choices is limited. This passivity also leads to apathy in voting and lack of participation in our political processes.[33]

Embracing the value of autonomy, individuals often use their market power to gather for themselves more of a particular good than is healthy for the balance of power between individuals and community as a whole. As one group has more of a particular good than needed, others who need access to that good may be kept from getting what they need. Greed corrupts the community as people keep for themselves more resources than are needed for security, for no other reason than just to have more.

ECONOMIC JUSTICE: A PRODUCER WORLDVIEW

As the ethical obligations of organizations are explored, the same four core ethical values are present, although with different names.[34] The values of rationality and sensibility are seen in the twin values of efficiency and growth. Thus, efficiency is a means to reaching the core values of consistency, faithfulness, and principled operations, guaranteeing the security or the organization. Firm growth is a function of the ability of the firm to meet the fluctuating needs of the community and thus related to the core value of sensibility, the ability to exercise prudence and flexibility to meet changing societal needs and wants.

The value of autonomy is seen in the right of each company to establish its own core values and operate the firm according to its own lights. As company owners determine the mix of product, identify customers, decide how to deliver the product, and cogitate over the myriad of decisions that need to be made, the leadership team chooses how they will put their unique mark on the company in the community. The value of equality is seen as the firm not only meets the stated needs of the community in the voice of the customers, but also in conversations about how to be both socially responsible as well as environmentally conscious.

CRITERIA FOR ECONOMIC JUSTICE

PRODUCER WORLD VIEW

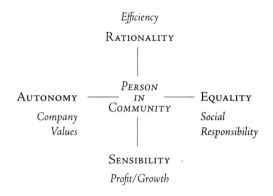

Thus, companies will find themselves in moving among the core values, working to keep them in balance, depending on the wisdom and skill of the team members and the vagaries of the economy. By tracking the twin indicators of efficiency and growth, leaders can assess the trajectory of the company.

The economic term for careful use of resources is efficiency, the ability to reach a desired goal with a minimum of effort, expense, or waste.[35] Deborah Stone, in *Policy Paradox*, asserts that efficiency is a means to the other core values. Even so, she notes that many people treat efficiency as a value in itself.[36] However, if ethics and economics are not to be set in conflict with each other, efficiency—using resources wisely—must be a handmaiden to the other core goals. If efficiency is seen as a primary goal, then the other core values may be sacrificed as abuse of power and greed come into play.

The same problem of abuse of power and greed can be seen in the relentless trajectory of growth on which many companies find themselves. Part of the drive is from the investment community that demands ever higher dividends and profitability. Part of the impetus is a result of the human desire to excel, which translates into growth. A real boundary condition is that if a company is not profitable, then it will fold. The underlying ethical question is two-fold. First, how much is enough? Does Microsoft really need to be the only player in the software market, or is there room for more providers? The bias against monopolies that has always been part of economic/business best practices militates against those who desire unrestrained growth for their own firms.

The second question is growth at what cost? One method of assuring high profits is seen with Walmart, who pays its employees notoriously low wages and benefits, demands deep discounts from its suppliers, and has profits that outstrip those of Target and Costco, who have reputations for being better employers and business partners.[37] Another indicator is determining whether people are being paid a living wage for the work being done. The Living Wage Calculator is maintained by Dr. Amy Glasmeier at the University of Pennsylvania. The site calculates the hourly wages needed to have a living wage in every county in the United States and compares the results to a poverty wage and minimum wage.[38]

Finally, if efficiency and growth are primary goals for an organization, the core values of the company and community that provide the underpinnings for the company may be neglected or

EVERYDAY ETHICS: *Making Wise Choices in a Complex World*

ignored, which may ultimately be a very high cost. While liberty and charity are needed for an economy to grow, even Adam Smith knew that liberty and charity could only be secured in a political system that assured justice, defense, and maintenance of public systems that were needed but might not be profitable, such as roads and education.[39]

As business leaders embrace the perspective of scholars such as Robert Greenleaf, who wrote *Servant Leadership*, leaders will rearticulate their roles in light of stewardship, assuring the well being of the company rather than gathering for themselves power and money.[40] The core value of equality manifests as companies explore the parameters of social responsibility. One shift has been the move from the shareholder theory of the firm to the stakeholder theory. The notion is that all of the stakeholders of a firm should be considered in the ethical and economic decisions, not just the shareholders.[41] Another emerging theme is the notion of Corporate Social Responsibility, where organizations share responsibility for the welfare of the community in which they find themselves.[42]

Economic Justice: An Ecological Worldview

Another way of looking at the intersection of economics and ethics comes from William C. Frederick in *Values, Nature, and Culture in the American Corporation*.[43] Frederick asserts that the business community has traditionally had three core values: *growth*, which depends on following one's gut and flexibility, is a sign of more successful economizing by the firm; *systemic integrity*, which brings the firm together as a whole through the autonomy of the firm to develop its own culture and values; and *economizing*, where success and failure is measured in monetary profit and loss and thus parallels rationality.[44]

Healthy growth would indicate that a firm is both efficient (using its resources well) and attentive (appropriately responding to the community by producing the goods and services that members of the community want). Thus, healthy growth requires a firm to be flexible to meet changing and emerging market preferences. Systemic integrity supports autonomy: the organization is seen as a whole as the company becomes the autonomous actor and members of the firm work together. Finally, the value of economizing (using resources to stay in business) is essential to the financial well being of a company. It doesn't serve a

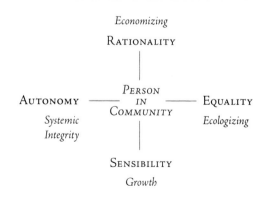

FREDERICK'S TERMS
PARALLELING THE
CORE VALUES OF BUSINESS

Economizing
RATIONALITY

|
PERSON
AUTONOMY ——— IN ——— EQUALITY
COMMUNITY
Systemic *Ecologizing*
Integrity
|

SENSIBILITY
Growth

company well to either squander resources on perks for the employees or to provide benefits that result in the company going out of business.

Frederick asserts that corporations have ignored the core value of equality, which he names as the value of *ecologizing*, defined as embracing those life-conserving values that build and maintain community.[45] Frederick further states that the ethical as well as the financial health of the corporation can only be maintained through working with other firms, both in sharing resources, such as information and effort, and in being part of a healthy community. Thus, in the economic life of a company, leadership's antennae must be out for two different variables, the appropriate use of resources and responding to change.

Initially, we must attend to the careful use of the company's resources to assure they are used appropriately to balance between the values of rationality and sensibility as well as between autonomy and equality within the firm and in the life of the stakeholders to which the firm has responsibility. Next, we must respond to changes in available resources and needs in the community: when fewer resources are available or when priorities of the community change, the growth and efficiency of a company will change.

Classically, the question of the allocation of community resources is described as a "guns or butter" conversation. Those monies that are put into the military, industries that provide military supplies, and agricultural subsidies to assure an adequate supply of food for the community are seen as supporting the goal of national or community security, in shorthand "guns." Those monies that are put into education, health care, housing, or food for the poor are seen as supporting the goal of equality, in shorthand "butter." The notion is that economic growth comes from the efforts of autonomous individuals and corporations who share their resources through taxes or direct charity to provide security or equality, guns or butter.

In a time of a threat to national security, firms that make weapons will experience growth as community resources are put into guns at the same time that firms that provide consumer goods might shrink as resources are withdrawn from butter. In a time of expanding wealth, the community resources might be put into increasing health care, day care, education or any other number of services for those who may have less access to individual resources. Those companies that provide such services and goods will thus experience growth as the community buys butter.

Clearly, times of imbalance and transition are times of great uncertainty for firms. In the months following the September 11, 2001 attack on the World Trade Center, American firms scrambled as resources were reallocated from butter to guns. The increased interest in security coincided with two other tumultuous shifts that had a profound effect on the economic structure of the community and demonstrated deep ethical flaws.

EVERYDAY ETHICS: *Making Wise Choices in a Complex World*

The first began in the early 1990s, where, as prosperity grew, people felt a need to emphasize autonomy by keeping their resources for personal use and making those who use services pay for them. Charity (especially in the narrow sense of almsgiving that was seen through efforts to privatize services that had previously been delivered by the government) also was favored by minimizing government interference with the running of businesses that manifested as a flurry of legislation designed to reduce regulation.

This shift was made at the expense of equality, reducing those taxes that provided resources for goods and services for all regardless of individual ability to pay. The shift to less regulation was also at the expense of rationality, which assured that external governmental controls were in place to militate against corporations having unbridled economic power. Even as the prosperity of the country faltered, the United States Congress passed more tax cuts to stimulate the economy, which favored autonomy and charity, while authorizing greater military spending and commercial protections, which favored security.[46]

Ironically, those changes were made during the second seismic shift, the bursting of the technology bubble with its economic ramifications.[47] As the revelation of those illegal and unethical actions that had led to an unprecedented increase of wealth for a few at the expense of the many sank into the collective consciousness, the stock market plunged, resulting in increased unemployment and less opportunities for firms. The ethical crisis exacerbated the economic crisis, which led to fewer individual resources available for purchasing goods and services. Then, when people did not have sufficient individual resources to buy goods and services, they had a greater need for a community safety net, which had been dismantled. As the resources of the community shrink, the question is which of the core values needs attention. Which of the core values are so out of balance that we need to recalibrate?

As we evaluate whether a company or individuals are using resources appropriately, the community tends to find ethical those companies that, within the constraints of available economic resources, maintain a balance among the four core value clusters. Stakeholders in a company do not expect raises, increases in benefits, or dividends at a time when the security of a company is threatened. However, stakeholders do expect some level of equality in sharing the burden of shrinking resources.

The executives at Enron would not have been vilified had they taken their financial lumps in terms of reduction of share value with all of the other employees. Cries of foul play were heard when the executives abused their power by exempting themselves from the downward slide of profit while either not informing the other stockholders of the economic problems or not allowing the other stockholders to move their money to minimize their own personal financial loss.[48] Martha Stewart was pilloried because she was seen as having received an advantage through information not available to the rest of the community as she took her money from one company and put her resources in another.[49]

Now, a mere decade into the 21st century, the global financial crisis of 2008 and the resulting government intervention to save banks and companies that were "too big to fail," show that increasing technology and economic sophistication have done little to reduce greed and abuse of power that have been themes throughout all of our globe's economic history.[50] Economists are fond of saying that economics is value-free. The implication is that Western rationality results in decisions that are value neutral. This assumption overlooks the fact that all of our decisions are in fact driven by our values. If economic theory is used to describe what is currently in place, economics is in fact value-free, a description of what is. However, as soon as economists move into the realm of predicting what change in resource allocation will cause what results, they enter the world of ethics: any change in resource allocation is in fact a value judgment about the best way to balance among the competing interests of the core values of the firm and the community.[51]

As Lynn Sharp Paine asserts in *Value Shift*, leaders and managers of companies must begin to see their task as maximizing both the ethical and economic well-being of the firm.[52] Thus, ethics should not be seen as an added bonus, to be considered only if the company is doing well financially. Rather, the goal of the firm is to assure that the core values of the company, which themselves are often in conflict, remain in balance as the financial fortunes of the company fluctuate. Then the company can attend to the triple bottom line—ethics, economics, and the environment.

CORE VALUES AND LAW

Ethics and law mediate among the core value sets and help assure their balance both in individual and corporate action. Personal ethics provide an informal foundation for moderating behavior. Our conscience provides internal structure, directing us as we decide which action is the right thing to do. Community norms provide external pressure to conform to the expectations of parents and other members of the society. The mild punishments for violating our personal ethics or community norms range from reproach to guilt. Being removed from the community, shunning, is the greatest threat.

Each of us is complex: a mixture of good and bad. We generally know what is right to do and we work to be good, virtuous citizens. We also are interested in assuring that in our corner of the world we maximize our power and wealth. Even in institutions whose mission is to help the downtrodden and mediate the presence of God to the people, leaders get caught by the desire to accumulate power and privilege, a desire often at cross-purposes with the organization's values.

EVERYDAY ETHICS: *Making Wise Choices in a Complex World*

Thus, we need both carrots and sticks: rewards for doing well and threats of punishment to keep us in line.

Political Structures

Political structures, whether in families, organizations, or nations, provide webs of accountability that help us maximize our tendencies to be good and minimize the temptations to transgress. Webs of accountability, whether informal peer groups or formal rules and regulations, can provide us with early warnings that we are about to go astray when we have been blinded by our own hubris or blind-sided by our naïveté or ignorance.

In a rapidly shrinking world where the current primary social organization is nation-states, the first question is the shape of the political structure of the country. Four different models exist across the globe. The first one is the liberal economic model, which values a free market. The second is neo-mercantile, which values nation-building and security. The third is social democracy, which values equality in sharing the social burdens and benefits. A fourth is a regulated market economy where the community has a restrained transfer of resources (bias toward lower taxes) in order to provide the moderated needs of security and social benefits.[53]

POLITICAL ORGANIZATION AND TAXATION POLICY

(Transfer of resources for security) *Neo-Mercantile*	*(Transfer of resources for the people)* *Social-Democracy*
Rationality/Autonomy	Rationality/Equality
Sensibility/Autonomy	Sensibility/Equality
Liberal Market Economy *(Minimal transfer of resources)*	*Mixed Economy* *(Restrained transfer to meet moderated needs of security and people)*

The United States is modeled on a market economy, embodying the values of autonomy and sensibility. In its pure form, the liberal economic model has a commitment to individualism, the free market, and private property. Proponents of this political and economic school of thought advocate an unregulated market and a small government. The belief is that because people are rational, economic persons, as they make their choices, the market will continuously recalibrate itself in accordance with its own internal logic. According to Robert Gilpin, "the rationale for a market system is that it increases economic efficiency, maximizes economic growth, and thereby improves human welfare ... the primary objective of economic activity is to benefit individual consumers".[54] The expectation is that a market economy will move, over the long term, toward equilibrium and inherent stability.

As Manuel Velasquez notes, a market economy is ethical to the degree that the following three requirements are met: 1) buyers and sellers are free to enter or leave the market when they wish, a market economy embodies "the negative right of freedom of opportunity;" 2) no one is forced to buy or sell that which they don't wish to buy or sell, including their labor, a market economy embodies "the negative right of freedom of consent;" and 3) power is shared among many firms, so that no one firm will be able to so dominate the market that it will be able to force others to accept its terms. Thus, a market economy embodies "the negative right of freedom from coercion."[55]

A cursory look at the world around us shows some of the serious real-world limitations in the assumptions underlying a purely unregulated market. First, as anyone who has ever tried to start a micro-enterprise will tell you, entering and leaving the market is neither inexpensive nor easy. The overwhelming majority of new businesses fail in the first year. Second, as those who are watching their jobs leave the United States and go to other countries will tell you, employees don't have the same market power as employers.

Finally, although some may argue that Microsoft simply had a "better mousetrap," the anti-trust litigation against Microsoft indicates that it used its market power to dominate the economy. When faced with true competition from Linux and lax enforcement of anti-piracy laws, even Microsoft blinked and offered its programs to Thailand at a lower price to assure that the next generation of consumers is raised on Windows.[56] Thus, while a market economy may establish a capitalist form of justice, maximize utility, and protect the negative rights of buyers and sellers, other important core values and forms of justice are not met, particularly those based on rationality (fair play) or equality (just deserts).[57]

One response to the problems of distributive justice in a market economy is seen in the policies of Europe and other communities that operate from a social democracy framework. The goal is to assure that people in their communities receive sufficient resources to provide basic needs. These communities may provide benefits in the form of vacations and pensions or may tax themselves to provide for health care, housing, and other human needs. Often, a very high rate of taxation is needed to support the requirements of the community, and at least in Sweden, the people don't seem to care.[58]

One response to the problem of a market economy inadequately providing for national security and a strong business infrastructure is to impose taxes to pay for national defense and provide government support for businesses. China is often named as the primary neo-mercantile economy in the world. While its military spending is often touted as growing, China wields formidable economic power through a tightly controlled economy. In addition, the low labor costs and huge population make it a formidable force.[59]

EVERYDAY ETHICS: *Making Wise Choices in a Complex World*

While the United States began squarely in the free market camp, over the years it has become what is known as a mixed economy—moving both toward the neo-mercantile point through military spending and business support and toward the social democracy point through its social spending. The unintended consequences of moving toward a mixed economy are seen in the increasing portion of the GDP (Gross Domestic Product) that is spent by the federal government. In the 1920s, approximately 3% of the GDP came from federal spending. From a peak of 44% during WWII, federal spending today accounts for more than 20% of the GDP.[60] Wanting to satisfy those who want guns as well as those who want butter, the United States spends for both sets of priorities.

To satisfy those for whom security and spending domestically for national defense is a priority, the United States has the largest military spending of any country in the world, with the total military spending reaching $722 billion in 2010, representing 46.5% of global military spending. In response to 9/11 and the escalating wars in Iraq and Afghanistan, the amount spent on defense has grown during the past decade. That amount represents about 29.8% of the national budget. An additional 13.6% is spent on interest for debt on past wars. Wanting to satisfy those who lean toward social democracy, at the federal level, 48% of the budget is spent on social security, Medicare, health, and education.[61]

A key variable in using personal ethics as a standard for public policy and law is that we have to find some way to mediate among the competing world views of individuals and organizations in the community. What we know from history is that the more homogeneous the community, the less likely that a legal structure is needed. So, the People's Republic of China has a minimal legal system because culturally its citizens are expected to fit in and follow the societal norms.[62] Because the United States is pluralistic, none of its systems are unified. Because US citizens value decentralized power, the system is diverse and complex. As Paul Spicker, an expert in social policy noted, "diversity and complexity come at a price, and despite—or perhaps because of—political hostility to welfare provision, the US system is also unusually expensive."[63]

The difficulty that any nation—or business—faces as it moves toward implementing a mixed economy is moderating benefits. A country cannot provide both all the safety that nervous citizens want and all the safety-nets that those who see the plight of those without resources want. Over the long haul, no company can provide a double-digit rate of return to its investors as well as a living wage, full health-care benefits, and generous vacations to its employees. Principled leadership and moderation of personal desire is required to balance among the competing demands to assure a healthy, sustainable economy or company. The challenge for those who would call themselves ethical is to model restraint and demand the responsible use of resources while caring for those without power.

LEGAL STRUCTURES

The multi-cultural United States, which values individuality and is pluralistic, relies on its legal system to resolve differences. When people have competing notions about what is or is not ethical behavior because of religious or cultural differences, or when the church or dominant culture is no longer able to enforce behavior, laws become necessary to mediate among competing personal and community worldviews. When members of the community do not agree upon the purpose for which resources should be transferred through taxation, public policy debates erupt that are couched in ethical language and claim legitimacy through appealing to the core values of the community. In these contested situations, ethics, which allow for the exercise of discretion, tend to become codified into law.

Law and ethics are seen as synonymous at the edges as the law defines the sand-box in which we live and work. Regulation, contracts, and litigation become the means to enforce our shared ethical values. A society's legal and ethical structures use both persuasion to enhance responsibility and coercion to enforce accountability as autonomy, equality, rationality, and sensibility are balanced and held in tension.

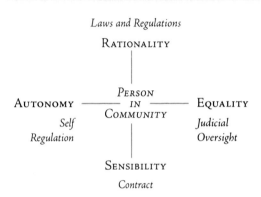

INTERSECTION OF LEGAL AND ETHICAL ACCOUNTABILITY

Laws and Regulations
RATIONALITY

AUTONOMY ———— PERSON *IN* COMMUNITY ———— EQUALITY

Self Regulation

Judicial Oversight

SENSIBILITY

Contract

Autonomy is enhanced through self-regulation when people choose to live by ethical codes.[64] Autonomy is also accepted when people have a high level of trust in each other. In those instances people do not need laws to do the right thing.

❖ As individuals seek to respect all persons, value both private and communal property, and then responsibly use power, values like integrity, honesty, and compassion emerge in the community.

❖ As businesses and other organizations articulate the core values that govern their economic strategies and are willing to hold themselves to a higher ethical standard than the law, trust in business evolves and transactional costs are reduced.

❖ As companies assure that all qualified applicants have access to jobs and that the benefits of the company (such as salaries, vacations, and other perks) are fairly distributed, those companies will be respected and may minimize their exposure to lawsuits and regulatory oversight.

However, if people or businesses do not embrace the ethical values of the community on their own or do not trust each other to keep their word, laws must be passed to define the norms (rationality) and to provide a method of enforcement (equality). Equality is enhanced through the laws that enforce our contracts and mete out punishments such as fines or confinement for violations of community norms that are found in the common law or in the regulatory scheme. The actions of the law in these situations are reactive, after the fact. Thus one who has violated the laws and expectations of the community is subject to court action.

For litigation to be effective at regulating behavior, the enforcement must either be frequent with low penalties (the chances of getting caught are high and the fines are low) or infrequent with high penalties (the chances of getting caught are low but the penalties are high, such as triple damages, large fines, jail time, and one's name all over the front pages of the paper). If the enforcement is inconsistent or infrequent with low penalties, people will consider fines as a cost of doing business, take the risk of getting caught, and continue engaging in illegal or unethical behavior.

Our laws and legal systems also reinforce equality by determining what redistributions of resources are required. This redistribution can happen through a tax system where property and income taxes are used to provide education for all members of the community or housing, food, and health care for those who are without money. Businesses may also be asked to absorb some of the social costs through requirements such as providing health care, worker's compensation, or family medical leave. The trick is to assure that our demand for both equality and predictability does not stifle innovation and initiative.

The law supports tolerance and flexibility, which enable people to negotiate contracts that represent the risk and the responsibilities they wish to undertake—whatever goods and services they want for whatever price their fancy desires. As long as people accept both the benefits and the burdens of those contracts, the community is strengthened. However, if people want the benefit of a contract (such as being able to engage in dangerous activities like whitewater rafting) without assuming the burden (possible death without compensation), the community will restrict their ability to choose. Many of us seem to want to decide how we want to live but then expect the community to pick up the pieces when the gamble goes sour.

During the 1980s, many savings and loans institutions failed because of risky investments. Some people had more than $100,000 in their favorite savings and loan institution. When the banks failed they lost any investment greater than the federal guarantee. Many wanted to maximize their return on investment and had not noticed that the community only guarantees a loss up to $100,000 through federal insurance. Those who expected more than the guarantee were very upset that they could not recover all their loss, even though they made the decision to take that risk. The public policy tension is finding the right balance between risk and protection of investments. Through our legislators, we determine when the cost of protecting people from the risks inherent in autonomy is too high for the community as a whole to survive. The amount of the federal guarantee represents the balance Congress struck.

Rationality is accomplished as legislatures pass laws and administrative agencies promulgate regulations that let people know their obligations to the community. Laws that are proscriptive (such as emissions standards to reduce environmental pollution or requirements for labeling packages) tend to promote rationality because they put businesses on an equal playing field. Carefully considered regulations can reduce the economic pressure that the market (both owners and consumers) place on companies to inappropriately minimize expenses. This pressure is felt by companies such as Walmart where owners want to maximize their return and consumers want to pay rock bottom prices. By having every business absorb the same social costs (such as minimum wage and requirements to provide health care) as part of doing business, employees, consumers, and the environment can be protected while companies thrive.

Rationality (predictability and fair play) is also enhanced through a redistribution of resources such as taxes or through voluntary behavior that restricts individual liberty in order to provide a safe environment. Pooled resources and taxes pay for military and police protection as well as provide subsidies to companies who manufacture goods that are essential to the well being of the community (such as steel and airplanes in wartime). Businesses and individuals are also expected to use personal resources for safety, whether through keeping sidewalks free from snow and ice or paying to create safe environments for employees. They are also expected to not poison the common environment such as air and water. Ultimately, we want to evenly enforce the laws while not requiring too much redistribution of revenue. We want to preserve the incentives for personal responsibility and accountability while assuring that the resources for equality are not shortchanged.

Because a community is always in flux regarding the allocation of scarce resources, maintaining the proper balance among the core values, individual and community ethics, and the law is imperfect.[65] A member of the community who believes that the law is unethical can force the community to reevaluate its stance. Dr. Kevorkian invited the United States into a conversation about the ethics of assisted suicide in the face of terminal illness. Oregon chose to modify its law to allow physicians and patients to make a decision about ending life. After considering this difficult situation, citizens of other states made other choices.

The reverse can also happen. The community can determine that a particular ethical value can no longer be tolerated and thus change the law to encourage a change of behavior. People are fond of saying that morality cannot be legislated, which is true: laws alone cannot change a person's heart. However, the law can force people to act differently. The Civil Rights Movement and the resulting legislation forced many people to stop overt behavior of discrimination. In the ensuing forty years since the passage of The Civil Rights Act (Title VII), a new generation has come of age that takes as given that we do not discriminate based on race, religion or national origin. Personal and communal ethics have changed in response to the requirements of the law. However, the debate still is active as to whether gays and lesbians will be entitled to equal treatment under the law. Whether heard in the seemingly never resolved conversation in both the courts and in Congress about whether the U.S. military's position of "don't ask/don't tell" is constitutional[66] or in discussions about whether the privilege of marriage should be extended to homosexuals, we still have not answered all of our ethical questions about allowing discrimination based on sexual orientation.

RELATIONSHIP OF
LAW AND ETHICS

An act may be ...

LEGAL *and* ETHICAL	NOT LEGAL *but* ETHICAL
LEGAL *but not* ETHICAL	NOT LEGAL *and not* ETHICAL

In the 1990s, Dr. Kevorkian appealed to the core principle of autonomy, the right of each person to choose how to live—and how to die. Currently the conversation about assisted suicide hinges on assuring that people who choose to die are in fact making the choice freely rather than being forced into a choice just to save health care resources. The Civil Rights Movement appealed to the core principle of equality, the right of each person to have access to the goods and benefits of the community. One question concerning the persistent remnants of inequality is whether individuals who have historically been disadvantaged are exercising sufficient autonomy, making choices that will assure that they maximize their potential as humans, or whether barriers to equality still exist.

In reaction to the destruction of the World Trade Center, the United States Congress passed sweeping new legislation, The USA PATRIOT Act,[67] which in the name of national security severely limits the rights of privacy and citizen access to public venues. The question remains whether the security gained from the new laws is sufficient to justify the tradeoffs in autonomy and equality.

The impetus behind privatization of government services and deregulation of segments of the economy is to encourage economic flexibility. In continuing conversations, voices in the community speak to persuade others that the ethics and/or law are not adequately balancing the four building blocks and thus the rules, or even the underlying assumptions of capitalism, must be changed. This fluid dialogue requires everyone's participation, as new situations and understandings of what it means to be a person-in-community are brought forward for critique and evaluation.

CONCLUSION

The perennial organizing questions that opened the chapter—questions concerning politics and economics, ethics, and technology—are answered differently in various communities depending on which of the four core values are seen to be out of balance and what preferred solutions make sense to the people. As each of us identifies our preferred stance on these issues, we can enter into conversation to fashion the best public policies to solve the emerging problems.

However, as we saw with the chart on page 61, because the underlying values for each of the forms of political organization and taxation are persuasive and have both benefits and burdens, we are often conflicted as we struggle to find that right mix of individual responsibility, community safety, and care for the lease advantaged. We want low taxes and a secure community. Or we want low taxes and safety nets for the poor and disenfranchised. Or we want low taxes and shared social goods such roads and national parks.

Unfortunately, because resources are limited, solutions don't come neatly tied up in the above packages. We must make hard choices as we discern how best to provide for the individual in community. These choices are often driven by our fundamental understanding of the nature of human beings and our role in the community. Thus our basic religious and ethical convictions drive our preferred ethics and public policy. Understanding this basic truth and knowing our own positions helps us mediate among competing values in order to make more consistent public policy decisions.

CONTINUING THE CONVERSATION

1. Find an article in your local paper or a news magazine that discusses both sides of a public policy question, such as minimum wage, moving jobs off-shore, or providing health care. See if you can identify which core values each side invokes as they make their arguments.

2. Identify an ethical or public policy issue that is present either in your professional life or in the public eye. Try to formulate the arguments for and against a particular solution in terms of the three public policy models—market economy, social democracy, or neo-mercantile.

3. Interview two people—one on each side of the debate. Interview one person who would tilt toward social democracy (often a strong, liberal Democrat) and one person who would tilt toward neo-mercantilism (often a strong, conservative Republican). Ask them why they favor one school of thought over the others. Also ask them how they begin to fashion compromises when faced with a public policy decision.

4. Write a brief description of your own beliefs about the role of public policy and ethics. What is the source of your political convictions? Have they been formed by your family? Your experience? Your religious beliefs? How have your political beliefs changed over time?

MATRIX OF TRADITIONAL WESTERN APPROACHES TO JUSTICE

Organizing Question	Individual (Autonomy) Politically Conservative	Community (Equality) Politically Liberal
The Absolute is ...	... TRANSCENDENT so we seek to recreate the ideal (heaven).	... IMMANENT so we celebrate the real in the here and now.
Human beings are ...	... FLAWED so will respond to rules to avoid punishment.	... BASICALLY GOOD but misguided, so will respond to relationship to assure respect.
Individuals should embrace ...	... INDIVIDUALISM so that through autonomy we can each creatively find the best way to live.	... COMMUNITARIANISM so that through consensus we can respectfully share a good life together.
Private property is ...	... NECESSARY FOR PEACE so individuals should be able to accumulate wealth and control its distribution.	... INSTRUMENT OF PROGRESS so individuals should be encouraged to share wealth and be a good steward for all.
Our community should be structured to emphasize ...	... INDEPENDENCE which means that we are egalitarian and admit people based on merit.	... INTERDEPENDENCE which means that we are hierarchal and admit people based on birth or their embracing our beliefs.
Our government should therefore be ...	... A DEMOCRACY WITH A TILT TO NEO-MERCANTILE so resources are transferred from individuals and redistributed to provide security to enhance autonomy.	... A DEMOCRACY WITH A TILT TO SOCIAL DEMOCRACY so resources are transferred from individuals and redistributed to provide opportunity to enhance equality.
Our global relationships should also emphasize ...	... INDEPENDENCE with agreements that assure individual agreements with countries or companies.	... INTERDEPENDENCE with agreements that assure inclusive considerations for the people in the countries.
Our relationship to the earth should encourage ...	... DEVELOPMENT to assure that individuals have resources to create wealth and thrive.	... CONSERVATION to assure that the planet is left intact for our children and grandchildren.

Give a man a fish,
and you feed him for a day.
Teach a man to fish,
and you feed him for a lifetime.

Chinese Proverb

CHAPTER 3

Stepping Stones and Safety Nets

BELIEFS ABOUT WHICH CORE VALUE should take precedence over another have evolved over the course of our civilization. Reviewing the trajectory of history shows that one thread of the conversation remains constant: seeking to understand the nature of the human person and the human condition, how we live our lives in community. As civilization moves through time, the assumptions about people and community that underlie the two core Western philosophical traditions—deontology and teleology—are continually rearticulated against technological innovations and scientific breakthroughs that drive changes in political, organizational, and economic structures. Our core beliefs about human nature, whether at our core we are fundamentally good or fundamentally bad, provide the underpinnings of public policy and laws as well as inform the emerging business culture that transcends national boundaries and ideologies.

Throughout history, two primary philosophical traditions have prevailed. Deontology (which includes theories based in duty or principles as well as many theories of justice) asserts that to determine the right thing to do, we should identify the duties and responsibilities of humans and assure procedural justice to protect individual rights. Teleology (which includes utilitarianism, consequentialism, and virtue ethics) asserts that we should focus on the goals and character of humans. Each tradition is grounded in very different understandings of humanity that then lead to very different policies about the treatment of people and use of property.

As philosophers explain their theories, they address the implications of their theories for our personal life, our own ethical compass, as well as the shared values that guide our common life of politics, economics, and business. As theorists place themselves in a particular tradition, they also explore how their theory has relevance to the problems of the day, how their ideas can help us with applied ethics, solving the very real dilemmas that face us all.

REPRESENTATIVE THEORISTS

Deontological Tradition ❖ *Teleological Tradition*

400-500 BCE	Plato	Aristotle
300-1300 CE	St. Augustine	Thomas Aquinas
1500-1700 CE	Martin Luther	Isaac Newton
1700-1850 CE	Immanuel Kant	John Stuart Mill
1800-1950 CE	Charles Darwin	John Dewey
1950- CE	John Rawls	Alasdair MacIntyre

As the chart shows, the two philosophical theories have been in conversation with each other over a long sweep of history: one school of thought would have a popular spokesperson and then an advocate for the opposite tradition would come into prominence. The modern era emerged with Martin Luther and the Protestant Reformation. As the dust was settling in the 16th century after the emergence of Christian Protestantism, a tradition that rivaled Catholicism, the question was asked: Is it possible to know "truth" through human reason rather than revelation from God?

At the beginning of what has come to be called the Age of Enlightenment, Immanuel Kant (deontology) and John Stuart Mill (teleology) explored how we could move from an ethic grounded in revelation and mediated through the church to an ethic grounded in reason and desire that was decided by individuals. They were deeply informed by René Descartes' dualism where "the soul is understood as mind, and human awareness as distinctively that of the thinker."[1] As Richard Tarnas notes, this understanding of the universe was a shift from the vibrancy of the medieval mind, where the universe was alive, to a belief that the universe was composed of "nonvital atomistic matter" that could be understood in mechanistic terms. To explain, Tarnas continues,

> Descartes enthroned human reason as the supreme authority in matters of knowledge, capable of distinguishing certain metaphysical truth and of achieving certain scientific understanding of the material world. Infallibility, once ascribed only to Holy Scripture or the supreme pontiff, was now transferred to human reason alone.[2]

Once the religious authority for social organization was undermined, the work of other seminal political philosophers such as Thomas Hobbes gave rise to the notion of social contract, where citizens agree on the system of governance by which they will be bound. The logical conclusion for the Enlightenment notions of self-governance was democracy and a liberal market economy, which in its pure form is unregulated.

EVERYDAY ETHICS: *Making Wise Choices in a Complex World*

In the 19th century, with the advent of mass production and resulting mega-organizations, social reformers highlighted the unintended consequences and problems of a liberal market economy. Reflecting on the labor unrest of the early 1900s and the Great Depression, John Rawls (deontology) explored how attention to procedural justice could mitigate against the myopia caused by a focus on individual goals. Alasdair MacIntyre (teleology) turned our attention to our character to correct for the shortsightedness caused by a focus on individual rights. These theories provided the underpinnings for a political shift towards a regulated economy with statutory protections for workers, consumers, and investors.

❖ *As humans, we are born into a family that tends to favor one tradition over the other. Whether considered in terms of religious or political preferences, our parents have a set of core commitments that they wish us to adopt as well. These core commitments define us and have the potential to energize and transform the self, the family, and the community. As we wend our way through life, we have the opportunity to first identify the salient elements of our birth tradition and then either reaffirm that tradition, change traditions, or nuance our beliefs by a thoughtful synthesis of the two.*

The above categorization of theorists accounts for the rationality-sensibility continua of the four ethical lenses. In each case, the theorists who identified with one or the other tradition began with shared assumptions. However, the other axis of the grid is the autonomy-equality continuum. That division helps us make sense of deeply held political differences.

CORE BELIEFS AND VALUE MANIFESTATIONS

Robert H. Nelson, in *Reaching for Heaven on Earth: The Theological Meaning of Economics*, looked at the sweep of history differently. His focus was on what he called the Protestant tradition and the Roman tradition. Those in the Protestant tradition favored an individual approach to ethics and economics. Those in the Roman tradition favored a community approach to ethics and economics. Nelson asserts that core beliefs about the human person, our relationship to the sacred, and our lives with each other provide foundations for our ethics and also our convictions about economics, law, and government. From a bird's-eye view, these core beliefs, whether conscious or unconscious, manifest as favored political and economic structures as well as public policy preferences. With a modicum of consistency, the assumptions we hold about human nature will also establish our theoretical grounding for business ethics and public policy.

While the representative theorists are placed in a particular tradition (individual or community) either through self-identification or based on their body of writing, Nelson notes that none of them fit squarely within a given school of thought. Over the course of their lives, each one may have grappled with weaknesses in their own tradition or appropriated ideas from the other. However, the two traditions are a good place to start in charting our own belief systems.[3]

Our belief systems depend on which core values inform our actions, define how we believe we should treat each other, and determine our policy preferences for the whole community. The assumption is that if we think clearly and act consistently, we will find ways to agree on what particular action is the "right" thing to do in a situation. Unfortunately, rather than discussing points of agreement and considering points of differences, many of us believe that if the other person just saw life the way we do, all this fussing and bickering would stop. However, each tradition has strengths and weaknesses, so we can make a persuasive argument for ethics and policies that flow from either.

REPRESENTATIVE POLITICAL AND ECONOMIC POSITIONS

Individual Tradition ❖ *Community Tradition*

Plato/Aristotle | Aquinas/Augustine

Kant/Mill | Rawls/MacIntyre

Those who favor the individual approach, what one student called "I-People," tend to favor what I call "stepping stone" policies. They believe that the best public policy provides incentives and structures for people to care for themselves, which they can use—or not. Slipping off and getting wet in the stream becomes an individual problem, not a concern of the community. Those who favor the community approach, "We-People," tend to favor "safety net" policies. They believe that the best public policy provides a safe haven for people to regroup after a difficult time complete with access to the resources they need to move forward. Because we are responsible for each other, We-People are comfortable requiring life jackets for all to assure that when one slips on a rock and falls into the stream, they don't injure themselves.

The saving grace is that in ethics and public policy, we often agree on *what* to do even if we don't agree on *why*. Usually, the best solutions are a blend of the two approaches, providing both safety nets and stepping stones—or, to use the example in the proverb that introduces this chapter, giving a woman a fish while she is taking fishing lessons. Of course, the question is always *how many* fish and *how long* the lessons should take to learn. Thus, the best public policy is hammered out when one group does not have a monopoly on power but shares power with other groups holding divergent beliefs and looking at the world through different ethical lenses.

The following listings are the representative core beliefs of people in the two traditions. Consider the text in the boxes as the endpoints on a continuum with many gradations in between. We each hold some of these beliefs very strongly and others more tenuously, which also impacts our action. Because each position contains some truth, we may try to reach a both/and position and thus mix and match beliefs.

We also have to carefully discern when the mixing results in a judicious balance rather than schizophrenic behavior caused by choosing a position that favors us this time and then moving to a different position when we would receive the benefit of a different policy. However, surveying the big picture helps us situate ourselves in the ongoing conversation about the state of the world and our response to it.[4]

EVERYDAY ETHICS: *Making Wise Choices in a Complex World*

Nelson begins by asserting that our worldview is grounded in our beliefs about the transcendent, our relationship to the sacred.[5] Thus we begin our survey by exploring the fundamental nature of what is considered sacred and the nature of humans. Then we will explore our understanding of community and our relationship to each other.

Whether acknowledged or not, these beliefs that define our core values are choreographed together in elegant if-then dance steps. These values manifest as our choices and actions, our ethics. As our dance evolves, we see whether we favor soloing in our own breakdance or participating in a line dance with others. In any event, whether we acknowledge our partners or not, all of us dance together in this amazing performance we call life.

RELATIONSHIP OF INDIVIDUALS TO THE SACRED

The foundation for all of our beliefs is our understanding of the sacred. Those in theistic traditions name this presence God. Those in non-theistic traditions, such as Buddhism, seek Enlightenment through meditation and other spiritual practices that take humans past the cycle of life on earth to Nirvana, where suffering ends for all time.[6] Those in the humanist tradition, who assert that human understanding and reason are suffi-

Individual Tradition ❖	*Community Tradition*
THE ABSOLUTE IS …	
… *TRANSCENDENT* SO we seek to recreate the ideal (heaven).	… *IMMANENT* SO we celebrate the real (here and now).

cient for us to know what to do, speak of matters spiritual without invoking a deity, but find the Spirit within each person.[7] While we may not agree on what "It" is, every tradition speaks of some energetic presence that is beyond each of us individually, which for the purpose of our discussion we will call the Absolute.

Individual tradition

CORE BELIEF:

The Absolute is believed to be primarily Transcendent, separate from creation. A persistent image for I-People is that of Nicole Oresme, a 14th century philosopher who described God as the great watchmaker who created the universe as a clock and then withdrew to let history unwind. In this view, the Absolute and/or Nature are seen as capricious and impersonal. Humans are powerless in the face of a predetermined destiny.[8]

MANIFESTATION:

I-People are often perceived as pessimistic because they see the great divide between what we as humans can be at our very best and what we do every day. I-People see the goal of life as recreating the ideals that are beyond us and despair of actually being able to reach our goal.

Plato's "Allegory of the Cave" presents the image of humans chained to a cave who see reality in flickering shadows. Plato asserts that we can free ourselves as we individually come to understand Truth. This individual change may lead, when necessary, to a radical reorganization of our community. This theme of radical change is threaded through the writings of idealists. Responsibility for facilitating change resides in the hands of the chosen enlightened leadership.

Community tradition

CORE BELIEF:

The Absolute is believed to be primarily Immanent, active in history and human affairs, and can be partially known through reason and experience. Humans are seen as being able to work with God and/or Nature in shaping our common destiny. People in this tradition often see themselves in conversation with Spirit as they choose how to live and shape community.

MANIFESTATION:

We-People are often seen as optimistic because they see the goal of life as creating heaven on earth. In theological language, these people seek to usher in the "Reign of God" through appealing to the reasonableness of humans as we celebrate and embrace the sacred nature of each of us. In secular language, these people are often considered utopians. Responsibility for change resides in the hands and hearts of each of us as we live out our birthright of sharing in the divine.

Individual Tradition ❖ Community Tradition	
HUMAN BEINGS ARE …	
… *FLAWED* so will respond to rules to avoid punishment.	… *BASICALLY GOOD BUT MISGUIDED* so will respond to relationship to assure respect.

STATE OF HUMAN NATURE

The next conversation concerns the nature of humanity: are we essentially good or bad? Our beliefs about human nature are informed by biology (nature vs. nurture), psychology (psychological wounding as a child that needs healing), as well as philosophy and theology (the nature of the human person). Regardless of what disciplines we use to get to the conclusion, we notice that humans have the capacity for both good and ill.

Our belief about the predominant nature of human beings—whether, as we mature, our tendency to do what is right outweighs our tendency to what is wrong, or not—determines what interventions we see as useful. If the goal is to assure that individuals behave well and follow the norms of our community, do we primarily need rules to keep us in shape (a pessimistic view of human nature) or healthy relationships to guide us through love and respect (an optimistic view of human nature)? The point is well made in a cartoon that shows two school children

EVERYDAY ETHICS: *Making Wise Choices in a Complex World*

giving each other a high-five. The boy tells the girl, "Wow! You only got an 'I'm disappointed in you.' I thought you were going to get punished!"

Individual tradition

CORE BELIEF:

I-People tend to believe that human beings are flawed and by ourselves we can do little to change that situation. As articulated by the Protestant reformers, the separation from God that comes from Original Sin can only be corrected by God's grace—which may or may not be given. Because even our minds are tinged with the stain of separation from the Divine, reason is not useful in making us better persons.

In the Eastern traditions, the human condition is escaped through Enlightenment, which after many cycles of life, allows us to escape the cycle of life and reach Nirvana. Humanists who believe in the flawed nature of humans find that a striking life experience may become a catalyst for change. Thus, those of us who unexpectedly experience discrimination may see that our beliefs about the differences among humans are not accurate and begin to work for change.

MANIFESTATION:

Given that I-People believe that change comes either through radical metamorphosis of belief or experiencing transforming circumstances, adherents tend to be pessimistic about the future of individuals and society. As reason cannot be trusted to keep us on the straight and narrow, people in this tradition favor rules so we all know what is expected. The threat of punishment keeps us in line.

Community tradition

CORE BELIEF:

We-People believe that humans are basically good. As articulated by Roman Catholic and liberal Protestant theologians, through our experience of God's goodness and being in relationship with others who are good, we can learn how to be ethical persons. Many humanists, who do refer to a God, believe that people are inherently good. The notion is that because we desire to stay in relationship with those who are important to us, we modify our behavior to stay in their good graces.

MANIFESTATION:

Because We-People believe that through experience and reflection we can determine the best way to live and imagine possibilities that enhance human existence, people in this tradition tend to be optimistic about individuals and society. "Agreeing to disagree" becomes their mantra as preserving relationships is important. Shame and the threat of exclusion from the community are used to keep us in line. We recognize someone in this tradition when, to discipline us, they sigh deeply and say, "I'm disappointed in you."

Individual Tradition ❖ *Community Tradition*	
THE IDEAL CAN BE REACHED …	
… ONLY AFTER DEATH SO we should work to minimize the effect of sin.	*… ON THIS EARTH* so we should work to make the world better.

RELATIONSHIP OF INDIVIDUALS TO THE IDEAL

A persistent question in philosophy and theology is whether we can achieve an ideal state on earth—whether we can find or create Nirvana or any of many other utopian visions on this earth or if we must wait until we enter another plane to find our ideal.

Individual tradition

CORE BELIEF:

I-People do not see any possibility of creating "heaven on earth." Because we are separated from the Absolute or the Ideal by sin or illusion, we must escape this plane and go to another world to evade pain, selfishness, and greed. In one popular version, our life on earth is a dress rehearsal for the real play, which will be heaven.

MANIFESTATION:

I-People tend towards asceticism, as they see this world and its gifts as inherently evil. The Puritan heritage of the United States, which historically has distrusted displays of opulence and expected us to not trust the experience of physical pleasure, calls us to live simply and not seek comfortable living. The money raised by our effort should go back into the business or the community. Warren Buffett, a multi-billionaire, would be a contemporary example of living into this value as he and his wife still live simply in their first home in Omaha, Nebraska, rather than in a mansion.

Community tradition

CORE BELIEF:

We-People are committed to creating "heaven on earth." Because we continually seek to do that which is good, we can choose to act in a way that will make this world a better place. We-People believe that compassion for others and creativity will solve our problems.

MANIFESTATION:

We-People tend towards hedonism as they embrace the gifts of this world and expect us to enjoy them. Thus, the good life is to be celebrated and the joys of good food, good drink, and good friends are to be savored. Because We-People believe that we can all work together to

EVERYDAY ETHICS: *Making Wise Choices in a Complex World*

make this world a better place, they value signs of progress and change that enhance the lot of our lives together.

CONDITION OF HUMAN SOCIETY

Once we know the nature of the Absolute, human beings, and our relationship to the Ideal, we determine the shape of our lives together, how we build community. With one tradition we have to strive to resist corruption, with the other we trust in our innate goodness. This belief determines how we interact with our various social institutions, from the work-place, to schools, to our government structures.

Individual Tradition ❖	*Community Tradition*
HUMAN EXISTENCE IS …	
… SHORT AND BRUTISH thus we should resist corrupting institutions.	… FUNDAMENTALLY GOOD thus we should calibrate evolving institutions.

Individual tradition

CORE BELIEF:

Because people are flawed, I-People find human existence harsh and cruel. In the words of Thomas Hobbes, unless we constantly strive to maintain the civilizing structures of community, life is "nasty, brutish, and short" as we are alienated from the sacred, ourselves, and each other.[9] Those who historians name as the protestors of history, from Martin Luther to Martin Luther King, Jr., have railed against corrupt institutions and demanded that leaders be held accountable for their actions or lose their legitimacy.

MANIFESTATION:

As each of us is responsible for finding our own truth, I-People favor autonomy and personal responsibility. We are asked to evaluate the evidence, identify what is true, make our choices based on that truth, and then accept responsibility for the outcome. I-People also value creativity and innovation. Because each of us has the potential for greatness, those who march to a different drummer are tolerated and brilliant eccentrics are revered. However, a persistent question is defining the line between individualism and anti-social behavior or willful insubordination.

Community tradition

CORE BELIEF:

Because we have reason, We-People believe that many of us can experience the good life. We-People believe that we can discover our true identity and work together to fashion a world where all people can thrive. People in this tradition value change within existing structures rather than wholesale reform.

MANIFESTATION:

As truth and the knowledge of what is good is revealed both in individuals and the community, We-People favor trusting the wisdom of experience and tradition in determining how to live. We come together and debate the issues and then agree to live by the ethical guidelines that emerge in that conversation. Because of the value of the whole body, creativity is tolerated within carefully constructed guidelines and the loyal worker who mirrors the company values is venerated. A persistent question for this tradition is defining the line between loyalty and mindless allegiance given that what is true and good for one person is not necessarily true and good for another.

Given the limitations of human understanding, we can never conclusively prove which of these sets of core assumptions provides the best foundation for life. In fact, because we are Persons-in-Community, both traditions are useful as we seek to make our way through this world.

Because we have to make choices in this world, each of us has a worldview (either articulated or unarticulated) that informs our actions while we strive to better understand and then live into the values of what is true and good. Ultimately, each must take Søren Kierkegaard's proverbial leap of faith as, with Guy Noir of Lake Wobegon fame, we continue to seek "answers to life's persistent questions."[10] The existentialists who wrote during the early 20th century and whose work provided important foundations for the postmodern movement claimed that in the face of uncertainty, humans have a profound responsibility to determine both what is good and what is true for themselves.

As Kierkegaard says, "It is the duty of the human understanding to understand that there are things which it cannot understand, and what those things are."[11] Though it sounds trite, as we wake each morning we each get to choose how best we will live. Acting in light of our best understandings, our core beliefs about human nature and community set the trajectory for our lives together.

Because human society requires that we learn how to live together, we use our foundational beliefs about human nature to establish governments, pass laws, and develop business and economic structures. As Nelson demonstrates, the different preferred ways to organize society reflect our varied beliefs about what is the best path of action, both as an individual and as a community.

Individual Tradition ❖ *Community Tradition*	
LAW IS ...	
... CORRUPTED PRODUCT OF HUMANS so government should be limited to provide safety.	*... NOBLE EMBODIMENT OF CIVILIZATION* so government should be expanded to provide opportunity.

ROLE OF LAW AND GOVERNMENT

From earliest civilization, people have codified the rules by which they agree to live and the punishments for their infractions. These statutes act as both carrot and stick, promising respect if one is seen as a good, law-abiding citizen and threatening punishment for violations of community norms.

Individual tradition

CORE BELIEF:

I-People who embrace Western rationality see the law as necessary to keep us from destroying both ourselves and others. Because we cannot know the truth by reason, human law is a rough approximation of divine mandates that are revealed to us by the Absolute or through inspired leaders. Thus, even though human law is a "corrupt product of human weakness and frail reason," law is needed to keep our selfishness from leading us to "theft, lying, cruelty, and oppression."[12] Government, too, assists in keeping us in line by assuring that our base natures don't take over to the detriment of the community. The primary function of government is to assure the safety and well-being of individuals and to protect us from invasion.

MANIFESTATION:

I-People favor limited government because institutions are subject to being corrupted. Contracts are favored over governmental regulation so that people can choose the conditions under which they want to be bound. The law should be restricted to that which is necessary to keep greed and abuse in check. The government should only be able to marshal resources to guarantee individual safety and to keep the nation safe. Punishment is the primary vehicle for enforcing infractions and assuring that people follow the rules.

Community tradition

CORE BELIEF:

We-People embrace the notion of natural law, those precepts that are written on the conscience and consciousness of all humans. Because the law is imprinted in all of us, the true law can be discovered through reason. The laws we have are thus the "noble embodiment of accumulated human wisdom [and put] diverse people under one rule of reason."[13] The American notion of fidelity to the rule of law, where we agree to follow the laws of the community without external coercion even if we disagree with them, flows from a commitment to the notion of natural law.[14] Government becomes the way that we organize our energies to assure the common good and monitor the distribution of resources.

MANIFESTATION:

We-People tend to see government as the way to assist in the goods of the community being given to all. The modern welfare state, which provides education, housing, shelter, and food to those without, flows from the core belief that a strong government should care for the weaker members of the community. Given that We-People believe that we will not violate the law if they have sufficient education and resources, access to adequate assets is seen as the way to assure that we follow the community norms. Rehabilitation is the preferred method of intervention after a is we violate the law.

Individual Tradition ❖ *Community Tradition*

PRIVATE PROPERTY IS ...

| ... NECESSARY FOR PEACE so individuals should be able to accumulate wealth and control its use and distribution. | ... INSTRUMENT OF PROGRESS so individuals should be encouraged to share wealth and be a good steward for all. |

PRIVATE AND COMMON PROPERTY

The proper use of personal property and land is an ongoing conversation in economics and law. The right to develop property for personal gain is in tension with preserving and caring for that which is held in common for the benefit of all. Protection of private property undergirds capitalism and the market economy. Without Adam Smith's notion of creating wealth by adding labor and creativity to raw materials, our world would be a very different place.

Individual tradition

CORE BELIEF:

I-People believe that private property is necessary to keep us from quarreling amongst ourselves. However, to avoid greed, we should not accumulate property for self-aggrandizement, but rather we should live simply and avoid any excesses of human pleasure. Ironically, Calvinism threw a weird twist into the conversation. John Calvin (and his successors) taught that since we cannot know if we are "saved," one marker of being part of the "elect" is financial success in the world. However, *enjoying* the wealth is suspect. Thus, we should give away our wealth to the community in the form of charity.

The early Puritans also had a bias against people inheriting property, as each of us was to show our mettle through working and accumulating enough resources to care for our self. Thus the Protestant work ethic that infuses the American ethos states that we are to work diligently to assure "salvation" but live simply because the world and its riches are tainted.[15]

MANIFESTATION:

Because government is corrupt, it cannot be trusted with either the care of wealth or its distribution. Given that wealth and private property are the results of individual hard work, I-People believe that we should be able to control our own wealth and property. Those who want wealth should work hard to earn it, especially in a land where each of us has permission to make our own way. While the tenets of Calvinism no longer hold sway as they did at the founding of our country, this core belief is the source of the deep distrust of material wealth that has marked much of the history of the United States.

Community tradition

CORE BELIEF:

We-People believe that private property should be used as an instrument for a better life for the community as a whole. As we care for our property and use it to increase wealth, all members of society can benefit. As we seek to increase our wealth through enlightened self-interest, we can move from scarcity to abundance.

MANIFESTATION:

Because wealth comes through the efforts of many, not just one, We-People assert that private property is to be shared for the common good. Community efforts such as parks, national forests, roads open to all, health care, and public schools benefit the entire community as we share our resources through taxation and the redistribution of wealth. All of us who are part of the community should have an opportunity to share in the good life. Thus, people in this tradition favor pooling wealth to protect and sustain the common good.

Historically we have believed that our country is well served with a strong middle class and few very wealthy or very poor citizens. Thus, our laws encourage individuals to earn as much money as possible, but wealth is taxed upon death to put the resources back into the community for the next generation. The current conversations about the "death tax," the abolition of which is grounded in the right of people upon death to give their wealth to their children, challenge this worldview. Also, with the erosion of labor unions and the growth of two-income professional families, current economic policies lead to a strengthening of the upper class, a diminishing of the middle class, a growing lower class, and increasing poverty.[16]

Our historical understanding of private property is being challenged in today's environment. As technology makes copies of music and literature available with the click of a mouse, boundaries between personal property and community property blur. As we face environmental deterioration, we know that no one really owns water or air. Deeds can't keep water in aquifers and air pollution does not stop at property lines.

The greatest challenge to a market economy is people cavalierly disregarding the fundamentals: we each pay for what we use in order to assure that those who produce the goods are able to sustain their businesses and earn a livelihood. The market economy cannot thrive if students purchase bedding and items for their dorms and then return all for full value at the end of the quarter: the stores that supply those goods will either go out of business or raise prices to cover the loss. The market economy cannot thrive if those who have contracts to produce goods then sell those same goods on the shadow market: those companies that have the contracts will withdraw the contracts and people will be out of work.

Fundamentally, ethics is the agreements that we have with each other about how we will live our lives. Business ethics is about the agreements that we have to assure that commerce flows freely and fairly among all the stakeholders. With a strong culture of ethics, behaviors that build trust and ensure fair play, laws are not needed to regulate behavior and contracts don't have to have draconian terms. If, however, we play the edges, trust is broken and the free market ceases to function efficiently. In a very real sense, each of us—from the unemployed person who takes money under the table, to the student who returns a book to the bookstore after reading it to save a buck, to the CEO who chooses to negotiate the harshest terms possible for a contract—chooses every day whether we will contribute to an efficient free market or not by the choices we make about paying for goods and services, the choices we make about how to do our work, and the expectations we have for returns on our investments.

Individual Tradition ❖ _Community Tradition_	
THE POOR …	
… _GET WHAT THEY DESERVE_ and thus we have no obligation to help.	… _ARE UNFORTUNATE_ thus we have an obligation to help systematically.

SELF-INTEREST AND THE POOR

The last set of core beliefs that helps us make sense of our assumptions about business and economics concerns the role of self-interest and the poor. Our ideas about working conditions, distribution of wealth, and the role of government or other institutions to assure a fair sharing of resources flow from our ideas about personal responsibility in community.

Individual tradition

CORE BELIEF:

Because we are each responsible for ourselves, those who do not do well financially just need to work harder and improve themselves.[17] Because we are each responsible for our own well-being, any lack is due to our own choices, not systemic problems in distribution of wealth. Individual charity is the best way to deal with poverty. Thus those of us with resources can choose who deserves help and who does not.

MANIFESTATION:

I-People have little sympathy for idleness and sloth. If we are poor we get what we deserve for not applying ourselves. Scrooge, from Charles Dickens's _A Christmas Carol_, exemplifies this kind of person. The opening of Scrooge's heart comes as the Ghost of Christmas Yet to Come confronts Scrooge's miserliness with his own words, "Are there no workhouses?"[18]

The current debate about a minimum wage versus a living wage highlights the tension inherent in this value. I-People tend to believe that the minimum wage is a more than satisfactory beginning point, and if we want to work for less than minimum wage we should be

EVERYDAY ETHICS: _Making Wise Choices in a Complex World_

able to negotiate that agreement. People in this group tend to believe that if we want to have more money and greater resources, we should improve their skills and work harder and that the economic system will expand to accommodate our diligence.

Community tradition

CORE BELIEF:

We-People have a more empathetic view toward the poor than I-People. Aware of the differences in ability and distribution of resources that are an accident of birth, theorists in this tradition assert that we who have abundance have an obligation to help those of us who are poor and to work to change the systems that create and sustain poverty.

MANIFESTATION:

We-People value systems that assure that all have an opportunity to share the "goodies" of the community. They believe that the government should intervene to assure that those of us with wealth and power do not take advantage of those of us without power or privilege. Citing the imbalance of power between employers and employees, this tradition asserts that those of us who work should be paid appropriately, not the lowest wage possible.

We-People were the primary movers behind the labor revolution in the late 19th and early 20th centuries, resulting in the right to collective bargaining and improved work conditions. We-People also provided the impetus behind the Civil Rights Movement that resulted in the passage of the Civil Rights Act of 1964, guaranteeing equality of treatment in the workplace for all workers. Those currently arguing for a living wage for all workers and holding owners of businesses accountable for work conditions tend to be part of this tradition.

This very brief overview of core beliefs and how they manifest illuminates the source of the debates about business ethics and public policy. Different people and varying groups have divergent ideas about life. Our core beliefs define what we consider to be ethical behavior. Our core convictions determine how we define justice, those conditions that we believe are required to assure fundamental fairness in the larger business and political arenas. Yet in spite of all these differences, we are supposed to live and work together with some semblance of harmony.

IMPLICATIONS FOR ETHICS AND PUBLIC POLICY

Over the past several decades, we have seen vitriolic policy debates about what are proper business ethics as well as about the correct government response to the problems. These discussions generate much heat but little light. Because we can't figure out ways to honor the beliefs of those with whom we disagree and because we don't want to be seen as waffling on the topics, we position ourselves on the ends of the political continuum and proclaim our position as the truth. In

Individual Tradition ❖	_Community Tradition_
OUR COMMUNITY SHOULD EMPHASIZE ...	
... INDEPENDENCE which means that we are egalitarian and admit people based on merit alone.	... INTERDEPENDENCE which means that we are hierarchal and admit people based on birth and/or belief.

the process, we lose the ability to find meaningful solutions that incorporate the strengths while ameliorating the weaknesses of each position.

The policy debate about access to jobs and education highlights the differences well. Those who favor independence believe we should follow the rules and hire people based on merit, considering only whether they have job skills that we need and thus are the best person for the job. For example, this group of people believe we should admit young people into universities based on their proven ability (grades) or potential (test scores). Those who favor interdependence will admit young people into top schools based on birth (being the child of a graduate, or a "legacy") or belief (assuring that people ascribe to a set of principles). The difficulty comes when we want to use merit for one category of people (women and minorities) and prerogative of birth for a second category (our own children).

The same conundrum is seen in the current debate about non-documented workers. Those who favor independence assert that because the workers are not admitted through the formal processes of immigration law, they should not be given legitimate social status. People chose to break the law in coming to the US, and so they should not be expected to be protected by the law. Those who favor interdependence note that, using our market power, those of us who are citizens hire non-documented workers to till our fields and clean our houses, we take their payments for taxes and social security, and simultaneously deny them or their children who were brought to the United States as toddlers the protection of the law that would come with legal status or the protection of the community that would come with belonging. If those of us who are citizens are not thoughtful and if we do not work at being consistent in our definitions and expectations, we risk being at best inconsistent or at worst hypocritical and selfish.

Individual Tradition ❖	_Community Tradition_
OUR GOVERNMENT SHOULD TILT TOWARD ...	
... NEO-MERCANTILE so that resources are transferred to provide security for the community to enhance autonomy.	... SOCIAL DEMOCRACY so that resources are transferred to provide opportunity for individuals to enhance equality.

A next logical question becomes the right use of community resources—regulation, taxes, and gifts. Those who believe in independence claim that private property needs to be in the hands of individuals who can use it as they wish. Therefore, our taxing policies should be designed to transfer wealth only for national security. Also, tax incentives are permissible for protecting business, in particular industries and agriculture that contribute to national security. However, because in general government structures cannot be trusted, we should have as few regulations as possible.

EVERYDAY ETHICS: _Making Wise Choices in a Complex World_

Those who tilt toward interdependence will assert that we need to assure that children, and by extension their families, receive food, shelter, health care, and education. They believe our resources should be transferred to those without economic power in order to provide these building blocks of opportunity. Further, we need government regulation to prevent the abuse of power by individuals seeking to maximize their own self-interest.

As we then move to the larger conversation, the global economy, the problems become even more complex. The conversation that is heard in the domestic arena is rearticulated on the global stage. Those who favor independence believe that companies can make whatever agreements they want with multi-national companies, as well as with companies and/or individuals in the global economy. If we choose to work for a few cents a day, that is our prerogative; if we don't choose to bargain for decent work conditions, that is our choice. Those who favor interdependence look more carefully at a balance of power and assert that those of us with great market power need to attend to the common good of those of us in other communities as well.

Individual Tradition	❖	*Community Tradition*
GLOBAL RELATIONSHIPS SHOULD EMPHASIZE ...		
... *INDEPENDENCE* with agreements that assure individual agreements with companies.		... *INTERDEPENDENCE* with agreements that assure inclusive considerations for the people in the countries.

The financial meltdown of 2009 showed the interdependence of banks and stock exchanges of the world. The growth of multi-national companies with manufacturing and service sites in multiple countries provide opportunities to move our thinking beyond our traditional national borders. Those who are talking about global business leadership are seeing an emergence of a global business culture and ethic, one that is not defined by cultural expectations or the country in which the company happens to be situated.

The conversation is increasingly not about an American ethic of business or a Chinese ethic of business but rather a global ethic of business: what are the expectations that we should have of each other as we build a culture of trust to assure the full flowering of commerce? Given that we don't have an effective legal system that crosses international boundaries, a vibrant, effective, and efficient global economy depends on building agreement through contract and a culturally independent ethic.

The final, and perhaps the most difficult, conversation requires that we sort out our relationship to our Mother—the earth. Historically, we were exhorted to use and exploit our natural re-

Individual Tradition	❖	*Community Tradition*
WE SHOULD ENCOURAGE THE ...		
... *USE OF NATURAL RESOURCES* to assure that individuals have resources to create wealth and thrive.		... *CONSERVATION OF NATURAL RESOURCES* to assure that the planet is left intact for our children and grandchildren.

sources to create wealth. Because we want to have access to inexpensive oil, we find ways to drill on national parks and in the wilderness. Because we see a better life created by individual homes on the desert, we divert water from our rivers. Because we love nature, we build our homes on the edge of the national forests and complain about fire. But mostly, because the danger doesn't seem real, we do not restrain our own desires to assure that our children will have resources for their lives.

When the earth seemed huge and the supplies unlimited, the policies made sense. However, we now know that the resources are not limitless. The 2010 oil spill in the Gulf of Mexico caused by the explosion of a deep-water rig owned by BP reminds us that our earth is fragile and we are responsible for our planet. While young people may divide on other areas of public policy, those in their mid-thirties often agree on environmental policy. Those who see themselves as staunch political and fiscal conservatives have questions about global warming and the politics of drilling in the Arctic. They are also clear that the intertwined policies of enhanced production to build healthy, growing businesses and patterns of personal consumption contribute to the problem. Because many have the nagging thought that we must completely revamp our assumptions for politics, economics, and business in order to address the environmental problems, people will set aside closely held ideas to find creative and compelling solutions.

Interestingly, a new movement is beginning: environmental peacemaking. Across the globe, "hostile countries that share borders are working together to save their common environments."[19] Because the stakes are high, countries are learning to cooperate to solve problems from jellyfish that are taking over the Caspian Sea to peace parks that are "created in transboundary areas with ecological significance" such as the Cordillera del Condor Peace Transborder Reserve in a section of rainforest between Peru and Ecuador.[20] This thoughtful humility allows for creative local answers to environmental problems.

THE EXCLUDED MIDDLE

As long as the task is seen as finding the right answers, the debate will continue endlessly. If the postmodern theorists are right and reason will never provide a definitive answer, the only resolution would seem to be radical relativism, where each of us gets to choose knowing that we don't have any provable criteria for determining what is good or better. However, that resolution doesn't bring comfort either. Many assert that a lack of guidelines allowed greed to have its day in the two financial meltdowns of the past decades—to the detriment of many of those without power. In their heart of hearts, many know that mindless relativism will not solve the problems of a global economy or environmental deterioration.

EVERYDAY ETHICS: *Making Wise Choices in a Complex World*

From Answers to Questions

As the postmodern debate matured, the existentialists demonstrated that all we know is our own existence, which takes us to nihilism—the belief that everything is pointless and absurd. The phenomenologists focused on the role of language in shaping our understanding of the world. Because reality can only be known through the concepts and the words we choose, everything depends on language and individual interpretation.[21] At that point, any shared understanding seems impossible. While the academic case made for these approaches is persuasive, it doesn't offer much hope to those trying to practice applied ethics.

Some ethicists, to escape the conundrum of trying to find certain foundations for ethical action when the pillars of the temple melted into unfathomable muck, acknowledged that the bulwarks of truth were contested and then chose to pretend that the dissolved foundations were in fact essential for coherent ethical analysis.[22] However, that approach isn't very satisfactory, either. We cannot learn how to live with contingent truth (the best that we know now) and constructed reality (individuals contextualizing their own lives) by pretending that the foundations for Truth are at best unknowable or at worst illusory.

Another set of theorists, whom some call constructive postmodernists, sought a systemic and holistic way to move out of the box of rationalism and foundationalism.[23] These theorists found that to make sense out of our current knowledge, we had to move beyond reason to include emotions, which give us empathy, and spirit, which impels humans to self-transcend the limitations of our narrow, often selfish, thinking. We had to find ways to synthesize the right-brain, external understanding of the world with the left-brain, internal understanding of the self.[24] We had to find a way to neutralize the belief that reason was the territory of strong, rational men and emotions were the purview of soft, illogical women. We needed both an ethic of reason and an ethic of care.[25]

This task has only emerged in the United States during the last half of the 20th century. For about the first two-hundred years of our existence, Americans had what Robert Wuthnow calls the "unitary self." We didn't have to worry about sorting through various assumptions to know who we were because we were born into a family that had well established religious and political beliefs.[26] Those family beliefs provided the foundations for our morals and the religious institutions reinforced our ethics. Because everyone participated in a religious community, even if nominally, the church was the location for teaching morals and ethics. In tightly knit communities, the values were monolithic and minimally contested.

Since the 1960s, the foundations of the monolithic traditions have been challenged. People are exploring wide varieties of traditions and becoming what some pundits call "cafeteria believers," taking morsels from varying teachings and practices to put together a smörgåsbord of personal beliefs. This exploration makes perfect sense in a postmodern world where we have the privilege of constructing our own reality. The result is the creation of what Wuthnow calls a "dispersed self … whose being is defined in a wide variety of encounters and experiences, including moments of interaction with sacred objects, such as trees and automobiles"[27] Thus, we not only have to determine our place in the world, but we also have to construct ourselves — determine who we are, what behaviors are important, and find meaning for both our personal and professional lives.

The feminist philosophers, such as Carol Gilligan, Adrienne Rich, Norma Haan, and Sandra Harding, began exploring the disconnect between an ethic of reason that focused on rules and an ethic of care that focused on relationship. The gauntlet was taken up by theologians such as Bernard Lonergan, a constructive postmodernist, who rejected the course of nihilism and phenomenology to chart a more promising passageway through the treacherous waters of radical relativism. What he proposed was that we not focus on trying to agree on the "Truth" with a capital "T" but rather acknowledge that all knowledge is contested as is the definition of what is the "Good" with a capital "G."

His solution was to change the perspective: we can ask good questions rather than focus on right answers. Lonergan asserts that all human beings have an "unrestricted desire to know" that manifests in our trying to make sense out of that which doesn't make sense. He claimed that we can discern between "good" and "better," and in fact have that responsibility as humans.

If Lonergan is right, then rather than trying to decide between the two traditions, we can use the wisdom of both traditions. Instead of fixating on either-or, we can approach the problems with a both-and approach that includes the excluded middle of dualism. As we ask questions together, seeking to harmonize the good and the true, we may not find the "Answer," but we may discover better answers.[28]

CONCLUSION

After hearing the litany of differences that opened this chapter, many people assert that the way to harmony is to resist being placed in neat categories or boxes. Practical experience teaches that many in fact use a blend of the ideas of both schools of thought in making ethical decisions. As we attend to our world, we can see that from the smallest unit of community, the family, to the largest nation-state or multinational corporation, the culture of these segments of life is determined by the overall worldview, the sum total of the core beliefs held by a person or an institution. We also know that those core beliefs are multi-faceted, and thus we resist one-dimensional solutions to complex questions.

By asking questions, we can see the implications of each position. We notice that each tradition has some truth and some good. We also notice that each position, if taken to excess, has problems. By not being overly attached to our positions, as we find better answers we can seek the balance found in a well-strung loom where both the warp and the weft are maintained in perfect tension. With this insight, as we weave the tapestry of our life, we can hold in tension the truth of the individual tradition and the good of the community tradition as we define our individual core beliefs and those held by the various communities in which we live and work.

As individuals assess situations and choose courses of action, they have the opportunity to hold in balance the prerogatives of individuals against the claims of the community. Faced with choices, people try to look at the problem from as many angles as possible to discern the best answer. As one person described it, rather than thinking in terms of taking positions at the ends of a teeter-totter, we can think of the process as assuring that the compact disk is balanced so it can play. Thus, our reason (our heads) can be informed by our emotions (our hearts). Then both can be balanced in the crucible of spirituality so that we can intentionally and compassionately work together. In the process we can know when to use stepping stone policies and when to use safety net policies so all members of our global community can thrive.

CONTINUING THE CONVERSATION

1. As you reflect on your own belief system, see if you can place yourself along the various continua that are part of this chapter. What are your core beliefs in each of these areas? Do you see yourself advocating consistency in how you expect yourself to navigate through this world as well as the policies you advocate in both private and public settings?

2. How are your beliefs the same or different that those of your parents? How is your worldview different from that of your parents or birth community? What knowledge and/or experiences have caused those changes?

3. Find an article in your local paper or a news magazine that deals with a current ethical situation. Does the article give the positions of both traditions? If not, which position is articulated? Are the reasons given for embracing a particular position clearly stated or are they assumed?

4. Read several articles about a current ethical problem or public policy debate. Write two op-ed pieces for a local paper. For one piece use the lens of the individual tradition for both identifying the reasons for the problem and fashioning a solution. Write the second piece with the lens of the community tradition. Which one was easier? Which one do you find more persuasive? How did you address the concerns of the other tradition in the process? Did you find yourself taking a middle ground to address the assumptions of both traditions?

THE BAIRD DECISION MODEL[1]
(Part 1)

BE ATTENTIVE

Attend to the context

Identify the decision maker

Pinpoint the ethical issue

BE INTELLIGENT

Determine the stakeholders

Explore the values in tension

Identify options for action

CHAPTER 4

Foundations for Decision-Making

MOST OF US GIVE LITTLE ATTENTION to the strategies we use to make ethical decisions. Relying on habit, we don't seem to realize that effective decision-making requires thoughtfulness on two fronts. We first need to explore what process we should use to resolve our thorny problems. We then need to ask what criteria should be applied to determine what actions are or are not ethical. Using undeveloped tools of reason and emotion, we hone our instincts as children while being socialized by our parents. Our nascent awareness of ethics gives each of us a rough sense of right and wrong.

Even though our embryonic principles of good behavior are usually inadequate for the task, we often use our childhood norms as touchstones when we make complex decisions in a rapidly changing world. Then, when we find ourselves in a surreal environment where no one appears to be behaving in ethical ways, we feel like Alice—we aren't sure where we want to go and we don't know if we can get there.

Making effective ethical decisions requires the use of strategies as precise as any other rigorous investigation for truth. Over the past two hundred years, those seeking better answers to difficult questions developed new methods of critical analysis. These processes not only unlocked the mysteries of the earth but assisted in studying the wonders of individuals, communities, and culture. Using the same tools of critical analysis as the scientists, philosophers and theologians strove to identify the criteria for norms—values translated into principles and goals—that should be followed if we want to be ethical persons.

Even though these scholars ultimately could establish neither foundations for a universal set of norms nor standard criteria by which the norms should be prioritized, the questions they asked and the world they envisioned help all of us to become more thoughtful ethical decision makers. As we learn to habitually exercise the tools of science that philosophers use to explore and explicate key principles and values, each of us can be better equipped to be a thoughtful and intentional ethical person-in-community.

Becoming an effective decision maker requires practice. A learner-centered approach to ethics encourages participants to use the Baird Decision Model along with at least two of the four different ethical lenses. This chapter presents the first two steps, which help frame the problem. The next chapter discusses the final steps where the decision is made. Together these two chapters highlight an effective process for making hard choices in a complex world.

DECISION STEP 1:   BE ATTENTIVE

BE ATTENTIVE

❖ *Attend to the context*

❖ *Identify the decision maker*

❖ *Pinpoint the ethical issue*

As we frame ethical questions, three preliminary tasks set the parameters of the problem: 1) attend to the context of the problem; 2) identify the viewpoint of the decision maker; and 3) pinpoint the ethical issue. These steps are like gathering all of the ingredients before starting to cook a meal. As more care is given to the preparatory stages, the cooking itself becomes pleasurable and less frenetic, which results in a delectable dinner when the process is complete. If the facts of the context are ignored, the answer may be incomplete or incorrect. If the role and viewpoint of the ethical decision maker aren't clearly delineated, then inappropriate actions may be taken. If the ethical issue is not framed correctly, the wrong problem might be addressed, leaving the original problem unresolved.

PART 1: ATTEND TO THE CONTEXT

The first task we have as decision makers is to relax, step back, and notice all of the wonderful and not so wonderful things in our world, the context in which we are living and taking action. This context has two elements: the objective facts in the situation and our own worldview, the lens with which we interpret the facts. Both elements must be considered to get a full sense of the context of the situation.

The facts of the situation

Ethical decision making requires that we pay attention to the facts of the situation. As people begin to consider ethical questions, each one brings different information and assumptions to the conversation. The facts that are present, the context in which they are placed, and the assumptions of the ethical decision maker determine the way the problem is approached and solved. A careful description of the situation is crucial if we are to have a clear sense of the problem.

In describing the situation, we should make every effort not to prejudge what is happening but use language that is as value neutral as possible. Thus, the words should be normative (e.g., a table; a policy; a person) rather than descriptive (e.g., an old, decrepit table; a selfish, self-serving policy; a thoughtful, altruistic person). By using value neutral language, we avoid the temptation to use emotion-laden words to bias the interpretation. While all of ethics is ultimately subjective, we can have controlled subjectivity by being as objective as possible in defining the problem.

The context provides an eagle's eye view of the problem where details can be clearly seen from a distance. A brief description of the situation's history is useful. What are the relationships, the expectations of the primary players? Exploring the various approaches to the problem and the concerns of those who are part of the decision may help clarify the primary conflicts. Again, as practical ethics always requires application of abstract ideas to specific situations, we should make the description of the context complete enough to give us a sense of the problem at hand but brief enough that the reader will not be overwhelmed with extraneous details.

In describing the situation, we always need to acknowledge that our worldview is both limited in information and colored by our own closely held values and perceptions. In framing the question, talking with others can assist us in widening our worldview. We also need to notice that different facts will be important depending on the ethical focus we choose. The essential elements of the context are contingent on the information needed to investigate a problem using a particular lens. As we get clarity about the contours of a problem, we begin to see the way that ethical beliefs both join and divide a group. These biases may be because of personal experience (e.g.,surviving the Holocaust), particular knowledge (e.g.,training as an accountant), or personal weakness (e.g.,tending to see everything as a personal threat to well-being).

Our personal worldview

To navigate the certainties and uncertainties of life, we look at our world, examine the received teachings about our physical home, we ask "what if … ." What if this idea that my parents taught me is wrong? What if my understanding of the human person is wrong? Often, questions arise because the traditional explanations do not provide adequate answers for what we know or experience. We might have new information or notice that the offered interpretation doesn't match our experience. As we ask these questions, the ultimate answers we are seeking result from the question "what is true and what is good."

Every new idea that we embrace impels us to action. Every action has both intended and unintended outcomes as well as expected and unexpected results. We note what happens, see what pieces of the puzzle fall into place and which ones still haven't found a home in the picture —and continue to ask more questions. When we get an insight, when the pieces of the puzzle that didn't fit suddenly do, we see that order emerge from the seeming chaos. Then, as when running through a field of thistles, to avoid the prickles we need to pay close attention to their own worldview as well as the particular problem before us, ever watching for the unexpected sticklers.

Our personal journey begins as we are born into a community and learn how to negotiate in this world through the received wisdom of our elders. While learning how to think and speak as toddlers, we also absorb our parents' understanding of the world. We learn how to communicate, and, more importantly, we learn to identify what, according to our parents, is real and what is not real as we make sense of the physical world. Part of the task of becoming an adult is reevaluating the "truths" our parents taught to assure that our perceptions are not clouded by their biases. The Peter, Paul, and Mary classic "Puff, the Magic Dragon" is poignant for we each remember when our magic dragons were sent away and we had learn to deal with another level of reality.

The first exile happens with our shift into the literal world of seven-and eight-year-olds when our pretend friends were permanently sent to camp. The more difficult transition is critically examining what we were taught by our families and community as we move into adulthood. From time to time we need to banish some of the comfortable prejudices that we inherited from our families. People who are raised with racism may have to learn that people from different ethnic groups are no better or worse than themselves. People who are raised believing that one religious truth is the only way, may have to learn that other faiths have elements of truth. For many, sorting out their inherited beliefs is a difficult but liberating process. Many of the beliefs may be reclaimed, but only after thoughtful consideration.

The interests and beliefs of our family also open doors in this marvelous, opportunity-rich world. One family may value the arts, so the children will be introduced to music at a very early age and encouraged to develop their talents in that arena. Music and literature set the trajectory for their careers. Another family may teach their children how to look at the physical world carefully and critically. Biology, ecology, and attention to detail prime them to become scientists. Those early years bend the twig and establish the shape for growth.

Because we build on the knowledge and experience of our families and the information available when we were born, each generation has a different understanding of the world. People born on the threshold of the Great Depression have a fear and respect for scarcity that differs from the expectation of abundance that Baby Boomers take for granted. Those who fought for racial and gender equality are hyper-sensitive to individual and systemic discrimination. Those born after the anti-discrimination laws were well implemented expect that people in the workplace will be rewarded according to competence, not privilege of race or gender.

Generations coming into adulthood now have no understanding of a world before computers and cell phones. The children coming up through our educational system will only know learning mediated by technology. As we grow to adulthood, we are profoundly molded by our family and our culture.

Our worldview includes an understanding of ethics—how to live in community with others. We, the children of each generation, accept the ideas of the elders as a given. Then we identify the next set of problems and seek solutions to situations that our parents just accepted as what is and cannot be changed. At some point, every generation questions the received wisdom and worldviews of their forebears. We

❖ RECEIVED WISDOM ABOUT ETHICS

If one properly reflects and is trained, one right answer will emerge as the correct ethical answer in a given situation.

begin to determine, both as individuals and as communities, whether what we were told about ourselves, others, and the world in fact matches our experience and understanding of our lives. For example, we may ask whether one economic or political system is really that much better than another. We may wonder whether acting only in our own self interest without considering the environment or other people really makes sense.

The dance that forms a person-in-community unfolds in an intricate set of if-then steps. We say, "if this is true…then this should follow." When we note that our expected result does not follow, we have questions. Why is this result different? What else do I need to know? What am I not seeing clearly? Is the explanation that I've been given for the state of the world really true? Like Hansel and Gretel, we begin fol-

❖ EVALUATING RECEIVED WISDOM

If with reflection and training one right answer will emerge, then we should not have so many differences of opinion and approaches to ethical issues. Why the difference?

lowing the crumbs of insight hoping to find our way back home where all makes sense.

As we walk the path, we ask, either at a conscious or unconscious level, what about our life is not working. What explanations of our world don't make sense? When a new idea appears, we consider whether it is worthy of adoption. As individuals and the whole community test new concepts, we learn whether our notions are grounded in some sense of truth. Once we get preliminary answers, we ask whether we are willing to change our worldview, to follow our dreams based on new data. A pitfall would be to get stuck in a romanticized but inaccurate version of reality and not embrace new opportunities.

A final question we ask is what difference it would make for us to accept this new idea. The change can be in our understanding of our self, our knowledge of science or society, or in the action that would be required. Given that our sense of self and our world is shaped by the beliefs we hold, the new ideas can be terrifying, exhilarating—or both. Like parasailing over the ocean, adopting new ideas and choosing a new trajectory for life—embracing a new worldview—gives us an expanded and slightly scary vantage from which to observe and enjoy life.

NEW IDEAS

❖ *What if multiple ways of doing ethics were equally valid depending on one's vision of a "good life" and understanding of the human person-in-community?*

❖ *How can the community accept many different views without having all of ethics devolve into nothing more than egoistic preference instead of common truths?*

❖ *What change is needed in our understanding of people and business to adequately balance the desires and needs of individuals against the desires and needs of the community?*

Working through ethical problems with others helps us identify our own ethical worldview, our core beliefs and core commitments. Core beliefs are those ideas that form the structure of our understanding of ourselves and our world; these beliefs are formed as we search for that which is true. Core commitments are beliefs that are held with passion and compel us to action; these commitments are formed as we search for that which is good. In the process, "love and truth have come together; justice and peace join hands." [3]

As we become more skilled at ethical decision-making, we come to terms with our complex world. We learn how to be true to our own beliefs and commitments, while understanding that they are provisional—at best, all we know at this particular time. At the same time, we strive to effectively work with others who hold different beliefs and commitments, learning from them as we share together the best of our knowledge of the world and work together to create the world we envision.

Embracing a cycle of tension and resolution, the hallmark of mature ethical decision-making, helps us to live peacefully and effectively as persons in this community. As we become more comfortable with the uncertainties of life, we can feel secure in the process of the continuous improvement of our belief system and celebrate the idea that the world is seen and constructed through our personal worldview. Taking up the challenge of noticing just how we construct our world, we can enjoy the habit of paying attention rather than avoiding truly seeing because we are afraid that new information might threaten us. We learn to attend to our environment, committed to seeing that which we don't expect and noticing that which we may not want to see.

Given that we tend to interpret the events in our life to enhance our own vision of the world, and given that all of us want to see ourselves as ethical, we must make sure that our ethical lenses are polished so our vision is clear. Those who find themselves in a competitive world where the goal is to acquire as many material toys as possible are particularly susceptible to flawed sight. Focusing on the physical world, they tend to ignore the spiritual realm, which emphasizes mindfulness and humility.

Cultivating the habit of awareness helps us carefully seek answers and consider our own biases. To be effective ethical decision makers, we need to develop our ethical sensibilities—

EVERYDAY ETHICS: *Making Wise Choices in a Complex World*

recognizing when either our own or the community's core values are in conflict. As we become more aware of the ethical values that are held individually and by members of the community, we can make more effective decisions.

All philosophers as well as spiritual teachers caution that we must examine our own selves with as much thoughtfulness as we do the world around us. What are our motives, our goals? What are our fears, our weaknesses? The temptation for each of us is to reinforce our preexisting worldview as we interpret the world around us rather than see every day, every opportunity, with fresh eyes. Learning to give up our attachment to being right in order to build and support an effective life, as well as our varied organizations, requires thought and commitment. In fact, giving up our attachment to being right and to promoting ourselves is the most difficult task of ethical decision making. Often we would rather face failure than admit that we are wrong.

Many of us are like the characters in the classic movie *The War of the Roses*, where the husband and wife, in the middle of a nasty divorce, refused to compromise, preferring instead to die together swinging on a chandelier. Many a company has gone bankrupt because the owners were more concerned about being right and amassing personal fortune and exercising privilege than being a responsible steward of the stakeholders' resources. Many employees have been fired because of their attachment to doing a job in a particular way rather than seeing where they could, with integrity, do the work as instructed. As we practice the discipline of awareness, of paying attention, we must learn to tell the truth about ourselves as well as others.

PART 2: IDENTIFY THE DECISION MAKER

Every ethical decision has someone or some organization responsible for carrying out the action. The temptation is to look at the ethical act either in a vacuum or from an omniscient point of view. However, people and organizations make decisions in particular places and times that affect specific sets of persons. Those people and organizations never have full information about the consequences of their choices and are limited by their knowledge and their best predictions about the results of their choices. Thus, ethical decision makers must place the problem in the context of their own information and belief systems.

In identifying the ethical decision maker, we must attend to who has the authority to act. From time to time, sending the decision to another desk is important. If the person confronting the problem doesn't have the proper authority, then consulting an ethics committee or sending the issue to a supervisor may be appropriate. At that point, the person refer-

❖ *Ethical decisions are always contextual: they are made in light of the ethical decision maker's understanding of the culture, expectations of the community, and the actor's own sense of what is right or wrong in a given situation.*

ring the problem is not making an ethical decision but rather a managerial one. After consulting with the appropriate stakeholders, the final ethical decision needs to be made by a person with the actual authority to choose a course of action.

Part 3: Pinpoint the Ethical Issue

Framing the ethical issue involves two distinct phases. The first phase is determining whether the problem at hand is an ethical issue. We need to distinguish among technical questions (questions about how to do something), aesthetic preferences (questions about personal preferences), and true ethical issues (questions about how our actions impact ourselves or others). The second phase is to frame the question precisely to highlight the conflict.

Framing an ethical problem as a question to be answered is very useful. Because the way we ask a question sets the trajectory for the decision, we must carefully select the language of the problem. The process involves both individual assessment of the conflict as well as the communal process of checking with others to assure that we are seeing the problem correctly.

Is this an ethical question?

Gordon Kaufman, in his book *In Face of Mystery: A Constructive Approach to Theology*, presents an elegant construct for determining whether an ethical issue exists.[4] Kaufman notes that for most of our lives we are unaware, acting out of habit and instinct. Then something happens that disrupts the flow of action: something is not quite right and we have to make a decision about what to do.

Ethical issues raise questions about the proper definitions of rights and responsibilities, appropriate ways to reach a goal, or a tension between individual and community obligations. Kaufman notes that as we attend to ethical issues, we must take responsibility for and be concerned "with acts as constituents and shapers of an ongoing web of action (morality)."[5] This conversation involves exploring what is appropriate action to promote goodness, right action, and justice. At the center, each controversy is a conflict in the categorization and application of core values.

Another kind of decision Kaufman calls "expedient reflection." This kind of thought is concerned with choosing the action that will promote a specific goal and discerning the best technique for accomplishing that goal. A nurse who is to give inoculations needs to be technically competent so that patients don't pass out from fear or suffer through clumsy work. Similarly, accountants need to know the rules of GAAP (Generally Accepted Accounting Principles) if they are going to competently complete an audit of a company.

We see moral reflection intersect with technical decisions as we determine whether we are going to complete our work with integrity. Issues such as plagiarism, falsifying documents, fraud, product safety, and inattention to safety in the workplace fall in this category. Much of the work in professional ethics concerns delineating how, for example, lawyers, accountants, and health care professionals, are supposed to meet their professional obligations. Ethical failure in the professional arena is often grounds for dismissal.

Another kind of decision involves aesthetic reflection. For this decision, the issue is elegance of process and outcome. How can the action be carried forward in a way that is aesthetically pleasing? Many of the decisions that upset us as humans are matters of simple personal preference. Learning to do our work elegantly is important. However, when we find ourselves fussing over the layout of an office, the typeface on a report, or the form of a project, we need to remember that these issues are not quite as important as those we consider ethical decisions.

Aesthetic decisions intersect with ethical deliberation around interpersonal concerns. Issues such as sexual or racial harassment, inappropriate dress, intoxication at company parties, and bullying fall into this category. Historically, breaches of interpersonal ethics have been tolerated more than breaches of professional or fiduciary ethics. However, with increasing concern for treating all people with respect, people are expected to behave well in the workplace and will be punished for not adhering to high interpersonal standards.

The distinction between these two forms of ethical violations was seen with the saga of Mike Hurd, former CEO of Hewlett-Packard and newly hired co-CEO of Oracle. Hurd was dismissed from HP after being accused of sexual harassment and falsifying expense reports. After a full investigation, HP determined that while the behavior of entertaining a contractor while on business trips didn't rise to sexual harassment, it did violate company policy. Hurd was immediately hired by Oracle.

Commentators noted that Hurd had more than tripled profit at HP through cost cutting measures and expanding their business. Daniel Indiviglio cynically noted that in decisions of hiring and firing, violations of ethics in the personal arena may not matter, but violations of ethics that affect the financial well-being of the company clearly do. In comparing Hurd with Bernie Madoff and Enron, Indiviglio states: "Instead of using their superior talent and expertise, such firms or individuals must rely on fraud to bring in profits. The business community has no use for mere thievery as a means to make money."[6]

What is the specific issue to be resolved?

An ethical question will present a set of conflicts. The clash may be between competing rights (e.g., the right of an employee vs. the right of an employer). The dissension may be between competing goals (e.g., the goal of efficiency vs. the goal of having a reputation for absolute honesty). The dispute may also be between competing notions of justice (e.g., the obligation of a corporation to distribute maximum return to shareholders and the obligation to pay employees a fair, living wage with appropriate benefits).

The conflict may also be about which virtues are most important in a particular role (e.g., integrity in telling the truth about a situation or loyalty to the company). The question will often involve not only competing values but a question about how to harmonize and balance the values in this particular situation. Because ethics is about choosing a course of action, the first task is to frame the issue as accurately as possible so that the conflict may be clearly seen.

DECISION STEP 2: BE INTELLIGENT

Be intelligent

❖ *Determine the stakeholders*

❖ *Explore the values in tension*

❖ *Identify options for actions*

As we learn to pay attention to the world around us, we must evaluate the information we found when we explored the context of the problem. We begin the process by being intelligent—working to understand what we see, expressing what we believe to be true, and considering all of the implications of our knowledge.[7] Being intelligent involves not only attending to our own worldview but also being sensitive to individual values as well as cultural and community expectations. As we engage in this next phase, three core questions will help us intelligently explore the ethical question so the best decision possible can emerge from our deliberations.

First, we have to identify the stakeholders, those who will be affected by our decision. Next, we ask what core values are in conflict. The tricky part of working through an ethical analysis is identifying the core values and seeing how they are in tension with each other. A good resolution involves fashioning a solution that addresses the underlying concerns of the core values. This solution requires that we find ways to honor both conflicting values rather than devolving into polarization. Ethical dilemmas are problems because two or more equally good values are in conflict. The temptation is to give only one value priority rather than trying to harmonize them. Finally, we must identify the options for action. Often this step requires thinking creatively about multiple possibilities, not just mindlessly doing what has been done before.

PART 1: DETERMINE THE STAKEHOLDERS

All ethical decisions are relational, because varying parties are directly affected by the choice. Thus, the next step is to identify the stakeholders. Be sure to include those who have to carry out the decision, those directly affected by the decision, and those whose interests are to be protected.

EVERYDAY ETHICS: *Making Wise Choices in a Complex World*

We need to remember that Monday morning quarterbacking by members of the organization and the community accompanies any important ethical decision. If we do not have the buy-in of the core constituents, then the right action may be ignored or subverted. Thus the context into which the decision will play out and the potential response of members of the community are always factors in the strategy.

During the last half of the 20th century, a shareholder theory of management emerged. That theory asserts that shareholders and owners are the only stakeholders with a direct interest in the ethical acts of the company's agents, and thus are the only interests to be considered. The belief is that the financial interests of these stakeholders should never be compromised by the ethical decisions of leadership. One weakness of this theory is that historically those who own shares in a company do not exercise control over the operations but vote with their feet by selling their stock when they don't like what a company is doing.

That trend is changing as large pension funds begin to exercise more control by pressuring boards of directors to take action. An example of the pressure that can be leveraged comes from the California State Teachers Retirement System (CalSTRS). CalSTRS, the third largest pension fund in the United States, joined with others to force President and CEO Michael Eisner to shed some of his leadership role in the Disney Corporation. CalSTRS also recommended that the investors form a committee to hold Disney accountable for the changes.[8]

STAKEHOLDERS

❖ *Tier 1: Shareholders*

❖ *Tier 2: Employees and customers*

❖ *Tier 3: Competitors and vendors*

❖ *Tier 4: Interested community members*

The stakeholder theory was developed in response to the inadequacies of the shareholder theory, which shortchanged the interests of the employees and other constituents. The stakeholder theory posits that to assure the financial and ethical health of the firm, the ethical decision maker should consider all stakeholders in the decision. Lynn Sharpe Paine, in *Value Shift*, reminds us that every problem has four different sets of stakeholders who are impacted by the choices of the organization and who have interests in the decision.[9] The first tier of stakeholders is the shareholders, those whose financial investment and ownership in the company will be directly impacted by the ethical acts of leadership and other employees. The second tier includes those immediately impacted by a company decision, such as employees, customers, and suppliers. The third tier lists constituents such as competitors and vendors.

By considering all of the levels of stakeholders, we determine who will be impacted by a decision and decide who has a legitimate claim to celebrate or critique the organization's actions. As we discipline ourselves to identify all tiers of interested parties, we can tune our social antennae. While the claims of all stakeholders may not be equal, all should be considered.

Falling under the broad rubric of Corporate Social Responsibility, the final tier addresses the concerns of the larger community that may be affected (e.g., labor policies or environmental policies). Those in the final tier may not be directly impacted by the decision but may have persuasive power in the community. As these fourth tier constituents clearly articulate their concerns, they may impact policy. For example, a person may care about whether a particular company uses child labor in Asia. If that person is not employed by the company, does not own stock in the company, and does not buy the company's products, the policy and underlying ethical values may not have any direct personal impact.

However, as Nike and others learned the hard way when the movement against sweatshops brought the issues to the forefront, a group of people who care passionately about a situation can force change. Companies therefore must be responsive to changing community expectations about acceptable corporate behavior. [10]

While considering the constituents, we also need to consider the role of these groups. For example, a legislative body or administrative agency might represent its own interest or it might be charged with representing the interest of the community as a whole. Thus, if the legislature is a constituent, we need to determine whether it is acting on behalf of itself or if it represents the people in the community. We should also look at the role of the persons involved because someone might represent the interests of another, such as an advocate or a formal agent.

PART 2: EXPLORE THE VALUES IN TENSION

Before we can identify and harmonize the values for a particular situation, we must become aware of the competing values that are inherent in any ethical dilemma. As individuals living in community, several overlapping sets of values come into play for any problem. While we have four broad categories of values, the specific content of those value sets is drawn from the communities in which we live as well as our own personal set of value priorities.

Our first value imprints are received from our family of origin. Each family has its own beliefs about what kind of autonomy a person should have or what constitutes fairness or equality. These ideas, which are ultimately passed on to us, are shaped by the religious and philosophical commitments of our forebears.

We get additional knowledge about what kinds of actions are ethical from the community in which we live. The more diverse the community, the more varied and disputed are the values in play. One reason for the surge in ethical conflicts is because of the diversity of our communities. When we live in a community that is racially, religiously, and economically homogenous, the values are shared and thus invisible. When the community becomes diverse, the differences in values and their priorities become very clear.

Someone who has not paid attention to the amount of privilege they have had (such as having parents who can make a large down payment on their house) may not see that those who do not come from that kind of wealth have different definitions of "fair" in getting affordable housing. Thus, in order to be effective ethical decision makers, we must attend to the similarities and differences between personal and community views.

A third source of values is found in the culture of the organization where we work and is articulated by the company's leadership team. The Ethics Resource Center asserted in its 2009 National Business Ethics Survey that "ethical culture is the single biggest factor determining the amount of misconduct that will take place in a business."[11] Companies are increasingly working to assure that the values stated during an employee's orientation are the ones that are lived out every day.[12] Thus, as we go to work we will have the opportunity to determine whether the organization in fact lives into the values we think are important. If we are very lucky, the actions that are expected and rewarded in the company are the same values stated in the mission statement of the organization and will harmonize with our own core commitments.

As seen in Chapter 2, the core values of the community can be placed into four broad categories that are in tension with each other. One tension is between the value of equality (assuring that members of the community are treated fairly) and the value of autonomy (assuring that each person has a chance to determine how best to live). The second tension is between rationality (where people know what is expected and what others will probably do in a situation regardless of the specifics of the situation) and sensibility (assuring that we consider the unique situation and thus have toler-

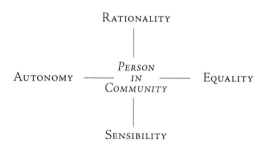

CORE VALUE SETS

RATIONALITY

AUTONOMY — PERSON IN COMMUNITY — EQUALITY

SENSIBILITY

ance and flexibility as we move and make choices in light of change and emerging conditions). As stated before, our task is often difficult because we believe that we have to choose between two good results, emphasizing one and excluding the other. However, as we make ethical decisions, we have the opportunity to fashion a solution that weaves together competing values.

The task is complicated even more when personal values conflict with the prevailing values in the community. Mediating the differences among people, communities, and cultures involves identifying the weight and priority that have been given to the different values. The underlying core values themselves are the same for each community, so the conversation about core values is similar across cultures. Thus, each culture (individual, organizational, and national) has to make its own choice about how to balance among the four competing core values.

In the United States, we claim that we value those who hold companies accountable for ethical behavior—whistle blowers. However, research that tracks the history of whistle blowers shows that our actions don't match with our values: those who reveal corruption in a company are often vilified and fired or marginalized.[13] These stories teach that loyalty to a company is in fact valued more than ethical transparency, no matter what the rhetoric. Which values are given priority in a situation to produce the best resolution will depend on individual beliefs and commitments as they are worked out in agreement or in tension with community beliefs and commitments.

As we engage the conversation, one criterion for reasonableness is the defensibility of the reasons that we use for the decision. Thus, if the reasons that are given are acceptable in a complex community, then the decision tends to pass muster. A second criterion is the authority underlying the action, be that legal (such as state statutes) or ideological (such as a particular theological or philosophical view). As we consider the components of the core values, any two or more of which may be in tension or conflict, we must clearly articulate the reason for the priority (for example, the rationale for emphasizing autonomy over security) and explicate our authority for acting (for example the U.S. Constitution rather than a conflicting local law).

The economics of the situation is also a factor. One element of the financial picture is what is called a boundary condition—we only have so much money in the bank and only certain available resources. Thus, within the financial constraints of the company, we have to make the most ethical decision possible. The second element has to do with how the resources of the company are distributed. In this regard, the four core values each have an economic factor that must be balanced along with the non-economic factors. We need to be sure not to bankrupt the company while doing good work. The goal is to do well while we are doing good.

CATEGORY LEVELS

META-CATEGORY—	*Animal* (*no specific image*)
NEXT CONCEPTUAL LEVEL—	*Cat* (*prototype image*)
NEXT CONCEPTUAL LEVEL—	*Siamese cat* (*concrete image*)

A final complicating factor is that as we balance these values we must consider the organization as an entity in addition to other individuals within the organization and members of the community. The balancing act includes not only the well-being of the company, but also the well-being of the employees. We are also invited to attend to the common good, to determine which actions will strengthen the community as a whole. The goal is to find that delicate balance between privileging the individual and the community so all persons can thrive and become whole.

EVERYDAY ETHICS: *Making Wise Choices in a Complex World*

Taken in isolation, the names of the core values and the two traditions that are historically the paths to maturity may not have much meaning to the ordinary person. Moving down one conceptual level gives us a more concrete picture of what kinds of issues are present in each of these categories. As Steven Winter reminds us in *A Clearing in the Forest*, we tend to articulate meta-categories that don't evoke any images or emotions.[14] As we identify the specific actions or items that are part of the category, we can wrap our minds around the more abstract notions. Autonomy as a concept may not have much meaning; however, the concrete right to spend our money the way we choose or say whatever we desire, even if it annoys people, strikes a visceral chord.

Identifying common value clusters

To help identify how the core values—rationality, sensibility, equality, and autonomy—might manifest as virtues in an organizational setting, a number of concrete situations and their attendant concerns and commitments are described below. We can use these examples to help us develop our ethical sensibilities as we explore the values that are present in every culture. While the following lists are by no means exhaustive, they represent the most common expressions of the value conflicts that appear in organizational ethics. As we work through various ethical problems, we have to identify the values in tension. Referring back to these lists might help in the quest.

The listing for each core value is divided into three categories: A) organizational concerns, which address the core values of the company or organization; B) individual concerns, which are the most often articulated values in the Western community; and C) stakeholder concerns, which help identify how others will be affected by the decision. The individual is separated from the organization to remind us that while we work for various organizations, we are members of more than one interest group. Therefore, our interests as employees may not be synonymous with those of our employers.

RATIONALITY: SAFEGUARDING EXPECTATIONS AND RULES OF THE GAME

This core value focuses on making sure that we have some sense of the rules of the game and that people will follow those rules. None of us likes to be surprised. Thus, even though we may not like the rule, we want to know what the members of our community expect of us. We want to know that agreements will be honored and contracts kept. We also want to be safe, both physically and financially. We want some assurance that we will not be injured and that we will get paid for our work.

Organizational concerns

STAYING IN BUSINESS: If revenues are down or a policy would break the bank, hard decisions have to be made. For example, as the cost of health care increases, companies that previously provided very comprehensive packages might find they cannot afford to offer the same level of care.

FIDUCIARY DUTIES: Employees are expected to put the concerns of the company ahead of their own interests. Profit taking or information sharing that puts the company at risk is a security issue. Thus, a key value is loyalty, where one avoids conflicts of interest. In management literature this particular characteristic is called "attitudinal commitment."

MINIMIZING WASTE: As a company needs to gain the maximum return while using the fewest possible resources, waste of time or resources is a concern. Whether avoiding abuse of telephones, the Internet, or office supplies, employers expect employees to put the interest of the company ahead of personal gain. The values in this cluster are efficiency and productivity.

Individual concerns

PHYSICAL SAFETY: The company is expected to provide a safe workplace. Safety includes the site itself—stairs, ventilation systems, and machinery—as well as protection against fellow employees—harassment, bullying or violence.

FINANCIAL SECURITY: We expect companies to assist employees in reaching economic security, having sufficient resources to care for themselves and their families. Minimum wage laws, laws about hours and conditions, and requirements for other benefits are some of the ways that companies are expected to help each person find economic security.

Stakeholder concerns

FINANCIAL INTEGRITY: Investors want to assure that the value of their investment is both preserved and returns a fair profit. This assures that neither they nor the company are put at financial risk because of bad management decisions, and that the company stays solvent so it is able to employ people in the community.

GOOD CITIZENSHIP: Stakeholders expect firms to follow the rules of doing business, such as abiding by GAAP and other laws, or, if they choose to violate the principles, to take appropriate responsibility for the inevitable consequences.

RESPONSIBLE CITIZENSHIP: Stakeholders are increasingly raising their voice to call firms to become responsible citizens in their treatment of the environment (sustainability) as well as the needs of the community (corporate social responsibility) around

EVERYDAY ETHICS: *Making Wise Choices in a Complex World*

them. Balancing financial responsibility with environmental and social needs requires careful thought and action.

SENSIBILITY: SAFEGUARDING THE ABILITY TO NIMBLY MOVE WITH EMERGING CIRCUMSTANCES — FLEXIBILITY, TOLERANCE, AND FREEDOM.

This core value is in tension with rationality. We are given much freedom to experiment and innovate as we set up our businesses. We have an expansive notion of sensibility as we tolerate different organizational structures and strategies. One of the hallmarks of American business is that we are expected to move gracefully with change. Thus, going out of business may not of itself be a bad thing if we are able to embrace new technology or opportunities to move ahead. We want to assure that all have the ability to change as needed to be more effective and efficient.

Organizational concerns

STAYING IN BUSINESS: Companies need to be able to change product lines, move locations, and reconfigure workforces. Thus, being locked into long term contracts or expectations of stability may hamper the ability of the company to rapidly adapt to change.

FIDUCIARY DUTIES: Granting the ability to move quickly often means that stakeholders should have little expectation that a firm will be particularly loyal to them. One question is whether the change is arbitrary and capricious or a careful response to changing circumstances. Another issue is whether the company has given adequate notice or met the cultural expectations before implementing change. A value in this setting would be due process, assuring fundamental fairness.

RISK TAKING: Companies are often rewarded for taking risk. Different individuals, companies, and cultures have varying tolerances for risk taking. A person who is allergic to risk would probably be well suited for government work rather than a seat on the stock exchange. America, as a whole, tends to be more risk friendly than other cultures.

Individual concerns

PHYSICAL SAFETY: People are expected to be alert, take personal responsibility, and protect themselves in workplace settings.

FINANCIAL SECURITY: Employees also want the ability to move, rather than to get locked into long term arrangements. The ability to make choices, move within the industry, and take personal risks is carefully guarded.

Stakeholder concerns

RESPONSIVENESS TO THE MARKET: When faced with difficult circumstances, stakeholders expect the company to be able to move quickly from a difficult situation in order to restore the company to health. The question often involves leaders determining what notice of a decision is appropriate as well as making choices that will not put the stakeholders at more risk than they have willingly embraced.

ANTICIPATING MARKET SHIFTS: Stakeholders also expect organizations to anticipate market shifts, both those that will bring added value to the firm as well as those that might cause the firm harm.

AUTONOMY: THE ABILITY TO CHOOSE FOR ONE'S SELF HOW BEST TO LIVE, BOTH IN TERMS OF RIGHTS AND RESPONSIBILITIES.

This core value is deeply embedded in the American psyche. Born in the image of the rugged individual escaping the oppression of a community that did not provide freedom of religion, speech, or economic opportunity, America is a nation committed to individual choice and the protection of individual rights.

Organizational concerns

MARKET AUTONOMY: Companies get to choose what products they want to sell, how they want to market those products, and what strategies they will embrace to ensure success. If leadership is unskilled and makes ill-informed choices, no one is expected to bail the company out of financial problems.

STRUCTURE OF THE ORGANIZATION: Companies are free to choose the form of business they wish—sole proprietor, partnership, corporation—based on their needs and preferences.

CLIENT BASE: Companies can choose the market segment they wish to pursue, which clients they wish to serve, and how they meet their client's needs and desires.

Employee concerns

The employees care about being able to retain as many of their privileges as independent persons as possible. Being treated as a responsible, engaged person helps employees find meaning at work.

PERSONAL LIVES: Employees' right to privacy ensures minimal interference with their personal lives (e.g., drug and alcohol restrictions, leisure activities). If a company resists a patriarchal approach to work, the leadership will embrace the notion that as employees give employers a fair day's work for a fair wage, what they do when they are off the clock should not matter.

Professional lives: Employees also expect minimal interference with their professional lives (e.g., cell phone or Internet use, clocking in or out, or not being required to do personal tasks for a superior). This value is described as the right to respect, appreciation, and being treated as an adult with inherent dignity.

Balance of power: While it is true that employees can either take a contract or leave it, most employees do not have great mobility. Thus, employees fear that they cannot easily say no to requests from superiors that may conflict with the employee's personal ethics. Watching the professional lives of whistle blowers crumble, colleagues fear that demanding that their employers be ethical will cost the employees their jobs. This value reminds us to neither abuse power nor be overbearing.

Stakeholder concerns

Stakeholders want to have enough information to make good choices.

SHAREHOLDERS AND INVESTORS: The company's financial partners expect transparency in the financial documents.

CONSUMERS: Those who buy the goods and services expect sufficient information about the product to assess the risks and benefits of the product.

COMMUNITY: The members of the community expect the company to be a good neighbor and also not abuse its power. Whether demanding tax benefits or polluting the environment, a company's exercise of autonomy is not expected to put the autonomy of the community at risk.

EQUALITY: FAIRNESS IN SHARING THE BURDENS AND BENEFITS

This core value is in direct tension with the value of autonomy. Those who value equality expect individuals to restrain their use of individual prerogatives in order to attend to the common good. As we structure our community, we want to assure that all persons have both equality of opportunity for living out their dreams as well as some rough equality of result in the distribution of benefits and burdens — the economic and political goods of the community.

Organizational concerns

SHARING BURDENS: The organization wishes to be treated fairly, like every other organization in the community. Thus, it does not expect to be taxed more or have higher safety or environmental requirements than other companies in similar industries. So, for example, all securities broker-dealers have higher duties of transparency than providers of retail products, but within each class, companies have the same responsibilities.

SHARING BENEFITS: Organizations expect equal opportunity to bid for business with other companies. Issues related to not giving benefits based on personal preferences, not inappropriately granting or withholding change orders, and fair treatment of stakeholders manifest under the goal of equality. An ongoing question is when companies should be treated as a person by the communities in which they are situated. Sometimes the law gives companies the rights of individuals and treats them as a person; other times they are treated as organizations with no inherent rights.

Employee concerns

SHARING BURDENS: Employees often focus on workload issues, safety risks, and treatment of differently situated persons (e.g., someone who has lots of kids and thus high medical needs, someone who has special medical needs, or someone who needs accommodations in the workplace environment). Making sure people are similarly treated while real differences are acknowledged is always a balancing act.

SHARING BENEFITS: Fair access to profits, salaries, and benefits—such as vacation, health care, and child care—is a major issue for employees. One rule adopted by companies considered ethical is that the highest-paid employee receives no more than 30 times what the lowest-paid employee receives.

Stakeholder concerns

SHARING BURDENS: Every community has formal or informal structures in place to help those who are less fortunate. Organizations who have as a goal to deliver quality goods and services at appropriate prices often find that balancing their social responsibility to help disadvantaged members of the community while still remaining profitable requires careful thought and discretion. The community expects companies to pay their fair share of the burdens through taxes as well as employment, thus issues of offshore tax filings or moving employment opportunities to foreign countries becomes germane when determining what is fair.

SHARING BENEFITS: Companies often come to a community because of quality of life features such as schools, affordable cost of living, and access to recreation. Stakeholders need to be sensitive to the fact that companies shouldn't expect to be treated differently than other folks. Conversations about tax subsidies offered to companies to induce them to relocate are particularly touchy as members of the community are torn between wanting the benefits that a company can bring while expecting the company to shoulder its fair share.

As we explore and articulate the different commitments in the community, it quickly becomes obvious that various people give different priority to the core values. We are all asked to discern between specific actions that are essential to meet the requirements of core values and strongly held commitments that would be nice to do but are not necessary given our ethical commitments.

Each of us has a different tolerance for the balance along the two continua. For example, someone may see loyalty as being critical for an organization where another may more highly prize individualism and independence. We all need to determine for ourselves what the appropriate balance is among the competing values and then negotiate that balance with other members of the community.

Determine the specific values in tension

The above cataloguing of how core values manifest as specific virtues is meant to enhance ethical sensitivity—being able to recognize an ethical dilemma when we see one. If we don't know what is prized in the culture, we unintentionally violate the ethical norms. As we become ever more sensitive to the ethical nuances of action, we can carefully identify the commitments in question and evaluate the consequences.

Many times we don't notice when ideals are in conflict. Ethical dilemmas don't generally announce their presence in Siren tones. Rather, problems creep up when we least expect them. Often the dilemmas are not obvious, as complicated situations have ethical questions buried in the facts, and then catch us in their sticky mess when we least expect it.

As stated earlier, an ethical question will usually be a choice between two competing good actions. We must attend to conflicts among competing good values in an organization and community. Does the person or the organization desire economizing behaviors, assuring the best productivity and return on investment, more or less than ecologizing behaviors, assuring that people and relationships are preserved?[15] Another set of questions might ask whether the individual rights of employees or customers are more or less important than the prerogatives of the organization. This conflict might play out in an organization with decisions about compensation, leave time, or benefits. Identifying the core values in tension helps sort out the possible options for action.

Ethical decisions do not usually involve determining whether or not to break the law. In our community, many people equate ethical action with following the law. However a core assertion of this text is that following the law is a secondary conversation. The primary conversation concerns indentifying what values and norms should be part of the community. Then we can work towards the goal of having the law match the norms of the community.

When an ethical standard is in dispute, people may choose to violate the law and engage in civil disobedience. However, using civil disobedience to draw attention to the disputed standard or unjust law is very different from playing the edges and hoping not to get caught. Because many of us like to get as close to the edge as possible to get an economic advantage, laws are passed to both define the playing field as well as arbitrate among competing ethical norms. Laws may be used to set the rules, if one uses the metaphor of business as a game. Laws may also provide clarification when standards are in dispute or be used to implement enforcement strategies when people don't follow the ethical norms of the community.

Discerning when a law is setting the parameters of the playing field and when it reflects a core value of the community will help leaders know when to play the edge and when to be squeaky clean. Practicing making decisions with hypothetical situations such as case studies and simulations helps us notice and evaluate our worldview concerning the core ethical commitments that are part of our community. As we solve various ethical problems, we can notice both what values are in conflict and which ideals are given a place of priority.

PART 3: IDENTIFY OPTIONS FOR ACTION

After determining the stakeholders and exploring the values in tension, the final step is to identify options for action. Applied ethical decision-making is about choosing among competing possibilities for action, including options that we believe are unethical. Many times we need to know why a particular choice does not pass ethical muster. Often, an option that at first blush appears unethical may in fact be the most ethical course of action. An option for action may include doing nothing, allowing continuation of the existing policy or course of action (or inaction).

The best options for action emerge after investigation and consultation. While research can never be complete, the final option for action is not more research. We must assure that we have consulted with all appropriate constituents to identify the best possible options. However, at some point a decision needs to be made.

Finally, good ethical decisions are creative solutions that elegantly harmonize competing interests. Knowing what different members of the community prefer helps us think outside of the box. For example, a company recently decided that it needed all employees to have ID tags to assure security. One of the long-time employees was a Muslim woman who came to work veiled. The question was how to respect her right of autonomy while respecting the right of the company for security. The solution was to have one ID card with the woman in a veil and another one with her face revealed. The photograph for the second ID card was taken by a woman; in the

EVERYDAY ETHICS: *Making Wise Choices in a Complex World*

event of a question, she was promised that only a female security officer would verify her identity. With a bit of care, the needs of both groups were met. As a bonus, the morale of the entire company went up as employees realized that they were valued as individuals.[16]

CONCLUSION

People often make bad decisions because they have not taken the time to carefully set up the problem. While going through the steps of being attentive and being intelligent feels tedious and redundant, failing to carefully evaluate the context of the problem will lead to an inferior decision. Finding the core values in tension requires that we become very aware of the context.

Often in the United States, minorities and women are more aware of the values in tension in an organization because they are trying to make sense of the system and learn how to move ahead. Anne Wilson Schaef noted that those who are in power in a situation tend not to notice the different elements of the context. Those who are working to fit into a system that is hostile or indifferent know all of the spoken and unspoken rules.[17]

Accurately evaluating the context also requires that we know ourselves very well. This knowledge should include an awareness of where we cannot see clearly because of our own biases and our own need to protect our power base. We all have a fear of failure and sense of inadequacy. Listening to those who don't just tell us how wonderful we are requires courage and integrity—essential qualities of respected leaders. In the process, we will be able to see how we can meet the triple bottom line of our organizations—economic success, ethical action, and environmental concern.

CONTINUING THE CONVERSATION

1. Reflect on your own belief system and review the list of how the core values manifest in a business setting. What values are the most important to you in a business setting? How have you either chosen an employer or shaped your work setting to make sure that those values are part of your work?

2. Find an article or editorial piece in your local paper or a news magazine that deals with a current ethical situation. See if you can identify all of the elements of the context in the story. Find a second article on the same topic and see how the information is contextualized differently. What beliefs and values are demonstrated by the way that the authors put the stories together? What is missing that might give the context a different spin?

3. Identify an ethical dilemma that you are facing or have seen in your workplace. Following the steps of this chapter, in a page or less, describe the context of the problem. Now, what do you notice about both what you chose to include and what facts you decided were not relevant? Was the process easy or hard? What did you learn about yourself in the process?

THE BAIRD DECISION MODEL
(Part 2)

BE REASONABLE

Hone critical thinking skills

Examine from multiple perspectives

BE RESPONSIBLE

Strive for ethical maturity

Act with courage

BE REFLECTIVE

Reflect on results

Seek continuous improvement

CHAPTER 5

Strategies for Decision-Making

IN THE 1960S, THE POPULAR CULTURE spawned the human potential movement. Replete with self-help books and seminars, this movement promises that as we learn to take responsibility for ourselves and the way that we live in this world, we can gain control over our lives and find meaning and happiness. Many have speculated about the reason for this surge of interest in pop psychology. Whatever the cause, the result has been that many individuals have spent thousands of dollars to learn more about themselves and how they can be effective at work and at play.

Bernard Lonergan describes this drive to understand ourselves and our world as common to all humans, the "detached, disinterested, unrestricted desire to know."[2] Lonergan asserts that this characteristic of people drives us not only to understand the physical world, to determine what is true, but also to seek the good—the good for ourselves and other people as well as the good of our institutions such as the economy, the family, and the earth.

The desire to know manifests first as relentless questioning. As we gather information about the world, we ask more questions. One set of questions is about the material world itself. What does science tell us about ourselves and our world? How do markets work? What processes will help me make my product and services better? How can I develop a product that will solve a particular problem? Another set of questions explores what Lonergan calls the spiritual, leading to questions about the proper ordering of values in our community.

Free will is the ability to choose how to live. While arguably we may not be able to choose the circumstances of our birth, each of us gets to decide what we will do with the life we are given. Some of the questions concern the probable outcomes of our choices, our reasons for our choices, and the values we consider important. Theologians and philosophers call this ability to choose the gift of free will. As humans, we can ask questions, contemplate results, and choose to either do that which will create good or that which will not. Because developing rational self-consciousness is an ongoing process, we have the opportunity over and over again to choose to act in light of our best understanding of the world and its consequences or to choose to act in a way that causes harm to our self, others, and the environment.

SELF-EFFICACY AND EFFECTIVENESS

	HIGH OUTCOMES EXPECTANCY	LOW OUTCOMES EXPECTANCY
HIGH SELF-EFFICACY	Motivated and productive	Engaged in social activism
LOW SELF-EFFICACY	Despondent and depressed	Resigned as powerless

Psychologists call embracing the privilege and responsibility of choosing how to live "self-efficacy." Albert Bandura defines self-efficacy as "a judgment of one's ability to organize and execute given types of performances."[3] Bandura's research demonstrates that those who have a strong belief in their own self-efficacy will be more motivated and proactive in the choices that they make about life than those who do not believe that they have the power to make effective decisions. People who have high self-efficacy and high outcome expectancies will tend to be productive and satisfied with their lives. Those with high self-efficacy and low outcome expectancies will protest and engage in social activism. Those who have low self-efficacy but think that they have some power over their circumstance will be despondent; or if they feel powerless, they will be resigned.[4]

Bandura's research also shows that the more accurate our assessments of the world around us and ourselves, the more likely we are to have high self-efficacy. As we combine Lonergan's method of learning about ourselves and our community with our knowledge and experience of the business world, our self-efficacy will increase. In the process, we will become both effective and ethical while finding meaning and satisfaction in our work. By asking questions (making sure we continually look for data that doesn't match our expectations), while we subject our own motives and desires to the same grilling, we will increase our self-efficacy, our ability to believe that we have control over our lives and our work. Fortunately, as our self-efficacy grows, we also increase the control we have over what we believe about ourselves and others and what happens in our professional and personal lives.

William Greider asserts that toxic work situations can create apathy and cynicism. Rather than finding the meaning in our work that we all crave, the deadening environment results in many of us having low self-efficacy in our professional lives. Whether we are on the floor of a manufacturing plant where we have power over a tiny part of the process or we are part of a system where we don't know whom we are serving and thus are not connected to our customers, even in a time of great surplus we may believe that we have little control over our economic lives and that we are powerless to affect either our personal work situation or the firms that employ us.[5]

The conversation about how to be an ethical person in business presumes that we believe that who we are and what we do makes a difference. If we believe that we have no control over the people or the systems in which we find ourselves, we stop questioning and resign ourselves to a tiny piece of our world. Much like the government workers in Nazi Germany who took responsibility only for their tasks, it is often easier not to ask what our actions do to help or hinder the greater good.

The way that officials in Nazi Germany managed to get good people to buy into the horrors of the Holocaust was by asking them only to do their small, bureaucratic part. Thus, when members of the Jewish community were sent to the concentration camps, all of the bills of lading (a legal document that lets people know what cargo is being shipped) were properly filled out, the fees for transporting "goods" were paid, and no one asked what impact those small bureaucratic acts had on the fabric of the community and the lives of millions.[6]

From time to time in American business, good people find themselves part of a system that does not create good for many people. While the evil we create may not be on the scale of the Holocaust, when we actually look at the wealth that has been lost through unethical practices causing the collapse of major American corporations or the lives disrupted through shady employment practices, we must place the responsibility somewhere. A delightful but unexpected consequence of the self-help movement may be that people will have the tools as well as the desire to stop their unknowing participation in systems that deaden their souls and lead to the destruction of the fabric of our community. As we choose to be as aware, responsible and proactive at work as we are in our personal lives, the ethics of business will be transformed.

After being *attentive* in identifying the problem and *intelligent* in exploring options, step three in the decision process shows us how to be *reasonable* in solving the dilemmas and then step four allows us to be *responsible* in our actions. By focusing on the perennial questions (see p. 38), we learn to see that which we otherwise would ignore. By subjecting difficult questions to the core ethical frameworks, we get a much more complete picture of not only the problems but also the strengths and weaknesses of potential options for acting. The last phase of the decision-making process also reminds us that we must act—and that not acting is in fact an action.

As we move our focus from a narrow consideration of only our own well being, to a wider look at the interests of those around us, and finally to the vantage point of working to improve systems—the institutions and organizations that provide the structure for our lives—we also become more ethically mature and wise. Often, these choices involve taking the road less traveled, the road that asks us to give to others out of our abundance, cheerfully subordinating personal interest to support the common good. Many who have taken the other road find, as in the words of Robert Frost, that it *has* made all the difference.

DECISION STEP 3:   BE REASONABLE

Ethics and morality are not just about determining the right course of action but also about choosing the best course of action and persuading others that the action is right. All of us must determine for ourselves how best to live. This knowledge emerges in conversation with our friends and co-workers in our own community. We are shaped by our own dreams and the community's expectations of us, as others either embrace or critique our worldview. The dialogue forms us and our community as we listen and strive to understand each other. As we intentionally engage in conversations about the balance between *autonomy*, doing what we believe is best, and *equality*, assuring that everyone else gets the same options, the boundaries between appropriate self care and selfishness are provisionally set. Many vigorous exchanges explore when our individual prerogatives need to be curtailed in favor of the company's financial well-being, or security. These dialogues determine both the content of what is ethical in hypothetical as well as real situations.

Be reasonable

❖ *Hone critical thinking skills*

❖ *Examine from multiple perspectives*

After exploring the context and determining the options for action, we evaluate the options. Even though an ethical decision is ultimately subjective, we want to be as objective as possible: we want to reach intentional subjectivity. Being a responsible ethical decision maker requires three intersecting bodies of knowledge. First, what are the analytical rules that will give the best result? Second, what is the ethical content that provides the basis of the decision? Third, what are the moral considerations that provide an essential filter? These steps help us to fairly evaluate the options and determine the ethical and moral criteria to judge the "rightness" of a course of action.

PART 1: HONE CRITICAL THINKING SKILLS

As we begin to identify values in tension and work toward a resolution, a host of skills is available that assist us in the process. After we experience the situation and become aware of the problem

EVERYDAY ETHICS: *Making Wise Choices in a Complex World*

and our own response, the next step becomes to understand and judge the situation to come up with the best response possible. The disciplines of philosophy and law, as well as science and engineering, have specific tools that help in both framing and analyzing problems. Time-tested tools of critical thinking can help us hone our analytical skills. Manuel Velasquez, in his text *Business Ethics: Concepts and Cases*, summarizes the skills necessary for ethical decision-making. Meticulously attending to these rules helps us find the best possible answer.[7]

Strategy 1: The logic of the argument needs to be rigorously examined; all of the unspoken moral and factual assumptions in the claims need to be displayed and critiqued.

Each section of an author's outline will contain an *assertion* that supports the primary thesis or argument. For example, in theology, the assertion might be that Christianity is superior to all other world religions. The rest of the article would then present the evidence to persuade the reader that the assertion is correct. Sometimes the author has made an *assumption* in the writing that is veiled. In economics, the underlying assumption might be that capitalism or socialism is the preferred system. Even though both ideas are contested, people may not provide an analysis for assumptions because they don't recognize the assumption or they believe that it is not contested. Be sensitive to the assumptions, both individual and cultural, behind the assertions as you work the problem. The assertions that we make might lose their appeal if others find the underlying assumptions flawed.

Many times we mask flawed assumptions by failing to clarify ambiguity in our statements. The most common cause of ambiguity is difference in definition. Many times we avoid clarifying our definitions because we don't want conflict. However, as all communication depends on assuring that people receive the same message, if we want to resolve the problem, identifying the similarities and differences in definition is critical. We can clearly see an example of this process by examining the conversation of a group exploring the morality of abortion.

If one person in the group assumes that a fetus is a human being (or even a potential human being) upon the first division of cells, the preferred ethical act (and underlying analysis) will be very different than if the person assumes that a fetus does not become a human being until some later point in the maturation process. However, few engage in this difficult task

ANALYTICAL PITFALLS

CIRCULAR ARGUMENTS	*Make sure that you do not argue one point by using the same point as validation.*
AD HOMINEM ARGUMENTS	*Do not attack a person (or their mental skills). Evaluate the argument itself.*
DIVERSIONS	*Don't go off on tangents or use glittering generalities to hide the reasoning or assumptions or to stir emotions.*
FALSE DICHOTOMY	*Don't set up the problem so that the reader is forced into believing that only two choices are available.*

of harmonizing definitions by listening to each other carefully enough to identify the underlying core assumptions about what makes us a human.

Often, as we identify differences in assumptions, the resolution of the problem becomes clear. Sometimes clarity means that we respectfully disagree on the core definitions. As we get better information, we note that which doesn't fit, enlightened by the beliefs and experiences of those with whom we have talked. In the process, we exercise the gift of civility rather than shouting at and denigrating each other. Many fear that unless we learn to respect each other and search for the highest common ground, we will destroy our community.

Strategy 2: *The factual information cited in support of a person's judgment must be accurate, relevant, and complete.*

Doing sufficient research to test our assumptions is time-consuming. We usually prefer to go with our biases or with data that seems to support our ideas. Whether we are looking at data about salaries, job mobility, discrimination in the workforce, or a myriad of other topics, we need to carefully check the sources of the data and ask how it was compiled. We also need to be careful about our own use of data as we move forward with our closely-held opinions. Carefully looking to see if our cherished notions can be supported rather than putting a spin on data to support our preferred vision of the world requires intellectual maturity.

VERIFICATION FOR BELIEF SYSTEMS	
Statistics	*Other authorities*
REASON	AUTHORITY
EXPERIENCE	TRADITION
Author's expertise	*Anecdotes*

Authors will use many different sources of *evidence* to support their assertions. The following are sources that are traditionally used to establish credibility.

❖ **Statistics:** Many authors use numbers to support their ideas. As we review statistics, we must be aware of the underlying data sets and the questions that were asked in obtaining the results. Statistics may be descriptive and tell us what is, such as census data. Other statistics are predictive and tell us what is forecasted, such as what the economy will do in the upcoming months. The difference in reliability between the two approaches radically affects decision making.

❖ **Author's Expertise:** Sometimes an author will rely on the persuasiveness of the argument and/or the author's own reputation as an authority in the field as evidence for the arguments. Careful evaluation of the data requires identification of the credentials, assumptions, and commitments of the author.

❖ *Authorities:* Other authors or works can be used to support the ideas of the author. Two questions are important. First, we must validate the expertise of the author. Next, we ask whether the author's statement is based on expertise or whether the writing is really just opinion.

❖ *Anecdotes:* Authors give examples of their point. People often will use a "poster child" for an argument, a specific case that depicts the worst possible example of the point being made. This example may represent a small percentage of those in a particular category, the statistical extreme, rather than a person whose case falls within an expected range of results. Testing anecdotes against statistics, we can notice fuzzy thinking and avoid false generalizations.

As each of us evaluates the premises used to support a claim, we judge them as credible or not credible. As we evaluate the evidence, we determine whether we tend to believe it as presented or whether we are skeptical and want further proof before we buy the argument. This process can be called "being careful whose voices you allow to get into your head." The evaluation and belief continuum might look like the chart on the right.

Some of us will accept information without challenge if our own knowledge is sparse. Others want multiple sources of verification. Some of us have favorite authorities—we always trust the writing of certain authors while distrusting others. Some of us have favorite viewpoints—we always trust someone who basically agrees with us while distrusting someone who disagrees.[8] We are neutral if the evidence has no impact on us at all.

VERY SKEPTICAL	FALSE
↕	↕
SKEPTICAL	NOT-CREDIBLE
↕	↕
NEUTRAL	NEUTRAL
↕	↕
ACCEPTING	CREDIBLE
↕	↕
VERY ACCEPTING	TRUE

Through the process of careful evaluation, we begin identifying our own strengths and weaknesses in a subject area as well as our own inclinations. As each of us learns how we evaluate evidence, we can begin to see where we are gullible or hypercritical. Through evaluation, we also can learn how to better structure our own writing and thinking in order to be clear and persuasive.

Strategy 3: The ethical and moral standards involved in our reasoning must be internally consistent as well as consistent over time.

The hardest task of ethical decision-making is to be consistent in applying the principles and values that form our belief system and rationale for action. For example, a student wrote a set of papers evaluating whether undocumented workers should receive free health care. She was adamant in her claim that every human being is entitled to health care, regardless of ability to pay and regardless of citizenship. She became frustrated with her low scores that resulted from her inconsistent thinking that led to an untenable position.

Finally, the professor told her that he would revise her grade if she assured him that any homeless person who showed up at her doorstep would be welcomed no matter how long the person wanted to stay or what kind of resources he might need. The student had a shocked look on her face as she told her professor, "I can't afford that." The teacher then rejoined that maybe the United States couldn't afford to pay for health care for everyone in the world. The issue of access to health care wasn't resolved. However, the student became clear that her reasoning would not be considered consistent while she advocated one set of behavior for the government (which receives its funds from taxpayers) without being willing to embrace that behavior herself.

Whether we are evaluating someone else's work or constructing an argument, the quality of our ethical analysis depends on the rigor with which we use our analytical tools. As we become more skilled in critical thinking, we become more effective participants in the business world as well as more persuasive leaders.

Part 2: Examine from Multiple Perspectives
The Four Ethical Lenses

Over the course of history, ethicists have tried to determine whether an ethical course of action flows from a set of principles from which we live (deontology) or from choosing to seek our preferred goals (teleology). The two approaches to ethics have been in conversation for thousands of years with no resolution in sight. The theories will be explained more fully in Part Two, illustrating that those who engage in the field of applied ethics—applying abstract principles and practices as well as goals and virtues to concrete situations—find that the criteria of either tradition can give a good result.

Each of us uses a preferred tradition when making decisions. We recognize our favorite perspective because the process will feel intuitive and seem easy. Our least preferred focus will be the one with which we struggle: we cannot believe that anyone could possibly use that approach for making decisions. In particularly difficult situations, we should use the vantage point of all four ethical lenses, so that we can check ourselves for bias or blind spots. Further, as we become skilled in describing the landscape of multiple traditions, we

THE *FOUR ETHICAL LENSES*
THE HUMAN TASK

	Principles	Justice	
RESPONSIBILITIES		RELATIONSHIP	
	LENS	LENS	
RESULTS		REPUTATION	
	LENS	LENS	
	Ideal goals	Virtues	

are able to speak with those whose primary tradition is not our own and avoid confusion while moving toward agreement or consensus.

To become skilled in decision-making, we can practice examining ethical problems using four different lenses. Two of the lenses come from the duty-based—*deontological*—tradition. The first is the Responsibilities Lens, which focuses on finding the principles, the rules that guide individuals to appropriate behavior. The second is the Relationship Lens, which focuses on justice, assuring that all in the community are treated fairly. When used together, these lenses help us determine what is true. Also, these two lenses allow us to harmonize our autonomy, our individual rights, and our responsibilities with the community's claim for justice and fairness.

The other two lenses come from the goal-based—*teleological*—tradition. The first, the Results Lens, focuses on ideal goals, achieving the highest possible goals for ourselves and others in the community. The second, the Reputation Lens, focuses on virtues, the qualities of character that allow us to be effective in the community. When used together, these lenses help us determine what is good. Also, these two lenses allow us to harmonize individual goals with the virtues we embody and our character, how we are seen and judged by the community.

The difficulty in any problem is clearly articulating what core values and commitments are in conflict and then determining which should be given priority in any given situation. Our ideas about the proper balance among the elements of the four core values (rationality/sensibility and autonomy/equality) will determine what we finally decide is the appropriate ethical action given a particular problem—intentional subjectivity.

Once our critical thinking skills are polished, we are ready to evaluate the problem against our core values and commitments. Just as a surveyor must measure from multiple vantage points to get an accurate read on the terrain, our personal morality and community ethics must be examined from three vantage points—intention, empathy, and integration—to give us a robust, three-dimensional picture of the best action in a particular situation. Examining a potential course of action from each point is necessary to move toward ethical maturity. No one dimension is sufficient by itself.

The vantage point of intention

The vantage point of intention allows us to discipline our mind, using the tools of reason to choose appropriate values and a consistent path of action. Using critical thinking skills, we apply ethical principles and criteria to a problem to help us choose the most

THE VANTAGE POINT OF INTENTION

❖ *Disciplining the mind to appropriately prioritize core values*

THE *FOUR ETHICAL LENSES*
THE VANTAGE POINT OF INTENTION

Reason and manage self	*Seek solutions from experts*
RESPONSIBILITIES LENS	RELATIONSHIP LENS
RESULTS LENS	REPUTATION LENS
Act/reflect from experience	*Reflect on core virtues*

ethical act. We learn to see clearly from this vantage point as we use our minds and discipline ourselves to pay attention to what is going on in the situation. As we work through the values and commitments of the four lenses, we learn to think carefully about our preferred course of action.

As we look at the four different strategies used to focus our intentional actions, we can see how each perspective provides a valuable frame from which to evaluate our intentions. As we develop the capacity to reason clearly, we can manage ourselves, doing what is right even if no one is watching. As we engage in the dialectic of action and reflection, we use our experiences to sharpen our intentions to reach our desired goals. As we seek solutions from experts, we learn to appropriate the best wisdom from our leaders and forbears. And finally, the core virtues provide aspirational direction—what would it mean to live a life of integrity, of justice, of responsibility. Like a kaleidoscope, each lens provides a slightly different perspective that hones our intentions, equipping us for ethical action.

The vantage point of empathy

The vantage point of empathy allows us to use our feelings and emotions to give us the drive to act on our core values and commitments. Without the power of our emotions, our ethical analysis can remain an academic exercise without any impetus to action. As we develop a fire in our belly to accomplish our goals or exercise responsible leadership, we can make a profound difference in the world.

THE VANTAGE POINT OF EMPATHY

❖ *Using feelings and emotions to fuel our core commitments*

During the past thirty years, the role of emotions in ethical decision making has been explored. If one reads about ethical decision making from authors writing before 1980, emotions had an adverse impact on the decision process. However, with the research of feminist scholars such as Carol Gilligan, Nel Noddings, and Norma Haan that was published in the 1980s, writings about the role of caring for another, an ethic of care, catapulted to center stage. The first response to the research was to assert that women tended to use emotion to resolve ethical issues and men tended to use reason. Then the work of scientists such as Candice Pert and Daniel Goleman in the 1990s showed that both women and men used their reason and emotions in decision making.

Now we know that all persons need to develop both their capacity to reason carefully as well as use their adult emotions to make good ethical decisions. Patricia Gorman describes the process of learning to make emotionally mature decisions as moving from using the "lizard brain," that part of our brain that responds from fear and greed, to the "wizard brain," that part of our brain that operates from empathy and cooperation.[9] That process requires that we develop strategies to move from emotions of fight-or-flight and survival to emotions that allow us to thrive in a complex community.

THE *FOUR ETHICAL LENSES*
THE VANTAGE POINT OF EMPATHY

Care for self and others	Care for those with no power
RESPONSIBILITIES LENS	RELATIONSHIP LENS
RESULTS LENS	REPUTATION LENS
Craft win-win solutions	Serve with gratitude

Emotion doesn't replace reason, but the harsh edges of actions seemingly demanded through reason become tempered through care and respect. In the Responsibilities Lens, our duties are tempered through finding ways to meet those obligations with care for ourselves and others. In the Results Lens, our single-minded pursuit of our goals is tempered through crafting win-win situations where all can reach their goals. The Relationship Lens's relentless quest for justice is tempered through caring for those with no power. Finally, in the Reputation Lens, embodying the virtues is tempered with service and gratitude.

Through the process, we learn to manage ourselves, which involves characteristics such as emotional self-control, transparency, and adaptability.[10] The claim is that the more we develop these skills, the more effective we are as leaders, whatever our positions may be in an organization. Thus, as we consider how to be moral, we discipline our emotions through empathy to nourish relationships. An ethically mature person will use both rational analysis as well as consider the emotional implications for the key relationships before adopting any course of action.

The vantage point of integration

During the past decade, the interest in spirituality at work and in every other facet of our lives has dramatically increased. Robert Wuthnow, writing about spirituality in America, states that "at its core, spirituality consists of all the beliefs and activities by which individuals attempt to relate their lives to God or to a divine being or some other conception of a transcendent reality."[11] Wuthnow finds that spirituality is an individual quest for meaning and is shaped by the larger community context. Thus in the current times, where ideas about ethics and morality are in flux, ideas about spirituality are

THE VANTAGE POINT OF INTEGRATION

❖ Balancing the head and the heart to make consistent, situation-appropriate choices

THE *FOUR ETHICAL LENSES*
THE VANTAGE POINT OF INTEGRATION

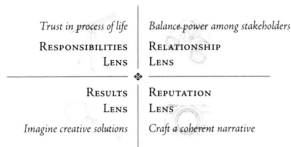

Trust in process of life	*Balance power among stakeholders*
RESPONSIBILITIES Lens	RELATIONSHIP Lens
RESULTS Lens	REPUTATION Lens
Imagine creative solutions	*Craft a coherent narrative*

also contested. Just as no single philosophical approach fits all, no single religious or spiritual framework meets all needs.

Daniel Helminiak, a Lonergan scholar, says that spirituality is the drive to become a whole human being, who is recognized by four characteristics. The first is accepting that the human spirit has an intrinsic impetus that will take us beyond ourselves and our preferences into a search for values that includes other persons and ultimately society and the sacred, however defined. The second quality is being open to moving beyond considering only ourselves in decisions. A third characteristic is movement toward personal integrity and wholeness. The final quality is that spirituality is a move to adulthood—thinking and weighing evidence for ourselves, judging and deciding for ourselves what we will do and so become.[12] Thus, spirituality is not tied to any one particular religious tradition and for some may be independent of any formal religious tradition or practice.

Perhaps the most difficult task of all is befriending our ethical shadow, that part of us that is hidden and conspires to bring forward our worst self, that self that is driven by fear. We begin by becoming aware of our blind spots, those places where we can be tempted to act unethically. The literature in ethics presumes that for most of us, our "best" self shows up most of the time. However, anyone who pays attention knows that from time to time we want to be petty, mean, selfish, and greedy. The practice of self-reflection helps us anticipate the appearance of our "worst" self and find ways to befriend our shadow side so that its warnings and fears can be acknowledged without allowing our shadow side to sabotage our desire to be ethical and whole.

BLIND SPOTS OF THE FOUR LENSES

Belief that motive justifies method	*Belief that process results in justice*
RESPONSIBILITIES Lens	RELATIONSHIP Lens
RESULTS Lens	REPUTATION Lens
Being satisfied with too little good	*Unrealistic role expectations*

Each ethical lens has a particular blind spot. As fully explored in *The Ethical Self* by Catharyn Baird and Jeannine Niacaris, if we don't learn to use the gifts of the other ethical lenses, we can become more unethical either because we are not aware or because we become unbalanced and fanatical. Further, each of the ethical vantage points has a blind spot. If we only view the situation from the Vantage Point of Intention, focusing on rational think-

EVERYDAY ETHICS: *Making Wise Choices in a Complex World*

ing, we become rigid. If we only look from the Vantage Point of Empathy, focusing only on emotions we become maudlin. And from the Vantage Point of Integration, an over-emphasis on either the individual or the community causes imbalance. Let's look at each lens a bit closer.

If we view ethical dilemmas only through the Responsibilities Lens, from the Vantage Point of Intention, we become so clear about the reasons for acting, we tend to believe that the motive justifies the method. As we narrowly focus on our motives, we may fail to consider the possible effects of our action. From the Vantage Point of Empathy, we may be so unaware of our emotions that we may not accurately match the information we are receiving from others with appropriate action, unintentionally causing upset and pain. Finally, from the Vantage Point of Integration, we can take on so much responsibility that we get lost in busyness and forget to reflect on whether the duties we have embraced support our meaning and purpose.

If we view ethical dilemmas only through the Results Lens, from the Vantage Point of Intention, we want to make people happy, and so we may seek only expedience and be satisfied with too little good. By not using the tools of rationality, we may forget to check out our obligations before we commit to a course of action. From the Vantage Point of Empathy, we may become hypersensitive to the emotional climate of the situation and forget to maintain consistency between our long-term goals and our actions. Finally, from the Vantage Point of Integration, as we try to respond to everyone, we can become angry and resentful that no one has paid attention to us. We forget that we are the one who chooses the goals and can change direction, if we desire.

If we view ethical dilemmas only through the Relationship Lens, from the Vantage Point of Intention, we become so focused on process that we forget the purpose of the process is to achieve justice and equality, not follow the process for the sake of the process. Remembering who the process is supposed to serve becomes important. From the Vantage Point of Empathy, we may not be able to find the appropriate emotional response. If we aren't paying attention, we may ignore the plight of those who are lost in the process. Finally, from the Vantage Point of Integration, we can make the process so obscure and arcane that we risk creating an overly exclusive system that is only useful for those who know the secret handshake. Our goal of achieving justice is lost in the minutia of the system.

If we view ethical dilemmas only through the Reputation Lens, from the Vantage Point of Intention, we can become lost in community expectations and set unrealistic role expectations for ourselves. We become self-righteous and demand accolades for our accomplishments. From the Vantage Point of Empathy, we may forget to look clearly at the benefits that come to us because of our role and think that we deserve the perks. Without clear thinking, we may not accurately assess our effectiveness in our role. Finally, from the Vantage Point of Integration, as we live more and more into the mask of our role instead of our authenticity as a person, we become afraid that someone will discover who we really are—a charlatan and a fraud.

Key in this process is learning to love ourselves and others. Balancing the four core values, if we look at our world with eyes of love, we learn to discern which value priorities are appropriate in a given situation. For example, the Responsibilities Lens coaches us (autonomy) that to love in a particular situation requires that we trust the process of life. That process includes assuring that justice is done and the rules are enforced (rationality) to help a person become a fully functioning responsible adult. The Results Lens encourages us (autonomy) to imagine creative solutions so we can show mercy (sensibility). The Relationship Lens reminds us—the community (equality)—to balance power among the various stakeholders, requiring that those of us with power and resources subordinate our rights to assure that others thrive (rationality). And finally, the Reputation Lens can help us—the community (equality)—craft a coherent narrative, the story that gives meaning to our lives (sensibility). Wisdom guides us as we discern which values should take precedence in a situation.

DECISION STEP 4:   BE RESPONSIBLE

Having completed the first three steps—being attentive, intelligent, and reasonable—we are ready for the fourth step, which is being responsible. To act responsibly, we must have two final filters before we take action. First, we need to be aware of and correct for our own personal bias, the way in which we engage the problem and what we bring to the table in terms of skills and expectations. Second, because the stakes are so high for any action given our technological prowess and our ability to profoundly affect the quality of the environment and community, many ethicists are calling us to attend to the common good.

BE RESPONSIBLE

❖ *Strive for ethical maturity*

❖ *Act with courage*

As stated before, we have two sets of competing values to balance. First, each of us is a person-in-community, so one task of the ethical decision maker is balancing the rights and responsibilities of the individual against the claims and prerogatives of the community. Second, we have to balance between our quest for what is true, using the tools of rationality, and our desire for what is good, using the gifts of sensibility. Ethical agility is the ability to find the appropriate values to highlight to resolve a particular ethical issue in a specific time and place.

STRIVE FOR ETHICAL MATURITY

Begin a conversation about ethical maturity and many will assert that all we need to know about ethics we learned in kindergarten—thus, trying to teach any of us how to make better ethical decisions is foolhardy. The four theorists whose work will be highlighted in this chapter (and who are introduced in the text box) assert that we can all grow in ethical, moral, and spiritual maturity. In the final analysis, we evidence maturity by responsibly evaluating courses of action, making choices, and carrying out our decisions.[13]

As various researchers have mapped the path of human development, different stages have been named and categorized. While the details differ, the theorists agree that as we embrace habits of growth, we have the potential to grow and develop into fully functioning, responsible adult humans. The theorists also agree that our maturity can be determined by listening carefully to the meaning that is given to the events of our lives and the choices that we make. As we become ethically mature, we notice that both people and the community are multifaceted and complex. Thus, while people at a lower ethical level may take the same action as someone at a higher ethical level, the reasons given for the action will be very different.[14]

MATURITY IN THE FOUR LENSES

Attend to proper use of reason –KOHLBERG	*Attend to right use of power* –HAGBERG
RESPONSIBILITIES LENS	RELATIONSHIP LENS
RESULTS LENS	REPUTATION LENS
Attend to wholeness –LIEBERT	*Attend to healthy relationship* –HAAN

Ethical maturity through The Four Ethical Lenses

A universal life goal for humans is for each person to become a fully functioning adult—living responsibly while nurturing and being nurtured by the larger community. Researchers who study the criteria that define adulthood have identified benchmarks and defined the stages of ethical maturity. Intriguingly, a theoretical school of thought parallels the key focus of each of the four ethical lenses.

As we use the conceptual tools of the lens, we can also use criteria of maturity to move from acting only to protect ourselves to considering a wider view of the community and looking toward systemic solutions to the problems. The research about why people in business do unethical things indicates that often individuals have high ethical standards but stumble when the system either encourages or rewards unethical behavior.[15]

If a person is rewarded for padding sales, the personal value of transparency in recording sales may lose out when faced with the question of whether to be honest in recording transactions. Because our need to belong is so strong, people are reluctant to speak up when it appears we have a view contrary to the majority.[16] Thus, personal values may be subordinated to company values, resulting in unethical behavior.

❖ *Responsibilities-focused ethics—learning to use reason effectively:* One theorist who studied our ability to effectively use reason is Lawrence Kohlberg.[17] Kohlberg's research focused on identifying the strategies we use for ethical decisions. He identified the stages of maturity that enhance our ability to find the principles of life through ever more sophisticated reasoning ability and careful use of the universal ethical principles.

❖ *Results-focused ethics—attending to wholeness:* Spirituality is a term that has many different meanings. Elizabeth Liebert, who focuses on spiritual development, defines spirituality as that which drives us to wholeness. The goal is for individuals to become self-aware and confident enough to make their own carefully considered decisions. Her approach to wholeness includes the notion of a "pacer," one who models ethical behavior and thus encourages others toward maturity.[18]

❖ *Relationship-focused ethics—assuring a proper use of power:* As we look at both doing an ethical act (ethics) and becoming an ethical person (morality), we increase our personal power. When the conversation turns to what acts are not only ethical but just (fair), the way that people use their personal and organizational power is important. Janet Hagberg traces the steps of personal power that parallel the steps of ethical and moral maturity and gives insight into our use of power as we seek justice and fundamental fairness.[19]

❖ *Reputation-focused ethics—striving to nourish relationships:* Ethical maturity uses the tools of empathy to build relationships. A thoughtful theorist in this arena is Norma Haan, who charts the motivations and choices of those for whom maintaining healthy relationships within each person's role is key.[20] Haan asserts that as we focus on relationships that strengthen the reciprocity between the individual and the community, we can be effective actors in the community.

As we consider the virtues that we wish to embody and think about how we want to be known in the world, we attend to ourselves as whole, not partitioned into work, family, and friends. Not only does each ethical lens provide a perspective on right action, but within each lens, the person using that tool can become ever more skilled at ethical decision making, ever more ethically mature.

Benchmarks of ethical maturity

Jane Loevinger mapped the developmental stages identified by various theorists and harmonized many of the traditions.[21] We will begin with the young adult, the stage of most high school

EVERYDAY ETHICS: *Making Wise Choices in a Complex World*

students and college freshmen, and move through the highest stage to which most adults in our culture ascend.

Characteristics of the Pre-Conformist Stage

The pre-conformist stage is marked by allegiance to our peer group. At this stage, we are just beginning to differentiate between ourselves and others. A key task of young adults is to evaluate the belief systems—the worldview—of their family and friends and then decide for themselves which pieces of that system to reaffirm or reject. Clearly, moving through this stage can be disquieting both for teens and their parents.

Attending to reason:
Kohlberg finds that people at this stage find that the right action is literal obedience to rules and authority. People want to avoid punishment and not do physical harm to others.

Attending to wholeness:
Liebert finds that people in this stage are impulsive, with a fear of retaliation even while they try to exploit others.

Attending to power:
Hagberg finds that people in this stage get their power from powerlessness, as they get others to take care of them. These people are dependent with low self-esteem. They are uninformed: helpless but not hopeless.

Attending to reciprocity:
Haan finds that people at this level of maturity will interpret experiences to validate their own self-interests. In terms of action, people will vacillate between compliance and thwarting, believing that others force them to act and they can force others to their will.

Trajectory for change:
As people begin to develop self-esteem and manage their fear of change and the world in general, they are ready to move to the conformist stage.

Characteristics of the Conformist Stage

We enter the conformist stage when we accept personal responsibility for our own actions. However, the responsibility will still be grounded in and affirmed by an external authority and will be supported by the approval of those significant to us.

Attending to reason:
Kohlberg finds that people at this stage find that the right action is serving their own or others' needs and making fair deals in terms of concrete exchange.

Attending to wholeness:
Liebert finds that people in this stage have a fear of being caught and externalize blame. They are wary, manipulative, and exploitative.

Attending to power:
Hagberg finds that people in this stage get their personal power by association. They find another person and learn the ropes as they figure out the culture. They are dependent on the leader or mentor as they begin to experience new self-awareness.

Attending to reciprocity:
Haan finds that people at this level of maturity will accommodate the interests of others when forced. They will trade to get what they want while they recognize that sometimes others must get what they want. The basic orientation is assuring that others get what they want, and individuals get what they deserve.

Trajectory for change:
As we begin to develop confidence, we can move beyond worrying about the approval of others and the need for security and begin to develop our own ethical compass. We begin taking responsibility for ourselves and move into the conscientious-conformist stage.

CHARACTERISTICS OF THE CONSCIENTIOUS-CONFORMIST STAGE

According to all of our theorists, the conscientious-conformist stage is the stage of most adults. As we begin to take responsibility for ourselves, we realize that because of unthinking adherence to an inherited worldview we have abdicated personal responsibility. Thus, we will begin to consider the source of our beliefs and form our own ideas about what is or is not ethical. However, even with attending to our own beliefs, most of us will adopt the community norms and not seriously challenge the status quo.

Attending to reason:
Kohlberg finds that people at this stage believe that the right action is playing a good (nice) role, being concerned about other people and their feelings. Keeping loyalty and trust with others is key. People follow the rules but don't consider the overall system perspective.

Attending to wholeness:

Liebert finds that people in this stage conform to external rules. They will feel shame or guilt for breaking the rules. As they mature, they will differentiate between norms and goals that are imposed by the community and those that are self-imposed. These people are aware of themselves as persons-in-community and want to belong.

Attending to power:

Hagberg finds that people in this stage get their personal power by the symbols in their lives, such as degrees, cars, money, or position. People at this level are egocentric, realistic, and competitive. As experts, they are ambitious and charismatic.

Attending to reciprocity:

Haan finds that people at this level of maturity will identify their self-interest as the same as the others' interests, thus identifying a common interest. The emphasis is on interpersonal exchanges based on sustaining good faith. People will compromise to include other persons they deem "good" and reject other persons they deem "bad." Thus, a person at this stage of development will try to be good so they will be able to claim receiving good things from others.

Trajectory for change:

The crisis for most people at this stage is one of personal integrity. Most people in America operate at this stage because they don't know they are stuck. At some point they have a personal or professional crisis that leads them to restructure their life according to their own understanding of the world and move to the conscientious stage.

CHARACTERISTICS OF THE CONSCIENTIOUS STAGE

The crises that propel us into the conscientious stage are never fun. Often, we are abandoned by the very family and friends whom we expected to provide validation for our worldview. At this point, we begin to take responsibility for ourselves and our world rather than having unbending commitment to our previously considered principles.

A persistent question (which is unsettling) is whether we are just being rebellious in making our own way or in fact we have moved to a higher level of maturity by taking a more systemic approach to the problem, even if it means going against the norms of the community. Finding a mentor at this point can help us sort through that question.

Attending to reason:

Kohlberg asserts that people at this stage find that the right action is doing their duty in society, upholding the social order, and maintaining the welfare of the society. Persons at this stage consider their individual relationships in terms of their own place in the system.

Attending to wholeness:

Liebert finds that people in this stage live by self-evaluated standards and monitor their own behavior by self-criticism and measuring action against long term goals and ideals. People respect the community and are concerned about maintaining it, as well as justice and caring for others.

Attending to power:

Hagberg finds that people in this stage get their power from reflection and are competent, reflective, and strong. They are comfortable with their personal style, are skilled at mentoring and show true leadership.

Attending to reciprocity:

Haan finds that people at this level of maturity will accommodate their self-interest to meet common interests. People will embrace a systematized, structural exchange based on the understanding that all persons can fall from grace. The balances are conscious compromises where a person commits himself to the shared agreements and rules of the community, and believes that he should have the same considerations and privileges as others.

Trajectory for change:

As people begin to mellow and learn to let go of their own ego, they become ready to make the final move to the compassionate inter-individual stage.

CHARACTERISTICS OF THE COMPASSIONATE INTER-INDIVIDUAL STAGE

Driven to define the purpose for our life, we move to this stage when we become willing to expand our belief systems beyond ourselves to find ultimate meaning. We are willing to embrace the worldview of others and see that the world is gloriously pluralistic in outlook and opportunities. When we reach this stage, we will still have intense commitments, but the actions we take to support those commitments will be more realistic and more tempered. We become gentle with ourselves and with others as we accept inner conflict and the complexity of reality.

Attending to reason:

Kohlberg asserts that people at this stage find that the right action is upholding the basic rights, values, and legal contracts of a society, even when they conflict with the concrete rules and laws of the group.

EVERYDAY ETHICS: *Making Wise Choices in a Complex World*

Attending to wholeness:

Liebert finds that people in this stage are tolerant as well as able to cope with conflicting inner needs. They respect autonomy and interdependence.

Attending to power:

Hagberg finds that people in this stage get their power from their purpose in life. People accept themselves and are calm and humble. As visionaries, they are confident of their life purpose and generously empower other people.

Attending to reciprocity:

Haan finds that people at this level of maturity will assimilate their self-interests into others' mutual interests to achieve personally and situationally specific balances. The belief is that one is a moral agent among other moral agents. Thus, people are responsible to themselves, others, and to the mutual interests. People at this stage realize that we are all connected to each other and thus part of each other's existence.

Trajectory for change:

Most theorists who look at personal development assert that one more level of development is possible. However, none are able to find examples of this next stage except perhaps the very greatest of moral leaders such as Jesus Christ, Muhammad, and the Buddha. Thus, the final stage is called the cosmic stage.

As we mature and begin to make sense of the world around us, we move through the various stages of ethical maturity. The theorists seem to agree that to move from the conscientious-conformist stage requires great intentionality because the Western culture hands out most of the rewards to people at that stage. We also must remember that rather than predictably moving lockstep through the stages, when we are threatened, frightened or confused, we may operate at a lower stage of ethical maturity. Because we have free will, we can either choose to make decisions at our highest level of ethical maturity or at a lower stage to protect our self or others.

A common fault is that we believe that we are further along the trajectory than we actually are, thus becoming blind to the opportunities for growth that are present. As we become self-aware, we can more accurately assess our ethical maturity and make conscious decisions to become more mature. As we learn to correct for the bias that is inherent in the ethical lenses as well as the bias that is present because of our level of ethical maturity, we make better ethical decisions.

ACT WITH COURAGE

In the mid-20th century, two images seared the consciousness of the Western world. The first was the mushroom cloud that filled the sky after the atomic bombing of Hiroshima, which starkly underscored the realization that we could destroy our earth. The second image was captured by the astronauts in outer space, a luminous blue globe, Earth, with land, clouds, and water —and no borders or delineations.

Leonard Shlain, in *The Alphabet and the Goddess: The Conflict Between Word and Image*, asserts that those images changed the trajectory of human existence.[22] For the first time in the human history our actions were not local and restricted in time. The actions of any one of us could have implications for generations, consequences that we could not foresee. As the full impact of the technological revolution was felt in the last half of the 20th century, many from all disciplines and walks of life began to question whether the commitment that the Western community has to individualism could in fact result in the destruction of civilization. In response, a call for a sustainable economy or community arose from many sectors.

Voices from every discipline—including economics, philosophy, theology, sociology, and ecology—suggested that we need to expand our horizons to explore what impact individual action has on the common good. The move towards considering the whole community, not just individuals, is gaining ever more acceptance. As Hans Jonas reminds us, we cannot look only to our own desires and preferences, because our acts have the potential of affecting people and generations far removed from us.[23]

The most insistent examples of our interconnectedness are the global economy and the environmental movement. First, as goods and jobs move seamlessly across the globe, we are called to pay attention to economic and social conditions in underdeveloped and undeveloped countries. Second, all of us are affected by issues such as global warming, scarce water, and air pollution. Traditional ethical notions of organizations attending only to their own bottom line will not meet the firm's responsibility to the larger community.

In the corporate world, paying attention to the common good falls broadly under the rubric of Corporate Social Responsibility (CSR). Proponents of CSR offer new criteria for determining the ethical behavior of a company, such as attending to the triple bottom line that measures and reports "corporate performance against economic, social, and environmental parameters."[24]

Be REFLECTIVE

❖ *Reflect on results*

❖ *Seek continuous improvement*

A telling feature of the value of socially-aware companies is that during the recent economic downturn, those companies that were identified as socially conscious kept their value much better than those that were not identified as being concerned with the common good.[25]

Theorists predict that in the very near future, companies will not be judged only on how much profit they return to their stockholders, but they will be expected to assure that the interests of all stakeholders are considered in their choices. We are each asked then to give from our abundance, to notice that we have resources and personal power. As we give of

EVERYDAY ETHICS: *Making Wise Choices in a Complex World*

ourselves we can work to assure that others without resources and power can themselves become fully functioning adults in a safe and clean world.

No one ever has enough information. No one ever knows all the ramifications of action. Yet, each of us must make choices. Acting with courage requires being as thoughtful as possible in evaluating the situation and then acting, knowing that more information will come forward and the results will be imperfect. As stated before, choosing not to act *is* acting. Thus, each of us is called upon to make the best decision that we can in the situation at hand, knowing that we are fallible human beings operating in an ever-changing world.

DECISION STEP 5:   BE REFLECTIVE

After we act, we begin again with the process of reflection and awareness. As we intentionally engage in the cycle, the promise is that change—growth—is possible.

REFLECT ON RESULTS

Every new action brings another set of questions. As we move from reflection to action and back again, we can see what results were good and which ones we want to avoid. We also see which principles were appropriate and which ones need to be reframed and nuanced in light of emerging knowledge. Thus, we transform ourselves by becoming ever more effective as ethical decision makers as well as more mature humans.

SEEK CONTINUOUS IMPROVEMENT

We see this approach in the contemporary management theories of Continuous Quality Improvement (CQI), pioneered by W. Edwards Deming. This movement helps organizations continually attend to their management processes in order to become ever more effective in delivering goods and services. Rather than assuming that bad apples are responsible for failure, CQI initiatives ask where the system unintentionally supported the undesirable result and how processes can be changed to get better results.

An example of CQI in action can be seen as hospitals are working to find ways to reduce mortality rates caused by lack of quality control. As reported by Arja Adair, the President and CEO of the Colorado Foundation for Medical Care, one physician noticed that he prescribed a particular set of treatments based on which symptom the patient mentioned first. He found that after hearing one or two indicators, he stopped listening and made a judgment about the appropriate treatment. When he began tracking his work, he discovered that he was prescribing different treatments for the same set of symptoms.

In order to minimize what this physician called treatment variations, he designed a process using a hand-held computer to enter the information that was given by the patient to assure more uniformity of treatment. He found that his results were better and the quality of care improved. However, many other physicians have resisted adopting this practice because they believe that using the computer takes all of the personal touch and art out of caring for their patients. Their personal pride, hubris, was such that they were willing to put patients at risk rather than admit that they might be wrong.[26] As this physician demonstrated, working through hypothetical problems helps facilitate the same sort of process of improvement in ethical maturity by helping us develop the habit of reflection and action.

As we go through life, we need to periodically stop and see whether we are moving toward wholeness. Are we in fact attending to our mind, nurturing our heart, and cultivating our spirit? The Baird Decision Model helps us correct for error and reinforce success. As we increase our self-efficacy, we have the potential to find meaning in our lives and joy in our work. As we continue to pay attention, explore our own response intelligently, judge soundly among competing understandings of ourselves and the world, and act responsibly, we can be ever more effective persons-in-community. If something doesn't work well, we can correct the action. As we get more information, we can change course. Honoring the innate drive within us that desires that which is good and seeks that which is true, we can become authentic human beings who are not just drifting through life. In the process, we can also help create an ethical and effective organizational culture.

CONCLUSION

As we work through ethical dilemmas, we should attend attend not only to the choices that we make but also our internal responses—our gut reactions—and our reaction to colleagues. The self-knowledge that is gained as we choose to act bravely marks the difference between being an effective ethical decision maker and choosing the other road—the well-travelled path of obliviousness. The good news is that as we learn to habitually act reflectively, the decisions become easier. As we practice a variety of decision-making techniques and strive for ethical maturity, we become more effective leaders in our community and more complete human beings.

CONTINUING THE CONVERSATION

1. As you reflect on your own ethical decision-making, how do you balance among ethical, moral, and spiritual concerns? How do you adjust for imbalance between rationalism and your emotionalism? On which side do you tend to fall in a difficult situation?

2. Find an article or an editorial in your local paper or a news magazine that deals with a current ethical situation. See if you can identify the reasons that were given for the decisions. What did the author use to justify the position that they took? Were you persuaded? Why or why not?

3. Identify an ethical dilemma that you have faced and resolved. Following the steps of this chapter, in a page or less, describe the criteria you used to resolve the problem. What did you use to justify the position that you took? Now, what do you notice about both what you chose to include and what information you decided was not relevant? Was the process easy or hard? What did you learn about yourself in the process?

PART 2

MAKING WISE CHOICES IN A COMPLEX WORLD

VANTAGE POINTS FOR ETHICAL MATURITY

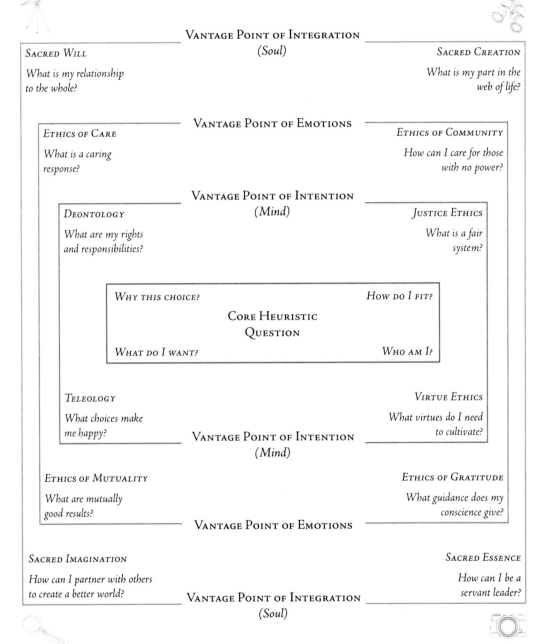

VANTAGE POINT OF INTEGRATION
(Soul)

SACRED WILL

What is my relationship
to the whole?

SACRED CREATION

What is my part in the
web of life?

VANTAGE POINT OF EMOTIONS

ETHICS OF CARE

What is a caring
response?

ETHICS OF COMMUNITY

How can I care for those
with no power?

VANTAGE POINT OF INTENTION
(Mind)

DEONTOLOGY

What are my rights
and responsibilities?

JUSTICE ETHICS

What is a fair
system?

WHY THIS CHOICE?

HOW DO I FIT?

CORE HEURISTIC
QUESTION

WHAT DO I WANT?

WHO AM I?

TELEOLOGY

What choices make
me happy?

VIRTUE ETHICS

What virtues do I need
to cultivate?

VANTAGE POINT OF INTENTION
(Mind)

ETHICS OF MUTUALITY

What are mutually
good results?

ETHICS OF GRATITUDE

What guidance does my
conscience give?

VANTAGE POINT OF EMOTIONS

SACRED IMAGINATION

How can I partner with others
to create a better world?

SACRED ESSENCE

How can I be a
servant leader?

VANTAGE POINT OF INTEGRATION
(Soul)

CHAPTER 6

Vantage Points of Ethical Maturity

A FTER COMPLETING AN ETHICS CLASS and considering the approaches of the various theorists, students often ask, "Which ethical theory is right?" The answer is: all of them and none of them. Just as Heisenberg demonstrated that looking for particles means that we find particles—that is, we find what we are looking for—all ethical theorists have a question that focuses their attention and shapes what they see. As theorists are situated within their own historical context as they respond to perennial questions, their writing is best understood as the next chapter in an ongoing conversation about how best to live in a particular time.

Philosophers and theologians who write about ethics and justice respond to the prevalent worldview of their time.[2] In addition, each broad historical period has a primary spokesman from all of the major ethical traditions.[3] Thus, each theorist responds to the inadequacies of the prevailing worldview (and those in the other primary schools of thought), addresses challenges presented by excesses and abuses of the current leaders and power structures, and incorporates new information about our world and humans that comes through science and technology.[4]

CHARTING THE CONVERSATION

The first task of philosophers is to answer the critiques and expose the weaknesses of currently accepted theories. Because historically the theorists tend to move between traditions, they show how all or part of their predecessors' worldview is flawed. In the process, a theorist might accept some of the writing of a colleague and reject other portions of the scholarship or tradition.

Although each generation of philosophers writes during a particular historical time, with the specific circumstances of that time and place coloring their work, they tend to place themselves within a larger tradition based on their core beliefs. In the process of situating themselves in the conversation, the theorists reappropriate the themes of their preferred school of thought in light of the problems and emerging knowledge of their generation.

Thus, John Rawls places himself in the tradition of Immanuel Kant and asserts that his work is supplementing Kant's categorical imperatives by adding a process through which those imperatives can be used in today's society. Alasdair MacIntyre claims that he is rearticulating the work of Aristotle by recovering a theory of virtue that is needed to make sense of ethics today.

The challenge for us is to determine an overall approach that makes the most sense for us and then live consistently in that tradition while working with people who embrace a different ethical tradition. A central thesis of this book is that we must humbly embrace the paradox of the human condition. Only as we continue to seek to find the "true" and the "good" will we continue to bring out the best of human potential. However, if we don't acknowledge that each of us only sees part of the whole, we will argue like the proverbial blind-folded people trying to define an elephant when each of them could only feel a leg, a trunk, a tail.

The task is for each of us to continue the journey of becoming ethically mature by learning from our own experience and each other rather than taking a position, holding on to it regardless of the evidence that our understanding of the world might be wrong, and refusing to budge. If we continue to stubbornly assert that our worldview and core beliefs represent "The Truth," we will exacerbate the divisions in our community and not be able to find consensus for action.

Further, rather than engaging in the hard work of finding wise solutions to complex problems, we will be content with mindless relativism, where we claim that no particular statement about what is right can trump a different understanding of what is right. However, most of us know that some answers to ethical dilemmas are better than others. The question is how to get to the better and best solutions. One approach is harmonizing the theories rather than holding them in opposition. The claim is that if we can learn to consider all the theories and

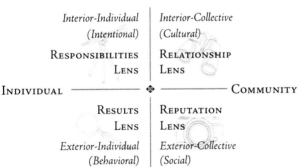

WILBER'S MATRIX

REFLECTION
ASCENDED WORLD VIEW

Interior-Individual (*Intentional*)	*Interior-Collective* (*Cultural*)
RESPONSIBILITIES LENS	RELATIONSHIP LENS

INDIVIDUAL ——————— ❖ ——————— COMMUNITY

RESULTS LENS	REPUTATION LENS
Exterior-Individual (*Behavioral*)	*Exterior-Collective* (*Social*)

DESCENDED WORLD VIEW
ACTION

work from a position of meta-ethics, a structure that holds the theories together, then we can reach better decisions.

To be able to hold a both/and approach to ethics, we need to look at how the two traditional ethical conversations complement each other, rather than see only how they are in opposition. Ken Wilber, a constructive postmodern Buddhist writer, provides a key. In his seminal work, *Sex, Ecology, Spirituality: The Spirit of Evolution*, Wilber asks, "How can you sympathetically align the traditions with one another?"[5] To answer the question, Wilber traces the evolution of individual and collective beliefs. He lays out a matrix that clearly shows the interrelationship of reflection and action in individual and collective community development. Expanding Plato's "Allegory of the Cave," Wilber asserts that for the past several centuries, the Western world in particular has focused on the exterior side of development, neglecting the interior. The result is what he calls

> a purely Descended world view. Spirit is simply identified with the Sum Total of exteriors, the Sum Total of the shadows in the Cave. We are so intent on proving that the shadows are one great interlocking order that we never move from these exteriors to the real interior, and thus we never find the genuine superior.[6]

He claims that we need to include the "Ascended world view," where the self-transcending nature of Spirit is added to the mix.[7]

Two insights emerge from Wilber's matrix. The first is that as we consider the world and then act, we move between action and reflection. The essence of critical thinking (a staple in our educational system) is learning to use the tools of reason to reflect on the authority and tradition of our culture as well as our own experiences after we choose to act. Then when the actions create new information, new data, we consider our total worldview again, modifying and changing our beliefs as needed. Thus, Wilbur's vertical axis moves between interior and exterior—reflection and action. In the process of continually tweaking our worldview we are able to become ever more effective, ethical people.

The horizontal axis moves between the individual and the community. Ethics is traditionally defined as an individual's moral standards. This definition masks the observation that, unless we live in a community, we don't have to worry about ethics. To make the point, this text defines *morals* as our personal value priorities and *ethics* as our shared expectations about how values will be translated into actions.

A way to put the conversation into sharper focus is to adopt the language of another set of constructive postmodern theorists: Herman Daly (an economist) and John Cobb, Jr. (a theologian) who coined the phrase "person-in-community." Daly and Cobb assert that "[t]he self that is to be understood is not a bundle of separate aspects, and it has no existence at all apart from its relations to its human and non-human environments."[8] They note further that "[i]n reality political, social, economic, and cultural aspects of human existence are indissolubly interconnected" and so rather than seeking learning where we continue to abstract knowledge into ever tinier boxes, we need to focus on a holistic synthesizing of our knowledge, impelled by the human desire to know.[9]

To make Daly and Cobb's abstract thought a bit more concrete, let's consider the multiple roles we all have. We are producers of goods and services: we work for companies who pay us for our contribution. We are consumers of goods and services: we take our wages and spend them to buy goods and services produced by someone else. If we only buy products that are made outside of our country, people in our communities are not employed and thus cannot pay us for the goods and services we produce. We are individuals: we live in our homes and choose our activities based on our preferences. We are members of a community. Without people making movies, we can't go and see them. Without our community paying for roads, we would be driving on dirt paths.

A recent news report highlights this interdependence. The residents of Obion County, Tennessee, contract with the fire department of South Fulton for fire protection. Each family is to pay $75 to have the fire team show up and put out the fire. One family chose not to pay the $75. When a fire broke out, the fire department refused to put out the fire. When the fire spread to a neighbor's field, the fire department put it out—they had paid their fees, their taxes if you will. The person who failed to pay the fee never thought his house would catch on fire and expected that someone would put the fire out even if he was a freeloader. But he didn't get to have it both ways: either he was a member of the community and contributed to the infrastructure or he was an individual who relied only on his own resources.[10]

If in fact we are persons-in-community, then the discipline of applied ethics should not just focus on the principles that individuals choose to adopt as they navigate their path through this world. Rather, the discipline needs to explore the synergy created between individuals and their communities through ongoing conversations that inform and moderate beliefs and actions. When should we be responsible for ourselves and when should we band together for mutual protection and support?

Wilber's horizontal axis, which moves between the individual and collective, helps us understand the balancing act that many have instinctively employed in sorting out for themselves how best to live. To be ethically mature, we need to attend to our internal development and our external reality—spirit and reason. We also need to attend to our lives as individuals while considering and enhancing the common good. In the process, we have the possibility of moving from an egocentric viewpoint to, in Wilber's words, "a world-centric, more holistic view," which embraces both historic ethical traditions.[11]

EVERYDAY ETHICS: *Making Wise Choices in a Complex World*

Joseph A. Petrick and John F. Quinn, apparently independent of Wilber, organized traditional ethical theories into a similar matrix. These management scholars asked the same question as Wilber but from a management perspective. Petrick and Quinn mirror Wilber's axis between individual reflection and action. However, they identify the points of the horizontal axis "control" and "flexibility" rather than Wilber's collective and individual.[12]

Petrick and Quinn note that deontology and teleology locate the control for action within the individual. These two theories focus on what each of us believes is right action for us. As individuals, we cherish flexibility as we nimbly move in community. However, control is needed if the community is going to have stability. Thus, individuals learn to follow the rules of the community as they accommodate the interests of others. Like Daly, Cobb, and Wilber, Petrick and Quinn argue for a richer understanding of ethics. They encourage business leaders to use the tools and insights of all of the theories to move against "ethical relativism in favor of an enriched but bounded tradition of moral pluralism."[13]

Interestingly, when the representative philosophers listed on page 72 are placed in the core ethical frameworks grid, the self-correcting nature of each tradition emerges. Traditional deontological theories (the Responsibilities Lens—asserting individual rights and responsibilities) are moderated by theories of justice (the Relationship Lens—disciplining desire for the common good). As one considers the personal entitlements that can lead to selfishness (Responsibilities Lens), one must assure that all have some ability to exercise the same or similar rights that lead to procedural justice, sharing, and generosity (Relationship Lens). As one works for justice (Relationship Lens), one

PETRICK AND QUINN'S MATRIX

REFLECTION

| *Deontological Theories of Ethics* | *System Development Theories of Ethics* |
| RESPONSIBILITIES LENS | RELATIONSHIP LENS |

FLEXIBILITY ——————— ❖ ——————— CONTROL

| RESULTS LENS | REPUTATION LENS |
| *Teleological Theories of Ethics* | *Virtue Theories of Ethics* |

ACTION

THEORETICAL EVOLUTION

RATIONALITY

Plato (427 – 347? BCE)	*Augustine (340 – 430)*
Kant (1724 – 1804)	*Rawls (1921 – 2002)*
RESPONSIBILITIES LENSS	RELATIONSHIP LENS
DEONTOLOGICAL	DEONTOLOGICAL

AUTONOMY ——————— ❖ ——————— EQUALITY

TELEOLOGICAL RESULTS LENS	TELEOLOGICAL REPUTATION LENS
Aristotle (384 – 322 BCE)	*Aquinas (1225 – 1274)*
Mill (1806 – 1873)	*MacIntyre (1929 –)*

SENSIBILITY

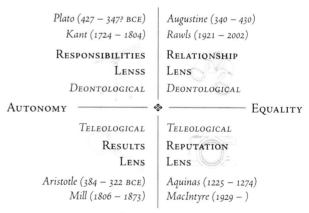

remembers that individuals have responsibilities to embrace that lead to the privileges of the community (Responsibilities Lens).

The traditional teleological theories of utilitarianism (the Results Lens—seeking the greatest good for the greatest number) and egoism (seeking happiness for oneself), which can lead to acting from expedience, are moderated by virtue ethics (the Reputation Lens—developing a good character). As one chooses to act to gain the goods of the community (Results Lens), one must reflect on how that action will affect one's reputation in the community and seek excellence (Reputation Lens). As one chooses to embrace one's roles in the community (Reputation Lens), one becomes a servant leader by asking what specific goals and actions will support individuals in that community (Results Lens).

As each tradition has evolved over our history, it appears that the excess of one generation is moderated by turning the theoretical coin over to see its other face. Thus, we can place the theorists in an evolving spiral around the matrix. The grand sweep of history appears to mimic the balance that many instinctively seek. Plato and Aristotle laid the foundation for modern ethics by focusing on the place of individuals in society. As Augustine and Aquinas rearticulated classical thought in light of Christian doctrine, they emphasized the prerogatives of community, the Church. The perceived excesses of the Holy Roman Empire were moderated by Kant and Mill in the emerging Age of Enlightenment with a reassertion of the rights of individuals to choose how to live. The excesses of individualism were tempered by the voices of Rawls, who made a claim for procedural justice, and MacIntyre who reclaimed the tradition of virtue ethics.

Wuthnow suggests that these shifts can be seen as the difference between a "spirituality of wandering" and a "spirituality of dwelling." When ideas and institutions are challenged or in flux, we must rely on our own resources to sort out what is true and thus we tend to be more pessimistic about the human condition as we see ourselves as pilgrims in an unfriendly land. During settled times, when institutions are strong and the community holds beliefs in common, we tend to be more optimistic and are willing to put down roots as we see ourselves connected to the larger community.[14]

The work of each of these theorists not only addressed the elements of their preferred lens but also included elements of the other lens of the larger tradition. So, Kant, while focusing on rights and responsibilities, foreshadows the work of Rawls as he talks about our responsibility to the larger whole. Mill, while focusing on the importance of individuals choosing what makes them happy, spends considerable time talking about character and virtues, the balancing lens explored by MacIntyre. In addition, each theorist responds to the strengths and weaknesses of the other theories.

Finally, as each theorist is placed in the context for which he is best known, we can see the overall pattern caused by different values having differing priorities as we choose to act. And then, as each of us becomes skilled in ethical pluralism, we can see the gift of the various approaches and learn to use the foundational question of each ethical theory to answer for ourselves the question of how best to live.

CORE HEURISTIC QUESTIONS

As we move from childhood to adulthood, we begin the journey with a set of inherited assumptions and beliefs about ourselves and our community. As discussed earlier, our worldview is informed by the authorities we find persuasive, the traditions we embrace, and our personal experiences, which are mediated by reason and emotion, and harmonized as we seek to make meaning out of our lives. Our assumptions shape our worldview, setting the course for our activities in life. The center of the Path to Maturity chart (p. 144) posits four heuristic questions—questions that allow us to discover the answers for ourselves—that each of us must answer, first as children and then as adults, as we begin to find our place in our community. These questions allow us to learn from our own process of reflection and answer the answers to questions that will help us find meaning and purpose in our lives.

CORE HEURISTIC QUESTIONS

Why this choice?	*How do I fit?*
RESPONSIBILITIES LENS	RELATIONSHIP LENS
RESULTS LENS	REPUTATION LENS
What do I want?	*Who am I?*

As youngsters, we begin life enmeshed in our family with no separate sense of self. The "terrible twos" represent the move from immersion in our family to the recognition of ourselves as separate individuals with desires and the ability to reason. As we have to figure out once again who we are within the larger community, we continue anticipating the perennial questions posed by our representative theorists. At each stage of our development, when faced with difficult situations, we ask the questions over and over again, hopefully maturing into a richer understanding of ourselves as persons-in-community.

WHY THIS CHOICE? (RESPONSIBILITIES LENS)

The question "Why this choice?" focuses our attention on our duties, motives, and reasons for acting. Although annoying for parents, the primary developmental task of children is to differentiate themselves from their family. This transition is signaled by the words "mine" and "no." One of my children has the "Rules of Toddlers" on her refrigerator: The only rule is: "Everything that is mine is mine and everything that is yours is mine." Parents help children sort out concepts like property and values such as respect for possessions and sharing by helping them figure out their rights and responsibilities as well as their motives for acting. If parents reinforce the claim that a friend can claim prior right to a toy truck because the friend owns the truck, even though the child may possess it, the parent plants the seeds of individual rights, in this case the right to private property. As parents teach their children to pick up after themselves, say "please" and "thank you," and share with others, they plant the seeds of responsibility.

As adults, we learn to examine our own motives for acting and determine what our obligations are to ourselves and others. Kant provides a key restraint on selfishness by asking us to consider whether the reasons we give for acting would be equally persuasive if those reasons were used by others in relation to us. Many writers assert that we cannot be held morally accountable for an act that turns out badly but was done with good intentions. Of course, what counts as "good intentions" is also contested. Is a good intention to act to maximize shareholder value ethically acceptable if this policy results in many of the employees not having sufficient resources (salary, health care, leisure) to live relatively good lives?

What Do I Want? (Results Lens)

The question "What do I want?" forces us to choose among competing goods—we can't buy everything we see, and we don't have time do everything we want. One of the most frustrating characteristics of being human is that we can't have it all: every choice precludes other choices. Robert Frost's poignant poem "The Road Not Taken," which opened Chapter 4, tells of a person making choices along life's way, promising to come back while somehow knowing that the path will never be traveled again. By asking this question, each of us has the opportunity in this moment to follow our heart's desire.

Mill's articulation of utilitarianism, which invites us to choose for ourselves how to live, is compelling because he asserts that we should not be locked into certain vocations or life circumstances because of our family history, birth order, or the family business. The lack of mobility in the Old World and the promise of new beginnings in the New World accelerated the crumbling of the feudal age where the first born got all the property and the business (or, if a woman, was married off to someone with property to manage the family fortunes), the second son was sent into military service, and the third son (and sometimes daughter) was sent into the service of the church.

This notion of self-determination was intoxicating. At the time Mill was writing, in England, licenses to do business were inherited. The idea of a market economy described by Mill and Adam Smith, where people could make their own choices about what services they wanted and what price they wanted to pay, was heady stuff indeed. While clearly some unintended consequences flowed from the move to a market economy, on the whole the founding fathers and mothers of America found the trade-off worthy.

How Do I Fit? (Relationship Lens)

The question "How do I fit?" reminds us, in the words of John Donne, that "No man is a island … every man is a piece of the continent, a part of the main."[15] As we are persons-in-community, determining how we fit is critical. While the images of the tenacious entrepreneur or the independent pioneer fashioning a living in the wilderness are compelling parts of the American mythology, those in the new economy and on the frontier depended on each other in a myriad of ways. The trappers needed customers for their pelts as well as suppliers from whom they could buy goods. Those on farms and in the towns needed goods as well as security from those who would threaten them. Wuthnow notes that as settlers and immigrants came to the United States, they built their communities with churches and institutions that provided a place for them to be and familiar rituals and celebrations that gave them a sense of belonging.[16]

Bill Convery, the Colorado State Historian, did a stint during college as a guide in one of Colorado's ghost towns. He reports that a persistent question asked by visitors (after inquiring at what altitude elk become deer—really!) was where the gun fights were held. Convery patiently explained that the frontier towns didn't see much action as "guns are bad for business." The first things the good founding fathers did was to pass laws, elect a sheriff, put up a jail, and prosecute those who didn't fit into the community.[17]

The story portrays businesses' persistent ambivalence toward government. While many in business prefer to be free from government regulation, they also depend on a legal system to assure that contracts are enforced, that debts are paid, and that goods get to market without being stolen. Thus, business owners and government officials have always had an interesting relationship: business asks government to protect it while asking that it also be left to run its affairs as it will.[18] Like the family in Tennessee who wanted it both ways, businesses shouldn't be able to claim the benefits of a regulated economy while avoiding the burdens of being part of a community.

Determining how and where we fit into the workplace is also an interesting question. Our parents settled into their jobs with the expectation that they would keep the same job for a lifetime. The rhetoric often masked the reality of changing economic needs. My father worked for Boeing as a chemist, and, noting the pattern of layoffs during economic downturns, our family sardonically affirms that Dad retired after twenty-five years, but, because of fluctuations in the economy and frequent temporary layoffs, it took him over thirty years to get his retirement pay.

Students are currently told that they should expect to change jobs five to seven times; clearly the expectation for finding a community at work among one's peers and colleagues is different. As blue-collar and white-collar professional jobs that used to be filled by Americans are outsourced to other countries—a result of developing a global economy—answering the question of what exactly creates a community becomes ever more important. Peering through the glasses of business owners, investors, and consumers, a global economy looks pretty swell. Looking through the glasses of an employee or a citizen, the picture is not quite as rosy. We forget that, depending on our particular role at a given time, all of us look through both sets of glasses, which makes determining where we fit even more problematic.

WHO AM I? (REPUTATION LENS)

The final question—"Who am I?"—is one of identity and role. As children, we take our identity from our families: "Daddy's little girl" or "Mommy's muffin." We learn that members of our families do certain things—we chew with our mouths closed, say please and thank you, and do not terrorize our younger siblings. We learn that we are expected to do well in school, excel in sports, or continue the family tradition in the arts or in work. While we usually think of identity as being positive, our families and community can also create a negative self-image. Children who are the scapegoats for all that is wrong in the family, or who belong to an ethnic group that is not fully accepted, have different issues surrounding their identity than those who are raised and nurtured in a loving family.

One of the most disturbing cases I ever had as a juvenile defense attorney was representing three high-school students who lived in my upper-middle class neighborhood. Two of the students found themselves in the wrong place at the wrong time breaking into the local elementary school and stealing computers. The third, the mastermind, had a father who fenced the stolen goods for the boys. The notion of a parent encouraging his child to engage in illegal behavior that would jeopardize that child's life and well-being was incredibly discouraging. As the child received praise from his father for stealing; the twig was bent.

Another example of the power of identity comes from a colleague who was raised in segregated Kansas City. He tells of discovering at the age of nine the world of those who were not able to be part of his life. He was at a BBQ joint and needed to use the restroom. To get there he had to go through the "colored only" section of the restaurant.[19] Even at age nine, he knew that all humans were worthy of respect. The realization that some people were not free to go wherever they desired based only on race profoundly shaped his sense of justice and deeply influenced his work

EVERYDAY ETHICS: *Making Wise Choices in a Complex World*

to make sure that, in the words of Martin Luther King, Jr., people would "one day live in a nation where they will not be judged by the color of their skin, but by the content of their character."[20]

As intimated by the examples above, each of these four questions leads to an ethical framework where we can explore the implications for being effective persons-in-community. Each question has intrigued successive generations of theorists and activists who have worked to find just the right balance among the competing values. The opportunity is for each of us to learn to be responsible ethical adults by intentionally engaging in the questions and then carefully choosing a course of action.

To see our personal trajectory of growth and to find our preferred tradition, we must go back to our cultural roots. This journey helps us understand both our own worldview and the way that we move through society. To make effective ethical decisions while living in our pluralistic community with its contested core assumptions, we must determine where we stand and where we want to go. As we embrace a holistic approach to ethics, we will have the opportunity to claim our own truth that will guide us as we make wise choices in a complex world. In the process, we can become fully functioning adults who nourish our reason, our emotions, and our spirit.

THE VANTAGE POINT OF INTENTION

The vantage point of intention invites us to use our mind, our reason, to seek that which is true and thus determine the rules of life by which we should live. Aided by the Gutenberg's printing press in 1436, as the Protestant Reformation (beginning in 1518) and the Age of Enlightenment (1700s) unfolded, the key impetus for individual rights emerged as ordinary people learned how to read and reason.[21] As people were expected to determine for themselves first their religious views and then their political views, the ability to read the Bible and discern its truth was viewed as critical. However, because the notion of the divine right of kings was still in play, the religion of the leader determined the religion of the subjects. In Europe, wars raged in community after community as the battle between Protestantism and Catholicism took its toll.[22]

As the political and religious agenda of the Protestant Reformation took hold during the 1500s, the politics of a given city depended on the religious persuasion of the leadership. If the leaders were Catholic, the established religion was Catholicism, all in the town were expected to be Catholic, and the economic and legal benefits went primarily to Catholics. Likewise, if the leaders were Protestant, all the benefits and privileges citizenship and business went to Protestants.[23] Minority religious traditions such as Judaism were excluded.[24]

The political changes were fueled by religious convictions and accompanied with much bloodshed. To help end the carnage, the Enlightenment philosophers posited that through reason alone one could determine the rules for living. Descartes' famous dictum "I think, therefore I am," introduced the notion of doubt as a beginning for the search for truth.[25] With reason providing the litmus test for truth, the authority of a church father or political leader could not substitute for careful thought and reasoning in a situation. As much of the fighting was fueled by religious zealots fanning the emotions of the people, philosophers, Kant in particular, extolled reason in decision-making, and declared the passions untrustworthy.[26]

❖ *The vantage point of intention*

Focus your mind through reason to find the rules of life.

Thus, most traditional approaches to ethics teach disciplined, critical thinking to help us focus our minds through using the tools of reason to determine the rules of life that we will follow. Using reason, we apply ethical principles and criteria to a problem to help us choose the most ethical act. As we explore the traditions further, patterns emerge and we see how the theorists approach the four core questions. One side of each tradition focuses on individual action; the other side highlights our responsibility to the community. Because we are complex individuals who live in community, and because we are often like the "little girl with the curl" from nursery rhyme days—"when she was good, she was very, very good, and when she was bad, she was horrid"—we need both sides of each tradition. To make an ethically mature decision, we must consider the problem from all angles to balance the tendency to excess, which is present if one ignores the complementary and corresponding parts of the ethical traditions.

The Vantage Point of Intention for the Person

The first two lenses help us discern what we as individuals should do. As responsible, self-managing adults, we are expected to have an ethical compass that allows us to determine the correct action in a particular situation.

❖ *Why this choice?*

As you seek to be responsible, consider your rights and responsibilities.

The Responsibilities Lens, as part of the deontological tradition (the study of duty), directs our attention to the perfection to which individuals should aspire. This strand of ethics focuses on each of us determining through reason our duties, both to ourselves and others. Ethicists who emphasize personal responsibility call us to consider our own obligations rather than blindly following the dictates of tradition, whether religious or political.

Kant, who is commonly associated with this school of thought, invites us to explore our motives—our reasons for acting—as we determine what we should do. Kant asserts that we have duties such as preserving our life and that of others, doing no harm, and loving each other. But even loving each other comes from a sense of duty, not because we feel like it. So a mother is expected to love her child, even if she doesn't particularly like the child.[27]

The Results Lens, as part of the teleological tradition, asks us to consider what will make us as an individual happy in the here and now, not in some unknown future. Mill, who is the primary spokesperson for this tradition, asserts that as we seek goals that will make us happy, we will become responsible members of our community. Hedonism, the ethical theory that one should seek pleasure, often gets a bad reputation because it can lead to short-term happiness but not long term goals. Anyone who has ever turned down going to a party in order to finish a paper knows the tension between hedonism—living for pleasure—and utilitarianism—making choices that lead to satisfying long-term goals. In the final analysis, Mill and others who invite us to consider the consequences of our actions exhort us to do what makes us, not someone else, happy.

❖ *WHAT DO I WANT?*

As you seek to evaluate your choices, consider your short and long term goals.

THE VANTAGE POINT OF INTENTION IN COMMUNITY

The second two lenses allow us to use our reason to create a community where all persons can thrive. The approach requires both looking at systems as we use reason to create thoughtful, fair processes as well as considering the qualities of leadership that are needed to create a culture of excellence.

The Relationship Lens, which is part of the deontological tradition, invites us to use our powers of reason to develop systems of justice to assure that the least advantaged in our community are protected and considered in the distribution of power and privilege. Rawls and others who focus on themes of justice invite us to see how with the roll of the dice we could be unable to care for ourselves and become disadvantaged.

❖ *How do I fit?*

As you seek to be fair, consider what determines a fair system.

Anyone who saw the pictures of the devastation of the floods from hurricane Katrina in New Orleans (2005), the destruction following the earthquake in Haiti (2010), or, on a smaller scale, the flooding in Nashville (2010), knows that any one of us could move from a place of privilege to disadvantage in the blink of an eye. Anyone who has ever faced a health challenge and needed to access health care knows how fast an academic question about who should receive health care becomes very personal and precarious.

The Reputation Lens, part of the teleological tradition, asks us to consider what virtues are necessary to have a good character. Each of us has different roles in our community with a variety of virtues that can be developed. MacIntyre and others who explore the role of character encourage us to pursue virtues such as integrity, justice, and courage, so we are not seduced by expedience and forget excellence. We are asked to consider which roles we wish to

❖ *WHO AM I?*

As you cultivate your character, consider what virtues you should develop.

take on, and then in conversation with others in the community, use our reason and determination to choose to behave in ways that represent the very best of those roles.

The Vantage Point of Intention for the Person-in-Community

In addition to the assumptions behind each tradition being contested, that is, not agreed upon by all theorists, much ink has been spilled in the battle over which ethical lens should take precedence over the others. Theorists who favor one of the four traditions over the others assert that if you follow the primary values of their path, the rest of the values will fall in place. In making the case for deontology trumping teleology, Kant notes that we need to consider the consequences, but he believes that they are secondary to doing our duty. John Stuart Mill and other consequentialists argue that we can only determine our duty by considering our goals and what makes us happy.

The question becomes a version of the classic chicken and egg conundrum: do we begin by figuring out our responsibilities and let the consequences fall where they may *or* do we consider the consequences and from there determine duty? Do we seek justice first or determine what is required by our role and within that role do what is right? In philosopher's terms: Is "the right prior to the good … in that its principles are independently derived" by reason or do we first determine "final human purposes or ends … conceptions of the good" and then choose to act?[28]

In a practical sense, we tend to get a better result if we consider both sides of the coin before acting. As we view our ethical life from the vantage point of intention, using our reason to explore all four of the heuristic questions will help us develop a rich, multi-dimensional worldview rather than a two-dimensional picture. Each framework encompasses a particular set of theorists and traditions that informs the process.

Each lens focuses on a particular ethical content—principles, goals, justice, or virtue—that help us determine the right answer for ethical dilemmas. Each ethical lens also has a process that helps us focus our analytic skills and correct for the bias that may be present in other parts of the ethical tradition. Those who engage in the field of applied ethics—taking abstract principles and goals and applying them to concrete situations—find that the criteria of all four traditions can give good results. The key is to use at least two of the four lenses in any analysis to compensate for the inherent distortion embedded in each lens.

THE VANTAGE POINT OF EMPATHY

The world of emotion, which had been marginalized by the emphasis on reason during the Age of Enlightenment, moved to center stage in the mid-20th century. Many different strands of research led to a reassertion of the importance of our emotions. Biologists began doing research on the physical effects of emotions on our bodies as well as on our thought processes.[29] Sociologists and historians noted that the atrocities of the Holocaust in Europe and slavery in the United States, which treated people as property and separated families, resulted from a strict attending to reason without seeing others as fully human.[30] As we dampened our feelings of empathy for other humans by not seeing them as fully human, we cruelly imposed rules that destroyed relationships and deeply wounded human lives.[31] The discovery that a well-disciplined mind does not necessarily have a clue about how to build satisfying relationships was popularized in the whole "Mars vs. Venus" dialogue between men and women.[32]

Another strand of research during the last half of the 20th century focused on how individuals make ethical decisions. Lawrence Kohlberg, who studied the ethical development of humans, demonstrated that through learning how to reason more effectively, people could make better ethical decisions. One of Kohlberg's important insights is the notion that ethical development continues over the course of a lifetime and is not finished at the knees of our mothers and fathers. As Kohlberg's research continued, his evidence seemed to indicate that women were less ethical than men: when faced with a difficult decision, women tended to try to preserve relationships rather than choosing actions dictated by rules that might damage rapport. According to Kohlberg's scheme where reason was king, this tendency showed a lack of ethical maturity.[33]

Women scholars took a measure of exception to the notion that women are ethically inferior to men. As research continued, Norma Haan demonstrated that while men tended to be taught to discipline their *mind* through the tool of reason, women tended to be encouraged to discipline their *emotions* using the tool of empathy.[34]

❖ *THE VANTAGE POINT OF EMPATHY*

Discipline your emotions through empathy to nourish relationships.

Haan constructed a model of ethical development based on people preserving relationships. The steps to ethical maturity paralleled Kohlberg's as people moved from a thought process that only considered the implications of their actions on the individuals involved to a process that included considering the systemic consequences for their actions.[35]

The two strands of thought were brought together by the work of psychologist Albert Bandura, who taught that to be a fully functioning adult in this world, one needs both rational and emotionally mature.[36] A useful analogy might be comparing ethical decision-making to playing a beautiful fugue: the melody line, our mind, is made whole by the counterpoint, our emotions. Effective decision-makers need both skill sets.

THE VANTAGE POINT OF EMPATHY FOR THE PERSON

The first two lenses help us move from using our "lizard brains," which respond to fear to using our "wizard brains," which allow us to experience empathy and compassion for others. As we learn to manage our emotions, they provide the focused energy we need to propel us to action, the impetus behind acting on our closely held commitments.

❖ WHY THIS CHOICE?

As you responsibly fulfill your duties, carry out your actions with care.

The values of the Responsibilities Lens are well represented by Carol Gilligan's work, *In a Different Voice*. Gilligan persuasively demonstrates that an ethic of relationship as historically exercised primarily by women is as valid as an ethic of rules that tends to be embraced by men.[37] Another seminal writer, Nel Noddings, calls the ethic that emerges from relationship an ethic of care. Noddings invites us to augment Kant's notion of the ethical act as the one where we do our duty with empathy and commitment. The counterpoint to "Why this choice?" is "*As you exercise your rights and responsibilities, respond to the other with care and commitment.*"[38]

❖ WHAT DO I WANT?

As you choose that which makes you happy, consider the happiness of others.

Just as an ethic of care that comes from emotional maturity tempers the excesses of individualism, an ethic of compassion and mutuality tempers excesses in the teleological tradition where people are tempted to operate from an ethic of expedience rather than embracing an ethic of excellence. For those in the Results Lens, rather than just asking "*What choices make me happy?,*" we consider the happiness of others as well. This action moves us from pure hedonism to seeking ideal goals such as liberty and freedom for all people.

Considering the happiness of others requires finding moral balance. Haan asserts that while happiness is important, one must also pay attention to the moral balance between people so that all may have a chance to achieve their goals.[39] For this framework, the key is to choose goals that will support others in also reaching their goals. Lonergan reflects this approach by asking us to always seek the highest good, that good which addresses the complex, interdependent goals of many in the community.[40] Thus, we are invited to think systemically about the ways we support others in achieving their dreams and how best to reach our own.

THE VANTAGE POINT OF EMPATHY IN COMMUNITY

The second two lenses allow us to use our emotions to create a community where all persons can thrive. The approach requires that we use compassion and express gratitude as we exercise leadership and participate in the larger community.

❖ HOW DO I FIT?

As you use your power to create a fair system, consider those with no power.

Theorists concerned with emotional maturity also explore the heuristic question of the Relationship Lens, "How do I fit?" The claims of justice articulated by Rawls expand from concern about an individual's ability to fairly negotiate a complex system to an awareness of how we are all profoundly connected to all people and nature. The study of ecosystems by Frederick revealed that healthy natural systems required cooperation in addition to competition according to the rule of survival of the fittest.

Management theorists then began speaking of an ethic of cooperation to nourish and sustain the ecosystems of the workplace.[41] An ethic of relationship explores the ways that we are all connected, which underscores our obligation to care for the community as a whole. So, one answer to the question "How do I fit" is "As I use my power to create just and fair systems, I will respond to the other people in my community cooperatively as an integral part of the community."

The question posed by the Reputation Lens, "Who am I?," focuses on what constitutes emotional maturity in the various roles of our life. Psychologist Charles Shelton states that the answer can be found as we each assert that "I am a moral person" and explore what that identity means for us. While developing virtues is important, Shelton suggests that being moral, which includes emotional maturity, is the critical characteristic of being human. Shelton asserts that we become moral by exercising our conscience and developing empathy, the ability to walk with another in life. A core practice for exercising our conscience is the practice of gratitude, being thankful for all the wondrous tangible and intangible things we have.[42]

❖ WHO AM I?

As you develop a virtuous character, serve others with gratitude.

Shelton and other developmental psychologists maintain that the self-regulation of our emotions is essential for ethical and moral behavior because reason does not attend to the feeling side of life. Emotions have the potential either to give our minds valuable information as we reason through problems or to cast us into a maelstrom of feelings. Through disciplining our emotions, we can heed their wisdom and not be overwhelmed by them. By listening to our minds and our hearts, we can become morally mature and have the tools to maintain moral balance. So the answer to the question "Who am I?" includes "I am a grateful person with a good character and a well-developed conscience."

The Vantage Point of Empathy for the Person-in-Community

The conversation began as a debate between men and women—men think and women feel. Although feminist scholars reminded us of the value of our emotions and introduced us to an ethic of care, we must be careful not to slide into an essentialist position—thinking is the realm of men and feeling is the realm of women. One reminder comes from the research that led to the formation of the Myers-Briggs Type Indicator™ demonstrating that men and women both fall along the Thinking-Feeling continuum. The new discipline of neuro-economics shows us that both men and women are not just "econs," robots who make perfectly rational economic decisions, but that we are humans and use both reason and emotions in our everyday life.[43]

While the term "feminist" has fallen on hard times in recent years, the dream of the women and the men who embraced the movement was that each of us would be able to fully exercise our reason and deeply feel. As we moved to human maturity, no one would be locked into an expectation of behavior based on gender. Fortunately, the precepts of radical equality have become deep enough in our culture that we no longer regard rational women or emotional men as an aberration. Each of us is called to view our behaviors from both the vantage point of reason and empathy as we make wise choices in our complex world.

THE VANTAGE POINT OF INTEGRATION

While an ethic of the heart complements an ethic of the head, the picture is still two dimensional. Neither the vantage point of intention nor the vantage point of empathy provides a sufficient perspective to allow us to find and navigate a path leading to success. Neither viewpoint provides a clear map to allow us to determine the rules to follow, choose goals that are satisfying, learn how to build good relationships with difficult people, or develop a good character. The perspectives provided by our minds and our emotions help us live a satisfying external life, moving effectively in our professional and personal life. However, neither of these worldviews addresses our internal life, the place where we find meaning and purpose.

❖ *THE VANTAGE POINT OF INTEGRATION*

Seek what is good and true to live a whole, integrated life.

To view our world in 3-D rather than 2-D, we must tend to our interior life, the spiritual realm. The third strand of questions asks whether it is possible to intentionally blend the interior world of spiritual maturity with the exterior world of emotional and intellectual maturity as one seeks to be ethical and effective in our professional lives. As we continue in our question to find and harmonize that which is true and that which is good, the answer turns out to be yes.

Bookstores are rearranging their shelves to make room for whole new sections about spirituality at work, and courses are flourishing in major universities that explore the gifts that our personal spiritual traditions, as well as those of others, bring to the table. The time is clearly ripe for a conversation about how spirituality influences the world of business. As the whole realm of business ethics is about how we treat ourselves and others in the workplace, exploring the realm of our deepest desires makes some sense. A careful review of the literature shows that each of the four core questions explored above has caught the attention of different authors. Thus, looking at the world through a spiritual lens reveals intriguing answers to the perennial questions with the added twist of how to nourish our souls.

The Vantage Point of integration for the Person

The first two lenses explore our individual response to the vantage point of integration. Until the 1960s, most people in the Western community identified themselves as Christians. Thus, the value structure of Christianity permeated the business world. However, in light of the postmodern shift that changed how we find what is true and what is good, people tend to have conversations about spirituality independent of conversations about theology. As Wuthnow notes, "At the start the twentieth century, virtually all Americans practiced their faith within a Christian or Jewish framework … . Now, at the end of the twentieth century, growing numbers of Americans piece together their faith like a patchwork quilt. Spirituality has become a vastly complex quest in which each person seeks in his or her own way."[44]

This individual journey has two different implications for the world of business ethics, implications that parallel the two ethical lenses with an individual focus. Reflecting the values of the Responsibilities Lens, spirituality has an ethical component in that our spirituality determines what we define as ethically binding, what rules constrain our behavior. Many people frame their ethical obligations in light of their duties to God. So, as we fulfill our duties, we do so with joy as we delight in following timeless, universal precepts.

❖ *Why this choice?*

As you fulfill your duties with care, remember to delight in your work.

Second, given that the two primary needs for human beings are to work and to love, as we learn from the Results Lens, our spirituality, the meaning we give to the whole of our lives, profoundly affects both what goals we seek in the business world and how we then fit into the whirlwind of commerce. Every spiritual tradition teaches that as we explore why we make the choices we make, we can become aware and learn to love and serve ourselves and others with delight. Then, as we go to our work, we can go with a spirit of joy rather than grumbling with discontent and discouragement.

❖ *What do I want?*

As you implement win-win solutions, remember that you are a co-creator of all that is.

For example, a woman who teaches reading to young men and women who have just been released from detention facilities finds much that is discouraging. The skills of the students are far below average, their lives hold little hope, and their circumstances are grim. Yet, the teacher finds comfort in the fact that maybe one of her students, as he or she is treated with dignity and respect, will find the way out of the box and acquire the skills to be a participating member of the community. That possibility keeps her going to work even as her students move in and out of the penal system.

The world of imagination helps us answer the question "What do I want?" Much of the literature on the spirituality of work invites us to envision a world where all are able to thrive as full human beings and then act to make that world a reality. As we take responsibility for creating our own work life, or at least creating our response to it, we can find meaning even in difficult situations. By the choices we make, we become co-creator of our lives, following the desires and intuitions placed deep in our hearts by someone or something larger than ourselves. So, the content of our ethical beliefs is determined in large part by the shape of our spiritual beliefs and practices.[45]

The Vantage Point of Integration in Community

The second two lenses allow us to use the vantage point of integration in order to see the big picture, and to find our place in that picture. Whether the image is one square in a large mosaic, or one note in a song that is to be played over 639 years, we make a difference, just like every other person who walks the face of the planet.[46] Spiritual maturity requires that we reason with skill, relate to others with care, and that we integrate the two through love—first by loving ourselves and then by loving all of creation.

❖ *How do I fit?*

As you participate in a fair system for all, remember that you are part of all that is.

As is the hallmark of the Relationship Lens, spiritual reflection is the process by which we take a stand for what we believe and search our own soul to find our biases and interests.[47] As we move beyond ourselves to serve those without power, people who may be our co-workers or women working in home industries in developing countries, we learn that true power comes from service. As we consider how we fit into the larger community, spiritual teachers encourage us to notice that we are not separate from each other but are part of the whole.

This approach has interesting and complex implications as we consider whether we should focus on local or global concerns, giving rise to the popular slogan "Think globally and act locally."[48] The solutions to global problems are not easy. The problems will not be solved by screaming at each other, becoming lost in fear, and circling the wagons. As those of us called to the work in the everyday world work thoughtfully together, we have the possibility of creating social, political, and economic systems that allow all people on our planet to thrive.

❖ *Who am I?*

As you gratefully and virtuously live into your roles, remember that you are special, just like everyone else.

Finally, as we consider our character through the prism of the Reputation Lens, theologian Mark McIntosh states that spirituality becomes "a discovery of the true 'self' precisely in encountering the divine and the human other—who allow one neither to rest in a reassuring self-image nor to languish in the prison of a false social construction of oneself."[49] With this definition, McIntosh reminds us that through blending theory and practice we are transformed.

Everyday Ethics: *Making Wise Choices in a Complex World*

Our work life, as much as our personal life, can become the crucible for growth and change and in the process more than an inconvenient interlude where we get the resources we need to live. By weaving the thread of spirituality through our work, these resources can help us discover what it means to be fully human. In the process, we find our personal center, essential for effective leadership. For each lens, the spiritual polish helps to sharpen the answers to the core questions explored through the vantage point of intentionality and empathy.

THE VANTAGE POINT OF INTEGRATION FOR THE PERSON-IN-COMMUNITY

Much of our study of ethics focuses on our relationships with others. As we take our final look at what is required to be mature ethical people in community, the vantage point of integration calls us to accountability for what Carl Jung calls our shadow side, that part of us which, according to many spiritual traditions, is driven by fear rather than by love.[50] All the ethical, moral, and spiritual frameworks have a challenge and risk that are subtle variations on a theme: I don't have to account to anyone. This hubris, arrogance that often comes from pride, has led to the downfall of many an executive.

Those whose ethical home is in the Responsibilities Lens are especially prone to believing that they can operate by themselves. Isolating themselves from the discipline of a community, they can become self-righteous and judgmental, finding excuses why they don't have to play by the same self-imposed rules as everyone else. Those whose home is in the Results Lens begin to believe that their way is the only way, and their goals are the only goals. They begin to make inconsistent choices between long- and short-term goals, reducing everything to a cost/benefit analysis. In the process, they live by expedience rather than excellence, doing that which is required to meet their self-directed goals.

HUBRIS INHERENT IN THE FOUR ETHICAL LENSES	
I can do it alone … *so I'm excused!*	*I know the truth …* *so I'm exempt!*
WHY THIS CHOICE?	HOW DO I FIT?
WHAT DO I WANT?	WHO AM I?
My way is the best … *so expedience is fine!*	*I am special …* *so I'm entitled!*

Those whose ethical home is in the Relationship Lens may over-identify with their group and begin to believe that they know "The Truth." As a member of the group, they can become authoritarian while believing that they are exempt from the community norms. Those whose home is in the Reputation Lens often believe that they are special and thereby entitled to indulgence, favoritism, and leniency. A contemporary example of this hubris was seen with the sentencing requests of Andrew and Lea Fastow, convicted for their role in the Enron scandal, who argued that they needed to serve consecutive jail terms so their children would not be without a parent.

Many who are less advantaged do not have the luxury of tailoring their jail sentences to their children's needs.[51]

The headlines of the business pages trumpet stories of highly respected business executives and those in the lower ranks who did not temper their preferred ethical tradition with awareness and moderation. Blinded by their own weaknesses, they ended up being the antithesis of what they desired while becoming that which they feared: unreflective, unfulfilled, isolated, and broken. As we use the disciplines of the spirit, noting where we are not whole and complete, we at least can mitigate against disaster.

At its core, spirituality is the drive to wholeness. Employing a wide range of practices that are primarily found in our religious traditions, we each need to ultimately find meaning for our lives. The difficulty is that while work is one of the two essential functions of being human, many of us find that, in the words of William F. Lynch, our employers only want our "technical selves," that part of us that does our work carefully and well.[52]

Our employers may not want our whole selves, that part of us that has families, worries about our children, lives in a community, values clean air and water, and have spiritual practices. Thus, we must each be ever mindful of the tensions that call us to park our minds, emotions, and spirits at the entrance of our offices. Those of us in positions of power must also be mindful of the choices we are giving our employees and suppliers who may not have the bargaining power that we do. As we consider fully what it means to find meaning in our work, we will create business environments where all can not only survive, but thrive.

THE JOURNEY TO ETHICAL MATURITY

The spiritual journey requires that we all walk an individual path and do our own work in community. Not surprisingly, the claim of many spiritual teachers is that as we do our work we will move beyond a focus on ourselves to a larger picture, one that includes all and compels us to compassionate action. Shaped by our response to the core heuristic questions about the nature of the world and the people in it, our core beliefs provide our lives with meaning and give purpose to our actions. Because our core beliefs are those ideas that we hold with affection, we often respond to the circumstances of our lives based on whether the events match our preferred world view and whether we believe that we can make a difference—our perceived personal power, or self-efficacy.

Those who believe that they have power often work to strengthen those institutions and situations with which they agree. Thus, if we believe that we are employed by an ethical company *and* we believe that what we do shapes that company, we can proactively work to strengthen the core values and assure that the choices made mirror those values. In situations with which we don't agree, with perceived self-efficacy we can begin to implement strategies for change. Sometimes we find that we only need to alter our perception of an event. Other times we are moved to actively work to change the beliefs and actions of people in an organization or community. Those who do not believe they have any personal power to make a difference (or choose not to exercise the power they have) can become apathetic, tacit participants in a system with which they either basically agree or disagree.

	Matches worldview	Does not match worldview
BELIEVE I HAVE POWER	Work to strengthen	Work to change
BELIEVE I HAVE NO POWER	Apathethic agreement	Perceive self as victim

We see this tendency when Boards of Directors offer CEOs very high wages and stock options stating that the market demands this level of compensation to get the "best and the brightest." Rather than making an independent determination that the salaries are out of line with those in the rest of the organization, CEOs accept the pay as a modern version of "the devil made me do it." Groupthink in the guise of market surveys is just fine when we are the recipients of the largesse. When those surveys don't advance our own interest, we are much more skeptical. In situations we don't like where we believe we have no power, we become passive-aggressive participants, giving lip service to the existing structures while doing our best to undermine them. We also can see ourselves as victims, powerless to do anything and demanding that others make our circumstances better.[53]

Clearly, commitment to our core beliefs both defines us and has the potential to energize and transform the self and community. The quest for self-knowledge has at its center the task of identifying core beliefs, determining whether those beliefs are in fact accurate and worthy of shaping us as persons, and then identifying the opportunities and barriers before us as we try to make consistent choices based on our beliefs about the right treatment of people, the right use of property, and the appropriate use of power. Theorists in all four traditions provide their understandings of the assumptions that inform our core values. These assumptions provide the foundations for our ethical beliefs as well as our political bent (conservative or liberal), economic preferences (capitalism or communitarianism), social (independent or interdependent), and spiritual (exclusive or inclusive) preferences.

None of these positions is black and white: they are tendencies on a continuum. However, the hardest questions are those that require that we choose between two competing actions, each of which will have a different bad result. In these situations, our core values will determine the outcome. We know that people who abuse alcohol may injure themselves or others at work.

On one hand, we may value autonomy, the right of each person to choose how to live. Thus, we might not intervene in the situation even if the person might cause damage to the company.

On the other hand, we may value the well-being of the community, and demand that all persons be subject to strict rules about drinking (limits of alcohol at lunch and random drug and alcohol tests at work), even though the vast majority of people don't abuse alcohol. Unfortunately, rather than carefully looking at the underlying assumptions that drive the decisions, many people choose actions based solely on perceived threats of possible legal liability.

Ironically, giving our power to corporate counsel (or any other external party) does not absolve us from responsibility for making an unethical decision or going against our core values. Rather, as we explore our own beliefs, see how they square with the prevailing beliefs in our community, and then act in accordance with our best understanding of what will reach our desired goals, we become responsible ethical participants in our community. As we take our desires and values—our intentionality, empathy, and spirituality—to the workplace, we soon learn that no one path is the only way to mastery.

In this day of ethical, moral, and religious pluralism, no one tradition has a prior or privileged claim on definitively stating what is good and what is true. Each tradition values the vantage point of intention as they offer a theory or belief that guides those in that tradition to use reason as they seek wholeness. Each tradition values the vantage point of empathy as they emphasize love or compassion as they seek wholeness. And each tradition has a set of spiritual practices that assist us in becoming integrated and whole human beings. The multitude of approaches provide variations on a theme: we are all threads of the sacred fabric called life and participate in weaving the next segments of the cloth, our civilization.

However, ethical and religious pluralism do not absolve us from the responsibility of living morally aware and spiritually enhanced lives. Through exploring the theories underlying each of the three different vantage points and developing the skills needed to master each in our business and professional lives, we can embrace life as a *process* with a series of *practices* that lead to integration rather than envisioning our life's quest as a search for an *answer* to be found through pursuing goals or following a set of *rules*. With practice and a dollop of grace, we can become comfortable and skilled in moving between the immanent world, where all is profoundly connected, and the transcendent world, where ideas are forms that are first imagined and then brought to reality.

The promise is that as mature individuals who have mastered the tools of reason, empathy, and love, we can give joyously back to the community and fashion a world where all can thrive. This promise does not just apply to our family and friends. This promise does not apply only to our social and community lives. This promise also applies to the world of commerce, the places where we earn our living and make our contributions to the whole. The question we each get to explore is whether we will contribute to the fulfillment of the promise of achieving integration and integrity in the offices and shops in which we work.

Everyday Ethics: *Making Wise Choices in a Complex World*

CONCLUSION

As we engage in intentional, empathetic practices that make us more effective ethical decision makers as we seek wholeness, we each change. We take our changed person and our expanded worldview back to the workplace and see the problems and opportunities of the day through a more perfect, cleaner lens. The world where goods and services are bought and sold is the world of reason and is governed by our intentionality. The world of customers and co-workers is the world of emotion and is governed by empathy. The crucible of Spirit is the place where we find our center. Placing our personal crucible within the blast-furnace of the business world, we can creatively transform the iron of the world of reason and the carbon of the world of emotion to create organizations with the beauty, strength, and durability of steel.

As we let joy, compassion, and gratitude permeate our soul, we find that the world of business becomes less frenzied and more satisfying. Doing the right thing becomes just a bit easier, and we revel ever more in the person we are becoming. By using the same tools for our common professional life that we use for our personal journey, we can learn to respect the path of each person and walk together towards integrity and wholeness. Celebrating our professional lives as a process that leads to ethical maturity, we hear more clearly what questions to ask to create a healthy, vibrant business community.

CONTINUING THE CONVERSATION

1. As you reflect on your own ethical belief system, how would you answer each of the four core contextual questions? What decisions about yourself or your experiences have shaped your answers to those questions?

2. Does the distinction between ethics as a discipline of reason and morality as a discipline of emotions make sense to you? Do you agree or disagree with that distinction? Why or why not?

3. As commentators were evaluating the high profile case of Martha Stewart that dominated the press in 2004, one made the comment that Stewart could not accept the fact that she made a mistake. Thus, instead of settling for a civil penalty to the SEC, she went to trial and was convicted of perjury. As you look at other high-profile cases dealing with breaches of business ethics, what was the hubris of those executives; where did they believe that they would not be held accountable to the community?

THE RESPONSIBILITIES LENS
CONCEPTUAL MAP

CONCEPTS	INTENTION	EMPATHY	INTEGRATION
Foundational Questions	"What are my responsibilities?"	"What is a caring response to this situation?"	"What is my relationship to the whole?"
Theory	Deontology	Ethic of Care	Ethic of Personal Responsibility
Representative Authors	Immanuel Kant W. D. Ross	Carol Gilligan Nel Noddings	Ronald Rolheiser Anthony de Mello J. P. de Caussade
Tools and Practices	Reason; research	Awareness; self-soothing	Individual piety; reflection
Key Phrase	"I am responsible."	"I am caring."	"I delight in my work."
An ethical act ...	... fulfills the duties and obligations of the ethical decsion maker	... is done with care and concern for others involved	... allows me to carry out my obligations with joy
My goal is to ...	... create a set of principles to determine duty	... develop the ability to evaluate emotions and respond from care	... be aware of participating in a sacred purpose
I have gifts of ...	... autonomy and responsibility	... commitment to caring for others	... living fully in the present, humility, faith, and trust
My blind spot is ...	... belief that motive justifies the method	... inability to accurately match data to emotional response	... masking pain with busyness
My vice is ...	... judgmentalism	... martyrdom	... alienation from my best self
I risk ...	... becoming autocratic	... cold-heartedness	... spiritual dryness
Hubris	"I am excused."	"I know what is best."	"I can do it alone."
My crisis is ...	... alienation	... exhaustion	... emptiness and isolation

Knowing others is intelligence; knowing yourself is true wisdom.
Mastering others is strength; mastering yourself is true power.

If you realize that you have enough, you are truly rich.
If you stay in the center and embrace death with your whole heart,
you will endure forever.

From the Tao Te Ching—33[1]

CHAPTER 7

The Responsibilities Lens

T HE FIRST ETHICAL LENS COMES FROM a long tradition
of ethicists who focus on the decision-maker's responsibilities. Drawing upon the traditions of Plato, St. Augustine,
and Luther, the earliest theorist in the modern era who focused
on the responsibilities of the individual is Immanuel Kant [1724-
1804]. As the history of modern ethics has unfolded, Kant is the
philosopher most people name as the theorist who marks the beginning of the Age of Enlightenment as well as the voice that determines the trajectory of the deontological tradition in the
modern era.[2]

❖   *What are my responsibilities?*

❖   *What is a caring response to this situation?*

❖   *What is my relationship to the whole?*

SEEING CLEARLY THROUGH THE RESPONSIBILITIES LENS

Working from the central concept that the ideal for ethics is to find the core rules by which we
should live, the Responsibilities Lens requires that each of us determine for ourselves what prerogatives and duties we have as adults in community.

THE VANTAGE POINT OF INTENTION

The theorists who are representative of this ethical lens, Kant and W.D. Ross, invite each of us
to consider what responsibilities we have as individuals in community. When we have to choose

CHAPTER 7: *The Responsibilities Lens*

171

among good options, this process helps us identify and prioritize competing values. Our mantra becomes "I am responsible."

Kant and other Enlightenment philosophers broke from the medieval traditions where the church, or some other authority, defined the privileges and obligations for each person. Thus, each resisted identification as indistinguishable members of a group and demanded to be viewed as an individual, a person with rights and responsibilities—just like every other person in the community. The theorists at the beginning of the Age of Enlightenment asserted that individuals as individuals have the right to self-determination.

Ironically, the notions of autonomy were grounded first in the Protestant Reformation. As Martin Luther protested the abuses and excesses of the Holy Roman Empire, he asserted that individuals could determine for themselves what scriptures said and thus they were responsible before God alone for their salvation. A corollary to spiritual self-determinism was that people could also decide for themselves how they were to be governed. The work of early Lutheran lawyers and policy gurus laid the foundations for the theory of social contract where each of us has the right to negotiate with each other to determine the shape of our community.[3]

The source of individual rights for the theologians was the belief that all persons are created in the image of God and thus are entitled to being treated with respect and dignity. This theme was carried forward in the Protestant tradition by theologians such as John Calvin and Richard Hooker. Theologians such as St. Ignatius of Loyola who were part of the Catholic counter-reformation articulated many of the same themes.[4]

Philosophers assert that we have individual rights and the right to self-determination because adults, unlike infants or animals, have the ability to reason. Those who agitated for equal rights for women and the abolition of slavery (as well as those committed to the goal of universal human rights today) used the core belief of the ability of humans to reason as the primary persuasive tool. Those in power (in the United States, free white males) made the argument that because women and Negroes lacked the ability to reason and to be taught, they should not be granted the political and economic autonomy they sought. Those who were charitable considered women and slaves as needing protection; those who were uncharitable considered women, and particularly the slaves, non-human and thus not entitled to any rights. Ironically, at the same time that slave owners in particular asserted their slaves could not reason, laws were passed prohibiting teaching any slaves to read or write.[5]

Of course, it has taken more than 250 years for every person to be given those rights, and for some groups the ideal is still illusive. But the theories of Kant provided ethical ammunition for the abolition of slavery, the emancipation of women, equal employment opportunities for all, and, currently, for the quest by homosexuals for full inclusion and rights within the community.[6]

The other major shift heralded by Kant's approach was using the tools of reason (and by implication the scientific method of testing assumptions) rather than the authority of scripture or proclamations of the monarchy or church, to determine the validity of any particular ethical principle. This shift laid the groundwork for the end of the notion of the divine right of kings as well as the eventual separation of church and state. As we moved into the post-modern era, we began to see the limits of science. Not every inquiry could be answered through the reductionist tendencies of the scientific method.

The responsibilities we embrace provide a tight corollary to our rights. The gift of self-determination means that we also are entitled to all of the consequences that come with that gift, including not being able to blame anyone else for what happens to us. If, in fact, we are able to exercise our rights of political autonomy, we get (in the words of political pundits) what we deserve. If we can make our own choices about our economic well-being, then we get whatever goods come to us as a result of our actions. Thus, we cannot demand more from others to make up for the shortfall of our own resources. Instead, we need to work harder, make better bargains, or be content with our lot in life. The freedom both to succeed and to fail granted when we embrace the notion of individual rights and responsibilities gave rise to the pithy folk exhortation "You made your bed, now sleep in it."

As with any enduring writer, Kant engages us in the perennial conversation about duty and inclination (or preference), obligations and virtues—in short, what emphasis is to be given to the various strands of thought that weave together to make the tapestry we call ethics. Although Kant's theories may not get us to universal truths that will hold for all people, the template he laid out for determining individual rights and responsibilities endures. As the tradition has matured, various ethicists such as W.D. Ross [1877-1971] have proposed a definitive list of duties. Even though all may not agree with the specifics of any given list, the *reflective process* by which we determine what core principles should govern our life remains fresh and relevant.

From the vantage of individuals reflecting on our place in the community, we can use strategies of critical thinking to consider what rights and responsibilities we can claim. The sticking point for many is that whatever rights and responsibilities (which tend to come in matched sets) are asserted for any one person need to be given to everyone else in the community as well. Thus, Kant's theories (and others writing in the same tradition) provide support for the idea of autonomy—we all get to choose how we wish to live and use our own resources.

THE VANTAGE POINT OF EMPATHY

Nel Noddings, in her seminal work, *Caring*, asserts that the source of moral behavior is twofold: a sense of caring directly for the other and a sense of feeling for and with our own best self. As we learn to care for others, we can also accept and sustain the feeling of being cared for. In describing the ideal, Noddings states that we move toward "our best picture of ourselves caring and being cared for."[7] Our mantra thus becomes "As I responsibly fulfill my duties, I will carry them out with care."

In response to being cared for by others, we commit ourselves to acting on behalf of the one for whom we care. We learn to care for others as we notice that concrete situations of caring and being cared for are good. Noddings and others in this tradition argue that as we care for others we are acting from a universal ideal: maintenance of the caring relationship.[8]

The theories of an ethic of care also call us to responsibility. Hans Jonas and other advocates of the common good note that, since we as humans have the power to destroy the environment and other nations, we must carefully consider the ramifications of our acts. Jonas asserts that we must consider public policy as well as our individual responsibilities when we act, because our actions can affect the very existence of our planet and civilization.[9] For example, as we soberly realize scientists have demonstrated that the climate changes that come with global warming are the result of human action, we must carefully weigh the goals of productivity and economic growth against the possibility of leaving our great-grandchildren a legacy that is on a trajectory to extinction.

The vantage point of integration

Many people ask whether it is possible to delight in our work, to find work that has meaning and is satisfying. One of the problems with a Kantian approach to life is that we can do the right thing, care for others, and still be miserable. Sometimes, our work becomes so segmented that we have no sense of how it fits into the whole or how it makes a shred of difference in our world. We often take on more and more responsibility at work, which leads to our lives being out of balance, putting more of our heart and soul into our work than our family or community life. As we learn to discipline our desires and seek what is really important, we can put our seemingly conflicting responsibilities into perspective. The final version of our mantra becomes "As I fulfill my duties with care, I will delight in my work."

A common refrain among students was that they don't want to see their work as a life sentence, as they perceived their parents did. Thus, they seek some way to find joy in their work. This anecdotal evidence was borne out by the research of Nash and McLennan, who found that people "want to live a life of meaning, they want to be more effective at problem solving, they need connection to other people; through it all they optimistically assume that in discovering this sacred, authentic self, they will find that it can be a rather noble self."[10]

Some choose to follow their own heart's desire in selecting their careers rather than living out expectations of their family. Some look for ways to serve rather than trying to climb to the top of an organization or make as much money as possible. Some find meaning and satisfaction as they are caring and civil to those in their workplace. Some find happiness by making the lives of their co-workers a bit easier as they work together to accomplish the goals of the organization.

The first question that writers in this tradition ask is how we can blend responsibility and joy. If the goal of life is to love and to work, as we find work which satisfies us, we can be happy. John Eldredge states that "desire, both the whispers and the shouts, is the map we have been given to find the only life worth living."[11] Ronald Rolheiser reminds us that "spirituality is, ultimately, about what we do with that desire." Our spirituality is what we do with our longings, how we handle the pain and the hope they bring.[12]

David Whyte, a poet who explores the intersection between spirituality and the corporate life, asserts that if we try to plan our lives, the young innocent heart of desire may turn all of our efforts to naught. Whyte found in his work that if our desire is not given its due, "our personalities can work all the hours God sends to no avail, pushing water upstream on a project which is destined to die no matter what we do ... the unawakened yet youthful soul is so entangled with the world and so physically alert ... that it need not to keep track of every detail in order to find its way in the world."[13] As Whyte describes the intersection of the wily mind and the innocent soul, when we are following our heart's desire he finds that we work out of "sheer joy"—that which we love gives us the energy to do the hard work. Thus, as we find ourselves looking at our professional lives from the vantage point of integration, we can "make an equal place in the psyche for both strategy and soul."[14]

The second question writers in this tradition ask is whether we are willing to become sufficiently disciplined to know ourselves and reach our heart's desire. As we use the tools of the Responsibilities Lens, we have to be ruthlessly honest with ourselves. We have to develop habits of awareness to avoid "excessive self-preoccupation" and "excessive focus on work, achievement, and the practical concerns of life" that can drain us of all our energy.[15] Thus, our workplace spirituality is the discipline by which we "both access that energy and contain it."[16]

We have seen many good businesspeople who, unable to contain the drive for power and greed, have self-destructed—often taking their companies with them. In the American culture, where the mantra is often "He who dies with the most toys wins," learning self-discipline as we follow a path that makes our heart sing feels counter-cultural. Our mentors on these paths are few. Yet, if we look carefully we can find those who found meaning in their work and satisfying relationships without getting seduced by power or sidetracked by greed.

CHARACTERISTICS OF THE RESPONSIBILITIES LENS

This lens focuses on whether the principles used to achieve our goals are appropriate, not whether the goal or the result is ethical. The entire focus is on whether we are accomplishing our responsibilities to ourselves and others so we can claim the rights or privileges that come with being a person.

To determine whether an act is ethical, we (autonomy) use our reason (rationality) to determine the universal principles by which we and others should live. Careful thinking and rational arguments are very persuasive as we weigh our own duties and obligations in the situation at hand. As we act responsibly and exercise our rights, we need to always remember that others are also persons with intrinsic human dignity. As we treat people with care and respect, we can carry out our duties with integrity and grace. As we seek transformation to become fully integrated human beings, we can discipline those desires that can lead to asserting rights that are not appropriate and to shirking our responsibilities. In the process, we find joy in our work and community.

QUESTIONS FOR DETERMINING RIGHT ACTION

❖ *Motives:* What are my motives and intentions in advocating one solution rather than another?

❖ *Principles:* What ethical principles are present in the conversation? Which of these principles should take priority and why? What are the criteria for determining which principles should take priority in this particular situation?

❖ *Autonomy:* How does this decision protect individuals from unwarranted interferences from government or other people in the exercise of that right?

❖ *Caring:* How does this ordering of principles demonstrate a caring attitude and respect for others?

❖ *Accountability:* How does this ordering of principles assure that I have held myself accountable for my reason for acting?

❖ *Balance:* How does this ordering of principles contribute to balance and joy in my life?

SECONDARY VALUES SEEN THROUGH THE PRISM OF THIS LENS

❖ *Life and safety:* Individuals have the right not to have their lives or safety unknowingly and unnecessarily endangered.

❖ *Truthfulness:* Individuals have a right to not be intentionally deceived by another.

EVERYDAY ETHICS: *Making Wise Choices in a Complex World*

- ❖ *Privacy:* Individuals have a right to do whatever they choose outside of working hours and to control information about their private life.

- ❖ *Freedom of conscience:* Individuals have a right to refrain from carrying out any order that violates those commonly accepted moral or religious norms to which they adhere.

- ❖ *Free speech:* Individuals have the right to criticize conscientiously and truthfully the ethics or legality of organizational actions as long as the criticism does not violate the rights of other individuals within the organization.

- ❖ *Financial transparency:* Individuals who invest in companies and others to whom the firm has a fiduciary duty have a right to fair, accurate reflection of the financial status of the firm.

- ❖ *Right to contract:* Individuals have a right to enter into contracts according to the terms that each party to the contract find agreeable.

USING THE RESPONSIBILITIES LENS

As we begin to work through an ethical issue using the perspective of people in the Responsibilities Lens, we begin with the human condition. People in this lens are very clear that each person is both "saint and sinner." Focusing on the fragmented nature of being a human, people in this lens are not particularly optimistic about the human condition or the

SNAPSHOT: AN ACTION IS ETHICAL IF IT

- ❖ *Fulfills the responsibilities of the agent.*

- ❖ *Is done with care and concern for other individuals involved.*

- ❖ *Allows one to delight in their work as they carry out their obligations.*

ability of people to choose to be good and do the right thing. Thus, people from this lens encourage the relentless seeking of the truth. Also, because people cannot be trusted to do what is right, we need a series of principles and rules to help us be on our best behavior.

Further, because people from this lens value the process of rationality, being able to explain why a particular position was taken is important. The steps of the analysis allow us to make a persuasive argument as to why we chose one option instead of another. The following set of questions helps us identify the responsibilities that govern our ethical choices. As we become more skilled, the analysis will become easier and we can begin to identify the core values that, for us, trump other competing values. However, even when we think we know the answer to the question, the discipline of working through the process can help clarify our thoughts.

To help understand the process, an abbreviated version of a real problem will be given in a set of text boxes. The problem that will be used in all four of the theoretical chapters explores whether or not an advertising campaign where the behavior portrayed could be viewed as bullying is ethical. After we look at the problem four times, the differences among the answers will prove intriguing. However, when a company wants to run an effective ad campaign, if members of the community resonate with the message even if the behavior advocated is questionable, the balance between selling the product and encouraging responsible behavior may not be clear. In each of the chapters, an abbreviated version of the analysis will be presented in the text. These examples will give us a feeling for the tools of each theory.

Step 1: Be Attentive

During the first step of the decision model, we pay attention to what is going on. This step is more difficult than we think. We have to pay attention to what our mind is observing, what we are seeing, and what we don't want to see. We also have to listen to our emotions. If we are not careful, our emotions can get hijacked and we wind up inappropriately reacting to a situation.

Attend to the context

As the Enlightenment philosophers established the primacy of reason over tradition or emotion, Kant spent much of his time exploring the role of reason in determining the shape of the law. *The Groundwork of the Metaphysics of Morals*, one of Kant's seminal texts, asserts that through reason we can discover the universal principles of life, the ethics by which we should all live. Thus, if "an action is really moral, it will not only accord with a law; it will be done because a law is acknowledged as absolutely and universally binding ... it will be ... 'ethics based on pure reason.'"[17]

In arguing for using reason, rather than personal inclination, as the final arbiter of what is right, Kant was aware of the fact that people have different skills and interests. Kant taught that we have a responsibility to help others develop their own skills of analysis, which would lead to autonomy. He also instructed that we should not act from our passions, our emotions, as those can be misleading.

One of the most troublesome examples that Kant gives of this concept is when he asks whether a husband who loves deeply an invalid wife and thus cares for her is more or less virtuous than a husband whose love has become cold and who nevertheless stays with his wife to assure that she receives the care she needs. Kant asserts that the one who stays from duty is more ethically meri-

CASE STUDY: FACTS AND ASSUMPTIONS

❖ *The VP for Sales and Marketing for G-BioSport North has recommended an ad campaign to boost sales among college age men. The ad campaign has two groups of college men playing intramural basketball. The team from one dorm is buff with aggressive athletes who gang up and taunt the scrawny and untalented team from another dorm. The scrawny team takes G-BioSport supplements and starts working out. The final shot is the revenge of the nerds—where they turn on the buff athletes who flee from the court in shame and humiliation. This ad was tested in the field and had a very positive response from the target demographics. However, just as the campaign is about to begin, I received a letter raising concerns about our new ad campaign from a watchdog group, Concerned Athletes Against Bullying (CAAB). After some research, I discovered that CAAB is an advocacy group with lots of resources behind it and it targets companies that directly or indirectly advocate bullying.*

torious than the one whose actions are motivated by love. While many may disagree with that particular standard, Kant gives the example to underscore that we should carry out our duties even when the action is uncomfortable, inconvenient, or financially disadvantageous. The ethical person lives by the principles, or maxims, that reason reveals.[18]

Kant argued that through reason we could find the universal principles of life that would guide our actions. While Kant's claims are subject to much critique, asking the questions demanded by the categorical imperative helps us determine the overarching principles of life that form our core personal values as well as those of our community. The principles are then applied to the specific situations to determine what we should do. In specific situations, the cultural context can be considered, though the context itself should not drive the final choice.

Identify the decision maker

The next step is to determine who is responsible for making the decision, the ethical agent. Each of the theorists has a different understanding of the self that is going to engage in the ethical decision. As Kant was striving to find universal principles, he knew that the ethical agent needed to be removed from the everyday circumstances of life. For Kant this means that "the notion of a subject [ethical agent] that is prior to and independent of experience, such as the deontological ethic requires, appears not only possible but indispensable, a necessary presupposition of the possibility of self-knowledge and freedom."[19]

This self is called a "transcendental subject," a self that is "the something 'back there,' a self that comes before any particular experience that unifies our diverse perceptions and holds them together in a single consciousness."[20] Kant invites us to move ourselves out of the particular circumstances in which we make the decision—the people, the times, the place—and determine principles that hold for all times and places. Using this theory, these universal principles then determine our actions. This approach has the value of leading to consistency, as the ethical decision maker treats all persons who are similarly situated the same.

Making a decision without considering anything about the particular context is not easy. We have to imagine our self as "any person." We don't have a particular gender, race, nationality, age, set of abilities or disabilities, or anything except being a human who is seeking universal principles that will apply to all people at all times.

Pinpoint the ethical issue

What central problem is to be resolved? Is this an issue concerning interpersonal tensions? Is the issue one involving appropriately completing one's tasks, one's professional obligations? As

❖ *Given that recent incidents of bullying have escalated in the community and the community is actively taking steps to stop and prevent bullying, should we run an advertising campaign that is certain to boost the sale of our product where the behavior advocated could be viewed as bullying and might draw negative community commentary.*

we phrase this issue into a question, we need to focus on the conflicting rights and responsibilities that are present. The intriguing part of ethics is that each lens uses a different set of criteria to scrutinize any given question. The Responsibilities Lens focuses our attention on becoming a fully functioning adult who acts from a sense of duty.

STEP 2: BE INTELLIGENT

As we move into the second step, we are going to do our first round of critical analysis. For this segment, we are going to sort through the data and begin honing in on the problem itself.

Determine the stakeholders

The next step is to identify the stakeholders—the people who will be affected by the decision. As we consider the stakeholders, we need to attend to the agreements among the parties. Those who use the Responsibilities Lens presume that individuals with equal power will be negotiating with others who also have autonomy. Thus, the contracts between the parties help determine the ethical obligations. Often, the agreements are *explicit*: the price set for goods, a certain number of hours to work. Just as often, the agreements are *implicit*: grading papers fairly, treating all students alike. In a financial setting, we expect the information on balance sheets to be accurate and complete without entering into an additional agreement.

❖ *Me, the CEO of the Company, who is the decision-maker*

❖ *The VP of Sales and Marketing responsible for creating and implementing the ad campaign*

❖ *Shareholders of the Company, whose stock value depends on the financial success of the company*

❖ *Employees of the Company, who depend on a fiscally sound company for employment*

❖ *Customers who like your product and might increase use because of campaign*

❖ *Kids who are bullied because your company appears to advocate bad behavior*

❖ *Members of the community who may critique the ad campaign and your company because it contributes to bullying*

In completing this step, we must examine the agreements with every constituent and determine what our responsibilities are to each. How we *feel* about the people involved is irrelevant. The strength of the process is that we do not make decisions based on whether we like another person or whether we feel like doing a particular act. The litmus test is whether we are following the maxim, the required principle for acting.

As Kant sorted out our responsibilities to the various stakeholders, he asked us to consider whether the duties we have are perfect or imperfect. Many ethicists distinguish between *perfect duties*—those obligations we have explicitly agreed to undertake—and *imperfect duties*—those actions that we could take but are under no obligation to take. For example, a physician only has an obligation to those patients they have agreed to treat. Even though many may need help, until the physician has taken a particular person on as a patient, they only have an imperfect duty to the general public to cure that person.

The second task, according to Kant, is determining whether we are assisting people in making the best decisions they can. As ethical decsion makers, our primary duties are to those with whom we have express and implied agreements. As further explained by Ross, we have a *prima facie* ethical obligation to honor the terms of our contracts. Often, however, we also owe a duty to people with whom we are not in direct contractual relationship. Thus, companies who trade on the stock market have a fiduciary duty to the general public to make sure the financial information is accurate. This duty, which arises out of an obligation of trust, flows to both those who sell and those who buy stocks.

We may also have an obligation to those with whom we are in relationship because of the social contract we have with each other not to act in a way that will adversely impact our ability to live and thrive. For example, increasing numbers of people are asserting that companies have an implicit duty as citizens not to put toxic materials into the air or water in order to assure that members of the community don't become ill because of toxins in the environment. Each successive level of duty—those with whom an actor is in contractual relationship, those who will be directly affected by the action of the company, and those who are indirectly affected by the action of the company—moves along a continuum from perfect duties to imperfect duties.

Explore the values in tension

In a Kantian setting, conflicts can arise on several fronts. We may have conflicting duties with different stakeholders. For example, we may have a duty of loyalty to one person that would prclude meeting the requirement of truthfulness and integrity with another person. We may encounter a person who asserts rights but doesn't embrace the accompanying responsibilities.

Because this lens favors *autonomy*, as Kant encourages us to assist others in becoming responsible adults, he would expect us to hold those persons accountable as each of us is to act responsibly. Further, as this lens favors *rationality*, Kant would probably not raise an eyebrow if we found ourselves upsetting people with whom we are in relationship in order to meet our obligations. As we meet the requirements of the categorical imperative, people who expect favoritism will most certainly be annoyed.

CASE STUDY: VALUES IN TENSION

❖ *The two values in tension are* AUTONOMY, *where the Company makes its own choices about how to sell its products, and* EQUALITY, *where the Company responds to community pressure and initiative to stop bullying. In order to be successful, to continue to employ individuals, and to offer our products to the public, our Company must advertise its products. On the other hand, bullying has become an issue in our community. We have a commitment, as a member of the community, to not advocate behavior such as bullying that creates an increased risk to the safety and well-being of the community.*

Identify options for action

The next step is to identify the options. Clearly one can choose whether to carry out an action or not. More interesting is finding complex solutions, those that meet as many of the core values as possible and reveal systemic solutions. Also, working through a problem that on its face looks unethical is intriguing. Sometimes, those options that appear to not meet any of the requirements of the template are the best.

Case Study: Options for action

1: Run the advertising campaign that is certain to boost sales but could be advocating bullying behavior.

2: Do not run the advertising campaign that is certain to boost sales but could be advocating bullying behavior.

Consider how ethically mature the identified options are. The least mature option protects us and our interests with no concern for others. The next level of maturity focuses on options that take care of ourselves and our buddies but don't consider the systemic implications of the action. Finally, the most mature and responsible option will consider all of the stakeholders and whether the institutions of the community (such as schools, hospitals, businesses, and government) will thrive.

STEP 3: BE REASONABLE

For this section of the decision process, the questions that are asked are specific to the lens. The point of this section is to show how people who favor this particular approach to decision making would answer the problem. Because each ethical lens prioritizes different values, the questions asked to determine the best course of action are different.

Hone critical thinking skills

For Kant, the point of critical inquiry was to honestly articulate the reason for acting. To begin the process, we are asked to determine the motives we have for choosing each option. Kant believed that we could identify our rights and responsibilities and begin to formulate key principles that would guide us in making our decisions by examining our reasons for acting. When considering our reason for acting, it helps to think in terms of the different values in the core value clusters. Is the reason for this option so people will have autonomy, to be able to make a decision with full information about the choices they are going to make? Is the reason part of the cluster of values surrounding sensibility, making sure that the organization's resources are used appropriately?

As Kant explains the notions of the categorical imperative, reason helps us determine the right act. The universal rule, which is identified through use of the categorical imperatives, is an *imperative* because it is a command of reason, a command that tells us what we ought to do. A categorical imperative is one that directly commands a person to engage in certain conduct that is objectively necessary without reference to any other purpose or end.[21] For example, a categorical imperative would be to respect human life, even if the end or the purpose might result in the abolition of the death penalty or the cost of a product being increased in order to assure that it is safe.

Kant contrasts the categorical imperative, that which we do because our reason tells us the act is our duty even if we don't like the results, and the hypothetical imperative, that which we do as long as we like the results that we get. An example might be a company that manufactured baby clothes with a coating that was supposed to retard flames. After testing, the company discovered that the product did not retard flames, but rather increased the likelihood of the sleepers catching on fire. The product could not be sold in America because of the laws concerning safety. However, the laws of Europe did not restrict the sales. If the categorical imperative tells us that we should always act in a way that respects human life, then the company would not sell the product in Europe, even though it could.

If we were operating against the hypothetical imperative, the ethical rule might be that the company will act in a way that respects human life as long as the financial consequences aren't too high and it doesn't violate the law (or won't get caught). Selling the baby clothes in Europe might pass the hypothetical imperative because the financial consequences for not selling the clothes are high and no law prohibiting the sale or establishing liability exists in Europe.[22]

In framing the reason, we work to get to the highest reason possible, a reason that would reflect the best of human action and understanding. If my reason for hurting you is to watch you squirm in pain, the action would be, by definition, unethical. Most of us are unwilling to be hurt by another person who only wants to see how we respond to pain. However, if I am a physician and want to remove a tumor, I must also inflict physical pain. In that case, the reason for inflicting pain would be to assure greater health and preserve life. We are generally willing to let a physician inflict pain to assure that we have greater health. Thus, the physician's motive for causing us pain in order to facilitate health would pass ethical muster.

From time to time, people in charge want to say the reason for their actions is "because I said so and I'm in charge." Those in leadership positions should use the prerogatives of authority with care. Using authority and loyalty as reasons for acting will chill any conversation about the best reason for a firm to act and discourage others from engaging in their own reflective process.

CASE STUDY: REASONS FOR ACTING

OPTION 1: RUN THE ADVERTISING CAMPAIGN

❖ The reason for running the advertising campaign is to responsibly meet the perfect duty (PRIMA FACIE duty) to our shareholders, employees, and customers to increase sales of our products to assure fiscal health. The competition is gaining on us. The advertising campaign will help us maintain and grow our market share.

OPTION 2: DO NOT RUN THE ADVERTISING CAMPAIGN

❖ The reason for not running the campaign is to honor our imperfect duty to the community to assist in the initiative to stop and prevent bullying. Bullying incidents in the community have recently increased in number and severity. The community is concerned about bullying and is taking steps to stop acts of bullying. As a Company we do not want to encourage bullying and we want to be a responsible citizen.

Evaluate the dilemma from the vantage point of intention

To apply the ethical content, we ask four questions which are embedded in Kant's categorical imperative and Ross's *prima facie* duties. These questions help us sort through the competing rights and responsibilities that individuals claim because they are members of the community.

First Question: What would happen if everyone adopted this reason for acting?

As Kant developed his theory, he articulated two categorical imperatives that assist us in finding the principles by which we should live. The first categorical imperative is universalizability: the person's reasons for acting must be reasons that everyone could act on, at least in principle.[23] The notion is that, as we reflect using the tools of reason, we should only adopt maxims or principles that are not inherently self-contradictory. The principle of universalizability challenges us to consider those universal rules that all persons can follow without the rule becoming inconsistent.

Kant illustrates this maxim by asking whether if, when we have our backs to the wall and we don't like the anticipated consequences of telling the truth, we can make a promise that we don't intend to keep. As Kant explores this situation, he concludes that we would not be content if everyone operated on the rule "I will make promises but only keep them if it turns out that the consequences are consequences that are acceptable." Kant rightly notes that the proposed universal rule would destroy itself as soon as it became the law: If I keep only those promises that turn out to have good ends, no one will know whether or not my promise would be kept. Thus, the whole idea of promises and contract would dissolve.[24]

On the other hand, one could universally adopt the rule "When I make a promise, I will keep it regardless of whether the anticipated or unanticipated consequences are those that I prefer." Thus, everyone would keep promises once they were made. The popular version of this rule is seen in the notion of business by handshake. The highest compliment of a person's integrity in our community is that a complex deal is discussed and sealed with a handshake—and then honored. Even if later the market changes or the legal situation shows that parts of the deal may not be advantageous, if we have adopted the handshake principle, we consider our word to be our bond. We would not try to use legal loopholes to escape the obligation that we made.

As Kant laid out the criteria of what he called universalizability, he invited us to move into systemic thought rather than just look at the impact of our decision on ourselves. While we are relatively certain that no reason for acting will ever be acceptable to all people in all cultures, asking this question helps us think about overall systems, not just the act.

For example, if we have superior knowledge in a situation, we may be able to use our position of power to press an advantage against a client or customer. While acting from superior knowledge and power seems to be a compelling motive for our choice, we need to consider what would happen if everyone drove an advantage in a negotiation based on superior power and knowledge. A recent example was seen as EchoStar took on Viacom for what it considered "extortion" for the price to be charged to carry the station in areas where CBS did not have local affiliates. The two companies went into a face-off to see who would blink first as the negotiation for the royalties to be paid broke down.

Viacom believed that it would be able to control the negotiations as EchoStar's customers would not tolerate disruption in their service. EchoStar, even though it was a smaller company with seemingly less power, believed that their customers would support their efforts to keep prices low. Within forty-eight hours of Echo-Star pulling the plug on Viacom's programming, a new unpublished contract was signed, with both companies declaring victory.[25]

CASE STUDY: UNIVERSALIZABILITY

OPTION 1: RUN THE ADVERTISING CAMPAIGN

❖ *The reason for running the advertising campaign is to effectively sell our product and increase brand awareness. Everyone could adopt that reason for acting in actuality and in principle. The market is very competitive. Market share and brand awareness is critical to the overall success of any business.*

OPTION 2: DO NOT RUN THE ADVERTISING CAMPAIGN

❖ *The reason for not running the ad is to be perceived as a responsible member of the community that does not offend people who are not our target customers or that does not advocate bullying in its ad campaigns. Everyone could adopt that reason for acting in actuality and in principle. As members of the community we want to assure the needs of the community are met. If we all know and consider the ramifications of our choices before we act, we can make sound decisions, contracts, and agreements.*

Kant would invite us to consider what happens if market power or superior knowledge that is not available to everyone is consistently used to take advantage of others. The result in American culture is lack of trust, increased transaction costs, and lawsuits. If someone has a reputation for always being a sharp dealer, then every transaction will be carefully examined by lawyers and accountants to make sure no advantage is taken, which drives up transaction costs. The next consequence is increased litigation because we don't trust each other.

Thus, rather than each of us taking individual responsibility for a deal gone sour, the one taking advantage of power will quickly blame the other person for the bad result. The line between strong market power and coercion is fine. Living on the edge of that line may cause overall systemic damage, which may mean that pressing an advantage just because we can is not ultimately a good way to do business.

SECOND QUESTION: *AM I WILLING TO HAVE SOMEONE ELSE USE THIS REASON IN DECIDING HOW THEY WILL TREAT ME?*

The second part of the first categorical imperative is reversibility: our reasons for acting must be reasons that we would be willing to have all others use, even as a basis of how they treat us.[26] Thus, the second litmus test we use when adopting a reason for acting is whether we would be willing to have another person use the reason that justifies our action to determine how that person treats us. If we articulate a reason for acting and are not willing for someone to use that reason in how they treat us, then the option is by definition unethical. Reversibility is a variation on the Golden Rule. We tend to say that we are to treat others in the way that we would want to be treated. If we are not careful, however, we focus on the result of the action rather than the reason for the action.

An example of this principle in action comes as we look at people treating some people differently than others. In deciding who is going to get a particular contract, would I be willing for the reason that a contractor signed a deal to be that the contractor felt more comfortable playing golf with one vendor rather than with me? Given that the social aspect of business is important, would I be content with the reason for someone else receiving a contract being that the contractor wanted to assure that the vendor was a person who not only had an appropriate product but was also accepted at the country club?

Case Study: Reversibility

Option 1: Run the advertising campaign

❖ *The reason for running the advertising campaign is to effectively sell our product and increase brand awareness. Given the right of companies to run ads and people to choose products, I am willing to have that reason be the reason that others would use in choosing their ad campaign, given myself as a customer. I value the right of consumers to be informed and make their own choices without excessive filtering from the community.*

Option 2: Do not run the advertising campaign

❖ *The reason for not running the ad is to be perceived as a responsible member of the community who does not offend people who are not our target customers or who does not advocate bullying in its ad campaigns. Given the right of companies to run ads and people to choose products, I am not willing to have that reason be the reason that others would use in choosing their ad campaign, given myself as a customer. I value the right of consumers to be informed and make their own choices without excessive filtering from the community.*

Many of us who seek competitive advantage are willing to use whatever tools and resources we have to get a contract. If that means being cheerful when we are crabby or social when we want to be alone, we would try to meet the needs of the contractor. However, in the final analysis, most of us want to be judged according to the requirements of the contract. Most of us would prefer that the reason for a contract going to another person be that the product or price is better, not that we play golf badly, are a boring dinner companion, or that our parents are not members of the right—or any—country club.

Many students miss the point of this step of the process by focusing on the *result* of the action rather than the *reason* for the action. Kant never expected people to necessarily like the result of the action—they just had to be willing for others to use that reason in how they were treated. For example, when I ask someone a question, do I prefer the unvarnished truth or a polite lie? Given that I make decisions about what I am going to do based on accurate information, I would welcome a hurtful critique if the reason for giving the data is to assure that I have complete information. If the reason for the hurtful information is retaliation or to make me feel badly, I would prefer that the person keep their counsel. This step of the process is very black and white. If I am not willing for the reason to be used in how I am treated, then the option is not ethical. Once the motive for acting is determined and the test of reversibility is applied, the path of action becomes clear.

THIRD QUESTION: *IF I ADOPT THIS OPTION, AM I TREATING PEOPLE THE WAY THEY HAVE FREELY CONSENTED TO BE TREATED? AM I ASSISTING THEM IN THEIR OWN PROCESS OF BECOMING FULLY FUNCTIONING ADULTS WHO CAN MAKE THEIR OWN CHOICES?*

This question asks whether we are acting from selfish reasons alone or to fulfill our duty to another. While Kant expected people to examine their motives and follow their own lights in determining individual rights and responsibilities, action always is taken in community. Thus, if I have to cause you misery in order to fulfill my duty to you and others, then the action would be considered ethical. If I have to have a deadline for accepting papers to meet my obligation to the univer sity and my syllabus indicates that I am not going to accept late papers, students have agreed to that condition by staying in the class. Then, if I refuse to accept a paper after a deadline, my reason for acting is not just for the selfish reason of easing my load but to assure that I treat both the student and the university as they have agreed to be treated.

The second categorical imperative states that an action is morally right if, and only if, in performing the action, we do not use others merely as a means for advancing our own interests, but also both respect and develop our capacity to choose freely for ourselves.[27] Kant was absolutely committed to the notion of autonomy and the value of the human person. In making this point, Kant talked about the difference between everything having a price or having dignity. Kant asserts that if we treat people as means to our own ends, we assume that people are interchangeable commodities who do not have dignity or value in themselves. If, however, we look at people as ends in themselves, we accord them dignity and respect, regardless of their monetary worth.

This tension is seen poignantly in the health care debate. When a child is born at 26 weeks of gestation, six weeks before full term, what resources should be used to keep that child alive? If the child has dignity and value as a hu-

CASE STUDY TREATING PEOPLE AS ADULTS:

OPTION 1: RUN THE ADVERTISING CAMPAIGN

❖ *Because the customers are able to choose whether or not to take the supplements and thus gain the benefits, we are in fact giving them choices that will allow them autonomy and respect while providing a bit of humor that any reasonable person would recognize as comic overstatment.*

OPTION 2: DO NOT RUN THE ADVERTISING CAMPAIGN

❖ *By trying to satisfy a small advocacy group, we are adopting a paternalistic attitude rather than giving people interesting information and letting them make their own choices.*

man person, then the life of that person should not be measured in terms of how expensive it will be to preserve life. However, we also know that even if we use the very expensive technology we have available, the prognosis for the person ever being mentally and/or physically independent is very grim.

Many premature infants who survive have diminished mental and physical capacities that drain the health care resources of the community and profoundly affect the lives and resources of the family. Does treating that baby as a person in its own right require using every available resource to keep that person alive? Or would treating that baby with dignity be the way that one of my students was treated when she was born several weeks premature? Her grandmother wrapped her in a blanket, placed her in a shoe box by the fireplace and waited to see if she would breathe and survive. The thought was that if the baby was strong enough to survive, they would feed and care for her.

We also see this tension in how people are treated at work. Many times it seems that employers really don't care about us as people, about the totality of us as full human beings. Thus, many people believe that they are being treated as means for the employer to make lots of money rather than as ends, persons who have value as human beings. If someone else can do the job more cheaply, perhaps an immigrant, an undocumented worker, or one who has less experience or qualifications, we are replaced—like cogs in a machine. Of course, if we shift the vantage slightly to consider our obligation to assure that others who are very poor have an opportunity to have an income, the act may in reality be ethical. For Kant, the reason for an act is key in distinguishing between ethical and unethical acts.

This problem is amplified as employees who embrace their role as an agent for the company tend to see their interests as the same as the employers' and thus don't notice the pattern. Without thinking systemically, we identify with the owners—the stockholders—of the businesses who are our employers rather than seeing ourselves as workers in solidarity—persons with the same interests—as other workers. Many times our concern is first preserving shareholder value, which often translates to giving the workers as little as possible while driving them to be as productive as possible. Ironically, the policies we advocate lead to small raises for ourselves or the outsourcing of our jobs to other nations. The categorical imperative becomes an interesting lens: are we willing to be laid-off or to take lesser compensation because others are willing to do the same work for less?

One problem with this tendency only to consider the owner or shareholder of a company when making a decision was eloquently explored by William F. Lynch, S.J., in *Images of Hope* when he asserted that the usual form of citizenship created by these exclusive cities of man is that of the ideal or the beautiful self we have earlier described. But the form of citizenship created by the technological cities of exclusion is that of the *useful self* . . . . Only the useful part of the human self gets into the kind of community we will describe by the name of formal or mechanical organization.[28]

Using the work of Christopher Argyris, a leading management theorist, as his foil, Lynch goes on to describe how American management theory glorifies strategies where managers assure that the worker is convinced that any discontent is the problem of the worker and not the nature of the work that is provided by the firm. Lynch asserts that "in addition to the usual charges that workers are lazy and lack goodwill, those on top respond with every measure save the kind that will nurture responsibility, autonomy, and, I would add, the good taste of the human self."[29]

Troubled by Lynch's indictment of American business, I began probing to see whether my students had bought into the notion of the "useful self" as the ideal for the business world rather than the "beautiful self." One telling exercise came as I was exploring the notion of gratitude and trying to dispel the notion of the self-made person with my seniors in a seminar on Economic Justice. I asked my students to list all the people who were responsible for them being in class that glorious September day. They listed parents, former teachers, and mentors in the community. One student even went back to the *Mayflower* and was grateful for his forebears who crossed the stormy Atlantic.

Not one of them listed the people in the cafeteria who made their breakfast, the cleaning staff who assured that the room was vacuumed and the boards were washed, the groundskeepers who mowed the lawns and tended the roses, or the library staff who facilitated the research for the paper due that day. To my students, all of the people who were necessary for their success at school were in fact faceless instruments—valued only for the services they provided, people who were a means to the end of an education and a diploma.

Conversations about the right treatment of workers, conversations that began with an invitation to actually *see* those who provide the infrastructure for our success, are often quickly marooned on the shoals of relative ethics. The notion that every idea is as good as another is the unintentional fallout from the nascent postmodern ethos that seems to permit students to embrace the philosophy that "anything goes" as long as I am able to autonomously seek my goals.

This conversation leads to the next implication for Kant's theory, the sanctity of contracts. One of the ways that we treat people as ends is by treating them in the way they have freely consented to be treated. Thus, if you and I negotiate on the price of my services or the goods I am selling, once we have agreed, no one else should be able to second guess the contract. This understanding of contracts presumes that we have roughly equivalent market power and have the ability to walk away from a contract. In reality, many people do not have that kind of market power and thus an inquiry into fundamental fairness and justice becomes important.

A preliminary step in determining whether we are treating people as they have agreed to be treated is identifying the agreements we have with each other, which was part of setting the context. So, we must examine the implicit and explicit agreements with each constituent and determine what responsibilities we have to each. A corollary to the agreements is whether in making those agreements we acted in good faith and did not abuse our power. Acting in good faith requires that we give people the information they need to enter into fair, appropriate contracts. If we keep information from each other, we cannot make good agreements.

Not abusing power means that we must be sensitive to forced agreements, where in truth people cannot make good choices. We are fond of saying that we embrace the notion of contract "at will," the idea that employers can lay us off when they desire and we can leave when we wish. However, we know that for the vast majority of workers, finding a job is much more difficult than being replaced. Thus, especially in a non-unionized setting, employers have a great deal more market power than employees.

When power is out of balance, we often are using the other person as a means to our preferred ends rather than treating the person as an end, a human being with autonomy and choice in how to live his life. The classic example is the medical experiments with 600 black illiterate sharecroppers who, in 1932, were recruited by the Public Health Service to participate in a study in cooperation with the Tuskegee Institute, where research was being done concerning syphilis. The men were told that participating was part of their patriotic duty. The conversations happened in the men's home churches, giving the experiments an even greater imprimatur of authority. Even after the researchers determined in 1945 that a cure for syphilis existed, the tests continued (which included no treatment for the disease) until 1972 to document the physical results of syphilis, to the great detriment of the men and their families. In this case, the researchers used the men as a means to their goal, or end, of compiling more data.[30]

CASE STUDY: EVALUATE DUTIES

As we consider our duties to our stakeholders, we have three groups to consider: shareholders, employees, and customers.

OPTION 1: RUN THE ADVERTISING CAMPAIGN

❖ *Our duty of fidelity to our shareholders is met by running an effective ad campaign. Our duty of gratitude to our employees is met as we move ahead with their good work that lives into the company values. Our duty of fidelity to our customers is met as we are truthful (within accepted bounds of hyperbole). Finally, we meet the duty of beneficence as we make their lives better through using our products.*

OPTION 2: DO NOT RUN THE ADVERTISING CAMPAIGN

❖ *Our duty of fidelity to our shareholders is not met if we scrap the campaign because we are turning our back on an effective campaign and spending resources reworking the campaign. We are not meeting the duty of gratitude by scrapping the work of a dedicated marketing team. While our duty of non-maleficence (duty not to hurt anyone) generally only extends to direct harm, if we did not run the campaign we would not indirectly harm people by appearing to condone bullying..*

A final consideration asks whether we are helping people make the best decisions possible. To accomplish this, we need to help people realize that they are rational human beings who can determine the best way to live. One indicator of a person's autonomy is the balance of power among the various stakeholders. If either party abuses power, which can result from an imbalance of information, education, or financial resources, then the other party may not be able to freely choose what she wants to do. Another indicator of balanced power is the presence of real options. A person who has no access to health care cannot choose to be treated for illness. Thus, for this step we look for balance of power and options.

Fourth Question: How does this option meet the requirements of traditional and personal ethical principles?

Many people assert that we all instinctively know the principles—the rules by which we should live. The difficulty is that unexamined instincts often lead to bad results. Thus, considering the concrete duties that become clear as we consider the categorical imperatives is useful.

While we may not agree on the list or the priority to be given to each rule, reviewing the lists of traditional duties as outlined by ethicists such as W.D. Ross can be instructive in the process of finding balance and prioritizing our options. While Ross doesn't assert that the following list is exhaustive, reviewing the commonly accepted duties can help us ensure that we are being responsible.[31]

- ❖ *Duties of fidelity:* Telling the truth, keeping actual and implicit promises, and not representing fiction as history

- ❖ *Duties of reparation:* Righting the wrongs we have done to others

- ❖ *Duties of gratitude:* Recognizing the services others have done for us and being thankful for our lives and our community

- ❖ *Duties of justice:* Preventing someone from distributing pleasure or happiness that is not in keeping with the merit of people involved (people should not give good things to bad people)

- ❖ *Duties of beneficence:* Helping to better the condition of other beings with respect to virtue, intelligence, or pleasure

- ❖ *Duties of self-improvement:* Bettering ourselves with respect to virtue or intelligence

- ❖ *Duties of non-maleficence:* Avoiding or preventing an injury to others; not hurting other people

Again, this list is most helpful in identifying the duties that seem to make sense for members of our community after people have attempted to identify universal principles. Noting that in different communities different behaviors might count for when we have met these duties, the list can help us assure that our core duties have been considered before we act.

As we resolve ethical issues from the vantage point of intention, using the Responsibilities Lens, the gift we bring to the community is thinking for our self and responsibility. As we become ethically mature, not only do we fulfill our duties but we do so without prompting or supervision. A Midwestern saying exemplifies this lens: after assessing a problem, we "just pull up your socks and do it." That responsible self is highly valued in the community and an important partner in solving the problems of an organization or a community.

Evaluate from the vantage point of empathy

As we reflect on the options, our next task is to consider whether that option can be carried out in a way that demonstrates caring for the other person. Ethical actions have two dimensions—*what* we do and *how* we do it. Modern theorists consider primarily what we should do and do not focus on method. When we use the Responsibilities Lens, the question becomes which option will fulfill the prerogatives and duties that we have voluntarily taken on in our community. However, if we are not careful, we can carry out an ethical option in a way that is hurtful to others.

The post-modern viewpoint invites us to consider the context of the situation and to look at those affected by a decision as whole persons with feelings and emotions. We are not expected to violate our duties and responsibilities, but rather to carry out those duties in a way that acknowledges the essential humanity of the persons affected by the decision. In an era of downsizing and firing, many employers decide to give people fifteen minutes to clear out their desks and escort them to the door. Others choose to give people time to say goodbye, help with résumés, throw a party, and let the grieving or celebrating run a course over several days. Those companies that dismiss people with integrity and care fulfill their responsibilities while the dignity of the person is maintained. The moral lens turns our attention to caring for others as we invoke our rights. We can either accomplish our duty in a wholly rational way or we can see others as humans and treat them with respect and care as we carry out our duties.

CASE STUDY: ACT WITH CARE

OPTION 1: RUN THE ADVERTISING CAMPAIGN

❖ *This option demonstrates care for the primary stakeholders as well as those to whom we have a perfect duty by increasing our customer base (thus providing needed benefits to customers) and increasing our profit (addressing the rights of employees and shareholders).*

OPTION 2: DO NOT RUN THE ADVERTISING CAMPAIGN

❖ *This option demonstrates care for our secondary stakeholders, those to whom we have an imperfect duty, by partnering with those who are working to decrease the instances of bullying in high school and collegiate environments. However, this option does not demonstrate care for the primary stakeholders.*

EVERYDAY ETHICS: *Making Wise Choices in a Complex World*

As we resolve ethical issues from the vantage point of empathy, using the Responsibilities Lens, the gift we bring to the community is caring. As we become ethically mature, not only do we fulfill our duties but we do so with a gentleness (sometimes a curmudgeonly gentleness) that shows respect for the other stakeholders who are involved. In these situations, often our actions speak louder than our words, as people understand that we are carrying out our duties with a profound sense of respect for all people involved. That *caring* responsible self is highly respected in the community as people know that we are not just looking out for our self but are concerned with others as we solve the problems of an organization or a community.

Evaluate from the vantage point of integration

The vantage point of integration is the place where we make peace with ourselves—our best self and our worst self. Each person has places of fear, anxiety, meanness and perversity. As we become ethically mature, we embrace and befriend what Carl Jung called our "shadow self." Often our shadow self has the intention to protect us, and if we listen to that voice too closely we wind up in self-sabotage.

Blind spot

Like a blind spot in the side mirror of a car, the ethical blind spots are those places where we can unintentionally act unethically. Because the Responsibilities Lens favors rationality, from the vantage point of intention, we may overemphasize rational thinking and become rigid in our thinking. Often, the cause of rigidity is the belief that the motive—our reason for acting—justifies the method used to carry out our tasks. Because we are so clear about why we are doing the act, we may forget that others also have free will and need to be included in the conversation. We also may focus on the act without considering the results, the consequences of our choice. While this lens calls us to responsible living, we must remember that often we have multiple ways to be responsible.

From the vantage point of empathy, we may fail to notice either our own emotions or the emotions of others. If we are insensitive to our own emotions, we may not accurately match the

---

CASE STUDY: ACT FROM YOUR INTEGRATED CORE

OPTION 1: RUN THE ADVERTISING CAMPAIGN

❖ *This option supports the core values of truthfulness in that the ad campaign does not misrepresent the product. It does not directly contribute to endangering the life or property of another. By running an engaging ad, we contribute to freedom of choice and conscience as people can choose whether or not to use the product or, in an unlikely situation, imitate the behavior in the ad.*

OPTION 2: DO NOT RUN THE ADVERTISING CAMPAIGN

❖ *This option supports the core values of truthfulness in that the ad campaign does not misrepresent the product. It does not directly contribute to endangering the life or property of another. By substituting another ad that might not provide information in an engaging way, we may indirectly be denying freedom of choice and conscience as people will not be paying enough attention to choose wisely.*

information we are receiving from others with appropriate action. In the process, we may unintentionally cause people upset and pain.

Finally, as we take on more and more responsibilities to fulfill our duties, we may get lost in the busyness of what we are doing and fail to ask whether all of the tasks are necessary and whether they contribute to the meaning and purpose of our life. Upon reflection, one can determine the core essential activities and then shed the "shoulds" of life that are duties imposed by others or holdovers from previous roles and responsibilities. Many a woman who has embraced a career has discovered that she doesn't have to clean her house within an inch of its life every week, thus actually freeing her up to have some personal time. The greatest gift that someone from this lens can give themselves is to periodically prune the to-do list so that it reflects the tasks that are essential and only a few thoughtful selections from the "nice but not necessary" column.

Vices and risks

The opposite of virtues are vices, which emerge as we take ethical risks and do not diligently work to assure that we are being ethical. From the vantage point of intention, a misuse of reason leads to carelessness of thought. This trait expresses itself in the Responsibilities Lens as a tendency to be autocratic and domineering as we claim absolute authority over a situation. We justify claiming the prerogative of authority through claiming that no one else cares about fulfilling their duties but us. As we become increasingly judgmental, we criticize everyone for their ethics, or lack thereof.

From the vantage point of empathy, as we become increasingly critical, we also may become cold hearted and embrace the mantra of "my way or the highway." Ironically, as people distance themselves from you because of our lack of empathy, we feel like a martyr—no one appreciates all that we do in meeting the needs of the organization or community. As we embrace our martyrdom, we become more and more prickly, thus isolating us from what we want the most: acknowledgment for a job well done.

Finally, as we become more and more bitter, our self-righteousness alienates us from our best self, leading to increasing spiritual dryness and frustration. As we alienate our self from those who care about us, the antidote becomes looking at the world from the vantage point of the Reputation Lens, learning to balance our excess rationality with sensibility and our care for our self with concern for the community.

Hubris

Hubris, excessive pride and arrogance, moves us from unintentional ethical wrongdoing to intentional wrongdoing. Those who act with hubris have a deliberate disregard for the ethical requirements of the community as they work to further their own agenda. For the Responsibilities Lens, from the vantage point of intention, hubris shows up as excuses—because of our privileged status, in particular situations we are released from our obligation to follow the rules. As we move out of integrity by not living into our own core principles, we silence the voice of our "best self" and become alienated from others.

As the press revealed the hubris of top business executives at the end of the 20th century, all had a myriad of reasons why they did not have to follow the accounting rules or provide financial transparency for their stakeholders. Even while they required people in the firm to be careful with resources, they lived lives of excess, believing somehow that the wealth was deserved and was their prerogative. Even while they paid themselves exorbitant salaries and bonuses, they forced vendors to deeply discount prices and paid employees as little as possible to demonstrate the company's commitment to efficiency and the bottom line.

California's Pacific Gas and Electric Company (PG&E) provided a stark example of this hubris when it awarded $83 million in bonuses in January and $89 million in bonuses in July of 2004. The startling part was that in addition to being a regulated monopoly, the company emerged in April from a three-year stint in Chapter 11 bankruptcy following the energy crises in California. While the rank and file received performance bonuses at 11% of their base salary, the seven top execs received up to 70% of their base salary. The Chairman received $1.7 million in the first round and $10 million in the second while the CEO received $906,000 in the first and $10 million in the second. John Nelson, a PG&E spokesman, defended the bonuses as money owed to the executive team for the work they did to bring the company out of bankruptcy. Nelson added, "It's not like customers' power bills would be lower if PG&E stopped handing out millions in bonuses. It's the profits of the company. We earned it."[32]

From the vantage point of empathy, to insulate our self from the judgment of our self and others, we dismiss both the emotions that manifest as disapproval and our conscience, that internal guidance we have to keep us on the right path. Ignoring the emotional maelstrom swirling around us, we are sure that we know best. When others refuse to follow, we begin doing everything ours self from a perspective of self-righteousness.

Finally, as we become more and more exhausted, we discover that trying to do everything alone leads to emptiness and isolation. The isolation may be subtle, as people distance themselves from us. Or it may be very public as we are shunned by those who used to be our friend. A contemporary example of this shunning can be seen in the decision by Warner Bros. to remove Mel Gibson from a cameo appearance in a movie. Gibson, once a highly-respected actor, was embroiled in a legal action where he was accused of domestic violence and extortion. The cast in the movie objected to Gibson's appearance, and so the offer to appear was withdrawn.[33]

Consider the critiques of the lens

One of the major flaws of the Responsibilities Lens is that it does not address the inequities that come from a difference in the original position—the discrepancy in wealth and power—between those who are born with access to resources and privilege and those who are not. Neither Kant nor the theorists who rearticulate his position in the 20th century, most notably Robert Nozick, advocate for a redistribution of resources based solely on need. For Nozick, the current distribution of goods in our community is the result of a myriad of legitimate transactions over time and thus the discrepancies in wealth are fair. Arguing for a minimal state (which is important because governments are responsible for the transfer of wealth through taxation and redistribution), Nozick argues that "whatever arises from a just situation by just steps is itself just."[34]

This position articulates what some philosophers call a principle of negative rights: we are entitled to whatever we get either because of our original position (the resources of our family) or because of how we choose to use the resources we inherit or have earned. Thus, if we agree to employment that pays minimum wage with no benefits, that transaction is fair because we had the freedom of contract to either take or leave that job. Again, the conversation becomes stark when we consider health care. Is it ethical for a parent to take a child to the hospital for care if the parent knows that he cannot pay for the care?

Those who advocate for negative rights would state that we should not incur any obligation for which we are not able to pay, including debts for health care. Those who believe that every person is entitled to adequate health care disagree vehemently with limiting access to health care based solely on the patient's ability to pay. Those who are in the philosophical camp of Nozick argue for limiting governmental regulations concerning our contracts (minimum wage, wage and hour laws, laws concerning safety) and reducing taxes. Those advocating for a minimal government believe that people should be responsible for their own well-being and not have any expectation of protection from bad agreements or being on the public dole. Those who advocate for more government involvement to assure the well-being of members of the community believe that the public policy positions of those who argue for a minimal state are mean spirited and selfish.

This conversation will be revisited in Chapter 9 when we look at Rawls's theory of justice, which states that we have an obligation to transfer resources and care for the least advantaged. Nozick does not agree with Rawls as he asserts that "justice is determined not by the patterns of the final outcome of distribution, but by whether 'entitlements' are honored."[35] Rather than including health care, education, food, and shelter as positive rights to which all persons in a community should have access, the only positive right that Nozick recognizes is the "right to acquire

EVERYDAY ETHICS: *Making Wise Choices in a Complex World*

and transfer property."[36] Thus, he advocates protecting the right to private property, a bedrock for a market economy. Nozick's mantra is "from each as they choose, to each as they are chosen."[37]

While this lens focuses on the rights and responsibilities individuals claim, we must note that all others in the community are entitled to the same rights. Of course, the difficulty is that we don't always notice that we must have a modicum of personal and financial power to exercise rights. To correct for the bias of assuming that all have the same opportunities and resources, as we rank the options, we should focus on balancing between achieving individual rights and responsibilities against all of the stakeholder rights and responsibilities. If the rights and responsibilities of either party are to be compromised, we should compromise on the side of the one who has the least power and the least ability to gain power.

STEP 4: BE RESPONSIBLE

Rank the options from least preferred to most preferred

Having determined the reasons for acting and then evaluated the options from the vantage point of intention (can everyone act on this reason [universalizability]; would I be willing for someone to use this reason in how they treat me [reversibility]; and am I treating people as ends and not means to an end?), the vantage point of empathy (am I showing that I care for others by how I carry out my duties?), and the vantage point of integration (am I making sure that my "best self" shows up in this situation?), we can then rank the options from least preferred to most preferred.

As we rank the options, we summarize why this ranking of options was chosen and demonstrate the primacy given to the core values. First we must show how we privileged autonomy—because each person is valuable in their own right, each person can choose how they want to live; however, once having freely chosen, a person is obligated to fulfill those responsibilities. Then, we show how we privileged rationality—as we logically assessed our duties, we identified our responsibilities in this situation without being overly influenced by emotion or desire.

CASE STUDY: RANK THE OPTIONS

OPTION 1: RUN THE ADVERTISING CAMPAIGN

❖ *This option meets all of the tests of the lens. In each instance the primary stakeholders, the ones to whom we owe* prima facie *duties, are given priority. Also, this option treats people like adults who are able to make their own informed choices.*

OPTION 2: DO NOT RUN THE ADVERTISING CAMPAIGN

❖ *This option does not meet all of the tests of the lens because it gives priority to the secondary stakeholders, ignoring our duties and responsibilities to the primary stakeholders. This option would meet the requirements of the lens only if the ad campaign directly advocated bullying instead of presenting a tongue-in-cheek revenge of the weak.*

Strive for ethical maturity

The final stage before acting is much like going through a checklist one more time—have we

❖ *By running the ad campaign as designed, Option 1, we are living into our core principles of supporting autonomy and free choice. We are not forcing anyone to purchase our product, but inviting customers to consider the merits of your product by presenting an engaging ad. The purpose of the company is to sell product, make a profit, and contribute to the well-being of the community through the benefit of the product. Option 1 clearly meets this purpose.*

corrected for any unintended bias that might have appeared? For this stage, a final look at the tools for analysis is useful. With the final check, we can make sure that the option we choose is the most ethically mature choice available to us.

From the vantage point of intention, we analyze our own course of action. For the Responsibilities Lens, we want to assure that the option is carefully analyzed and researched. We have gathered the available data and subjected it to critical methods of inquiry to test for accuracy and truth. We also want to assure that we are being responsible in managing ourselves, taking responsibility for accomplishing our duties without nagging from others.

The vantage point of empathy is used to negotiate differences with others. For this lens, the ability to self-soothe, to smooth our own ruffled feathers when others see the world through a different lens than ours is critical for working effectively with others. This tool helps when others don't share our sense of duty or understand our motives.

❖ *After consideration, I will authorize running the ad as presented. Through this action we are providing valuable information to our clients and contributing to the fiscal health of the company. We are treating our clients like fully-functioning adults who can both make good choices about their health as well as treat others in the community with respect, as each lives out their own core values.*

Finally, we use the vantage point of integration to test our course of action against our personal meaning and purpose of life. As we learn to trust the process of life, we can develop the tools of humility, faith in ourselves and others, and trust that all will work out well. This tool helps us weather the inevitable storms of life when others don't see things our way.

Act with courage

After we make our choice, we should be able to communicate our decision to others. Creating a short statement that could be placed in a memo to others in the company or a press release helps us learn to articulate our ethical decisions so that we answer the core questions of the Responsibilities Lens.

BE TRUE TO THE PERSPECTIVE OF THE ETHICAL LENS

Remembering that this vantage point is like looking through a telescope, taking a long view, the option we choose should reflect the ideal values that are important for human beings. As the ethical decsion maker, we act as a "transcendent self" who has no particular identity and does not consider the particulars of the situation. The preferences of individuals, including ourselves, are not important as we fulfill our responsibilities. Prior experience is not persuasive as we chart our course of action. Our concern is identifying the ideal principles that apply to all people in this situation.

We are also going to choose the option that will stand the test of time, grounded in principles that will hold for all times and places. And, as we consider the stakeholders, we assume that they also are people with equal power who are negotiating with others who have autonomy. Each person will try to make decisions that reflect the timeless principles, so no one abuses power and everyone is treated the same.

FOLLOW CHECKLIST FOR ACTION

As we move to action, using the perspective of the Responsibilities Lens, we will:

- ❖ *Focus* on the ideals we want to accomplish. The purpose of ethical action is to help create a world where the principles for right living are followed.

- ❖ *Ask* people how they want to be treated. Each person is an individual who deserves respect. By asking them how they want to be treated and what behavior counts as living out the shared core principles, we can tailor our response to meet our obligations and their desires.

- ❖ *Treat* people as "fully functional adults." Assume that every person is committed to being responsible and living out their personal core values, which includes accepting the consequences of their actions.

Because most of the work in ethics is persuasion, we should be able to articulate clearly what choice we have made and why. After giving a bit of background information to set the stage for the problem, we can frame the statement so that we answer the core questions of this particular lens. What are our *reasons* for choosing this action? Having examined our motives, how are our *duties*, *rights*, and *responsibilities*, both our own as the ethical decision maker and those of all the other stakeholders, fulfilled? How does the way that we propose to carry out this action demonstrate caring for the stakeholders involved? How does this action fulfill our own need for *meaning and purpose* in life?

STEP 5   RETURN TO AWARENESS

Every action has a reaction. That reaction will be both from others and from ourselves. So, after we act and the dust has had a moment to settle, we turn back to determine whether our course of action was in fact wise.

REFLECTION

❖ *As we learn more about bullying and the whole question of the decline of civility in our community, the role of advertising in setting acceptable norms in the community is a recurring question. We wish that people weren't quite so responsive to the slap-stick humor that provides the foundation for this advertising campaign. Perhaps with more thought, we can find an ad campaign that reinforces positive behavior instead of quietly endorsing uncivil action.*

What improvements could we make on our process of ethical analysis? Did we like the result? What were the problems with the process? What are the sticking points with the process, where we were not comfortable with the way the decision was unfolding? What were the unintended consequences?

Reflect on results

As we reflect on the results that come from our actions, we can put strategies in place to become ever more ethically mature. Ethical maturity occurs as we move from only thinking of ourselves to noticing how our choices impact others as well as the institutions of our community. As we grow in ethical maturity, we seek solutions that are systemic and will improve life for as many as possible.

From the vantage point of intention, personal growth and maturity is defined as identifying the core principles that become our lodestar and fulfilling the duties that flow from those principles. Those duties are carried out whether or not anyone is watching. As we become familiar with our own emotions and those of others, from the vantage point of empathy our responses are tempered with care as opposed to us becoming a bulldozer that imposes our will on others. Finally, as our vantage point of integration matures, we will learn to live from the deep knowledge that we are participating in the unfolding of an overarching purpose that is larger than our individual life.

Seek continuous improvement

The process of continuous improvement involves evaluating the result of the action. As we take action in our life based on the lens, we can watch for intended and unintended results. Also we should watch for new questions or answers that were not complete. The trajectory for maturity is not necessarily smooth, but as we attend to our rights and responsibilities, we can get there. As we treat people with respect and dignity, we consider to what degree autonomy can be respected. This process will call us to accountability for paternalistic and autocratic behavior while caring for those who legitimately cannot care for themselves.

As we are called to balance, we need to address whether we are being overly responsible or not responsible enough. As we learn to live fully in the present, attending to our own desires and our inner child, we can avoid the problem of busyness for the sake of busyness or becoming self-righteous as we try to meet all of the spoken and unspoken requirements of the community virtuously. If we do not attend to our spirit as we do our work, we risk becoming bitter and brittle. Duty without joy provides naught but dry bread and water for sustenance. As we seek tastier fare, we can learn how to be responsible while treating ourselves and others with compassion.

Everyday Ethics: *Making Wise Choices in a Complex World*

CONCLUSION

The Responsibilities Lens invites us to consider how to live a responsible life. Beginning with the phrase *I am responsible*, which embodies the vantage point of intention, we learn to be adults who consider our motives as we act. To avoid becoming legalistic and autocratic, we learn to be compassionate, or, from the vantage point of empathy, *I am caring*. As we learn to use both our heads and our hearts, caring for others while assuring that they too are granted autonomy, we can see the world from the vantage point of integration and *delight in our work*. Balancing rights and responsibilities with caring and autonomy requires careful thought. With practice and discipline, we can use the tools of this lens to act with discretion and wisdom when faced with difficult choices.

CONTINUING THE CONVERSATION

1. Using either the first problem in the *EthicsGame Core Values* simulation or another fact pattern, analyze the situation using the Responsibilities Lens. Was the problem easy to do, indicating that this might be your preferred method of working ethical problems? Was the process difficult, indicating that this may not be your ethical home?

2. Read an op-ed piece in your local paper or a national paper and find examples of Responsibilities Lens ethics. In what ways did the author appeal to the right of contract and negative rights? What distinctions were made between rights and equality of opportunity for all people? How did the author explore the motives of those making the decisions and taking action?

3. Review the chart that opened this chapter, paying special attention to the gifts of this tradition. Considering both your own life as well as others who make decisions using the vantage of this tradition, what are the strengths of the Responsibilities Lens? Give examples of situations in which you have seen excellent results as someone used the viewpoints and processes of this lens to make a decision.

4. What strategies can you put in place to help you begin to strengthen your own mastery of this lens? How can you help the organizations in which you work, whether paid or volunteer, ask the core questions to help them make better ethical decisions?

5. Again, review the chart that opened this chapter, this time attending to the weaknesses of this tradition. Considering both your own life as well as others who make decisions using the vantage of this tradition, what are the weaknesses of the Responsibilities lens? Give examples of situations in which you have seen problematic results as someone used the viewpoints and processes of this lens to make a decision.

6. What strategies can you put in place to help you recognize and attend to the imbalance that comes from an inappropriate appropriation of the Responsibilities Lens, whether concerning abuse of power or hubris in your personal and professional life? How do you know when you are improperly using the tools of this lens? How can you help the organizations in which you work, whether paid or volunteer, ask the core questions to help them avoid imbalance or hubris?

THE RESULTS LENS
CONCEPTUAL MAP

Concepts	Intention	Empathy	Integration
Foundational Questions	"What do I want?"	"What are mutually good results?"	"How can I be a partner in creating a better world?"
Theory	Utilitarianism	Harmonization of Good	Sacred Imagination
Representative Authors	John Stuart Mill Jeremy Bentham	Bernard Lonergan Frederick Ferré	William Lynch Rosemary MacNaughton
Tools and Practices	Experience; action and reflection	Awareness; self-efficacy	Imagination
Key Phrase	"I have choices."	"I seek win-win solutions"	"I am co-creator of what is"
An ethical act …	… has good results	… creates the greatest happiness for the greatest number of people	… serves the greater good, resulting in harmony and satisfaction
My goal is to …	… identify the goals of life	… creatively imagine solutions that lead to higher goods	… be aware of participating in a sacred plan
I have gifts of …	… self-directed choices	… respect for others, living with ambiguity, and integrity	… optimism, enthusiasm, flexibility, and hope
My blind spot is …	… expedience and being satisfied with too little good	… maintaining consistency between actions and self-views	… becoming angry and resentful
My vice is …	… greed	… freeloading	… pride
I risk …	… reducing all to a cost/benefit analysis	… ignoring imbalances of power	… losing perspective
Hubris	"Expedience is fine!"	"I know what you need and want"	"My way is the best/only way."
My crisis is …	… failure	… guilt	… discouragement

What happens to a dream deferred?

Does it dry up like a raisin in the sun?

Or fester like a sore—And then run?

Does it stink like rotten meat?

Or crust and sugar over—like a syrupy sweet?

Maybe it just sags like a heavy load.

Or does it explode?

Langston Hughes[1]

CHAPTER 8

The Results Lens

The NEXT ETHICAL LENS COMES FROM the tradition that focuses on the decision-maker's goals and objectives. Because the emphasis is on each of us choosing to act in a way which makes us happy, the lens is called the Results Lens.

SEEING CLEARLY THROUGH THE RESULTS LENS

This particular tradition has had much criticism for not attending to concepts of justice as well as the deontological tradition does.[2] However, the *reflective process* by which one determines what key goals are important and worthy of pursuit for individuals and how to preserve the goals for the community remains fresh and relevant.

CORE HEURISTIC QUESTIONS

❖ *What results do I want to achieve?*

❖ *What are mutually good results for all in this situation?*

❖ *How can I be a partner in creating a better world?*

THE VANTAGE POINT OF INTENTION

Drawing upon the traditions of Aristotle, St. Aquinas, and St. Ignatius of Loyola, the earliest theorists in the modern era who focused on the right of people to pursue the goals that make them happy were John Stuart Mill and Jeremy Bentham. Their theory, known best as utilitarianism (which embraces the theories of hedonism[3] and consequentialism[4]), states that as individuals choose what will make them happy, the greatest good for the greatest number will emerge. For

Mill and Bentham, achieving the greatest good defines an ethical action. The underlying concept endures—that we each get to choose how we will live and pursue the ends, the goals, which make us happy. In this quest, all people are to be included so that segments of the local and eventually even the global community do not have to live with dreams deferred.

Working from the central concept of ethics as finding the goals that will create the most happiness for the most people, the Results Lens invites each of us, as ethical decision makers, to determine for ourselves what goals are worthy of pursuit. This school of thought matured as Mill and other Enlightenment philosophers were breaking from the medieval traditions where the church, or another authority, told each person what his or her role would be based on family structure, economic status, and gender roles.

Mill and Bentham put forward the notion that each of us has the right to choose what makes us happy, both as individuals as well as a community. While the foundations were laid in the 1800s, it has taken more than two hundred years for us to come into a fuller appreciation of the right of individuals to choose how to participate in the community based on their own preferences rather than an assigned role.

Linda Kerber sketched one stark example of the tendency to limit women's participation based on role as she traced the history of women being able to fully participate as citizens in our community. One of the chapters in her seminal work, *No Constitutional Right to be Ladies*, followed women's attempts to be systematically included on juries, one of the last barriers to full civic participation. Kerber recounts the following conversation, which took place in the House of Representatives in 1966:

> Emmanuel Celler of New York—who had been supporting women's voluntary service for many years—rose in the House of Representatives to assure Martha Griffiths of Michigan that he was willing to support compulsory service for women if he could be reassured on one issue: "Frankly, I am caught between the urging of the gentlewoman from Michigan and a male stakeholder, who expects a hot meal on the table when he returns from work. Is it the gentlewoman's desire to come between man and wife?"[5]

Not until 1975 did the Supreme Court find that to meet the constitutional requirement of "a jury of peers," women needed to be systematically included in jury panels, even if that meant that they might not be home to prepare dinner.[6]

Mill, who ardently supported the rights of both women and men to be full participants in the community, articulated a theoretical basis for each of us following our own dreams rather than those dictated by roles. Intriguingly, people do choose to embrace traditional roles. However, we must always be careful to verify that people are making a free choice. Mill reminds us that even though we are part of society, we are not just interchangeable cogs but individuals with dreams that should not be deferred.

In the process, Mill reminds us that we cannot stop when we have satisfied our desires of the moment. Mill also invites us to seek the ideal goals, such as liberty, equality, and democracy. We are sometimes asked to put aside our individual preferences for the higher good. As anyone who has stayed inside on a beautiful day to finish a paper or project knows, we sometimes have to endure short-term pain for long-term gain. In a similar vein, those of us with access to power may be required not to press our advantage in order to allow those with less power to realize their dreams.

The theories of utilitarianism also provide the foundation for our market economy. Just as we each can choose what we want to do, each of us can choose how we wish to use our resources. Adam Smith, a contemporary of John Stuart Mill, used these foundational ideas to nurture the notion of a market economy. Smith is best known for his theory of the "invisible hand" by which goods would be distributed appropriately as individuals made free and non-coerced economic choices.[7] Classic liberal economic thought holds that individuals are the basis of our community. As each of us rationally maximizes our self-interest (presuming full information of our options and opportunities) and does that which makes us happy, the market reaches equilibrium.[8]

The notion is that we will not pay more for something than it is worth to us; we will not work for less than we think we are worth or than an individual employer is willing to pay. In this economy, we will have full information of our options and opportunities. Thus Adam Smith and the economists who have followed in this tradition use the philosophical foundations of utilitarianism to justify their political and economic theories and policies of what has come to be known as market economy.[9]

THE VANTAGE POINT OF EMPATHY

As each of us learns that we can live our lives the way we choose, we can become heady with the freedom of autonomy. However, we note that we make our choices in a matrix of personal relations, a community that cooperates and is bound together by its own needs and a drive to move toward the common good.[10] These relationships are not isolated and theoretical. Rather, they are infused with the whole range of emotions that come as one embraces a dream, works to make that dream a reality, and then finally succeeds or fails.

Along the way, we discover that some goals give us as individuals a particular good. Then we learn that we can work with others to harmonize our individual goods so that others may also get their heart's desire. In one case, this shift may be from making sure that we have a job to making sure that others are employed as well. Another example may be noticing that we had good mentoring and thus want to put in place programs to assure that all new employees receive an orientation that will enhance their ability to succeed.

Constructive postmodern theorists point us to the common good by asking us to consider how to move to greater good. Frederick Ferré asserts that self-interest encourages us to be resourceful as we find ways to survive and thrive. According to Mill, choosing to survive and be satisfied is even better. The best is to find a way to survive with "complex, harmonized satisfactions."[11] Ferré believes that as we seek to maximize the good for all members of the community, we can begin to militate against the problem of evil. As individuals limit their vantage to only their personal happiness rather than the overall happiness of a community as a whole, we wind up focusing only on narrow self-interest rather than thoughtfully attending to the interests of the whole.

Working towards these complex, harmonized satisfactions is the goal of good leadership. Daniel Goleman, who introduced the notion of Emotional Intelligence, identifies one style of leadership as coaching, where the leader helps people identify their strengths and weaknesses then works with them to harmonize their individual goals with the goals of the organization.[12] Effective coaches manage themselves by being emotionally aware, empathetic, and authentic. Then they are able to work with others without either micro-managing or putting the goals of the organization ahead of the goals of individuals.

Bernard Lonergan asserts that one of the results of our unrestricted desire to know is a yearning to also seek the good. This desire propels humans into a quest for the good that is

> dynamic … [with] its own normative line of development, inasmuch as the ideas of order are grasped by insight into concrete situations, are formulated in proposals, are accepted by explicit or tacit agreements, and are put into execution only to change the situation and give rise to still further insights.[13]

For Lonergan, the practical, concrete trajectory for ethical growth begins by acknowledging the provisional state of our knowledge. The ideal ethical person acts bravely with imperfect knowledge as they explore concretely, in the here and now, how to live a life that is fully human and offers others in the community the opportunity to do the same. The focus for the vantage point of empathy is considering how to find our own happiness while developing empathy for others so they can also find happiness. As we act, we consider not only ourselves but also others.

The vantage point of integration

The vantage point of integration allows us to creatively find ways to meet both our own goals as well as others. Phoebe Snow, a folk singer from the 60s, laments in a song called "Harpo's Blues,"

EVERYDAY ETHICS: *Making Wise Choices in a Complex World*

"I hate to be a grown up and live my life in pain." Many people think that as we pursue our goals, the most we can hope for is survival—keeping body and soul together. If Lonergan is right that the goal of being human is to know and to learn, we progress not only by seeking the individual goals of survival, but by moving toward those "terminal values" that parallel Mill's ideal goals.[14]

Terminal values allow us to think beyond ourselves and our projects, to become, in the words of Lonergan, "self-transcending," which is defined as "the achievement of conscious intentionality."[15] As we consciously choose goals that move not only our selves but also our compatriots along the way toward maturity, we are able to see beyond the seeming pain of the day toward the larger good. In the process, we can realize that what seems like failure may in fact be a gift.

A young man who was nervous about his work once asked my husband how being fired can be good. My husband recounted a situation of being "fired"—reassigned—while serving in the Air Force. While he was devastated in the moment, he realized some five years later that but for the reassignment he would never have received the next promotion. Thus, what seemed like a bad result was exactly what was needed in the larger picture of his overall career. He thus learned that one can never be sure what should be considered a success and is truly a failure. Being committed to the terminal value of integrity as he refused to condone racial discrimination on the base to which he was assigned resulted in what looked like a set-back but was ultimately a step forward on his desired path.

This tale is told on a larger stage as we consider the flash-point of the Civil Rights Movement in America when Rosa Parks, a black woman, refused to give up her seat on a bus to a white person. The segregation laws in Alabama required that African-Americans sit in the back but relinquish their seats to white people who would otherwise have to stand. Parks was active in the National Association for the Advancement of Colored People (NAACP) and worked with Dr. Martin Luther King, Jr. The local NAACP chapter was considering how to highlight the effects of discrimination and trained people in how to respond when faced with discrimination. While the event itself was not planned, the emotion galvanized the local Black community. Hundreds of African-Americans joined in the boycott, putting aside their own goals of getting to work efficiently to seek the greater goal, the ultimate value of liberty and dignity.[16] In the process, the national community was compelled to face its own goals for a diverse community and the way that it treated its neighbors.

Progress of the sort described above is not inevitable. We must learn to keep our egos in check by remembering that our goals are not the only ones worth considering. If we are not careful, we can delude ourselves into believing that our self-centered actions and goals are the only ones that count. If we do not learn to moderate our seemingly insatiable need for "more" as we seek higher salaries and more perks, we do not learn to temper our greed. If we use the tools of reason to justify inaction and personal acquisition, we blind ourselves to the long-term consequences of our policies and choices.[17] As we come to terms with the very human frailties of greed and pride, we can move beyond expedience caused by reducing everything to a cost-benefit analysis and turn towards excellence.

CHARACTERISTICS OF THE RESULTS LENS

This lens focuses on whether or not the goals that we choose to pursue are ethical, not on the underlying principles or rules. The entire focus is on whether we are following our true heart's desire in pursuing the good things of life.

To determine whether an act is ethical, we (autonomy) use our feelings and intuition (sensibility) to determine the choices we should make that will contribute to our happiness and, by extension, the happiness of all. Our personal experiences help us sort out what action will get good results. Our imagination is also important as we visualize various options as we discern the course of action we want to act. As we choose actions that will get good results, we can pursue a path that will create the greatest happiness for the greatest number of people.

In this tradition, we act from the vantage point of empathy as we harmonize our goals with those of others. Knowing that relationships with others are alive with feelings, as we make choices that bring us happiness or as we notice that our goals and dreams are thwarted and so change direction, we work together to move toward the common good.[18] The vantage point of integration allows us to creatively find ways to meet both our own goals as well as those of others. As we mature, we come to terms with the need to choose among competing goods, choices that mean that one good path must be chosen over another equally good path. Each choice requires change. Even if, after reflection, we choose the same goal, we are satisfied. In the process, we use our spiritual energy to fuel the process of change while maintaining the integrity of the social structures of which we are a part.[19]

QUESTIONS FOR DETERMINING RIGHT ACTION

❖ *Goals:* How does this result help my long-term self interest while allowing for concern about the well-being of others?

❖ *Greatest good:* How does this result produce or tend to produce my greatest good, and then, by extension, the greatest amount of satisfaction for the greatest number of stakeholders?

❖ *Ideal goals:* How does this result promote or tend to promote those goals that are part of human happiness (e.g., health, wealth, friendship, knowledge)?

- ❖ *Harmonized goals:* How does this result move toward harmonizing goods for other individuals in the community?

- ❖ *Responsible choice and creative change:* How does this result support responsible choices and move toward creative change?

SECONDARY VALUES SEEN THROUGH THE PRISM OF THIS LENS

- ❖ *Maximizing satisfaction:* The ethical decision maker should aim at maximizing personal satisfaction, which will contribute to the satisfaction of the organization's stakeholders.

- ❖ *Efficiency:* The members of the organization should attempt to attain their goals as efficiently as possible by consuming as few resources as possible and minimizing the external costs that the agency imposes on others.

- ❖ *Loyalty:* The employee should use every effective means to achieve the goals of the organization and should not act in a way that would jeopardize the goals.

- ❖ *Avoiding conflict of interest:* The employee should use every effective means to achieve the goals of the organization and should not get into situations where personal interests conflict significantly with the goals of the organization.

USING THE RESULTS LENS

As we begin to work through an ethical issue using the perspective of people in the Results Lens, we begin with the human condition. People in this lens believe that with nurturing and support, people can make choices that will help them become happy, productive members of the community. People in this lens are optimistic about the human condition or the ability of people to choose to be good and

SNAPSHOT: AN ACTION IS ETHICAL IF IT

- ❖ *Has good results*

- ❖ *Creates the greatest happiness for the greatest number*

- ❖ *Serves the greater good resulting in harmony and satisfaction of many individuals*

do the right thing. Thus, people from this lens encourage the relentless seeking of what is good. Of all the lenses, this one gives more autonomy to individuals to live their lives according to their own lights.

Because people from this lens value sensibility, following our heart, being able to explain why a particular action contributes to their happiness is important. The steps of the analysis allow us to make a persuasive argument as to why a particular option was chosen and why others were not. As we become more skilled, the analysis will become easier and we can begin to identify the core values that, for us, trump other competing values. However, even when we think we know the answer to the question, the discipline of working through the process can help clarify our thoughts.

To help understand the process, we will use the Results Lens to look at our problem about the tension between responding to community concerns about bullying and running an effective ad campaign that seems to advocate bullying. We will see how the values of this lens assist the decision process of a company that wants to run an effective ad campaign if members of the community resonate with the message, even if the behavior advocated is questionable. Again, the balance between selling the product and encouraging responsible behavior is often not clear.

Step 1: Be Attentive

During the first step of the decision model, we pay attention to what is going on. This step is more difficult than we think. We have to pay attention to what our mind is observing, what we are seeing, and what we don't want to see. Those of us with a preference for the Results Lens tend to interpret what we are seeing through our prior experiences and sense of self. We also have to listen to our emotions. If we are not careful, our emotions can get hijacked and we wind up inappropriately reacting to a situation.

Attend to the context

As we use the template for the Results Lens, we are asked to consider what makes us happy — what allows us to thrive. Those who write in the utilitarian tradition focus on both what makes an individual happy while also considering what provides the greatest aggregate happiness for all. If the focus is on each individual maximizing his own happiness, we see ethics mimicking Adam Smith's invisible hand, which is the bulwark of a market economy. The underlying assumption is that each of us makes choices based on what will lead to our happiness. We can see an example of this by looking around at students in an MBA class.

While many students think that learning for the sake of learning is pretty exciting, most people who give up their time and money to get an education are deferring the happiness of

Case Study: Facts and assumptions

❖ *The VP for Sales and Marketing for G-BioSport North has recommended an ad campaign to boost sales among college age men. The ad campaign has two groups of college men playing intramural basketball. The team from one dorm is buff with aggressive athletes who gang up and taunt the scrawny and untalented team from another dorm. The scrawny team takes G-BioSport supplements and starts working out. The final shot is the revenge of the nerds—where they turn on the buff athletes who flee from the court in shame and humiliation. This ad was tested in the field and had a very positive response from the target demographics. However, just as the campaign is about to begin, I received a letter raising concerns about our new ad campaign from a watchdog group, Concerned Athletes Against Bullying (CAAB). After some research, I discovered that CAAB is an advocacy group with lots of resources behind it and it targets companies that directly or indirectly advocate bullying.*

EVERYDAY ETHICS: *Making Wise Choices in a Complex World*

a fat bank account or an active social whirl to acquire new information, a better job, or another credential. As choices are made, if people believe that an MBA will be a stepping stone on the way to their dream, they will sign up for classes and the program will thrive. If, however, people no longer value, for example, a Masters in Information Systems because the jobs in the information technology field are drying up or moving off-shore, then the classes disappear because of lack of interest.

One temptation is to reduce this lens to a cost/benefit analysis. While the financial issues are important, other goals of life that are harder to define are, according to Mill, more important to consider. Thus, the joy of a cultivated mind or freedom to make choices cannot be reduced to cost. Elections are expensive, but the right to participate in a democracy is seen as bringing greater happiness than reduced taxes. Thus we agree to tax ourselves to pay the expenses that are needed to guarantee free elections.

Another temptation is to focus only on short-term happiness, pleasure and pain, which is called "hedonistic" utilitarianism. In their formulation of utilitarianism, Mill and Bentham ask us to focus on ideal goals or ends such as truth, beauty, or freedom. The school of thought that seeks the ultimate goals of life is known as "ideal" utilitarianism.[20] Embracing long-term ideals, we then find ourselves avoiding expedience to reach short-term financial gains as we seek those goals that are truly important.

A final characteristic of the teleological tradition to consider as we attend to the context is that the theorists emphasize that we are born into a community and shaped by that community. Because we are social beings, Mill asserts that we each want to have harmony between our feelings and goals and those of our fellow humans.[21] Thus, we find ourselves attending to the community in which we participate to see what are considered noble goals and consequences worthy of pursuit. Mill, like all seminal theorists, expects members of the community to continue to think and grow as they mature as human beings. While the temptation may be to look only at what gives immediate short-term pleasure, Mill encourages each of us to work for unity, which is the motivation and strength of the utilitarian ethic, as we build communities and advance civilization.

Identify the ethical decision maker

As always, the ethical decision maker is the one with the authority to act. However, for this lens we move to a very personal decision with a person who lives in a particular time and place with specific desires and goals. Rather than the "transcendental person" of Kant who operates without awareness of time or space, Mill brings us into the rough-and-tumble world of reality. One of the primary differences between the deontological tradition, which focuses on ideal persons and situations, and the teleological tradition is the focus on the real circumstances and desires of a particular community.

This particular approach fits well with a postmodern understanding of how we each create our reality. Postmodern thinkers emphasize that each of us chooses what we will see in our world around us and how we will name the event. Being aware of our belief systems and noting how those beliefs inform how we behave help us make effective decisions. However, we must be careful not to look at a new situation and then assume we are seeing the same thing we did before. A supervisor tells the story of coaching an employee into more acceptable behavior at work.

At the six-month review, the supervisor didn't see any change in behavior. The employee pointed out all the behavior that had changed that was invisible to the supervisor because the supervisor wasn't looking at a new picture—but relying on old images of behaviors. To use a contemporary example, we need to continually visit other people's Facebook™ pages so that we have a current picture of who they are and what they are doing.

Case Study: Issue

❖ *Given that recent incidents of bullying have escalated in the community and the community is actively taking steps to stop and prevent bullying, should we run an advertising campaign that is certain to boost the sale of our product where the behavior advocated could be viewed as bullying and might draw negative community commentary?*

Pinpoint the ethical issue

What is the central problem that must be resolved? What are the different goals that can be pursued? Do some only focus on what will make us happy today (hedonism) or do some focus on long-term, ideal goals? As we phrase this issue into a question, we consider whether the problem focuses on a decision that impacts only our own happiness or whether in a leadership role we are making a decision that will impact the happiness of others.

If the problem concerns only us, we need to focus on what will create our happiness as adults crafting the good life. If the problem concerns actions that will impact others, we need to focus on what will create the greatest happiness for the greatest number of people. As theorists for this lens assert that because each of us desires to be happy, the Results Lens focuses our attention on making choices that will lead to greater happiness.

Step 2: Be Intelligent

As we move into the second step, we will complete our first round of critical analysis. For this segment, we are going to sort through the data and begin honing in on the problem itself. Some may find that the process of analysis is annoying, reducing a decision to a series of calculations. We must remember that the theory of utilitarianism gained ascendancy during the Modern Period, a period of time when philosophers were using the tools of science to resolve philosophical and ethical issues. Thus, we are invited into a rational process to measure what will make us happy.

Determine the stakeholders

As we work through our problem, we are making a decision that impacts others as we are trying to influence their behavior by giving them a choice that will make them happy.[22] For this analysis, we focus on two elements of the stakeholders — the number of them in any given category and the impact that our decision will have on them. The reason for identifying the number of persons in each stakeholder group is to determine that group's *influence factor*. To the degree that individuals concur about what action creates happiness, people will make the same choice. With the criterion being to maximize overall good, those with the largest number in the group will determine what is ethical.

This number is more about the difference in size of groups than about precise data. Thus, if one group has 10 people and another group has 100, the option that makes the 100 happy may eclipse the happiness of the 10. For those who are Star Trek aficionados, Mr. Spock was the quintessential utilitarian. Facing his own death, a death caused by bringing the main engines back online in a radiation-filled section of the *U.S.S. Enterprise* in order to save the lives of his shipmates, Spock states, "It is logical. The needs of the many outweigh the needs of the few." The line was finished by Kirk: "Or the one."[23]

To determine the influence factor of any particular group, we begin by establishing the approximate number of people who are affected by the action over a specific span of time. In the example with which we are working, the time frame was the length of the marketing campaign.

❖ *Me, the CEO of the Company, who is the decision-maker*

❖ *The VP of Sales and Marketing responsible for creating and implementing the ad campaign*

❖ *Shareholders of the Company, whose stock value depends on the financial success of the company*

❖ *Employees of the Company, who depend on a fiscally sound company for employment*

❖ *Customers who like your product and might increase use because of campaign*

❖ *Kids who are bullied because your company appears to advocate bad behavior*

❖ *Members of the community who may critique the ad campaign and your company because it contributes to bullying*

CALCULATION OF INFLUENCE FACTOR (IF)

CONSTITUENT	NUMBER X	IMPACT (1.00)	=IF
CEO	1	0.1	0.1
VP Sales	1	0.2	0.2
Shareholders	335	0.6	201
Employees	300	0.0999	29.7
Customers	250,000	0.00004	10
Kids	1,000,000	0.00005	50
Community	7,500,000	0.00001	75

Next we determine the impact of any particular decision on each of the stakeholders based on our best knowledge (see the third column of the adjoining chart). So that the weighting of the influence factor is fairly distributed, when we add up the impact factor for all of the stakeholders, the total impact is always 1.00. As we consider the impact for each group, we include estimating the strength of the group's economic and political voice, as well as any direct impact on their personal well-being. As stated above, at the end of this step, the numbers in column three, the impact column, need to add up to 1.00.

Finally, the influence factor is calculated by multiplying the number of stakeholders by the impact factor. The difficulty in a utilitarian analysis is that a decision that has a tiny impact for a large group may outweigh the interests of a few. The expectation is that if the few are not happy with the choice, they can make other personal choices. If the issue is small, like what brand of a particular product to buy, we can choose another brand. If we only have one brand, a monopoly situation, then making another choice becomes difficult. Also, most of us would have to be really unhappy with our lot in life to make a major choice like relocating to another country if we don't like the policies or opportunities of our country of birth.

For example, one student considered whether technical climbers should be able to put permanent bolts in the rocks in national parks. Currently, the United States has a population of 310 million souls, each of whom has a tiny interest in preserving national parks.[24] Even if as many as 50,000 people are technical climbers with a strong interest in placing permanent bolts in rocks, the minute interest of the 310 million citizens in keeping those rocks intact will significantly outweigh the more direct interest of the technical climbers. Thus, a utilitarian analysis of the problem suggested that no bolts should be placed in national parks.

However, because large groups are not monolithic, the non-climbing group may need to be divided into smaller groups of those in favor of—or not in opposition to—permanent bolts under certain conditions. Some portion of citizens will value pristine parks. Some non-climbing citizens may find the sport interesting and be perfectly willing for fixed bolts to be in the rocks as long as one set of bolts serves all technical climbers. These citizens may argue that because the ordinary person cannot see the bolts, their enjoyment of the park will not be compromised.

The whole point of market surveys and polls is to try to get some sense of the different interest groups in a population. If the information of a company or political group is wrong, they will not get support for their product or policy. One only has to think of the legendary Ford Edsel, which was built without noticing a change in the buying habits or needs of car owners, and thus was a marketing failure. Just as in the hypothetical case of non-climbing citizens' attitudes about permanent bolts for technical climbers, groups of apparently unified stakeholders may need to be divided into smaller categories to accurately calculate the influence factor for a particular course of action. Again, good data helps us identify the various groups.

As the United States began reconsidering security policies after the destruction of the World Trade Center on September 11, 2001, the question about whether the needs of the many should outweigh the needs of the few came into sharp relief. The issue was whether American citizens who happen to be of Middle Eastern descent or have Arabic surnames should be automatically subjected to greater scrutiny as they boarded airplanes than others with a different ethnic heritage. One school of thought said that because those who masterminded the hijacking of the planes used in the 9/11 attacks were from the Middle East, then subjecting all who were part of that ethnic group, in effect engaging in racial profiling, made perfect sense and was ethical.

Others said that all citizens should be subject to the same level of scrutiny because terrorists come from all different races, such as the act of a Caucasian American in the bombing of the Alfred P. Murrah Federal Building in Oklahoma City.[25] In any event, the security concerns of all citizens to be able to fly safely clearly outweighed the interest of any one citizen not to be subjected to the annoyance of a thorough search of shoe soles and luggage. The rules, however, are subject to constant tweaking based on the tolerance and concerns of the flying public.

Explore the values in tension

With a utilitarian perspective, the conflicts will arise as stakeholders identify competing goals each of which is expected to lead to someone's happiness. One set of conflicts arises when people focus on short term rather than long-term happiness. Mill never allows us to wallow in our own selfish notions of happiness. Mill advocates attending to seeking ideal goals, not fleeting hedonism. Mill also asserts that the community is always happier when people have cultivated a noble character, a character created by making consistent choices over time that lead to a particular way of being. Seeking to create an ethical character allows us to look at the whole fabric of our lives, not just individual threads in the momentary weaving of a small segment. Mill believes that the qualities of self-consciousness and self-observation will assist us in determining the rules of behavior that will allow for all persons, if not all creation, to find happiness.[26]

Another set of conflicts may arise with different ideas about what makes for an ideal community. Honest communication and dialogue helps to uncover the differences and find ways to resolve seemingly conflicting values. Those who teach skills of conflict resolution and mediation advocate beginning by listening to what each person desires in a given situation. At its best,

CASE STUDY: VALUES IN TENSION

❖ *The two values in tension are* AUTONOMY, *where the Company makes its own choices about how to sell its products, and* EQUALITY, *where the Company responds to community pressure and initiative to stop bullying. In order to be successful, to continue to employ individuals, and to offer our products to the public, our Company must advertise its products. On the other hand, bullying has become an issue in our community. We have a commitment, as a member of the community, to not advocate behavior such as bullying that creates an increase risk to the safety and well-being of the community.*

the political process of democracy allows for engaged citizens to share their ideas of what goals should be pursued and the balance between individual and community (governmental or organizational) action. Of course when people become more attached to their position and being "right" rather than seeking mutually satisfying goals, the result is political stalemate.

While engaging in this exercise of speculating about what makes people happy might seem pointless, any time an ethical decision maker makes a decision, the other stakeholders who are affected by the decision either ratify the decision through their words or actions or not. Generally, people don't give us notice about their choices and preferences; rather, they "vote with their feet." If they are unhappy with choices made by the leadership, they leave the firm, choose other products, or find other suppliers. The more accurate we are in evaluating the stakeholders' criteria for happiness, the more likely it is that we will also get the results that we want.

Case Study: Options for action

1: Run the advertising campaign that is certain to boost sales but could be advocating bullying behavior.

2: Do not run the advertising campaign that is certain to boost sales but could be advocating bullying behavior.

Identify options for action

Having surveyed the problem, the ethical decision maker has to come up with a beginning array of possible options. The process of decision-making requires that we test the possibilities against the abstract principles and values revealed through the perspective of the lens. The final evaluation of the problem will probably lead to refinement of the options as well as precise action that moves toward harmonized goals.

One characteristic of those who are more ethically mature is that they look for options that will not only satisfy individuals but will also make the system as a whole function better. Thus, the more skilled a person becomes in ethical decision-making, the more nuanced the solution will be. Some negotiated options look like compromise for the sake of compromise, where everyone gets a little something but the overall result is not good. However, skilled mediators teach us to listen carefully to identify the goals of each person affected by the decision and then work to fashion an option that meets as many of the needs as possible. Thus, the result is not a naked compromise but a "win-win" solution where every party gets what is important at the same time that the integrity of the overall system is maintained.

Step 3: Be Reasonable

For this section of the decision process, the questions that are asked are specific to the lens. The point of this section is to show how people who favor this particular approach to decision making would answer the problem. Because each ethical lens prioritizes different values, the questions asked to determine the best course of action are different.

Hone critical thinking skills

One critique of utilitarianism is that it supports a mindless calculation of pain and pleasure. Jeremy Bentham, who was of a methodical bent, proposed a system of calculation where we add up points for what makes us happy and then subtract the points for pain to determine what we should do. While it is tempting to dismiss the process as arcane, most of us do a cost/benefit analysis as we work through tough decisions. The analysis often includes considerations other than the merely financial, such as quality of life values, balancing our happiness with others in our family, and concern for the community.

When we choose not to take a promotion because we would have to be away from our families too much or choose to work in a non-profit setting to assist those who are less fortunate, we are weighing the relative value of our choices. The appeal of this theory is that those who may not understand why someone would choose to minimize financial wealth while seeking happiness in other quarters, they are free to find happiness where they will.

Mill invites us to thus consider both qualitative happiness as well as quantitative happiness. Mill was committed to the notion of a strong community where people were free to choose how best they wanted to live. The notions of liberty and personal independence were central to his thoughts about the greatest good for the greatest number. He was a visionary in the areas of women's rights, for example, advocating that when *all* people are free to manage their own property and be responsible for their destiny, all of us are happier.

He also advocated people sacrificing for others as long as that sacrifice resulted in a greater sum total of happiness for the community. Mill would assert that each of us should consider limiting our power in order to assure the well-being of the collective interests of the community. In making leadership decisions, CEOs and others can move from only considering how to maximize shareholder value to being a good citizen and attending to the well-being of employees.

At this point we can also consider Maslow's hierarchy of needs. Abraham Maslow first put forth his theory of motivation in 1943. He claimed that each of us works our way up a pyramid beginning with psychological needs, which if we are lucky are met through our family of origin, and then safety needs, social needs, esteem needs, and finally the need for self-actualization.[27] The choices we make depend on where we are on the hierarchy as well as the opportunities that we have.

One CEO of a non-profit that was part of the health care system was advised by the health care consultant to include greater health care benefits for the top three employees of the company than the rest of the employees. The rationale was that all of the other CEOs were giving more benefits to the leadership team than the rest of the employees, so the policy was acceptable. This

CEO refused. He asserted both to the consultant and the Board of Directors that the culture of the organization was built on all people being valued the same and thus being treated equally by being given the same choices about health care coverage.

By all people having the same options for health care insurance, those at the top remained aware of the changing health care costs and coverage and those in the heart of the organization knew they were valued. The leadership exhibited by this CEO means that in other tough times employees will be willing to sacrifice for the good of the company. All have a sense of being valued as they work together to make the organization successful.

We begin by making sure that we make the best choices possible to assure our own good life. Then, those of us called to work with individuals, especially the young, can help them meet their foundational needs on Maslow's pyramid by giving them self-confidence and the tools to succeed. Those of us working in business can have policies that help those who would otherwise not be employable find work or who would not have fresh groceries have good food. And finally, those of us who work at a policy level can be sensitive to the unintended blocking of choices that will lead to a dream deferred, as Langston Hughes describes, that might just explode.

Evaluate from the vantage point of intention

To apply the principle of the greatest happiness for the greatest number, we have to determine what makes each of the stakeholders happy. In this particular sense, the goals to be sought are those ends that make people happy in light of their core values. Each of us must balance for our core values in terms of personal goals, the goals of the community as a whole, and our own tolerance for pain, unintended and unpleasant consequences. Some of us are willing to tolerate great pain because of the adrenaline rush (think of a favorite stockbroker) while others prefer a more sedate life and are risk averse.

After identifying the stakeholders who will be affected by the decision, the next task is to determine what makes them happy. The first criteria to consider are the deal breakers. For each stakeholder, we need to determine what core ideal goals are not negotiable. A goal that is non-negotiable is grounded in a value that is so important that the person will not take an action that goes against that particular core commitment.

Many who have worked relentlessly to assure that all people are treated equally will not take any action that knowingly leads to discrimination. Those who have a passion for the well-being of children will not embrace any strategy that puts children at risk. If we are lucky, the stakeholder will be self-aware enough to identify the non-negotiable values. Further we must watch out for competing non-negotiable values; as the popular saying goes, "you can't have your cake and eat it too."[28] As we prioritize our core commitments, we must be aware of mutually exclusive

CRITERIA FOR HAPPINESS

Constituent	Criteria
CEO	The CEO is happy if the company is profitable.
VP Sales	The VP of Sales is happy if the campaign is successful and they make their numbers.
Shareholders	The shareholders are happy if the stock value increases.
Employees	The employees are happy if they retain their employment and the company maintains its reputation so they are not seen as working for a despicable organization.
Customers	Customers are happy if the information about the product is accurate so they can make informed buying decisions.
Kids	The kids in this community are happy if they are free from bullying.
Community	The community is happy if their children are protected both from bullying and from becoming bullies themselves.

demands that can't both be met. Often, many of us are not that aware of the conflicts and so we have to listen to each other to determine what is important.

The next set of goals is those that are preferred but are not necessarily deal breakers. Most of us have a set of goals that are important that we try to achieve. The more resources and personal power we have, the more we are able to reach those goals. However, when we can't reach our goals, we compromise. In these situations, the ethical decision maker must be aware of what has come to be called the tipping point. Popularized by Malcolm Gladwell's book *The Tipping Point*, the source of the idea comes from physics. In physics, the tipping point is that point at which an "object is displaced from a point of stable equilibrium to a new, different place."[29]

As we apply the notion of tipping points to ethical decision making, at some point the unhappiness of a given person or group reaches critical mass. Something becomes the proverbial "last straw that broke the camel's back."[30] Thus, the tipping point is not a fixed point or specific value but rather an event or happening that makes us say "no more!" The example given earlier in the chapter of Rosa Parks is an example of a tipping point that ignited the national Civil Rights Movement. For Rosa Parks, the tipping point came when, exhausted after working all day, she was asked to give up her seat in the front of the "colored section" of a Selma bus for a white person. When she refused the unjustified request, her subsequent arrest galvanized the Black community to action with a bus strike that ultimately led to the end of segregation.

For ease of calculation, a technique has been developed to calculate happiness. Assume that all stakeholder groups get ten units of happiness. Economists call these units of happiness *utils*.

CALCULATE HAPPINESS UTILS (OUT OF 10)
OPTION 1: RUN THE ADVERTISING CAMPAIGN

CONSTITUENT	UTILS	RATIONALE
CEO	8	The campaign is certain to be successful, but the CEO may feel the heat from a community backlash.
VP Sales	10	The campaign is certain to be successful.
Shareholders	9	The campaign is certain to be successful, but a community backlash could hurt share value in the long term if it led to a boycott.
Employees	4	Employees, who are certain to retain their employment whether or not the campaign runs, are more immediately concerned with knowing the company they work for is respected. That said, a failure with this campaign could start the company down a path that leads to future layoffs. Employees are also concerned about share value, but that is considered in their inclusion in the shareholder category.
Customers	5	Customers will receive the same information about the product whether it is through this particular ad campaign or another.
Kids	1	Though the likelihood of bullying may be slim (represented by the low Influence Factor), the effects of even one incident represent significant unhappiness (thus the low number of utils).
Community	2	They won't feel the direct result that the kids might, but the ad will affect the community through whatever impact it has on the kids.

So, each stakeholder group begins with ten utils of happiness. As we review the options, we decide how happy each option will make each group. The scale runs from one util—very unhappy —to ten utils—blissfully happy. We need to remember to look at both the identified deal breakers and tipping points. So, as we calculate the utils of happiness generated by any given decision, we begin by assuming that if one is blissfully happy the option will generate ten utils. We deduct utils of happiness to the extent that an option does not make us happy.

The rationale for the allocation of points is as important as the allocation itself. A person reviewing our calculations should be able to see the relationship between the criteria for happiness identified in the previous step and the units of happiness any given option generates. Calculate the happiness points for each option under consideration.

While the process may feel arbitrary, we make the decision based on our best understanding of the goals that advance the core and secondary values of the stakeholders. The goal is to be objectively subjective. By using the best data we have available and then making a calculated estimation of what we value, we will make a decision that will make our heart happy. As we make

EVERYDAY ETHICS: *Making Wise Choices in a Complex World*

CALCULATE HAPPINESS POINTS (OUT OF 10)
OPTION 2: DO NOT RUN THE ADVERTISING CAMPAIGN

CONSTITUENT	UTILS	RATIONALE
CEO	4	The CEO won't feel the same direct impact the VP of Sales or the shareholders will, and the public relations credit of running a respectable campaign will go to them.
VP Sales	1	Any loss of sales suffered from a refusal to run an effective campaign will be blamed on the VP of sales.
Shareholders	2	Refusing to run an effective campaign may not directly cause stock to go down, but missing an opportunity to raise share value creates, effectively, the same net result.
Employees	6	As the company's reputation is maintained, employee happiness will be maintained; however, there may be some temporary morale loss if the product launch is unsuccessful. Again, employee concerns about share value are taken into account in the shareholder utils.
Customers	5	As before, the information customers receive will not change.
Kids	10	Naturally, the kids do not have the same attachment to company share value and reputation (save for the few whose parents are in the shareholder or employee groups), so this option creates no unhappiness.
Community	9	The community will be happier with this option, as it works to prevent the deleterious influence of media that tacitly supports bullying.

policy decisions for others, and as we make a calculated estimation of what they value, we will create a good policy. If we are wrong, we will find out sooner or later and, hopefully, be able to correct the trajectory of action.

Lest we think that no one goes through this process, we can think of every market survey in which we have participated or every opinion poll that is conducted. An effective market survey measures what people value and anticipates then what public policy or business decision will be supported with market choices, votes, or other action. If someone launching a product is wrong about what customers need or want, the product will fail. If we misread an employee's tolerance for invasion of privacy or moving jobs offshore, we will have people walking out or protesting in other ways.

Finally, do the math to decide which option generates the most utils. This step involves multiplying the Influence Factor (IF) by the number of utils, generated in the previous two charts to calculate the *weighted utils* of happiness. Add the weighted totals for each stakeholder group to get the grand total of weighted utils of happiness for this option. The process of calculation is

CALCULATING THE GREATEST GOOD
Option 1 compared with Option 2

Constituent	IF (x)	Utils	=Weighted Total Option 1	Utils	=Weighted Total Option 2
CEO	0.1	8	0.8	4	0.4
VP Sales	0.2	10	2	1	0.2
Shareholders	201	9	1,809	2	302
Employees	29.7	4	118.8	6	178.2
Customers	10	5	50	5	50
Kids	50	1	50	10	500
Community	75	2	150	9	675
Total weighted utils			2,180.6		1,705.8

repeated for each option.

This process is a hybrid between the calculus of Jeremy Bentham and the idealism of John Stuart Mill. The reason the process is effective is that it forces each of us to consider the various stakeholders as separate from ourselves. We often believe that everyone has the same interests that we do when in fact their interests and values are very different. The other point of this exercise is to show the tyranny of the majority. As we consider that the United States was born in opposition to the perceived tyranny of the King of England, and the founding fathers and mothers had great faith in the ability of individuals to choose for themselves the practices and policies that would lead to happiness and prosperity, we begin to understand the foundational culture of the US. With protections for the minorities embedded in the Bill of Rights, the first ten amendments to the Constitution, those early policy makers knew that if the majority considers only its narrow self-interest as it acts, they can trump the minority concerns every time.

As we resolve ethical issues from the vantage point of intention, using the Results Lens, the gift we bring to the community is the capacity to make thoughtful, self-directed choices. We will be motivated from within rather than mindlessly responding to external rules and regulations. As we become ethically mature, not only do we make effective choices but we do so without undue responses to external rules and regulations. In the process, we give up our victim status exemplified by the saying "the Devil made me do it." That autonomous self who takes responsibility for their own choices and the consequences of their actions is highly valued in the community and an important partner in solving the problems of an organization or a community.

Evaluate from the vantage point of empathy

As we reflect on the options, our next task is to consider whether that option can be carried out in a way that creates "win-win" situations for all of the stakeholders. Ethical actions have two dimensions—*what* we do and *how* we do it. Modern theorists consider primarily what we should do and do not focus on method, the way that we carry out our ethical obligations. When we use the Results Lens, the question becomes which option will create our own happiness. However, if we are not careful, we can carry out an ethical option in a way that does not treat others as people who are entitled to make their own choices for happiness.

As we resolve ethical issues from the vantage point of empathy, using the Results Lens, the gift we bring to the community is creativity in finding mutually satisfying goals. As we become ethically mature, not only do we seek our own happiness and that of others, but as we become comfortable with people making their own choices, we are able to live with integrity. In these situations, often our actions speak louder than our words, as people understand that we genuinely respect the ability of all people to choose for themselves how they want to live. That creative responsible self is highly respected in the community as people know that we are not just looking out for ourselves but are concerned with others as we solve the problems of an organization or a community.

Evaluate from the vantage point of integration

The vantage point of integration is the place where we make peace with ourselves — our best self and our worst self. Each person has places of fear, anxiety, meanness and perversity. As we become ethically mature, we embrace and befriend what Carl Jung called our "shadow self." Often, our shadow self has the intention to protect us, and if we listen to that voice too closely we wind up in self-sabotage.

From the tulip mania that peaked during the winter of 1636-1637, when the price of a tulip bulb plunged from 5,200 guilders to 52 guilders, to the dot-com bubble, to the meltdown of the banking and financial industry in 2009, many ethical scandals come from people becoming greedy rather than paying attention to their own long-term goals and acting in the community's best interest.[31]

CASE STUDY: ACT TOWARD GREATEST GOOD FOR GREATEST NUMBER

❖ *In this case, the saying "the needs of the many outweigh the needs of the few," does not hold. Prioritizing options to meet the needs of the larger group of stakeholders is always tempting, but cases like this reveal the importance of going through the full analysis instead of following an instinct to protect the many. Here, the consequences from running a single advertisement are, to a single member of the community, insignificant, whereas the impact to the smaller groups of individuals whose livelihoods may rely on the success of the company is greater. Note, however, how close the results are.*

CASE STUDY: ACT TOWARD HARMONIZED GOOD

❖ *Working for "win-win" solutions is not easy. However, the data shows that a relatively small portion of the market who will be watching these ads are in fact kids. Given that the ads will be run during college football games, catching the attention of the predominantly male audience is critical. Also, because the perceived bullying action is subtle, people might not even notice or name the behavior in the ad as bullying.*

BLIND SPOT

Like a blind spot in the side mirror of a car, the ethical blind spots are those places where we can unintentionally act unethically. Because the Results Lens favors sensibility, from the vantage point of intention, we may underemphasize rational thinking and forget to check out our obligations before we commit to a path of action. Often, the cause of inconsistency between our stated values and our actions is our deep desire to make people happy and avoid conflict. As we work to make everyone happy, we can wind up making no one happy and being satisfied with too little good. By using the touchstone of our core principles, we can balance the ability to react quickly to changing circumstances with the more structured responses that come from considering our duties as well as the impact on the larger community.

From the vantage point of empathy, we may become hypersensitive to the emotional climate of the situation and thus find ourselves emotionally hijacked by other stakeholders. As we try to find emotional balance in the maelstrom, we can remember that other people are responsible for their own emotions and their responses to the situation. We are responsible for assuring that our responses are appropriate, not making sure that others behave well. If we are not careful, we may forget to check our course of action against our long-term goals as we work to find happiness in the short term.

Finally, as we become more and more responsive to others in order to pursue our many faceted heart's desires and roles, we may become angry and resentful that no one has paid attention to us. We have spent all this time trying to make others happy; why doesn't anyone try to make us happy and pay a bit of attention to our needs? Upon reflection, one can determine the core essential activities and then shed the "shoulds" of life that are activities and emotional burdens imposed by others or holdovers from previous roles and responsibilities. Learning to let others be responsible for their own happiness as we attend to ours is wonderful. From the perspective of this lens, the greatest gift that we can give ourselves is to periodically prune the to-do list so that it reflects the actions that will help us truly achieve our heart's desire and not live into someone else's idea of what will make us happy.

VICES AND RISKS

The opposite of virtues are vices, which emerge as we take ethical risks and do not diligently work to assure that we are being ethical. This trait expresses itself in the Results Lens by leading to the vice associated with this lens—greed, where we never have enough. From the vantage point of intention, a misuse of reason leads to carelessness of thought, where we forget to attend to the highest expression of the lens. The path of empathy becomes cluttered with boulders of greed as we become focused on acquiring "stuff." When we do not pay attention to imbalances of power and opportunity, we become blind to the inequities among humans. We then do not seek opportunities to share with others from our abundance.

The greed of a few at the top who are not attending to the long-term health of a company can cause the market system to reach a breaking point as well. Then, as a period of prosperity crashes to an end, ordinary people receive the full brunt of the tremendous loss of money and jobs that are caused by aggressive accounting techniques and greed. After the proverbial fox has raided the henhouse, people demand greater accountability from business executives, whether in the form of prison sentences or more regulation.

Had business leaders in power worked to assure that African-Americans fully participated in the economic life of America, Title VII of the Civil Rights Act of 1964 would not have been needed. If the citizens of America truly embraced the notion that every person has the opportunity to follow their dreams, we would not have persistent racial discrimination that thwarts opportunities or a patchwork of immigration policies and practices that exacerbate racial tensions.

Had the financial moguls of the late 20th century attended to well-identified financial "best-practices," the Sarbanes-Oxley Act would not have been passed. If those with financial power in American business had attended to what created the greatest happiness for all of their stakeholders, they would have moderated their own quest for personal happiness with a modicum of self-sacrifice and restraint and avoided Congressional intervention and takeover of their companies. Because they did not, we now face a recession that economists tell us is as bad as the Great Depression of the 30s, and it will take at least another decade to get us to financial health.

Had those who knew that the assumptions behind the hedge funds and financial modeling were flawed restrained their use of the suspect practices, the flood of government bailouts and banking regulation that were birthed in 2008 and 2009 would not have been needed. Had all of us as citizens not gotten caught up in ever-increasing values of pension funds and houses, rates of growth that we knew or should have known were unsustainable, we would not have been complicit in the economic debacle. As it happens, the cost of compliance with the law and rebuilding an economy is much higher than the cost of being ethical in the first place.

HUBRIS

Hubris, excessive pride and arrogance, moves us from unintentional ethical wrongdoing to intentional wrongdoing. Those who act with hubris have a deliberate disregard for the ethical requirements of the community as they work to further their own agenda. For the Results Lens, from the vantage point of intention, hubris shows up as willfully playing the very edges of the law to acquire more goods and power, just because we can. The first decade of the 21st century saw an unprecedented display of hubris as a number of CEOs recklessly put not only the United States but also global economy at risk.

Joe Nacchio deliberately misstated the company value of Qwest in order to line his own pockets.[32] Ken Lay recklessly required employees to invest in the company 401(k) plan even as the CEO knew that the value was crashing.[33] And thousands of upper- and mid-level banking officials participated in the hopelessly complex system of authorizing and trading sub-prime loans that contributed to the crash of the global financial market.[34]

From the vantage point of empathy, if we assume that we know the desires of others, we may find ourselves leaders with no followers. When our projects fail, we can become overwhelmed with guilt when confronted with our failures. As stories of business failures emerge, we also find that the suicide rate for men who have experienced professional failure is very high. In 2001, the United States Surgeon General announced that four of every five suicides are men, and the taking of their life is often in the face of a business or professional failure.[35]

Finally, as we become more and more overwhelmed, we discover that living from the assumption that our choices are the best or only ones to be made leads to profound discouragement and makes achieving our goals ever more elusive. To cope, we withdraw from others and may even become recluses. Ironically, some of the most outwardly successful people, such as Howard Hughes and J.D. Salinger, end up being very peculiar people as they find that having sought success in the public eye, all they really want is to be left alone with a few close friends.[36]

As we reflect on the options, we can ask whether we are treating others and ourselves with inherent dignity. Are we moving toward the greater good (which means moving from our own self-interest into the greater good for the community)? This process is different than compromising. It requires the hard work of listening to each other and finding ways that each person's desires can be met. Often, what people initially say they want is just the cover over a deeper desire. By entering into a process of discernment where we ask questions to uncover the true dream, we can come to individualized solutions.

For instance, having a well-paying job may be important either for status or for providing for a family. A very high-paying job may be required to meet the goal of status whereas a more moderate income may meet the goal of providing for a family. Accomplishing harmonized goals may require that we come up with innovative solutions. However, in the process, we will become co-creators of our destiny and discover that being an adult does not necessarily mean that one has a life sentence to live in pain.

Consider the critiques of the lens

The first weakness of the Results Lens is that people who use the tools of this lens easily rationalize their actions and become expedient rather than pursue excellence. Thus, as we become busy

EVERYDAY ETHICS: *Making Wise Choices in a Complex World*

with our projects, we must thoughtfully ask whether we are embracing excellence rather than being content with expedience. In the process, we must not be blinded by our own selfishness or greed, which often are realized at the expense of others. Another bias is considering only cost. While the financial side of the conversation is important, we must attend to overall happiness and good—not just the bottom line.

- ❖ *Expedience* judges people in terms of the acquisition of riches, power, status, and prestige while *excellence* judges people in terms of standards established in the community for values such as awareness, maturity, and competence.

- ❖ *Expedience* requires only that a person act to maximize satisfaction of his own wants and needs while *excellence* requires that a person seek goals in light of the virtues embodied by the community.

- ❖ *Expedience* requires that a person identify the strategies to acquire goods and become skilled in using those strategies to get ahead while *excellence* requires that a person continue to progress in reaching the ideals of the community and recognize what is the highest perfection.

- ❖ *Expedience* requires only that a person follow the rules of justice until the rules change while *excellence* can be defined independent of the current rules.

Thus, people who are expedient may operate from a narrow standard of getting the job done while people who strive for excellence have personal moral values that are harmonized with the ethical standards of the community at large.

A second, more persistent problem with this lens is that we can ignore poverty and economic class inequalities by failing to notice that people really don't have equality of opportunity to make good decisions that would then lead to equality of result. A persistent belief is that those who have less have just made poor decisions. Refusing to look at the political and economic system as a whole leads to the assertion that those who are poor just make worse political and economic decisions that those with more money—thus locking the poor into a cycle of poverty.

Equality of opportunity begins with access to education. Historically, in the United States, providing for education is a local issue. Recently, we have seen an increase in federal spending in education. While a healthy debate exists as to whether increasing per capita expenses in education results in better outcomes, those who have worked in public schools will attest that socioeconomic differences are a high predictor of how children will achieve and then, by extension, their opportunities as adults.[37]

The data on state and federal funding does not include resources provided by parents. As we look at schools in different socio-economic situations, we see wide variations of available resources. For example, when John Elway, a star quarterback for the Denver Broncos, had children in elementary school, he donated a car for the PTO auction. Parents in other demographic areas did not have those resources, which meant that the schools did not have discretionary funds for music and art programs, teacher's aides, or other educational supports. The data also doesn't account for lower achievement caused by mobility, mobility often required because parents don't have stable employment situations. Students who change schools three to five times during an academic year have a very difficult time maintaining grade levels.[38]

Research shows that on the whole, given the choices available, those of lesser economic means are just as wise as those of greater means. Sometimes good choices are not available. Many studies have demonstrated that poor people make worse choices about food in part because the stores in their neighborhoods don't stock healthy options or even fresh fruits and vegetables.[39]

Finally, as we become more and more attached to our own results, we lose perspective. We may forget that we did not achieve our accomplishments alone. Others have helpers along the way and they deserve recognition and reward for their contribution. Whether we stand on the shoulders of parents or teachers who set our sights on college or supported us pursing "a Big, Hairy, Audacious Goal" or took advantage of community resources in the shape of schools, libraries, and museums, each of us begins where others left off.

The chapter began with a poem by Langston Hughes concerning the disappointment of "dreams deferred." Mill asserts that everyone has the right to seek what makes us happy—not just those with power or privilege. We often forget that we have people who help us and thus we need to help others. We forget that we build on the hopes and dreams of our parents and grandparents and thus need to attend to the hopes and dreams of our children, all of our children. We need to attend to systemic barriers that keep people from being able to find happiness, resulting in deferred dreams.

Taking a wider view, we can explore the relationship between the systems in our community that keep people from making good choices to individuals just choosing badly. These conversations range from those who demonstrate that people are left out of the economic conversation, to those who talk about systemic barriers for those who want to move out of poverty, to those who assert that people just make bad choices.[40] As we pay attention to imbalances of power and access to resources, we can use the tools of the Relationship Lens so that we can balance our excess sensibility with rationality and our care for concern for the community. In the process, we can assure that all people have the ability and opportunities to make good decisions.

Step 4: Be Responsible

Rank the options from least preferred to most preferred

Having determined the utils generated by our actions, we can see which option truly generates the greatest good for the greatest number. As the options are ranked, we summarize why the ranking of options was made and demonstrate the primacy given to not only individual happiness but also the happiness of the community. Sometimes, options will generate very close numbers when the utils are calculated. In those situations, the ethical decision maker can choose whichever option they prefer as the difference is negligible. In other cases, while one option may generate the highest number of utils, another option may be chosen that meets the harmonized goals of the community.

As the options are ranked, we summarize why the ranking of options was made and demonstrate the primacy given to the core values. First we show how autonomy was privileged—because each person is valuable in his or her own right, each person can choose how best that person wants to live. However, once having freely chosen, a person is obligated to live with the consequences of the choices. Then we show how sensibility was privileged—as we imagined the goals we wanted to accomplish, we chose a path that would lead to the fulfilling of our heart's desire, without being overly constrained by rationality or obligation.

Strive for ethical maturity

The final stage before acting is much like going through a checklist one more time—have we corrected for any unintended bias that might have crept into our analysis? For this stage, a final look at the tools for analysis is useful. With the final check, we can make sure that the option we choose is the most ethically mature choice available to us.

From the vantage point of intention, we analyze our own course of action. For the Results Lens, we want to assure that we consider the interplay of action and reflection based on our own experience. As we evaluate whether or not a particular course of action will reach desired results, we can quickly and nimbly change direction to adjust to changing data or circumstances. We also want to assure that we are both celebrating our accomplishments and accepting the consequences of our choices, without blaming others for undesirable results.

Case Study: Rank the options

❖ *After calculating the weighted utils and considering whether the campaign contributes to harmonized good, running the ad campaign provides the greatest happiness for the greatest numbers. While the community represents a greater number of people, the effects of the campaign are negligible compared to the more significant impact to the company and its employees.*

Case Study: Strive for ethical maturity

❖ *By running the ad campaign as designed, Option 1 I am living into my core principles of supporting autonomy and free choice. I am not forcing anyone to purchase my product, but inviting customers to consider the merits of my product by presenting an engaging ad. The purpose of the company is to sell product, make a profit, and contribute to the well-being of the community through the benefit of the product. Option 1 clearly meets this purpose.*

The vantage point of empathy is used to negotiate "win-win" solutions while caring for ourselves. As we practice this skill, we develop the tool of self-esteem, the belief that our ideas are good and that our voice will be heard. Our passion for the goal will then fuel action to get results. This tool helps when others don't share our vision and we want to inspire people to action.

Finally, the vantage point of integration is used to test our course of action against our personal meaning and purpose of life. As we use our imagination, we can envision new ways to create solutions that honor the essential humanity of each person involved as well as the integrity of the planet itself. This tool helps us weather the inevitable storms of life when others don't see things our way.

Act with courage

After we make our choice, we should be able to communicate our decision to others. Creating a short statement that could be placed in a memo to others in the company or a press release helps us learn to articulate our ethical decisions so that we answer the core questions of the Results Lens.

BE TRUE TO THE PERSPECTIVE OF THE ETHICAL LENS

Remembering that this vantage point is like looking through a magnifying glass, taking a short view, the option we choose should reflect the practical ideal values that are important for human beings. As the ethical decision maker, we are a particular person who has a unique identity and considers the specifics of the situation. Our own preferences as well as those of others are important as we pursue our dreams. Prior experience is persuasive as we chart our course of action but not necessarily someone else's to-do list. Our concern is identifying the ideal goals that will make us happy as we walk on this beautiful planet.

We will choose options that are appropriate for this time and place, grounded in the specific needs and desires of the primary stakeholders. And, as we consider the stakeholders, we assume that they also are people with dreams and desires they want to fulfill. Each person will try to make decisions that will make them happy and take responsibility for their own choices, so power is not abused, and everyone has an equal opportunity to achieve the good things of life.

FOLLOW CHECKLIST FOR ACTION

As we move to action, using the persective of the Results Lens, we will:

❖ **Remember** to make choices that will contribute to our happiness. The purpose of ethical action is to imaginatively create a world where the people can pursue good results.

- ❖ *Focus* on the abundance we want to create. As we expect good results to come from our actions, our expectations will be fulfilled.

- ❖ *Provide* what makes people happy. Remember that each person has different goals and criteria for happiness.

- ❖ <u>*Hold*</u> people accountable for their choices—no victims allowed. We encourage people to think through the consequences of their choices and then honor that choice without rescuing them from the outcomes, whether good, bad, or ugly.

Because most of the work in ethics is persuasion, we should be able to articulate clearly what choice we have made and why. After giving a bit of background information to set the stage for the problem, we can frame the statement so that we answer the core questions of this particular lens. What *results* are we trying to achieve? How does the way that we propose to carry out this action contribute to *mutually good results* for all of the stakeholders? The goal is to assure that as many people as possible are able to be happy with the choices they have as they pursue their own goals. How does this action help us *partner with others* to create a better world? Asking this question allows us to contribute to both developing our own sense of accomplishment and using our imagination to help strengthen individuals and the group.

Step 5: Return to Awareness

Every action has a reaction. That reaction will be both from others and from us. So, after we act and the dust has had a moment to settle, we turn back to determine whether our course of action was, in fact, wise. What improvements could we make on our process of ethical analysis? Did we like the result? What were the problems with the process? What are the sticking points with the process, where we were not comfortable with the way the decision was unfolding? What were the unintended consequences?

Reflect on results

Ethical maturity occurs as we move from only thinking of ourselves to noticing how our choices impact others as well as the institutions of our community. As we grow in ethical maturity, we seek solutions that are systemic and will improve life for as many as possible.

CASE STUDY: REFLECTION

❖ *As we learn more about bullying and the whole question of the decline of civility in our community, the role of advertising in setting acceptable norms in the community is a recurring question. I wish that people weren't quite so responsive to the slap-stick humor that provides the foundation for this advertising campaign. However, I feel comfortable giving priority to the value of individuals choosing for themselves what will support their idea of the good rather than me. And, I feel good about finding a message that will both pique the interest of our customers and contribute to the well-being of the campaign. Perhaps with more thought, we can find an ad campaign that reinforces positive behavior instead of quietly endorsing uncivil action.*

From the vantage point of intention, personal growth and maturity is defined as becoming clear about what is important to us and consciously making choices that will accomplish those goals. As we become familiar with our own emotions and those of others, from the vantage point of empathy as we attune to the needs of others, we will seek innovative ways to assure the development of our community and the world as a whole. Finally, as our vantage point of integration matures, we will learn to live from the deep knowledge that we are co-creators of our own experience and choices as we live in joy and personal peace and harmony.

Seek continuous improvement

The process of continuous improvement involves evaluating the result of the action. As we take action in our life based on the lens, we can watch for intended and unintended results. Also, we should watch for new questions or answers that were not complete. The trajectory for maturity is not necessarily smooth, but as we attend to the goals, harmonized values, and our ideals, we can get there. As we take responsibility for our own self-directed choices as well as respect the choices of others, we will learn to live with ambiguity and integrity. In the process, we will learn how to maintain consistency between our actions and our self-concept.

As we are called to balance, we need to address whether we are being overly attached to our goals or whether we are detached from our everyday lives enough to see the bigger picture and consider the higher good. As we become aware of being part of a larger community, we can become optimistic and enthusiastic about participating in the community as a whole. We will also be aware of our tendencies toward pride and control, believing our way is the only way, and being attached to our own desired ends. We will make sure that we carry our own weight in the community and not freeload on the good will of others. If we do not attend to our spirit as we do our work, we risk becoming angry and discouraged. We will also notice where we have power to help others reach their dreams. In the process, we will discover the joy of helping others rather than attending only to ourselves.

CONCLUSION

The Results Lens invites us to consider how to live a joy-filled life. Beginning with the phrase *I have choices*, which embodies the vantage point of intention, we learn to be adults who consider our own dreams and desires as we act. To avoid becoming a flighty dilettante, we learn from the vantage point of empathy, *I am consistent*. As we learn to use both our heads and our hearts, caring for others while assuring that they too are granted autonomy, we can see the world from the vantage point of integration and *delight in being a co-creator of what is.*

Balancing pursuing our goals with responsibility and consistency requires careful thought. With practice and discipline, we can use the tools of this lens to act with creative wisdom when faced with difficult choices. With detachment, caring more about the people and the process than the result, we help everyone have a shot at realizing their dreams.

CONTINUING THE CONVERSATION

1. Using either the simulation or another fact pattern, analyze the situation using the Results Lens. Was the problem easy to do, indicating that this may be your preferred method of working ethical problems? Was the process difficult, indicating that this may not be your ethical home?

2. Read an op-ed piece in your local paper or a national paper and find examples of utilitarian thinking. In what ways did the author appeal to the "greatest good for the greatest number" as a justification for the policy direction? How did the advocated policy balance the goals of those in power against those who do not have as much opportunity to reach their goals?

3. Review the chart that opened this chapter, paying special attention to the gifts of this tradition. Considering both your own life as well as others who make decisions using the vantage of this tradition, what are the strengths of the Results Lens? Give examples of situations in which you have seen excellent results as someone used the viewpoints and processes of this lens to make a decision.

4. What strategies can you put in place to help you begin to strengthen your own mastery of this lens? How can you help the organizations in which you work, either paid or volunteer, ask the core questions to help them make better ethical decisions?

5. Again, review the chart that opened this chapter, this time looking for the weaknesses of the tradition. Considering both your own life as well as that of others who make decisions using the vantage of this tradition, what are the weaknesses of the Results Lens? Give examples of situations in which you have seen problematic results as someone used the viewpoints and processes of this lens to make a decision.

6. What strategies can you put in place to help you recognize and attend to the imbalance that comes from an inappropriate appropriation of the Results Lens, whether concerning abuse of power or hubris in your personal and professional life? How do you know when you are improperly using the tools of this lens? How can you help the organizations in which you work, whether paid or volunteer, ask the core questions to help them avoid imbalance or hubris?

THE RELATIONSHIP LENS
CONCEPTUAL MAP

CONCEPTS	INTENTION	EMPATHY	INTEGRATION
Foundational Questions	What is a fair system?	What is appropriate subordination of my own rights to those of the group?	What is my place in the web of life?
Theory	Justice Ethics/ Communitarianism	Moral Ecology	Sacred Creation
Representative Authors	John Rawls Amitai Etzioni	Robert Bellah William Frederick	Robert C. Fuller
Tools and Practices	Tradition; group activities	Evaluation of emotional climate of group	Commitment to justice, service
Key Phrase	"I am fair."	"I use power wisely."	"I am part of all that is."
An ethical act …	… is consistent with a good character for a particular role	… is made with awareness of the interplay of mind and emotions	… supports and enhances the meaning I have given to my life
My goal is to …	… create a set of processes to assure a just and fair community	… reach the correct evaluation of an event based on group response	… be aware of my place in a sacred community
I have gifts of …	… inclusiveness and an innate sense of fairness	… compassion and interconnectedness with others	… generosity and a forgiving heart
My blind spot is …	… an overconfidence in process	… difficulty finding the appropriate emotional response to an event	… masking pain with exclusiveness
My vice is …	… ambition and abuse of power	… groupthink	… elitism
I risk …	… authoritarianism	… emotional entrainment	… over-identifying with the group
Hubris	"I am exempt."	"I don't have to evaluate emotions of others."	"I have the *Truth*."
My crisis is …	… separation	… resenting demands of others	… lack of meaning and isolation

Let justice roll on like a river,
righteousness like
a never-failing stream!

The Prophet Amos[1]

CHAPTER 9

The Relationship Lens

THE THIRD ETHICAL LENS CALLS US BACK to the deontological tradition where we look at the decision-maker's responsibilities. However, the question now moves from a consideration of the individual alone to seeing how that individual fits into the community. Further, we need to determine what responsibilities we all have for assuring that the community and its supporting institutions are healthy.

SEEING CLEARLY THROUGH THE RELATIONSHIP LENS

John Rawls, drawing upon the idealist traditions of Plato, St. Augustine, Luther, and Kant, as well as the social contract notions of Thomas Hobbes, represents the philosopher on the theoretical edge of the postmodern world that began to move us toward a consideration of the community through a moderation of individual rights.

CORE HEURISTIC QUESTIONS

❖ *How do I fit into my community?*

❖ *How do I care for those with no power?*

❖ *What is my place in the web of life?*

THE VANTAGE POINT OF INTENTION

Rawls places himself in the modern tradition of those who consider the social contract as foundational for our community. However, he critiques Hobbes's notion that we subject ourselves to the community because of a self-serving desire for security. Thomas Hobbes, who is known as the father of the theory of social contract, argues that "if a citizen in a relatively secure state desires to commit an illegal act and is confident that he can avoid detection" there is no reason for him either ethically or morally to refrain from acting on that desire.[2]

Rawls suggests that meeting our agreements should not depend on our particular situation. The core of Rawls' theory is twofold. First, we should be committed to social agreements regardless of our original position, the position of our birth—our nationality, gender, race, and economic position. As we consider the claims of others to the resources needed to thrive, we make commitments that last in perpetuity, beyond our own particular interest. Second, our ignorance about the intricacies of a particular rule should not govern whether we follow it. Rather, as we learn more about our responsibilities to the community, our commitment to the underlying social contract will grow.

If we define ethics as finding the correct process by which decisions should be made and our rights and responsibilities exercised, the Relationship Lens focuses our attention on what social agreements we would make if we didn't know who we were in the community and wanted to assure fundamental fairness for all. Rawls asks us to make our decisions from an impersonal position as an *ideal observer* where we choose to act without knowing anything about ourselves or others in the community. In that role, we are asked to consider whether the agreements we make would satisfy us if we found ourselves as the least advantaged in the community. Rawls thus anticipates the postmodern approach to ethics where the process by which the rules of the community are decided is more important than the actual rules themselves. Rawls understands that while the rules may change, the process will help us avoid acting only out of our own self-interest.

As we apply the template for the Relationship Lens, we use our mind and the tools of reason to see how we fit into our community and what relationships are important to sustain. The sticking point for many is that whatever process we choose is to be applied equally to all persons in the situation. Rawls entreats us to consider the whole community, in particular the claims of those who are least advantaged, as we make choices about how best to live.

THE VANTAGE POINT OF EMPATHY

While Rawls calls us to consider what an ideal observer would do in a given situation, Robert Bellah and William Frederick invite us to personalize the conversation. Rather than taking a position that is removed from the actual hustle and bustle of the real world, those who are part of the communitarian movement invite us to consider not just how our individual acts affect us but also how those acts support a healthy community and vibrant institutions.

Bellah and Frederick both use the concept of *moral ecology* to call us to greater responsibility for the community. Ecology, in sociological terms, is the study of the relationships and adjustments of humans to their geographical and social environments.[3] For Bellah, moral ecology is the notion that we must understand that "the individual is realized only through community" so we should consider how to build and maintain healthy institutions that are the matrix from which healthy character is formed.[4] Frederick reminds us that corporations must attend to those life-conserving values such as fairness, unselfishness, and restraint, that both create and sustain human collective life.[5] The vantage point of empathy of the Relationship Lens invites us to see ourselves as part of an ongoing web of life where our business systems and institutions support the community as well as the individual.

This lesson was learned by one of my students who was an ardent individualist, believing that he did not need anyone else to make it in this world. He was absent from class for several weeks and then came to me with an explanation and an apology. He had been very ill. But for a close friend who nursed him through the illness and put his physical interests above her own needs, he literally would not have survived. He said that as he lay on his bed, he thought about his assertion in class that he (and by implication, everyone else) could make it on his own, and realized that he was wrong: he needed the larger community to thrive.

As we consider the Relationship Lens, the first of two lenses that call us to accountability for the community, the reaction of many is that any sharing of resources or providing opportunities to those who are disadvantaged is communism or socialism, and thus to be avoided. Ironically, many who make this claim are people of deep faith who do not explore how the Judeo-Christian tradition (as well as the traditions of other faiths) calls us to responsibility for others. In the Jewish community, practices such as gleaning (leaving part of the harvest) to provide for the poor or prohibitions against usury to assure that businesspeople didn't gouge consumers were woven into the fabric of the community.

The Christian community began by sharing the resources of all members, allowing the poor to thrive. Much of the New Testament focuses on our financial responsibilities to each other. In the basic economic unit of our community, the family, resources are shared according to need, not finite or prioritized based on contribution (otherwise children and college students would have a difficult time). As the communal life of the early church unfolded, Christians discovered that trust is an essential element of a healthy community.[6]

For every community, the basic economic unit is the family. One student squirmed as he had to acknowledge that in his family basic Marxist principles applied: the parents who had much because of their abilities provided for the children according to their needs, including him, who depended on his parents for his tuition and living expenses.[7] However, once the circle expands beyond the immediate family, we do not seem to trust that others truly need the resources or that they will use them appropriately. At that point, many become miserly in their sharing with others.

As the United States embraced the radical individualism that was a logical outgrowth of the theories of Kant, Mill, and Hobbes, whose theories deeply informed our Declaration of Independence and governmental structures, we adopted the philosophies of the Responsibilities Lens and the Results Lens, often forgetting to put in place structures to help those who were not advantaged. The idea was that people could use their brains and their brawn to provide for themselves and their families. Any needs in the community could be provided by the extended family or the religious and charitable organizations. The structure of the economic and social institutions were not to be regulated by the government, rather we would use our power of contract to moderate the excesses of the institutions.

In the beginning of the 20th century, a tipping point was reached, and society began to tilt toward the perspective of the Relationship Lens. As businesses grew during the Industrial Revolution (late 18th and early 19th centuries), many began to acknowledge the powerlessness of the everyday person to bargain with business organizations. The religious community joined with those in the Labor Movement and called upon businesses to temper their power by providing appropriate wages, safe working environments, and setting fair prices. As individual businesses believed they needed to push for their own economic advantage, they resisted those changes unless the bottom line was enhanced. The response was an increase in governmental regulation after the stock market crash of 1929 to assure that the excesses of businesses were tempered and some mechanism for caring for the disadvantaged was in place.

At the beginning of the 21st century, we are seeing a renewed call for businesses to be socially responsible as the questions of a hundred years ago are revisited. Added to the current mix are issues related to environmental responsibility. Members of the community are asking what responsibility an organization has to provide for the needs of its workers, including health care and sustained employment. What is the responsibility of an organization to assure that it doesn't damage the environment or community? What responsibility does an organization have to help the community in which it finds itself? How do we balance between the need to stay in business and the responsibility for caring for all of the stakeholders, including the community?

As explored in Chapters 2 and 3, polarizing the conversation into advocating for only an unregulated market economy or pushing for absolutely all resources being shared is not useful. Instead, Rawls and Bellah call us to consider how to balance the needs of individual autonomy and responsibility with the challenges of working together. Strong institutions are needed to educate our children and provide those amenities that require collective action. For example, no individual or groups of individuals alone can guarantee that airplanes can fly safely. The air traffic controllers employed by the Federal Aviation Administration and all the related organizations that are supported by tax dollars reduce accidents and keep the air space safe. The difficulty is finding the balance between rewarding individual initiative and assuring that the community is strong. Different communities find that balance in various ways, thus conversation and commitment to both the individual and the whole are essential.

THE VANTAGE POINT OF INTEGRATION

Those who are committed to justice for all find themselves part of the ethical tradition that emphasizes systemic integrity and control. In the United States, the religious groups that have been responsible for raising these issues are the historic justice communities, the Quakers and Mennonites, those who are part of the Catholic Social Thought community, the Bahá'is, and the Black churches, whom champion the call for civil rights. As we listen to voices from these faith communities, we begin to realize that all of humanity is profoundly connected—we are each part of all that is. At that point, the differences among us begin to dissolve and we understand that if our brother or sister hurts, we hurt as well. We are then called to consider the subtle connections of dependence, independence, and interdependence.

Healthy dependence comes when we acknowledge our needs, whether as children, the physically or mentally challenged, or the elderly who cannot provide for themselves. Those of us who seem fully capable still need mentors and teachers to help us navigate new situations and community structures to make our lives enjoyable. Roads, sewer systems, judicial systems, schools, and parks need to be maintained by all, based on individual ability to pay, not just usage, for the community to thrive. Unhealthy dependence comes when we do not take responsibility for doing what we can to better our situation and care for the whole. Healthy independence flows when we are as responsible as possible for ourselves both physically and economically. Unhealthy independence comes when we do not acknowledge that we cannot survive on our own.

Even fur trappers, who lived alone for months in the untamed wilderness of the West, needed someone to buy their pelts and make goods such as clothes and weapons so they could ply their trade. Often, we ignore the claims of those upon whose work we depend, such as janitors, technicians, and farm workers. We say that they should work to make their lives better as we scheme to pay them as little as possible for their efforts. And, when we ignore these claims for fair wages and respectful treatment, we are more prone to exploit those without economic power or political voice.

Those who embrace interdependence know that we all need each other. At the same time, we are each responsible for assuring that we carry out our own part of the bargain as well. Thus, as we seek interdependence, we acknowledge when we need others and when we need to act on our own. Recalling the image from outer space of the blue globe we call our home, we remember that no boundaries were present, no nations were seen—we are all one. As we learn that the environmental changes of one continent affect the environment of another, we begin to realize how we are all profoundly connected. As we then commit ourselves to work for others, in addition to ourselves, we can stand in awe of our wonderful life together. In the process, we can learn to receive the gifts of generosity and forgiveness.

CHARACTERISTICS OF THE RELATIONSHIP LENS

This lens focuses on whether the systems of justice used to achieve our goals are appropriate, thus assuring that those without access to power have an equal opportunity to thrive. This lens calls us to carefully balance the tension between individual achievement and community well-being.

To determine whether an act is ethical, the members of the community (equality) use our reason (rationality) to develop processes that will assure justice for all. The first form of process is known as due process, getting notice and participating in the decision. The second form is known as substantive process, making sure that people know the rules. As we act thoughtfully with others, we need to always remember that protecting fair systems for resolution of disputes is the bedrock of a healthy community.

In this tradition, people looking from the vantage point of empathy deeply understand that they are a member of a community and thus must work within that community in order to have healthy institutions. A society depends on institutions such as schools, churches, hospitals, and businesses to thrive. Those organizations provide continuity for the people in the community as well as a safety net for those who are having a hard go of life.

Often, supporting our core institutions means being shaped by them and being held accountable to them. Rather than just going off on our own, we find that we need the support and love of others to work through the difficult time. We see clearly from the vantage point of integration as we find our place within the web of our community. At times we need to share from our abundance; at other times we must receive from others as we do not have particular resources. At times we need to move into leadership roles; at other times we need to be served by others. At times we need to teach others and hold them accountable for their agreements; at other times we need to be taught by others and reminded of our obligations. As we move through our life, spiritual wisdom lets us know how we fit at this particular time into the ongoing fabric of society.

QUESTIONS FOR DETERMINING RIGHT ACTION

❖ *Process:* How does the process that is used to implement the decision assure that all stakeholders are considered and heard in this choice?

- *Healthy institutions:* How does this decision support my responsibility for assuring that the community and its institutions are healthy and effective?

- *Support of the organization:* How does this decision enhance the achievement of the organization's goals, responsibilities, and values?

- *Enhancement of relationships:* How does this decision enhance the relationship of my organization to the community at large?

SECONDARY VALUES SEEN THROUGH THE PRISM OF THIS LENS

- *Fair treatment:* Persons are to be treated in accord with the social agreements that have resulted from our analysis as an ideal observer. Those who are alike in relevant respects should be treated similarly; those who differ in some respect relevant to the job they perform should be treated differently in proportion to the difference.

- *Fair administration of rules:* Rules should be administered consistently, fairly, and impartially for all members of the community.

- *Fair compensation:* People should be paid fairly for their work. All people who are similarly situated should receive comparable wages and opportunities for advancement.

- *Fair blame:* No individual should be held responsible for matters over which they have no control.

- *Due process:* Every member of the community has a right to a fair and impartial hearing when he or she believes that personal rights are being violated.

USING THE RELATIONSHIP LENS

As we begin to work through an ethical issue using the perspective of people in the Relationship Lens, we begin with the human condition. Because of our tendency toward selfishness, Rawls invites us to consider what processes and procedures we would put into place in our community if we did not know who we were or what our role in the community would be. Rawls is concerned with ethics as fundamental fairness, which for him is a fair distribution of both the burdens and benefits of the community. Rawls also invites us

SNAPSHOT: AN ACTION IS ETHICAL IF IT

- *Creates fair systems for resolution of disputes and creation of policy*

- *Cares for all members and institutions of the community, especially in the allocation of resources*

- *Contributes to each member of the community knowing that they are part of "all that is"*

into a process that he calls "reflective equilibrium," in which we constantly balance the needs of individuals against the needs of others in the community. Rawls and others who are part of the social contract/justice traditions, ask us to consider those who are least advantaged—those without access to power and privilege.

Further, because people from this lens value the process of rationality, being able to explain why a particular position was taken is important. The steps of the analysis allow us to make a persuasive argument as to why we chose one option instead of another. The following set of questions helps us identify the systems of justice that inform our ethical choices. As we become more skilled, the analysis will become easier and we can begin to identify the core values that, for us, trump other competing values. However, even when we think we know the answer to the question, the discipline of working through the process can help clarify our thoughts.

To help understand the process, an abbreviated version of a real problem will be given in a set of text boxes. This is the third time that you will have explored whether or not airing an advertising campaign where the behavior portrayed could be viewed as bullying is ethical. As we move to an analysis that privileges the community as a whole, the differences among the answers will prove intriguing. However, when a company wants to run an effective ad campaign, if members of the community resonate with the message even if the behavior advocated is questionable, the balance between selling the product and encouraging responsible behavior may not be clear. Again, an abbreviated version of the analysis will be presented in the text. These examples will give us a feeling for the tools of each theory.

STEP 1: BE ATTENTIVE

During the first step of the decision model, we pay attention to what is going on. This step is more difficult than we think. We have to pay attention to what our mind is observing, what we are seeing, and what we don't want to see. Those of us with a preference for the Relationship Lens tend to interpret what we are seeing through lenses of the authorities we favor or our prio interpretation of events. We also have to listen to our emotions. if we are not careful, our emotions can get hijacked and we wind up inappropriately reacting to a situation.

Attend to the context

As we begin our analysis, we will pay attention to what is going on but without attachment because we don't know who we might be. Rawls calls this state being behind a "veil of ignorance": at any given time we might be the person with power and at another time we might have no power. Rawls suggests that we begin by evaluating the stakeholders in light of each person's access to knowledge, resources, and power. We are asked to determine who is the least advantaged in a situation and then work our analysis from there. We have to be careful because the least advantaged person may not be immediately obvious.

One Director of Human Resources related a conundrum in which he discovered that power may lie in unexpected places. A woman came to him and wanted to report an incident of sexual harassment. The woman asked that the conversation be confidential; the HR director knew that he had an obligation to the company to report sexual harassment and discipline the person who was responsible. Initially the woman appeared to be the least advantaged. However, by requesting that the HR executive violate the company rules and put the company at risk in exchange for the information, she was actually wielding considerable power. The director was the least advantaged: he had to decide whether to help the victim who did not want to operate within the protocols of the company or put the company at risk. This example shows that someone who may appear to be the least advantaged in the abstract, in the actual circumstances may have a great deal of power. Thus, as we consider the context in which the decision has to be made, we need to attend to the resources available to all persons and the nuances of power that attend the situation.

We also have to be careful not to make the middle manager the one who is always the least advantaged. Every person is pressured by various stakeholders to meet their needs. Often, those in the middle of organizations believe that if they don't accede to the pressure of the people at the top they will lose their jobs, and in fact our record of how we treat whistle-blowers in our community would seem to indicate that the fear has some merit. Yet those in the middle of organizations have power of position and conviction that can help them shape the system and the processes to assure that justice is done. Sometimes, attending to justice does require that we hold those in positions of power responsible for their actions and call them to accountability. Wisdom and the counsel of others can help us navigate these difficult situations. We must remember, however, that Rawls does not ask that we just protect ourselves, but that we look out for those who are truly without personal power.

Case Study: Facts and assumptions

❖ *The VP for Sales and Marketing for G-BioSport North has recommended an ad campaign to boost sales among college age men. The ad campaign has two groups of college men playing intramural basketball. The team from one dorm is buff with aggressive athletes who gang up and taunt the scrawny and untalented team from another dorm. The scrawny team takes G-BioSport supplements and starts working out. The final shot is the revenge of the nerds—where they turn on the buff athletes who flee from the court in shame and humiliation. This ad was tested in the field and had a very positive response from the target demographics. However, just as the campaign is about to begin, I received a letter raising concerns about our new ad campaign from a watchdog group, Concerned Athletes Against Bullying (CAAB). After some research, I discovered that CAAB is an advocacy group with lots of resources behind it and it targets companies that directly or indirectly advocate bullying.*

Case Study: Ethical agent

❖ *As the CEO of the company, I have to sign off on the ad campaign proposed by Vice President of Sales and Marketing. As I consider my choices in this situation, I want to make sure that I fit into my community. I want to care for those with not power. I also want to discover my place in the web of life.*

Identify the ethical decision maker

Imagine that we are the subject of a science-fiction movie. We are hovering in space, not connected to our bodies, and looking down at a business setting. We have a vague notion that we know something about that setting, a situation where people are scurrying around trying to solve some difficult problems. We also have a sense that we might be one of those persons—but we don't know which one. We know that we are looking at a business, an organization that manufactures something to sell to others or that provides services for people. We know that in this business, people sometimes get along and sometimes they fuss with each other. We have a sense that if we cooperate, we might be able to get good results. We also know that people measure success by how much money they make, and so we have some understanding about economic theory. Basically, we know enough about this situation to make some intelligent guesses about how people will respond to the answers chosen for the problems they face.

Watching, we notice that people don't particularly care about what other people do; they are *mutually disinterested*.[8] If someone says they want to get ahead in an organization, people will support her in that decision. If another person wants to slow down a bit to care for his family, people will generally support that decision as well. People tend to be *rational*, in that they want more of the basic goods of life and are willing to do what is required to get more of the good things, whether products or additional leisure time.[9]

We also notice that when they cooperate, they seem not to be *envious*, preferring to gain in primary goods even if others gain more than they do.[10] A bit skeptical about this last insight, we remember reading somewhere that people who are envious prefer that no one get a particular good if they can't have it.[11] A thread through all of the Harry Potter books is the envy that Snape felt toward James Potter, Harry's father. Snape and James competed over everything, from honors at Hogwarts to Lily, Harry's mother. The envy causes Snape to align with Voldemort, preferring the dark side rather than life without Lily. However, Snape's love for Lily allows for his ultimate redemption.[12] This complexity of human nature makes the idealistic approach of Rawls suspect.

However, as we make the decision, we know that we have to make a decision that will affect all of these people—and we don't know who we are. How will we make a decision that each of us is willing to embrace whether we are the CEO or the groundskeeper?

The above scenario plays out the notion of being an ideal observer who operates behind a veil of ignorance. Rawls asserts that if we focus only on our own self-interest, we in fact do not attend to the needs of the community as a whole. Go-

CASE STUDY: ISSUE

❖ *Given that recent incidents of bullying have escalated in the community and the community is actively taking steps to stop and prevent bullying, should we run an advertising campaign that is certain to boost the sale of our product where the behavior advocated could be viewed as bullying and might draw negative community commentary.*

EVERYDAY ETHICS: *Making Wise Choices in a Complex World*

ing behind the veil of ignorance is difficult. However, if we try to see the world from another's point of view, we can make decisions that move toward a systemic solution rather than just achieving individual happiness.

Pinpoint the ethical issue

What is the central problem that must be resolved? As we look at the problem, Rawls wants us to consider the systemic issues as well as the individual issues. We need to attend to processes that create or perpetuate injustice. Rawls asserts that if we reach procedural fairness then we will have substantive fairness.

CASE STUDY: STAKEHOLDERS

STEP 2: BE INTELLIGENT

As we move into the second step, we are going to do our first round of critical analysis. For this segment, we are going to sort through the data and begin honing in on the problem itself.

Determine the stakeholders

The next step is to identify the stakeholders—the people who will be affected by the decision. Building on the notion of being behind the veil of ignorance, Rawls next invites us to consider which constituent is the least advantaged in the situation. In our community we have power from three sources: access to autonomy, knowledge, and economic resources. As we determine what social and economic inequalities are present, we are called to rank the stakeholders from the most advantaged to the least advantaged in terms of the situation to

- ❖ Me, the CEO of the Company, who is the decision-maker

- ❖ The VP of Sales and Marketing responsible for creating and implementing the ad campaign

- ❖ Shareholders of the Company, whose stock value depends on the financial success of the company

- ❖ Employees of the Company, who depend on a fiscally sound company for employment

- ❖ Customers who like your product and might increase use because of the campaign

- ❖ Kids who are bullied because your company appears to advocate bad behavior

- ❖ Members of the community who may critique the ad campaign and your company because it contributes to bullying

determine who has inequality of voice and inequality in access to resources that then results in inequality of power.

Persons who are autonomous feel free to speak up and have their voices heard. They believe that they are independent actors and thus can, in some measure, control their destiny. To the degree people are marginalized or silenced, either because they do not believe that they have a right to speak or because they are not invited to the table, they will lack autonomy.

Access to resources includes both knowledge and money. People who know what resources are available, what systems are in place to access the help, and how to negotiate the various systems of our community have a great deal of power. People who have knowledge are better able to gain for themselves the goods that are important to them. Knowing what opportunities are available helps people get ahead. Public libraries provide those with limited economic resources crucial access to knowledge. Economic resources clearly open doors. Those with more access to economic resources, have more flexibility and the freedom to make a variety of choices in their lives than those without similar access.

People who do not have autonomy or resources lack power. A core touchstone for a just act, an ethical action, is how well it cares for those without power. A key concern for ethics is assuring that we do not abuse our economic or personal power as we carry out our work. Images of firemen hosing innocent children rather than allowing schools to be integrated in accordance with the law seared the minds of many and fueled the Civil Rights Movement. While we know that the work of police officers is dangerous, we cringe when we hear of an officer who, rather than using a search warrant, uses brute power to intimidate a person into a search of their premises.

CASE STUDY: VALUES IN TENSION

❖ *The two values in tension are* AUTONOMY, *where the Company makes its own choices about how to sell its products, and* EQUALITY *where the Company responds to community pressure and initiative to stop bullying. In order to be successful, to continue to employ individuals, and to offer our products to the public, our Company must advertise its products. On the other hand, bullying has become an issue in our community. We have a commitment, as a member of the community, to not advocate behavior such as bullying that creates an increase risk to the safety and well-being of the community.*

Explore the values in tension

Etched deep into the American consciousness is the notion that, as individuals do well, the community will prosper. Bellah reminds us, in describing the game of Monopoly, that an unrestrained market economy allows those with power to leverage that power into more resources and more power. As Bellah notes, "a game that begins with equality of resources among all players ends with only one winner and the rest dispossessed."[13] Thus, given the rules of the economic game, those who are rich get richer and those who are not suffer.

Those of us raised in our liberal market economy would consider winning the game of Monopoly representative of our lives: we consider our economic gains and losses as indicators of individual skill rather than seeing that our fortunes dependent on the fabric of the whole. However, at the very minimum, in addition to a plethora of legislative enactments, we depend upon an independent judicial system to uphold the integrity of contracts and to arbitrate among competing claims when someone has been physically or economically damaged. And then as the Wall Street meltdown in 2008 reminded us, when our fortunes are in the stock market and traded with portions of mortgages, none of us is exempt from the effects of community action. Even those who were thoughtful and careful found their retirement plans reduced by more than 50% in the aftermath of the scandals.

Identifying the spoken and unspoken agreements that are maintained by the various institutions is not always easy. We need to also acknowledge the way that the community as a whole exercises its shared power through governmental action that establishes and protects our prerogatives. For example, as the United States established its claim to the western part of the nation, those who moved west relied upon an institution called homesteading in which the government promised that the settlers would get the title to the land by simply living on it and farming it for five years, without attending to the claim of the land by Native Americans who were already living on or using the land's resources to survive. We have systems of subsidies (reduced rates for grazing, logging, and drilling for oil and gas on public lands), we have protections for property (copyright and patent laws), we have protections for people (minimum wage laws, unemployment insurance, and safety requirements).

All of these policies arise as we correct for abuses in application of the Responsibilities Lens and the Results Lens, to prevent individuals with power from ignoring the claims of the community and its institutions in the distribution of resources and economic benefits. From the perspective of the Relationship Lens, questions arise about the relationship of the individual to the community. When should we subordinate our own desires and goals in order to assure that the community as a whole may flourish? When can we legitimately make a claim against community resources and when should we depend on what we have provided for ourselves? What processes should be in place to make sure that justice is in fact accomplished? How can we assure that power and access to resources are appropriately balanced among groups and individuals in our community? Rawls's theory thus becomes a valuable resource for determining public policies as we navigate the shoals of determining how best to share resources and allocate responsibility. The challenge in the process is to appropriately balance between equal opportunity and equality of outcome, finding a result that all consider as close to fair as possible.

CASE STUDY: OPTIONS FOR ACTION

1: RUN the advertising campaign that is certain to boost sales but could be advocating bullying behavior.

2: DO NOT RUN the advertising campaign that is certain to boost sales but could be advocating bullying behavior.

Identify options for action

The next step is to identify the options. Again, the ethical decision maker has the opportunity to choose from an array of options. Many times, our experience provides us with a good first cut of available choices. As we seek guidance from others and see how different people have handled similar situations, our option set becomes richer. As we frame options, we look for those that address the processes and systems in place and that highlight the tension between supporting a healthy community, its institutions, and the individuals who are part of that community. Rawls requires that we look at the system as a whole, both spoken and unspoken processes that establish and enforce the community norms. Thus, in framing the options, we look to what systems are in place and how they need to be changed or maintained. Remember that even the lack of specific processes, as well as informal (as opposed to written) processes to enforce community norms, is a system.

STEP 3: BE REASONABLE

For this section of the decision process, the questions that are asked are specific to the lens. The point of this section is to show how people who favor this particular approach to decision making would answer the problem. Because each ethical lens prioritizes different values, the questions asked to determine the best course of action are different.

CASE STUDY: *REFLECTIVE EQUILIBRIUM*

❖ *The interests of the community that wishes to have engaging information about products has to be balanced against the interests of the kids, who might either decide that low-grade bullying is acceptable or who might be on the receiving end of the bullying. The kids are the least advantaged because they might be the ones who are bullied. They also have fewer skills of discernment to notice that the ad is not really promoting bullying but the sale of the product. We need to protect the least advantaged, the kids, without unduly burdening the most advantaged, in this case the company who is running the ad. We don't want to unfairly interfere with the Company's right to market their product.*

Hone critical thinking skills

We begin the analysis by identifying the stakeholder who is the least advantaged and then determine how their interests can be balanced against those of the advantaged. Rawls does not focus on rigidly determining the principles that we are supposed to follow or calculating happiness as a guide for what we should do. Rather, Rawls suggests that in complex situations we need to balance among the competing claims of the stakeholders. He advocates using a process that he calls *reflective equilibrium.*[14]

After we have considered the situation from behind the veil of ignorance, we identify principles that will lead to justice. As we actually test those principles against the concrete situation in which we find ourselves, just results can emerge. When we deliberate about what to do, we consider what tweaking is needed either in pruning the rules or stretching the protocols as the situation requires or changing the stipulations about the original positions. Rawls advocates a back and forth iterative method of testing, in which "eventually we shall find a description of the initial situation that both expresses reasonable conditions and yields principles that match our considered judgments duly pruned and adjusted."[15]

As we practice the process of reflective equilibrium, we become more skilled at both attending to situations where the least advantaged have not been considered and noticing nuances in the context that were not seen before. This skill requires wisdom and discretion. Leaders in our

EVERYDAY ETHICS: *Making Wise Choices in a Complex World*

community are expected to exercise discretion as they carry out their responsibilities. Discretion carries with it the expectation that we will be prudent in our decisions and carefully consider the implications of action. This critical thinking skill enables us to make better decisions.

Evaluate from the vantage point of intention

Rawls's process asks four questions that we can use to evaluate our options.

FIRST QUESTION: WHAT ARE THE BASIC LIBERTIES TO WHICH EVERY MEMBER OF THE COMMUNITY IS ENTITLED?

Rawls writes from the tradition of democracy and so is interested in assuring that his system of ethics upholds the basic principles of a free, self-determining society. The first task is to define what basic liberties all persons should have because they are part of our community. As Rawls asserts: each person is to have an equal right to the most extensive total system of equal basic liberties compatible with a similar system of liberty for all.[16]

This statement is much more narrow than it first appears. The notion is that everyone has exactly the same access to rights that everyone else has. When we think of a list of rights, we tend to think of what are called positive rights—rights to food, shelter, and education. But no one has the same amount of any of these things. We don't even have access to the same amount of air. Those who live high in the mountains don't have as much oxygen as those at sea level and those who live in industrial settings have lots of pollution in their air.

The rights that all of us can claim are procedural rights. Thus, we have a right to notice, to participate in the decisions that affect us, and to have our contracts honored. When Rawls talks about a "total system of equal basic liberties," he invites us to assure that the process by which decisions are made includes everyone. As we design processes for determining what action will be taken, actions that will affect the well-being of our stakeholders, we must assure that people have a right to a voice and to a vote. We need to remember that the right to participate is not a right to a veto. Rather, it is a right to notice, to comment, and to have a meaningful voice.

CASE STUDY: BASIC LIBERTIES

- ❖ *Two primary liberties are the right to notice, to have information about one's life from which one can make deliberate choices, and the right to voice, to comment about the situation.*

- ❖ *Safety itself is not a basic liberty. Different amounts of safety are given to people based on where they live and their ability to fend for themselves. As a community that values autonomy, we cannot put in place the social structures that would give everyone the same amount of safety, and so this benefit is distributed unequally.*

This right to notice and to voice are the bedrock upon which democracy is formed. As we all know, pure democracy, where everyone has a right to participate, is burdensome—whether in a political or organizational setting. To alleviate some of the time-consuming requirements of pure democracy, we often opt for representative democracy—making sure that a representative of various stakeholders is present at the table when decisions are being made.

Those of us who are asked to represent the interests of a group must remember that we speak for others and not just ourselves. Thus, our personal biases and concerns cannot override the interests of the group for which we speak. One mistake that is often made is not including every constituent in the decision-making process. We assume that those of us with resources know the issues and concerns of those without resources. We assume that those of us with power can voice the fears of those without power.

For an option to be ethical, it must include a process of comment for all individuals or groups who will be affected by the decision. If the option does not include a meaningful process for assuring that all have a voice in the decision, the first step may be to slightly change the process for decision making to assure full participation. Adding the process for notice and voice may make a decision that looks unethical, in fact, ethical, as all are willing to embrace the same option that the decision maker presented.

SECOND QUESTION: DOES THIS OPTION MEET THE REQUIREMENTS OF THE "JUST SAVINGS PRINCIPLE?" [17]

> We are able to meet all of our needs in the immediate time, but meeting those needs and desires may result in an irreversible depletion of our resources. When we are viewing the problem from the position of the ideal observer, we don't know to what generation we belong. We may be our own children or grandchildren.

The Western states are in the middle of a vigorous conversation about the right use of water. As communities in Colorado, New Mexico, Arizona, and California grow, a fierce battle rages for who is going to get what water. The mantra of growth fuels conversations about drilling more wells or finding ways to bring water across mountains. However, we are finding that the water is not inexhaustible. The Ogallala Aquifer is not being replenished as quickly as water is being taken out.[18] The Colorado and Rio Grande rivers are at all-time lows; urban, environmental, recreational, and agricultural uses all need to be balanced to sustain our way of life. Given the precariousness of our water supply, is it appropriate for local governments to issue building permits when a developer can identify a five- to ten-year source of water or should a longer trajectory be taken? Should we protect the jobs of builders and satisfy our need for large, individual homes when the land may not be able to support that kind of development? Should we buy water from farmers and leave the land fallow rather than assure our own food supply?

CASE STUDY: JUST SAVINGS PRINCIPLE

❖ *Both options meet the requirement of the just savings principle in that no extraordinary resources are required for either option.*

EVERYDAY ETHICS: *Making Wise Choices in a Complex World*

These questions are incredibly complex, as people in disparate communities with varying interests may advocate for different solutions. As individuals in community contemplate various courses of action, the constraint of the just savings principle advocated by Rawls provides a useful touchstone for our reflective process and choosing a subsequent course of action. This principle claims that if an option does not adequately provide for our children and grandchildren, that option is unethical. We must assure the good of future generations as we attend to our own needs.

THIRD QUESTION: DOES THIS OPTION ARRANGE THE SOCIAL AND ECONOMIC INEQUALITIES SO THAT THEY ARE ATTACHED TO OFFICES AND POSITIONS THAT ARE OPEN TO ALL UNDER CONDITIONS OF FAIR EQUALITY OF OPPORTUNITY?[19]

This question is also a process question: Is everyone informed of the opportunities and thus able to make choices about whether or not to participate? With this criterion, Rawls wants to make sure that we move to equality of opportunity rather than focusing on equality of result.

Some are confused by Rawls use of the term "offices." He does not limit the word to political offices, but is talking about all of the various roles that we have— from employment opportunities, to seats on Fortune 500 boards, to slots in prestigious universities. The term is very broad, reaching to all of the various possible opportunities we have.

Title VII of the Civil Rights Act of 1964 demonstrates this principle in action. The law was passed as Congress was made painfully aware of the systemic barriers that kept African-Americans out of the mainstream of political and economic life.[20] An African-American colleague recounts that, before Title VII was passed but after the Supreme Court declared segregation unconstitutional in *Brown v. Topeka Board of Education*, African-Americans were routinely placed in trade classes and not in college-prep courses. Further, they were not counseled about preparing for college but rather actively discouraged from considering higher education. Thus, he didn't hear about the Scholastic Aptitude Test (SAT), which was required for admission to universities. He saw a sign in the hall and decided on a lark to take the test to get out of a half-day of school. He received a score of 1600—a perfect score—and

CASE STUDY: EQUALITY OF OPPORTUNITY

OPTION 1: RUN THE ADVERTISING CAMPAIGN

❖ *Running the ad does give the viewers equality of opportunity. All who watch the ad can choose whether to purchase the product as well as model the behavior that is in the ad — or not. The only slight disadvantage would be kids who might not be able to protect themselves against those who would imitate the slightly humiliating acts that are modeled in the ad.*

OPTION 2: DO NOT RUN THE ADVERTISING CAMPAIGN

❖ *This option might make the company the disadvantaged party in that they would not have equality of opportunity to run the most advantageous campaign to maintain or grow market share.*

soon received offers for scholarships and ultimately earned a Ph.D. in psychology. But for that sign, he never would have known of the opportunity and requirements for a college education.

As companies and schools determine whether they have met the requirements of the law, they have to ask whether they have made the information available to all who might want to apply. Are the criteria for hire applied the same to all persons? Once people get jobs, do they have the same opportunities for advancement? The emphasis is not on mindlessly filling quotas but rather assuring that those who wish to advance have the opportunity to do so.

Again, the systemic barriers can be subtle. A woman who was a trade representative to an agricultural association went to the national meeting. She had taken golf lessons so that she could fully participate with the men, who were the vast majority of those at the conference. When she went to sign up for her tee time, she was told that women had never played golf with the men at this meeting and would not be starting now. She was more than welcome to play with the women, but the "wives tournament" was scheduled for the same time as the business meeting at which she was presenting. As a young executive, she was not prepared to face this level of systemic discrimination. At one level, golf is only a game; however, all who are familiar with business in America know that much gets accomplished on the links, if nothing more than cementing important relationships that facilitate business. If women are systematically excluded from the social events, they will not be able to do their jobs as well.

Rawls does not expect a quota system, nor does he require cranking numbers to assure equality. While looking at the spread of people in particular jobs or income brackets might be instructive as to how well the goal of equal access to opportunity is met, we are asked to carefully look at the stated and structural barriers to equality.

FOURTH QUESTION: DOES THIS OPTION ARRANGE THE SOCIAL AND ECONOMIC INEQUALITIES SO THAT THEY ARE TO THE GREATEST BENEFIT OF THE LEAST ADVANTAGED? [21]

Even when we attend to the systems and make them as fair as possible, inequalities still exist. In these situations, we are asked to reconsider two previous steps. The questions to be addressed are: who are the least advantaged and what kinds of policies do we need to put into place to assure that the inevitable inequalities of life do not unduly disadvantage the least advantaged?

As we recollect life behind the veil of ignorance, we have to ask whether we would be willing to be that person and take our chances at getting the good things in life. At this point, we need to revisit the difference between negative rights and positive rights. The Responsibilities Lens emphasized negative rights: the community would provide certain goods as long as no transfer of wealth was required. Any other goods that we purchased would be with our own nickel.

Rawls invites us to consider the role of positive rights, where assets need to be transferred from the most advantaged to the least advantaged in order to give them a fair opportunity in this life. The system that considers only negative rights assumes that all of us begin with about the same resources, sort of like the proverbial Monopoly game where we all start with a token and $200 in the bank, described above. The notion is that those who were strongest, smartest, and most ambitious will then rise to the top. Those who rise to the top will do so on merit, not by an accident of birth. The Darwinian notion of survival of the fittest meshes well with this ethical philosophy.

The difficulty is that we all know in our heart of hearts that we may not be the brightest and the best—everyone has gifts and talents as well as flaws and weaknesses. First, we know that we are born into a specific family. The very way our body gets put together depends on whether our mother took good care of her body while she was carrying us and on our family genetics, from both our father and our mother. We have no control over whether we are born into a family where the mother was healthy, took all of her prenatal vitamins, and had access to good health care or whether we are born into a family where the mother was an alcoholic, or lived in a rural area with limited health care. In this situation, because the baby has no ability to care for itself, it is the least advantaged. If any of us were behind the veil of ignorance, we would want the best shot at health, so we could be self-sufficient. Thus, many people support transferring community wealth to provide preventative health care for pregnant women and well-baby care for newborns.

As adults, we know that our ability to care for ourselves depends on both receiving good care when we are children and a solid education. Thus, the next place where we might consider transferring wealth is for preschool and quality K-12 education for all people. Not only does each of us need the best education possible, but the community needs to assure that we have well-trained productive people who will carry on when members of the current workforce are no longer able to work. In each stage of life, some do not have either the physical resources or monetary resources to have a shot at getting the good things of this life.

Thus, we see that the process of attending to the least advantaged both invites us to consider where we need to pool our resources as well as notice where life is most fragile. Rawls reminds

CASE STUDY: SOCIAL INEQUALITIES

OPTION 1: RUN THE ADVERTISING CAMPAIGN

❖ *The concern is the subtle message that taunting someone for being weak and then the victim becoming strong and retaliating is condoning that particular behavior in the larger community. As people get their social cues from the media, running this ad does subtly endorse low-level bullying, thus putting at risk those who are weak and defenseless.*

OPTION 2: DO NOT RUN THE ADVERTISING CAMPAIGN

❖ *This option disadvantages the company who has put time and resources into designing a campaign that promises to be successful. However, the company probably has more resources to tweak the ad than those who are weak and defenseless have from changing a culture that allows or condones bullying action.*

us that the decisions always have to be made in dialogue with others who are affected by the decision. We need to consider the tradeoffs as we assure that each of us has enough incentive to work and to care for ourselves at the same time that all persons have an opportunity to become self-sufficient adults.

CASE STUDY: ACT WITH CARE —

OPTION 1: RUN THE ADVERTISING CAMPAIGN

❖ *This option does not show care for the system as a whole. While the influence on the kids and those watching the ad campaign might be small, we are not contributing to an overall culture where all people are respected and those without strength or power are protected. As the community is holding itself to ever-higher standards of behavior, not running the campaign supports a process of change within the continuity of moving toward socially responsible advertising.*

OPTION 2: DO NOT RUN THE ADVERTISING CAMPAIGN

❖ *This option demonstrates care for the community as a whole. It supports creating a healthy community where all are honored and protected. Again, from small impacts big change comes. By having the courage to assure that the ads protect kids and support them becoming healthy, respectful adults, we are contributing to the creation of the greater good.*

Evaluate from the vantage point of empathy

We next determine which of the remaining options contributes best to an ecology of care, a value that notes that we are all deeply interconnected. As we look at ecology of care, we note that this is perhaps the place where Americans are the weakest. We have been so careful to assure autonomy that we fail to notice that our very institutions become frayed if we don't pay attention to them.

Frederick (see Chapter 3) took the lessons of biology and the emerging study of environmental ecology and applied them to our business organizations. He noted that, while the notion of survival of the fittest is true on the margins of biological systems, within the ecosystems themselves, rich interdependencies allow many different species to survive. Whether one looks at the remora, tiny fishes that clean the backs of dolphins, or plants and insects that are mutually interdependent, we see that no species is radically independent and thus able to survive by itself. Surprisingly, we also notice that those ecosystems that lose their diversity are in fact weaker than those teeming with a variety of life. If one species gains preeminence over the others, the entire system weakens.

A parallel is seen in business life. Our antitrust laws are based on the economic notion that our economy does better when we have a variety of products and choice. However, each person really hopes to be the next Bill Gates and corner a particular market. The lessons of nature play out in the computer world as we track the viruses that attack the Microsoft products while ignoring Apple products: if all of us have the same operating system we are as vulnerable as a forest that only has one kind of tree. Thus, we need to nurture diversity and cooperation within our communities. As we view the problem from the vantage point of empathy, we decide which option (with appropriate procedural modifications, if necessary) best accomplishes the following ecologizing values:

EVERYDAY ETHICS: *Making Wise Choices in a Complex World*

LINKAGE: THOSE CONNECTIONS THAT GIVE LIFE, PROVIDE SHELTER, CREATE SAFETY NETS

"Linkage extends the realization of genetic potentialities … permits an efflorescence of life forms … nurtures collectivities of organic beings … and regularizes and patterns the interactions that life units have with and within their oftentimes threatening environments."[22] Many times, the institutions of our society provide the connections that support life. Institutions such as families, churches, social organizations, professional groups, and even book clubs provide a place where relationships can be nourished. If we are lucky, the institutions in which we work provide us with a support structure where we can grow and mature, learning our craft while we become more effective in our work. Our task then is to assure that we support and strengthen those institutions that nourish us.

DIVERSITY: CREATED BY OPTIONS THAT SUPPORT VARIABILITY AND A DIVERSE LIFE WEB, A DIVERSE CONTEXT[23]

Many of us like to clone ourselves at work. We want to have people around us who think like we do, have the same values, and make us comfortable. However, what we know is that if only one voice is heard, other vantages are lost, and other options are foreclosed. As difficult as listening to other people may be, both the organization itself as well as the individuals within it do better when we have many different cultures and ideas represented.

We also want to do over and over again that which we do well. What diversity teaches, however, is that multiple approaches to the same problem may in fact result in a better solution. The tension is between "sticking to our knitting," as management guru Tom Peters advised, and looking at a variety of ways to accomplish our goals.[24] Many universities are facing this situation as more students want their education delivered in multiple ways. Online education, accelerated classes, and community-based learning are starting to make the old model of a professor in front of a room obsolete. Each method of delivering education has strengths and concerns. None is by definition more legitimate than another.

HOMEOSTATIC SUCCESSION: A PROCESS OF CHANGE THAT OCCURS WITHIN CONTINUITY

How well will the option allow for the ongoing evolution of the community?[25] As we attend to diversity, we also have to attend to change. The most healthy organizations are those that understand the life cycle of a business and a product. As one product is reaching maturity, another is being nurtured and brought online. As one set of senior executives is reaching their peak, another set is being mentored so that leadership continues. Change that is too rapid disorients people and often has disastrous results. No change leads to stagnation. An excellent leader is one who has a vision of change and gradually changes the culture and puts the structures in place to achieve that change.

COMMUNITY: *CREATED BY OPTIONS THAT ARE ABLE TO ACHIEVE THE NECESSARY DEGREE OF INTEGRATION AND COOPERATION TO MAKE LIFE TOLERABLE*[26]

We are social creatures. As we gather around coffee cups and giggle in cubicles, each of us needs to be wanted and included. One strategy used by slave owners to maintain control on the plantations was to forbid their slaves to communicate, fearing that through communication they would be able to strategize for freedom. The enslaved African-Americans learned to build community through their songs and quilt patterns, which often transferred essential information about how to reach the North as well as strategies for emancipation. For example, the innocuous folk song encouraging people to "follow the drinking gourd" was shorthand for following the North star to freedom.[27]

The worst punishment in our jails is isolation. The worst working conditions in our companies and factories are those that result in us becoming automatons and not full human beings who are part of a community. As cheesy as company functions may seem to those who are introverts, the T-shirts and parties provide opportunities for people to play as well as work together. We get a sense of belonging to a community that then enriches our work life.

Evaluate from the vantage point of integration

The vantage point of integration is the place where we make peace with ourselves—our best self and our worst self. Each person has places of fear, anxiety, meanness and perversity. As we become ethically mature, we embrace and befriend what Carl Jung called our "shadow self." Often, our shadow self has the intention to protect us, and if we listen to that voice too closely we wind up in self-sabotage.

BLIND SPOT

Like a blind spot in the side mirror of a car, the ethical blind spots are those places where we can unintentionally act unethically. Because the Relationship Lens favors rationality, from the vantage point of intention, we may focus on process and become so locked into that process that we forget the purpose is to achieve justice and quality. Remembering who the process is intended to serve helps us not become rigid. While this lens calls us to justice, we must remember that often we have multiple ways to find justice.

From the vantage point of empathy, we may find that discerning the appropriate emotional

    EVERYDAY ETHICS: *Making Wise Choices in a Complex World*

response to an event may be difficult. If we don't pay attention, we might ignore the plight—and real emotional distress—of those who are lost in the system. Remembering that people are not just cogs in a machine helps us put a human face next to our processes.

Finally, as we refine the processes over and over, they may become so arcane that no one knows how to navigate them. If the systems are overly complex, they become exclusive where only those in the know are able to benefit from the system. This is a critique that is often leveled at the American tax system: the rules are so hard to follow that only those with access to skilled accountants are able to accurately complete the forms. The goal of achieving justice is lost in the minutiae of the system.

Vices and Risks

The opposite of virtues are vices, which emerge as we take ethical risks and do not diligently work to assure that we are being ethical. From the vantage point of intention, a misuse of reason leads to carelessness of thought. This trait expresses itself in the Relationship Lens as a tendency to be overbearing and authoritarian to get your way. This path leads to the vice associated with this lens, ambitious abuse of power as we do whatever is needed to climb the hierarchy. As Timothy Clark, a leadership consultant, noted, "The ambition to govern one's fellow beings tends to view leadership as the pathway to a glittering world of personal reward. And so under pretense of leading, those of unbridled ambition seek it out and then let us down. Hence, we observe a teeming gallery of venal characters auctioned to the highest bidder."[28]

Another risk that we run as we use this lens is that we will become authoritarian and paternalistic. While we must attend to the institutions, we must avoid embracing the notion that "father knows best." Assuring full participation assists in this process. This balance is difficult because we all want someone to tell us what to do—as long as they also have the responsibility for the outcome. One management trainer describes this shift of accountability as the monkey on our back. When people become paternalistic and take responsibility for directing the actions of others, they have taken on the "monkey." A key responsibility of leadership is placing responsibility and accountability on appropriate shoulders.

Case Study: Act from your integrated core

Option 1: Run the advertising campaign

❖ *This option does not bring the needs and concerns of the least advantaged of the community to the forefront. By clinging to our "right" to run whatever kind of campaign we want, we separate ourselves from the community and convince ourselvesf that those below us really don't deserve the justice that we say is our passion.*

Option 2: Do not run the advertising campaign

❖ *This option brings the needs and concerns of the least advantaged to the forefront. We are not imposing our will on others and have the possibility of discovering that our meaning in life includes not only lots of sales but also contributing to the well-being of the community and the most vulnerable members of that community, our children.*

I once gave an assignment to a class to practice shared decision-making—to give responsibility for a decision to those who were actually affected by the decision. One student, a retired Army sergeant, was absolutely convinced that the process would not work. He was the manager of a company that manufactured seat belt buckles. The company was getting new equipment and had to make a decision about how to rearrange the plant. To humor the instructor, he created a committee and had them meet in his office. It turned out that two of the senior women who were on the assembly line and on the committee commuted together. They kept working at solving the problems both in the car and in the meetings, and then they talked to everyone else in the plant. Thus, when the committee was finished with its work (which did take longer than it would have had he made the decision), the decision was better than the one he fashioned and he already had buy-in from all of the employees. He was (reluctantly) converted.

Another bias to watch for is entrainment, where we all get so caught up in the excitement that we forget to ask the hard questions for fear of squelching enthusiasm. While we all like team players, many a disaster has happened because people didn't believe that they were able to speak up in the face of impending disaster. Another opportunity for entrainment occurs when it is not politically correct to question the party line. Again, as we track the demise of companies at the end of the 20th century, many in the organization believed that they would either be silenced or ostracized if they didn't parrot the party line. Thus, no one was able to effectively push the question of whether the accounting practices of Enron were appropriate. No one effectively questioned whether cutting health care benefits was right. No one challenged million-dollar bonuses for those at the top while those at the bottom were not earning enough to pay rent, let alone care for their families. Avoiding "groupthink" at the same time that one is a good team player requires wisdom and attention.

Also, from the vantage point of empathy, as we become increasingly ambitious, we use groupthink and emotional entrainment to blind others to our raw ambition. Thus, those we serve do not hold us accountable for our excesses. For example, in 2009 the United State had the highest income disparity ever in its history,[29] and those with wealth were still living high and making expensive, esoteric demands on their vendors. As a *Time* food editor noted, those with money have "also turned paying more into a moral cause no right-thinking chef could argue against ... as they have had to increase their budgets to find the obscure variety of beet grown only by Shakers or the cow that has been massaged ...before being slaughtered with love."[30]

Finally, as we over-identify with the group, where our position becomes our identity, we become elitist, believing that we deserve the good things we have rather than noticing where abuse of justice has resulted in us having benefits to which we are not really entitled. Joan Rivers, a comedian, hosts a cable TV program entitled *How'd You Get So Rich?* Rivers notes that everyone interviewed has attributed their wealth to their great work ethic. Peter Fedynsky responds,

EVERYDAY ETHICS: *Making Wise Choices in a Complex World*

"There are no programs, however, called *How'd You Get So Poor?*" Robert Hawkins, a professor at New York University, says that "people in impoverished areas lack some of the fundamental opportunities enjoyed by the rich."[31]

As the traditional middle class increasingly feels the effect of the growing income gap, those at the top need to remember that they are part of a community. As one commentator said when reviewing the salary gaps, "I think $900,000 would be plenty to support a lavish lifestyle for anyone. The bottom line is that socialism gets a bad rap. A spoonful of socialism might be the right medicine for corporate America because the greed thing has got to stop."[32]

HUBRIS

Hubris, excessive pride and arrogance, moves us from unintentional ethical wrongdoing to intentional wrongdoing. Those who act with hubris have a deliberate disregard for the ethical requirements of the community as they work to further their own agenda. For the Relationship Lens, from the vantage point of intention, hubris shows up as exemption from the processes—because of our privileged status, in particular situations we are exempt from the rules based on our privileged position.

Hiding behind the fact that we are not including ourselves, we become separated from our best self and others. As the health care debate rages, some see this hubris playing out with members of Congress and top leadership of organizations who provide for themselves excellent health care benefits while expecting those with much fewer means to bear the brunt of an increasingly expensive health care system. A mark of leadership is where the top echelon of executives has exactly the same health care policy and options as the rest of the employees. If we move out of integrity by not creating systems of justice, we silence the voice of our "best self" and become alienated from others.

From the vantage point of empathy, as we distance ourselves from the emotional pain of others, we believe that we don't have to evaluate the effectiveness of our work or the system as a whole. When others aren't grateful for what we do, we become increasingly resentful of their demands.

Finally, as we become clear that we have "the Truth," we impose our will on others, regardless of their concerns. We become increasingly isolated from others leading to increased paranoia. An MBA student who was part of Joe Nacchio's Qwest leadership team reported to the class that toward the end, Nacchio took to having meetings in the hall to assure that the conversations were not bugged. Employees were expected to sleep with their computers on and rush down to headquarters in the middle of the night if summoned. When the house of cards fell around Nacchio, this student was not surprised. Nacchio's behavior had become more and more erratic and paranoid as the end neared.

Consider the critiques of the lens

Those who are part of the social contract school have often been called utopians, because they envision a world where people get along, seemingly in defiance of human nature. Even those who are sympathetic to the theories of Rawls and others note that we have problems to overcome in order to implement the ideas.

First, we have human nature. As Karen Lebacqz notes, Rawls presumes that we will be able to put aside the human tendency toward envy in order to let some have a bit more so others can share in the wealth. As we look over the sweep of history, the tendency is for people to want just a bit more before they start sharing with others. A short story entitled "Rocking Horse Winner" by D.H. Lawrence chronicles the story of Paul, who rides his rocking horse to the death, betting on races where he is "sure" which horse will win, in order to stop the whispering in the house saying "There must be more money! There must be more money!"[33]

The next barrier becomes institutionalizing the principles, which may lead to a small dose of socialism. The business leaders best known for trying to implement the ideas of Rawls are Ben Cohen and Jerry Greenfield of Ben and Jerry's Homemade Ice Cream Inc. fame. Though Ben and Jerry's is well-known for having a very narrow salary range, where the top employees made no more than 5x the amount of the lowest paid employee, Hanna Rosin notes that even that gesture masked the fact that Cohen and Greenfield were multi-millionaires because of their stock options. With the options, they could afford to have their salary capped at $81,000 per year. As the founders worked to move their social mission into the streets, they had some successes and also some failures.

When an inner-city initiative where recovering addicts made pumpkin pies got swept up in the Ben and Jerry's company, LaSoul Bakery borrowed money to meet the contracts. When the ice cream flavor didn't sell, Ben and Jerry's decreased and then cancelled the orders. The company was left with half a million dollars of debt, contributing to the failure of the company. While some say that "Ben and Jerry are nothing more than New Age scam artists," Rosin notes that maybe Cohen and Greenfield have "scammed themselves. They believe that they haven't sold out … [but] the company is built … on little white lies, mutual delusions that keep everyone happy. In the end, Rosin notes, that the "politics are utterly conventional, if not Wall Street Republican."[34]

Finally, as we imagine taking Rawls's notions into the political sphere, we realize that deep cultural differences create different opportunities for implementing any of Rawls's ideas. Currently, Sweden would be one of the countries that is closest to the ideals of Rawls. Sweden is known for having very generous social benefits and a tolerance for high taxes. The Swedish Social Democratic Party came to power in 1887. Sweden's history does not include a feudal economy,

EVERYDAY ETHICS: *Making Wise Choices in a Complex World*

a history of serfdom, or a history of slavery. Grounded in a rural economy and with a tilt toward socialism birthed during a protracted famine in which by 1930 up to one-quarter of its citizens had emigrated to the United States[35], the citizens of Sweden have a culture that emphasizes taking care of each other.[36]

To support the social programs, currently Sweden has one of the highest tax rates in the world, with national income taxes peaking at 59.15% and a sales tax of 25%.[37] Sweden's population has historically been non-diverse, with issues of multiculturalism occasioned by an increase in migration only surfacing toward the end of the 20th century.[38] Finally, Sweden only pays 1.5% of its GDP on military spending.[39]

In contrast, the citizens of the United States, who have a deep suspicion of anything that smacks of socialism, are willing to have expensive social programs in order to preserve local control and individual choice. During the period of time that Sweden turned to Social Democracy, the United States was grappling with the end of slavery, reconstruction of the South after the Civil War, expansion to the West, and a huge economic growth triggered by the Industrial Revolution. Buoyed by one of the greatest periods of immigration, the political and industrial leaders of the late 19th and early 20th centuries rejected the claims of socialism. Even though the United States had many groups pushing for universal education, increased access to health care, and equal access to wages, the value that prevailed was the notion of the "self-made man," the expectation and belief that hard work and the market economy would be the solutions to inequities in results.

Unlike Sweden, who did not get embroiled in the Cold War, the United States has also taken on the responsibility for maintaining a huge military presence around the world. As we look at the priorities as measured by tax rates and spending, the United States has a top national income tax rate of 35%, an additional 12% for Social Security, and no national sales tax.[40] We then add an average of 10% for state and local taxes, although the actual amount varies greatly by state.[41] Finally, The United States pays 4.1% of its GDP on military spending, which represents 44% of all federal spending. 19.7% of federal spending goes to health care and 11.8% of the budget goes to responses to poverty.[42]

Clearly, the two nations have very different value priorities as reflected in their overall public policy. As we consider the gauntlet thrown by Rawls to protect those who are least advantaged, and as we reflect on the bruising battle for something resembling universal health care in the United States, with a compromise bill passed in 2009 that still is the subject of much criticism, we realize that the task discussed in macroeconomics classes of balancing "guns and butter," military and domestic spending, is far from easy. When we add the claims of the environment and the push toward sustainability to the list of considerations, the conversation becomes complex, indeed. However, thinking about the problem and engaging in thoughtful conversation about how the interests of all citizens and the environment can be met is worth our time and energy. If, however, those of differing viewpoints do not engage in civil discourse to seek sometimes small scale and sometimes larger solutions to the problems, we will end up with an angry stalemate that serves no one.

STEP 4: BE RESPONSIBLE

Rank the options from least preferred to most preferred

Having determined what liberties are essential, we rank the options from least preferred to the most preferred. We begin from the vantage point of intention: Are the basic liberties met, will our children have an inheritance, do we have equality of opportunity, and have we privileged the least advantaged? Then, from the vantage point of empathy: Have we demonstrated care for the members and institutions of the community, particularly in the allocation of resources and power? And, finally, from the vantage point of integration: Will the option contribute to each member of the community knowing that they are part of all that is?

As we rank the options, we summarize why this ranking of options was chosen and demonstrate the primacy given to the core values. First, we must show how we privileged equality—assuring that our processes are fair to reach equality of opportunity, and as much as possible, equality of result. Then, we show how we privileged rationality—as we logically assessed our systems, we carefully attended to both procedural and substantive due process without being overly influenced by emotion or desire.

CASE STUDY: RANK THE OPTIONS

OPTION 2: DO NOT RUN THE ADVERTISING CAMPAIGN

❖ *This option will both protect the least advantaged and support the building of a healthy community. This option also supports building a healthy company as you become known for caring about all of the members of the community, not just yourself. By considering those with no voice, the kids who watch the ads on TV, you are helping them, even in a small way, build a healthy image of self and community.*

OPTION 1: RUN THE ADVERTISING CAMPAIGN

❖ *This option does not meet the tests of the lens. If you run the ad, you will not be supporting those with no power and no voice. The power of advertising to shape a community must be acknowledged. You don't get it both ways. If people pay attention to the ads, which is the point of the campaign, their expectation of how to treat others in the community is also influenced.*

Strive for ethical maturity

The final stage before acting is much like going through a checklist one more time—have we corrected for any unintended bias that might have appeared? For this stage, a final look at the tools for analysis is useful. With the final check, we can make sure that the option we choose is the most ethically mature choice available to us.

From the vantage point of intention, we analyze our own course of action. For the Relationship Lens, we use our skills at finding the best of traditional solutions, op-

EVERYDAY ETHICS: *Making Wise Choices in a Complex World*

tions chosen by others in similar situations. In this way we are able to help ourselves and others become self-actualized as we reach our desired goals.

From the vantage point of empathy, we are able to read the emotional climate of a group and work well with others to discern the best course of action. As we learn to read the emotions of a group, we can assure that those with no voice or little power are represented in the conversation. As we develop our skills, we are able to speak with courage to assure that justice is done.

Finally, we use the vantage point of integration to test our course of action against our personal meaning and purpose of life. As we bring the needs and concerns of the least advantaged of the community to the forefront, champion their cause, and work to assure that they are protected, we find satisfaction.

Act with courage

After we make our choice, we should be able to communicate our decision to others. Creating a short statement that could be placed in a memo to others in the company or a press release helps us learn to articulate our ethical decisions so that we answer the core questions of the Relationship Lens.

BE TRUE TO THE PERSPECTIVE OF THE ETHICAL LENS

Remembering that this vantage point is like looking through a set of binoculars, we seek justice as we look around our own community. As the ethical decision maker, we take a middle position, not knowing who we might be in the situation, and seek a result where we would be willing to be any of the people in the situation. In the process, we are able to fulfill our duties in service to the ideals of a perfectly just community. We act from a passion for basic fairness—assuring that all within the community are treated with dignity and respect. We work to assure that all in the community have enough of the basic goods and services needed to thrive, regardless of their financial position or status.

We are also going to choose the option that will allow people to make choices that contribute to justice now and in the foreseeable future. We know that none of us really cares what choices the other person makes. However, as we support the life choices of others, those of us with autonomy, knowledge, and money will pay attention to those without power to assure they are helped.

FOLLOW CHECKLIST FOR ACTION

As we move to action, using the perspective of the Relationship Lens, we will:

❖ *Remember* to always ask the question: What additional processes and safeguards do we need to assure fundamental fairness for all people, from the executive suite to the mailroom?

❖ *Make sure* that representatives for all of the stakeholders are at the table when making decisions for the well-being of the community. Remember that each voice is important.

❖ *Listen* for clues as to where people perceive that injustice is being done. Pay attention particularly to those who don't have a voice because of lack of power, resources, or position.

❖ *Make sure* that the processes have a purpose and fulfill that purpose. Nothing suppresses justice faster than red-tape bureaucracy that winds up creating more injustice.

Because most of the work in ethics is persuasion, we should be able to articulate clearly what choice we have made and why. After giving a bit of background information to set the stage for the problem, we can frame the statement so that we answer the core questions of this particular lens. How does the process that is used assure that all stakeholders are considered and heard in this decision? How does this decision support my responsibility for assuring that the community and its institutions (schools, health care systems, religious systems, and government) are healthy and effective? How does this decision enhance the achievement of the organization's goals, responsibilities, and values? And finally, how does this decision enhance my relationships with others?

CASE STUDY: STATEMENT OF ACTION

❖ *After consideration, I will not authorize running the ad as presented. I am aware of the subtle power of advertising to shape community expectations about behavior. While the ad may be effective with our target audience, I believe if I pointed out to them the subtle messages around bullying that are in the proposed ad, their support would evaporate. Doing my part to support a civil, safe community for teenagers and youth is more important than the comparatively small amount of resources it will take to rework this ad.*

STEP 5: RETURN TO AWARENESS

Every action has a reaction. That reaction will be both from others and from ourselves. So, after we act and the dust has had a moment to settle, we turn back to determine whether our course of action was in fact wise. What improvements could we make on our process of ethical analysis? Did we like the result? What were the problems with the process? What are the sticking points with the process, where we were not comfortable with the way the decision was unfolding? What were the unintended consequences?

Reflect on results

As we reflect on the results that come from our actions, we can put strategies in place to become ever more ethically mature. Ethical maturity occurs as we move from only thinking of ourselves to noticing how our choices impact others as well as the institutions of our community. As we grow in ethical maturity, we seek solutions that are systemic and will improve life for as many as possible.

From the vantage point of intention, personal growth and maturity is defined as living easily within and working to create a fair and just community. As we become familiar with our own emotions and those of others, from the vantage point of empathy, we will use our emotions responsibly to be able to convince people of a preferred path without resorting to emotional entrainment or blackmail to get our own way. Finally, as our vantage point of integration matures, we will learn to live in a community that is comprised of all people from all times—present, past, and future. As we realize that, we honor the memories of those who have gone before by working to build a community where our children can grow and thrive.

CASE STUDY: REFLECTION

❖ *As I learn more about bullying and the whole question of the decline of civility in our community, the role of advertising in setting acceptable norms in the community is a recurring question. Balancing the cost of developing a new ad campaign against the possibility of being misunderstood is intriguing. However, I feel comfortable making a choice that prioritizes those who are the most vulnerable to being shaped by messages from the community—the children. That having been said, I also want to respect the intelligence and free will of our customers who are probably looking for a little humor. As we move forward, I don't want us to be preachy and want to find ways to encourage civility.*

Seek continuous improvement

The process of continuous improvement involves evaluating the result of the action. As we balance between assuring people have an equal opportunity to achieve their goals and attending to the equality of result, we respect individual rights and goals as people work within the structures of the community. The Relationship Lens requires that we carefully balance between the prerogatives of individuals and the needs of the community.

One trial attorney described the process over time of making sure that settlements for personal injury cases were appropriate. If the settlements were tracked, the pattern would look like a sine wave. When the

SELF-CORRECTING PATTERNS OF SETTLEMENT

SETTLEMENTS TOO HIGH ...
... insurance companies do not settle

SETTLEMENTS TOO LOW ...
... defense attorneys do not settle

insurance companies are too miserly with their offers, attorneys take the cases to trial. If attorneys demand too much, insurers take the cases to trial. Going to trial is always a risk because neither party can predict what a jury will do. However, those cases that are litigated reset the calibration as both the results of the case and the rationale given by juries reflect the values of the community. Those who are in the business also constantly calibrate their antennae, noticing where in the curve the current offers are. In this way, the interests of those who are injured are always balanced against the need to place appropriate blame and the need to shoulder responsibility.

As we are called to balance, we need to make sure that we don't over-identify with a group to the exclusion of an individual. As we realize that none of us, neither individuals nor communities, have a corner on the truth, we can make sure that we attend to the good of the whole without trampling on the needs of the few. A mark of spiritual maturity is moving from following a process for the sake of process while demanding that our own needs are met to joyously serving others while being committed to justice. If we truly serve others, we will put aside our own ambitions and needs for power to make sure that the least advantaged have a possibility of getting the good things of life. In the process, we will find joy in our work and meaning for our lives.

CONCLUSION

The Relationship Lens invites us to consider how to live a life in relationship with others, how to be a person-in-community. The focus for this lens is always fundamental fairness—what is required to thoughtfully balance the needs and prerogatives of the community against the needs and prerogatives of the individual. As we ask that question, we can move beyond technical fairness to genuine fairness, learning when we need to subordinate our own individual rights to that of the group or when the group needs to celebrate the individual idiosyncrasies of a particular person.

One key to this conundrum is noticing what annoys us. Often, if we are not threatened by the individual behavior of a person or celebrate the demands of the group, we have resolved the underlying issues and concerns and can fit into the web of life. However, if someone is very annoying rather than just different, we can see what questions or concerns we have about ourselves and how we belong to this group. When we accept ourselves—both gifts and flaws—we fit easily into different groups and find our own niche in the ongoing web of life.

CONTINUING THE CONVERSATION

1. Using either the third problem in the simulation or another fact pattern, analyze the situation using the Relationship Lens. Was the problem easy to do, indicating that this might by your preferred method of working ethical problems? Was the process difficult, indicating that this may not be your ethical home?

2. Read an editorial in your local paper or a national paper and find examples of justice thinking. In what ways did the author appeal to the fairness of the process assuring notice and voice for those affected? In what ways did the author explore whether the needs of the least advantaged were considered? How did the author balance the needs of the organization and institutions against the needs and desires of individuals?

3. In light of issues raised by this lens, reflect on ways that you attend to imbalance that comes from an inappropriate appropriation of the Relationship Lens, whether concerning abuse of power or hubris in your personal and professional life. How do you know when you are improperly using your personal power? How do you know when your life is not in balance? What strategies do you have to bring your life back into balance?

THE REPUTATION LENS
CONCEPTUAL MAP

Concepts	Intention	Empathy	Integration
Foundational Questions	What is a good character?	What is a healthy, functioning conscience?	How can I be a servant leader?
Theory	Virtue Ethics	Morality of the Heart; Emotional Quotient	Sacred Essence
Representative Authors	Alasdair MacIntyre	Charles Shelton Daniel Goleman	Parker Palmer
Tools and Practices	Personal reflection; community conversation	Empathy; gratitude; self-awareness	Fellowship; intimacy; attention
Key Phrase	"I am virtuous."	"I serve others."	"I am special … just like everyone else."
An ethical act …	… creates a fair system	… cares for people and institutions to assure fair allocation of power and goods	… contributes to each person knowing that they are part of "all that is"
My goal is to …	… cultivate virtues within a tradition	… empathize and integrate my emotion and intellect	… become aware of my sacred identity
I have gifts of …	… personal virtues and principled leadership	… sensitive conscience and emotional maturity	… gentleness, empathy, and a long view of life
My blind spot is …	… unrealistic role expectations	… lack of self-awareness	… over-committing to role and losing self
My vice is …	… hardness of heart	… unreflective action	… refusal to make commitments
I risk …	… becoming self-righteous	… failing to manage my emotions	… becoming engulfed and overwhelmed
Hubris	"I am entitled."	"I know that I'm good."	"I'm special."
My crisis is …	… being misunderstood	… losing my authority	… losing the center of meaning

*I have a dream that my four little
children will one day live in a nation
where they will not be judged by the
color of their skin but by the
content of their character.*

Martin Luther King, Jr [1]

CHAPTER 10

The Reputation Lens

THE FOURTH AND FINAL ETHICAL LENS, the Reputation
Lens, focuses on the virtues that a community believes should
be cultivated by a good person; thus, this lens requires that
we explore the world of character, virtue ethics. An integral branch
of the teleological tradition, with this lens our focus spirals back to
the teachings of Aristotle and St. Thomas Aquinas, who emphasize
the charge to become a person of good character as we live out our role in the community. Those
who write about virtue ethics remind us that becoming a person of good character embraces our
whole life and can become a quest that occupies us until our death.

CORE HEURISTIC QUESTIONS

❖ *What is a good character?*

❖ *What is a healthy, functioning conscience?*

❖ *Who is my neighbor?*

SEEING CLEARLY THROUGH THE REPUTATION LENS

This tradition distinguishes itself by focusing first on moral agents and their lives. The tradition
doesn't dictate specific motives or duties, as seen with Kant, who invites individuals to reflect on
their rights and responsibilities using the Responsibilities Lens. Neither does this lens mirror the
work of Mill and ask individuals to actively pursue their goals for happiness using the Results
Lens. Finally, although virtue ethics has a community focus, the goal is not to determine how to
act in community as seen in Rawls's invitation to fashion a just community using the Relationship Lens. Rather, the Reputation Lens invites us to reflect on how we want to be viewed by
others in the community and what qualities are essential to be a good citizen.

THE VANTAGE POINT OF INTENTION

The core questions direct our attention to what kind of person we want to be, what we want our character to be, and how we want others to see us—in essence, our reputation. This lens compels the ethical decision maker to engage with members of the community to determine what human qualities are important.[2] Clearly, as we determine what virtues we will embrace, certain obligations follow and we will choose specific goals. The question is what process comes first and receives emphasis: examining the character from which the action flows or choosing actions that then determine character.

Virtue ethics, or character ethics as it is often called, focuses on the central qualities that are required for us to fulfill our obligations in the community. Given that we are born into a community and take on certain responsibilities, we naturally strive to develop the virtues that are required by our various roles. The tension in defining ourselves by our roles is to assure that we can meet the requirements of excellence without becoming ultimately defined by our roles rather than by who we are as a person.

This balance is delicate. Who we are is shaped profoundly by the roles we assume. None of us has an unrestrained choice in the matter. Some are limited because of real or perceived constraints or opportunities created by gender or nationality. Our access to resources and opportunities makes a difference. Finally, we are influenced by our own personal dreams, preferences, and choices. At the height of a career, a person who is trained in the law but chooses to teach is different than that person would have been had they chosen a life in the courtroom; the skills and the character requirements for an effective teacher are different than those required by a good litigator. Thus, as we choose roles and modify our actions based on the response of ourselves and others, we attend to our character and our reputation. The Reputation Lens invites us to consider both our own sense of who we are and how we are viewed by others, both as individuals and in our roles, and not judge ourselves only by our accomplishments.

Working from the central concept of ethics as attending to the development of our character, the Reputation Lens requires that we determine for ourselves what kind of a person we want to be and how we want to be seen by others. The conversation centers on how we define ourselves in light of the expectations that the community has for a "good" person. Essential to this process is that we see ourselves as moral and strive to meet the criteria of ethical behavior that is both self-imposed as well as that which is expected by the community. This tradition reflects the essential optimism of the teleological tradition that says that as people are placed in community they will respond to love and acceptance by becoming good people.

EVERYDAY ETHICS: *Making Wise Choices in a Complex World*

THE VANTAGE POINT OF EMPATHY

We also are required to hone our reflective skills to become emotionally mature and flexible. If we are comfortable with our place in the community, we manage ourselves while understanding and empathizing with others. We become moral persons as we develop an internal sense of "ought-ness," which is the result of a life history that incorporates "who we are, who we are becoming, and who we desire to be" in light of the virtues and a healthy conscience.[3] Further, we become moral persons as we develop self-awareness (emotional self-awareness, accurate self-assessment, and self-confidence) as well as self-management (demonstrating emotional self-control and exercise of core virtues, such as transparency, adaptability, and optimism).[4]

As we come full circle in studying all of the primary theories of ethics, one quality is implicit in each of the theories—that we each take personal responsibility for who we are and what we do. If we are ruled by laws, we check to see who is watching over our shoulders and aim for compliance in the letter of the law rather than celebration of the spirit of the rule. As we mature and become grounded in our core beliefs, we learn to do what is right because it is right, not to avoid getting caught or punished. A morally mature person embraces self-regulation and self-efficacy. Self-regulation, choosing to be self-disciplined and directed by a carefully considered internal sense of values, gives us the ability to be guided and motivated to do those things we know need to be done. Self-efficacy, knowing that we have the tools we need to be effective, gives us the confidence that we need to act effectively and make a difference in our world, providing an essential link for the continuity of our community.[5]

THE VANTAGE POINT OF INTEGRATION

In one scene of the popular movie *Romancing the Stone*, a novelist who is trying to rescue her sister is stranded with an expatriate American who is following his dream. He describes his passion, a sailboat. As he goes on about his life in Columbia where he is working by himself to reach his goal, she says to him, "That sounds lonely, Jack T. Colton." As we follow our individual dreams, we find that we are back where we started—in community. In America in particular, with our mobility and our busyness, we may become lonesome because we have not put the time and energy needed into being part of a community, instead striving to do everything ourselves. As we learn to see ourselves as part of the larger whole, realizing that we don't have to do it all and that there is plenty of work for everyone, we can be gentle with ourselves and savor the joy of working with others. While being a free-wheeling individual sounds wonderful, to thrive as a person-in-community, we need to see each other as neighbors and friends: we are indeed our brothers' and our sisters' keepers.

In a business world where we cut our teeth on competitiveness, seeing each other as neighbors may seem farfetched. However, we can have healthy competition at the same time that we recognize that we are profoundly connected and that, at the core, no one is more special than anyone else. With this realization, we can give up our fear of failure and settle into enjoying the work we have been given to do. We can develop healthy relationships and networks as we each follow our heart's desire. In the process, we find our spiritual center, which keeps us in balance when the world goes crazy and helps us maintain the long view, the perspective that keeps us from being overwhelmed by all of the changes of this life.

CHARACTERISTICS OF THE REPUTATION LENS

An act is ethical if it is a virtuous act, consistent with the habitual development of sound character traits including habits of thoughtful reflection, good intentions, and noble human virtues. Using the Reputation Lens, a moral person is one who makes decisions or judgments based on his conscience, an internal sense of "oughtness" about how one should live or what one must do, and one's core beliefs. As we develop a good conscience, we can embrace the qualities of a good character deeply within our person and not just wear the virtues as a mask that can be shed when we believe that others are not watching. Then, rather than being motivated by what others think of us, we can be motivated by our core beliefs—notions or ideas that are held with affection and result in passion or action. These commitments define us and have the potential to energize and transform both us and our community.[6]

By focusing on the core commitments of our life, we can make choices about what path we want to follow rather than be swayed by those around us. Asking ourselves what is important and what we would be willing to go out on a limb to pursue is essential. While zealots may make us uncomfortable, if we don't have any commitments that inspire us to action, we miss an opportunity to leave our footprint on the sands of time. The spiritual balance is found by asking, "Who is my neighbor?"

Once we have attended to the core question of identity, the Reputation Lens invites us to consider those with whom we share this glorious planet. Many religious teachings emphasize that all human beings are our neighbors. Thus, as we attend to our own identities and lives, we have some responsibility to those persons. Those from the humanist traditions recognize that each person is worthy of respect and inclusion in the community. In the process of meeting those in our neighborhood, we discover that we are special—just like everyone else. All people have relationships that are important to them and want to make a difference in their world. As we see the sacred essence of each person, we can learn to live with gentleness towards ourselves and others as we walk our personal path.

QUESTIONS FOR DETERMINING RIGHT ACTION

❖ *Essential qualities:* What are the qualities that a good human being should have?

❖ *Core virtues:* What respected human virtues (e.g., temperance, humility, industry, resolution, and sincerity) are demonstrated by this decision?[7]

❖ *Role requirements:* How does this decision demonstrate the virtues of a person who is respected in this role (e.g., competence, loyalty, diligence, and fairness)?

❖ *Professional virtues:* How does this decision demonstrate the qualities of a person in this profession (e.g., commitment to public service, self-regulation, trust, and integrity)?

SECONDARY VALUES SEEN THROUGH THE PRISM OF THIS LENS

❖ *Integrity:* A person should develop habits of truthfulness.

❖ *Justice:* A person should seek to do that which will promote the fair treatment of people in terms of compensation for work done or contribution to the community. A just person also assures that the resources of the group, both opportunities and assets, are distributed fairly.

❖ *Courage:* A person should embrace the opportunity to demonstrate the highest qualities of the individual or profession even if others choose another path.

❖ *Civility:* A person should always behave in a way that respects the inherent dignity of people and encourages their development as persons.

USING THE REPUTATION LENS

While many contemporary philosophers write about virtue ethics, Alasdair MacIntyre is a paradigmatic philosopher in this tradition. In *After Virtue*, MacIntyre describes the history of this ethical tradition and provides a contemporary process that guides the discssion to help us determine what qualities count for being a virtuous person. Evaluating an ethical option using MacIntyre's process involves dialogue between the person making the ethical decision and the community.

SNAPSHOT: AN ACTION IS ETHICAL IF IT

❖ *Is consistent with a good character for the particular role*

❖ *Is made with an awareness of the interplay of mind and emotions*

❖ *Supports and enhances the meaning you have given to your life*

MacIntyre considers the problem of ethical relativism in his review of both the deontological and the teleological traditions. He asserts that ethical relativism can be avoided as the community embraces the core values of humanity—integrity, justice, and courage—fostering the development of sound character in individuals. When, toward the middle of the 20th century, philosophers began to quietly admit that the Enlightenment project, a belief that reason and science could find the certain foundations for truth, appeared to have failed (a claim with which many perceptive scientists agree), it seemed that no criteria for ethical action could be established. MacIntyre claims that as we embrace our roles and seek to become people of virtue, we can find our ethical bearings. This action is not done in isolation; none of us gets to decide on our own the shape of our role in the community or the exercise of the virtues. Rather, the community itself shapes our understanding of the expectations that accompany our roles. We each determine how best we should live, not in isolation but in conversation and dialogue within the community.

MacIntyre also states that those who are part of a particular practice are responsible for maintaining the integrity of the work. Because MacIntyre sees institutions as potentially corrupting, those of us in a particular profession must work together to assure that the virtues are embodied and celebrated in our political and economic life. The integrity of any particular profession depends on individuals to maintain and demand excellence rather than succumbing to the subtle pressures of expedience. Thus, a primary value of the Reputation Lens is that it militates against any of us basing decisions solely on the bottom line, doing whatever is required to reach the goals that are desired.[8] Rather, as we seek the goals of life, we are invited to consider what a good person in our role would do and seek excellence rather than mere expedience.

As we make our choices, each of us will be asked from time to time to explain why a particular option was chosen and why others were not. To demonstrate how to accomplish this task with integrity, the same problem and overall template will be used as with the other ethical lenses, but the ethical content will come from MacIntyre and others in the virtue ethics tradition. The reason for the repetition of process is the belief that as we practice, our skill increases and the process of analysis becomes easier. As we look at problems from different angles, we will learn to balance between what we believe are the marks of a good person and the expectations of the community while honoring our own personality. As we "exercise our conscience" and strive to be the best that we can be, our reputation for excellence will be enhanced.[9] However, even when we believe that our character is sterling and our reputation is stellar, the process assists us in correcting for personal bias and self-delusion.

STEP 1: BE ATTENTIVE

During the first step of the decision model, we pay attention to what is going on. This step is more difficult than we think. We have to pay attention to what our mind is observing, what we are seeing, and what we don't want to see. We also have to listen to our emotions. If we are not careful, our emotions can get hijacked and we wind up inappropriately reacting to a situation.

Attend to the context

MacIntyre asserts that three conversations inform the context of an ethical decision. The first is the practice in which we engage. That concept will be developed later. The second is what MacIntyre calls the "narrative order of a single human life."[10] One of the gifts of feminist and postmodern scholarship is the notion that each of us has the ability to construct for ourselves a life based on the stories that we tell about ourselves. Mary Catherine Bateson opened the door to the conversation in *Composing a Life* by noticing that each of us not only has different seasons of our lives but also defines who we are by the way we talk about our life.[11] To see what is important, listen to the strands of conversation when you tell people about yourself. Are you strong or pig-headed? Are you deliberate or slow? Are you a leader or a team builder? As we begin to look at an ethical problem, we must attend to our own narrative as an ethical decision maker as well as the narrative of the people and companies with whom we are working.

Listening to the stories, the narratives, people tell about themselves is fascinating. One person may come from a family of strong-minded women—just ask. This family believes that being fiercely independent, economically independent, and a bit "uppity" are marks of strong women. Thus, she may highlight in her narrative those times when she went against convention, was able to move with ease in a "man's world," and took care of herself. Another person may come from a family that values civic service and see himself as "pulling himself up by the bootstraps." He may spin a story about how he walks in the steps of the men in his family who toughed it out on the prairie, were "pillars of the community" as they served on school boards, and were successful in business. Reflecting on the stories of both one's family as well as those of the community is a useful exercise.

Seeing which story lines have been incorporated into one's script for life can help us sort through core values and commitments as well as the subtle and not-so-subtle messages about what is expected of us in the roles we embrace. *Secretariat*, a movie about Penny Chenery, who managed the family stables and shepherded the training of Secretariat, the Triple Crown Winner in 1973, has a scene where the owner of Sham, the closest contender, makes a crack about Chenery being a "housewife" and thus out of her league. While Chenery was married with four children, she also graduated from Smith and was one semester short of an MBA from Columbia University. And therein was the tension. That last semester was the showdown from the predominant social message for women immediately following WWII.

In the words of Kate Tweedy, Chenery's daughter, "no matter how smart and capable they [women] were, no matter what they did during the war, the only acceptable role for them now was to be a wife and mother." [12] Like many women of her generation, pursuing the narrative of becoming a successful businesswoman meant that she was not able to continue the narrative of being a successful wife. During the mid-point of the 20th century, the virtues of each role and expected behaviors were too incongruent to allow one person to maintain both.

Organizations also have a narrative, a story about the characteristics and virtues that are important to them and the values that they hold dear. Often, the personality of the founder forms the central story of the organization. One example is seen in the book *Pour Your Heart into It* by Howard Shultz, founder and CEO of Starbucks. [13] The chapters lay out his corporate philosophy. One telling story underscores why the company provides health care for all employees who work 10 hours a week or more. Shultz remembers when his father was injured on the job, had no health care, and the family almost didn't make it. Shultz vowed that if he got the opportunity, no one who worked for him would ever be in that situation. This story is often part of the narrative told at employee orientation as one joins the "Starbucks family."

MacIntyre states that the third conversation involves identifying and steeping ourselves in the moral tradition that shapes our life. As we examine the four central ethical lenses that inform both our personal and business ethics, we note that each of the ethical lenses comes from a moral tradition that purports to assist us in knowing what action is the right action. The lenses focus several thousand years of conversation as people consider the nature of human persons, the goals for the community, and how we should best live in community. Each lens has A) content, certain kinds of beliefs that define them, B) a set of practices that help us understand them, and C) people in the community who support us as we learn how to be better ethical decision makers. [14]

While the ethical lenses give us a chance to view different ways of looking at problems, if we are not careful, exploring the different traditions becomes an excuse not to grow. To become mature ethical people, we need to find a community that can support us in our growth as we go deep into the practices of that group. Traditionally, churches, mosques, synagogues, and ashrams have provided the structure and support for use to mature as we learn to balance the gifts of the four ethical lenses. Currently, others find that support groups and seminars provide the structure needed to explore their strengths and weaknesses. Additionally, our workplaces and relationships provide a proving ground for our lessons and show us where we've grown and where we need to focus next.

Thus, if the quest for justice is one of our core commitments, we may choose to be formed by traditions that are informed by teachings on economic and social justice. If we find a particular religious tradition meaningful, we will immerse ourselves in those thoughts and practices as we learn to be a good person. While no one path is the only way to find truth and achieve ethical adulthood, people who seek to grow in moral maturity often find that they need to go deep into one tradition and have their hearts and minds transformed in the crucible of a particular set of beliefs and practices while being sensitive to the perspectives and requirements of other traditions.

Identify the decision maker

For the Reputation Lens, the role of the decision maker determines the virtues and values that take priority. As we choose to act, we ask what qualities we expect a person in this role to demonstrate. As we return to our CEO in our problem about the marketing campaign, the focus shifts slightly. The CEO, the decision maker, must first identify his role in the problem at hand. This ethical tradition asserts that each of us is defined by our role.

CASE STUDY: ETHICAL AGENT

❖ *As the CEO of the company, I have to sign off on the ad campaign proposed by Vice President of Sales and Marketing. As I make this decision, I want my actions to demonstrate a leader with a good character. I want to have a conscience that is at ease. Finally, I want to make sure to ask, "Who is my neighbor?" and consider their values as I choose a path forward.*

The legal profession illustrates this concept well. In a criminal case, three attorneys are involved: the prosecutor, the defense attorney, and the judge. Each of them brings forward different virtues based on their role. The prosecuting attorney must zealously present his case to the court. The defense attorney must assure that the presumption that the defendant is innocent until proven guilty is maintained throughout the trial, by assuring that all evidence that would point to the defendant not being guilty is brought forward. The judge must evenhandedly assure that the rules of the courtroom are followed and the law is fairly applied. The judge (and, by extension, members of the jury) cannot go on a quest to find evidence: that is the role of the prosecution and defense. Each player in the drama has a role that is clearly defined by the practice of law.

Every profession has similar role constraints and expectations. Thus, as an ethical decision maker assumes responsibility for deciding a course of action, the decision maker must determine what core ethical values should be brought forward in light of the core virtues that should be cultivated by persons-in-community in that particular role. One of the key questions each of us must confront is what kind of a person we are: what exactly *is* our character and our reputation in the community? Because none of us likes to think ill of ourselves, learning to seek and hear the unvarnished truth can be difficult—but enlightening. The truth may even save a career.

Pinpoint the ethical issue

What is the central problem to be resolved? As we shape the issue into a question, we need to focus on the conflicting role expectations of the players in this situation. As stated above, the Reputation Lens encourages us to examine what a good person, a person of high virtue, would do in a particular role.

STEP 2: BE INTELLIGENT

As we move into the second step, we are going to do our first round of critical analysis. For this segment, we are going to sort through the data and begin honing in on the problem itself.

Determine the stakeholders

As the conversation evolves between us, the ethical decision maker, and the stakeholders who are impacted by our decision, we will also need to consider what our stakeholders expect of a virtuous ethical decision maker in this situation. Thus, as we list the stakeholders, we need to include a description of the competencies that the stakeholders expect the *ethical decision maker* to bring to the table. In framing this conversation, we must remember that the stakeholders don't always expect to be happy but they do expect the agent to act within the constraints of the role. Thus, if a good teacher is fair and impartial, a student will understand and accept getting a low grade for a paper that is inferior in quality.

CASE STUDY: STAKEHOLDERS

❖ *Me. the CEO of the Company, who is the decision-maker*

❖ *The VP of Sales and Marketing responsible for creating and implementing the ad campaign*

❖ *Shareholders of the Company, whose stock value depends on the financial success of the company*

❖ *Employees of the Company, who depend on a fiscally sound company for employment*

❖ *Customers who like your product and might increase use because of campaign*

❖ *Kids who are bullied because your company appears to advocate bad behavior*

❖ *Members of the community who may critique the ad campaign and your company because it contributes to bullying*

Explore the values in tension

Virtue ethics highlights three arenas of difficulty. The first is a conflict in expectations of the role itself. Different people may have different expectations for a person in this role and thus we must clarify what exactly a person in this role *should* do. The second is a conflict between excellence and expedience: we are often called to do that which is expedient, that which will get a result quickly or with the greatest return, even if the virtues of the ethical decision maker or the organization are compromised. The Reputation Lens calls us to focus on excellence. The third problem that may arise is a conflict between the role expectations and our vision of our self as a good person, or a good member of the larger community. Virtue theorists remind us that at the end of the day, who we are as a total person is what matters.

As Harry Potter grows up during the seven volume series chronicling life at Hogwarts and an archetypal battle between good and evil, the initial choice of direction is made as Potter is placed in Gryffindor instead of Slytherin. Each of the Houses has a set of virtues associated with it, virtues that match with the core values of the students at Hogwarts. Thus, the placement gives the new students clues about expected behavior. In each volume of the series, Potter has to choose between expedience and excellence, with each test becoming more and more difficult and ethically complex. The final choice is whether Harry is willing to die for the good of the community. As Michael Austin comments about the paradox, "those who, like Voldemort, put self above all else end up worse off than those who often put the common good above the self. The best life is the moral life."[15]

Identify options for action

Again, we must act, even in the face of difficulty and lack of clarity about the outcome. In framing options with this lens, the focus will be on the role expectations for the ethical decision maker. While our framing of the options should not include value language, being attentive to the vantage point with which the ethical lens will examine the problem helps. The ethically mature option in this ethical lens will focus on the balancing of individual virtue and serving the common good, where sacrifices are made for the good of all.

Case Study: Options for action

1: *RUN the advertising campaign that is certain to boost sales but could be advocating bullying behavior.*

2: *DO NOT RUN the advertising campaign that is certain to boost sales but could be advocating bullying behavior.*

STEP 3: BE REASONABLE

For this section of the decision process, the questions that are asked are specific to the lens. The point of this section is to show how people who favor this particular approach to decision making would answer the problem. Because each ethical lens prioritizes different values, the questions asked to determine the best course of action are different.

Hone critical thinking skills

MacIntyre gives an elegant process for determining the characteristics that mark an ethical person. He begins by defining a *practice* as

> any *coherent and complex form* of socially established cooperative human activity through which *goods internal* to that form of activity are realized in the course of trying to achieve those *standards of excellence* that are appropriate to, and partially definitive of, that form of activity, with the result that *human powers to achieve excellence*, and human conceptions of the ends and goods involved, are systematically extended. (Emphasis added)[16]

The first seminal concept is that a practice is a coherent and complex activity. To illustrate, MacIntyre distinguishes between tic-tac-toe, which is easy to learn and has little strategy, and chess, which is strategically complex and has many rules. An individual event—playing a game of tic-tac-toe—is not a practice. However, the discipline of learning how to be a skilled chess player and embracing the qualities of a chess grandmaster would be a practice. So, we need to distinguish between doing something sporadically and plunging into the practice to learn the rules and master the skills that mark true mastery.

As each of us looks at our own profession, we must seek the macro-definition, the big picture of who we are and what we do. Each one of us fails at times as we strive to do better. Because our practices are complex, we can always improve. Thus, we never really completely master a practice; we just continue to get better as we intentionally hone the skills that are the hallmarks of the practice. Rather than getting caught in the micro-minutiae of daily living, we learn to always keep our eye on the ultimate goal, a life that has meaning and purpose and is lived out within the context of our roles.

The second integral characteristic is that a practice is socially established and cooperative. All theorists in this tradition emphasize that we alone cannot determine the qualities that mark a good person in a particular role. Rather, our practice is continually nuanced in the lived conversation among members of the community. An interesting observation is that we may have a practice that is exercised in the privacy of our home but is still socially established.

For example, one who loves blues piano learns to play music in a particular way with certain rhythms and the distinctive walking bass that marks the movement of the piece. That person may never presume to play outside of the confines of his own music room but his playing is still being shaped by the masters of the practice, pianists who define the essence of what it is to be a blues pianist. A corollary is that sometimes we either are not good enough or others don't value our

EVERYDAY ETHICS: *Making Wise Choices in a Complex World*

practice enough to pay us to do it. Thus, restaurants are classically staffed by starving artists who are honing their disciplines while supporting themselves by serving others.

We also have multiple practices—parent, child, employee, citizen. We are called to consider what to do when the requirements of one practice conflict with the requirements of another. A perennial problem for many of us is balancing the demands of our work against the demands of our families. Thus, a pressing question for many young parents is when they should cut back on professional demands in order to attend to the needs of their children. Negotiating the boundaries and balance between professional and family responsibilities involves both the parents of the children as well as employers. Conversations such as availability of flex-time and day care begin to help us sort through the tangles of this issue.

The definition of our practices is refined through dialogue and experience. As we listen to the wisdom and stories of others, the expectations that we and others have about the obligations and characteristics of our practice become more clear. As the needs of a discipline change, the role expectations are also modified. Thirty years ago, managers were expected to be in charge and direct the life of the company. Currently, managers are seen as facilitators of a team, accountable to the whole company and individually responsible for carrying out their part of the organization's mission. Continually attending to how the practice is evolving helps us remain fresh in our work and current in our skills.

From time to time, we find that we cannot live within the constraints expected of us in a particular role. We have to ask two separate questions as we chafe against the stated role requirements. The first is whether we are fundamentally unsuited for the expectations of the role. Those who hate conflict will not make good supervisors. Those who hate pressure should not seek out jobs on Wall Street. Those who cannot manage deadlines should not get a job as a reporter for a newspaper. As we learn to know ourselves, our talents, and our limits, we can find roles that enable us to flourish and thrive rather than thwart us in our work.

The second question considers whether the role constraints themselves are inappropriate. If the role does not allow for all who are qualified to engage in that practice to be welcomed, we must be willing to challenge the parameters of the role. The long line of litigation in order to assure not only access to a practice (such as women and minorities demanding to be able to go to professional school) as well as equality within the practice (such as lawsuits for equal pay or equal opportunity for promotion) reminds us that pioneers of courage have challenged traditional boundaries in order to allow entry into varied practices to those who have historically been denied access.

Sometimes the role requires that we go against our core ethical commitments. This situation is perhaps the most difficult for each of us as we struggle to clarify whether the role requirements are in fact appropriate: should we fight to change the practice or leave it altogether. For example, being a soldier may require killing another person. Those who are fundamentally opposed to killing have the opportunity to become conscientious objectors and fulfill their obligation to the community through other forms of service. Those who are absolutely committed to financial transparency may bristle at a rule that says that salaries of all employees should not be shared across an organization. We must remember that even rebellion is a conversation with a community.

Many people who find themselves doing unethical things often justify their actions by saying "I'm just doing my job." In these situations, we may be like a frog placed in cold water that boils to death as the water is slowly heated rather than jumping out as it would have had it been placed in hot water. One management theorist states that each of us needs to write our own ethics exit card. What he means is that we need to know our core values so that when we are asked to go against those commitments we decline and leave. His assertion is that if we don't know our own personal bottom line—what we absolutely will not do under any circumstance—we are in fact unethical because we have no guiding principles or values by which to live.

Evaluate from the vantage point of intention

When the meaning of MacIntyre's complex sentence that defines a practice is examined, we see a set of basic steps that help us to determine proper ethical action. The conversation always begins with the ethical decision maker, who determines the contemporary shape of the practice that has been historically given.

DETERMINE COMPONENTS OF THE PRACTICE, AS DEFINED BY THE ETHICAL DECISION MAKER

MacIntyre invites us to determine the core competencies of the practice in light of four elements: 1) the standards of excellence, 2) rules, 3) internal goods, and 4) external goods that define and partially constitute the practice.

Many ethicists assert that our primary ethical obligation is to be competent—to meet the threshold requirements of our work. Thus, the criteria developed by MacIntyre can help us determine competence in our practice. We come into roles that have been previously established and designed by the community. We then add our own proficiencies, expertise, and vision. Thus, in conversation and community, the ethical decision maker and stakeholders continue to shape the practice and move it toward excellence.

CASE STUDY: INITIAL STEP

❖ *Work the process in two parts. First, eliminate the options which do not meet the threshold competencies. Then prioritize the remaining options based on the virtues and desired unity of life.*

Standards of excellence: What are the standards of excellence that mark the practice of the ethical decision maker?

To learn the standards of excellence in our chosen practice, we begin by looking to other practitioners in the field to see the benchmarks. MacIntyre encourages us to look at two faces of excellence, that of the finished product and that of the performance or skill needed to create that product. The conversation about the quality of a product can be related to the current trend to identify best practices and standards in our field and engage in continuous quality improvement.

As we adopt these strategies of improvement, we are part of a conversation for excellence. For example, the bar has been raised for professional presentations by the emergence of technology and PowerPoint™ presentations. Through graphics, presentations can be much clearer than those that are just spoken or rely on earlier forms of technology, such as an overhead projector. If we choose not to use the technology, our oral presentation must be even more compelling than is ordinarily required so that we can meet the new community standards.

Case Study: Standards of Excellence

❖ *In the context of the marketing campaign, I am committed to assuring that the products sold are safe and that they are of the quality advertised. I also havw an obligation to lead the company so that it makes a fair profit on the goods sold, a task that requires both getting the product effectively to market as well as thoughtfully managing the expenses of the organization.*

Excellence of performance can be seen in the quality of research, the care with which a presentation is constructed. We want to avoid having a beautiful, technology-enhanced presentation that has no content. Skilled presenters know that they must have a great deal more background information than they can ever present. A test of excellence is how many questions can be fielded before the expert gets to the end of his knowledge.

As noted, the perennial task is the quest to be as good as we can be. As MacIntyre explored the parameters of virtue, he sharply distinguished between excellence, which is the hallmark of a master, and expedience, which may involve cutting corners and may result in shoddy work. One set of distinctions was presented in Chapter 8. Another more nuanced version is below.[17]

If we reduce utilitarianism to a cost-benefit analysis rather than retaining the richness of ideal goals as envisioned by Mill, we find ourselves in the trap of expedience. The temptation to slide into expedience is very strong when companies are judged on short-term results rather than long-term returns. However, the quest for excellence cannot be achieved if one has a knee-jerk reaction and changes course based on the vicissitudes of the stock market. By constantly attending to the tension between expedience and excellence, we can discern when we need to relax the quality of our work just a tad to get a product out because we can never achieve perfection and when we need to be ruthless in our attention to detail.

- *Excellence* is judged in terms of standards established within and for some specific form of systematic activity and is best thought of in terms of role in community. *Expedience* is judged in terms of the acquisition of riches, power, status, and prestige—goods that can be and are objects of desire by human beings before they consider excellence and independent of any desire to excel.

- *Excellence* inherently strives for progress in achieving those qualities that mark excellence and also for progress in identifying our ideas and recognition of the highest perfection. *Expedience* inherently strives to identify those means that will be effective in securing goods and becoming effective in using the means to secure those goods.

- *Excellence* defines justice in terms of merit and what we deserve, using the same standards for all. *Expedience* defines justice in terms of reciprocity and effective cooperation with the other person.

- *Excellence* recognizes that someone who breaks rules generally hurts himself. *Expedience* believes that someone who breaks rules generally hurts other people.

- *Excellence* is a virtue that is definable independent of and before the establishment of enforceable rules of justice. *Expedience* is a virtue that is defined as following the rules of justice until the rules change and thus has no independent ethical content.

- *Excellence* has as a reason for acting, the goal of achieving excellence and being subject to the virtue of justice. *Expedience* finds the reason for acting to maximize the satisfaction of its own wants and needs.

RULES OF PRACTICE: WHAT ARE THE RULES THAT WE MUST FOLLOW?

The first category of rules is those that define the practice. For example, one who plays jazz uses a certain set of scales and rhythms that are different from those of Mozart's concertos. The second category of rules limits the practice such as codes of ethics, professional codes, or laws. Sometimes we want to challenge the professional codes or the law because they are (arguably) unjust. If the preferred option requires civil disobedience, going against these rules, we need to be willing to count the cost and assure that we are responding to a higher or more complete understanding of ethical behavior rather than just rebelling or demanding our own way. Often what poses as civil disobedience is just a person trying to play the edge and not get caught.

EVERYDAY ETHICS: *Making Wise Choices in a Complex World*

Every practice has inherent rules as well as explicit rules. Building on the example of public speaking, a good presentation has a coherent outline, congruent examples to illustrate the points, and good supporting data. As people learn the rules of the practice of public speaking, they master skills such as pacing, voice quality, and organization. A presentation may also be subject to external rules—length of time, appropriate content, depth of research. Those who choose to flout the external rules often have to be very, very good in order to get past the expectations of the audience and the gatekeepers of the practice. Anyone who has ever tried to change the way a practice "has always been done" knows that innovation is simultaneously encouraged and discouraged. On one hand, people say that they like innovation in order to keep a practice fresh and people engaged in the work. On the other hand, meeting the requirements of the practice means that one must be sensitive to the historical character and requirements of the practice. Walking the tightrope of remaining true to the practice while bringing in fresh ideas is difficult.

INTERNAL GOODS: WHAT ARRAY OF INTERNAL GOODS—SATISFACTION, FEELING OF A JOB WELL DONE, ABILITY TO MAKE A DIFFERENCE—IS IMPORTANT TO US IN THIS SITUATION?

A person who is not skilled at public speaking but who actually gets through the presentation will feel very good about the accomplishment, regardless of the opinion of others. We each have areas where we are stretching to become better as we perfect our practice. One of the core questions we must ask as we seek to improve at a practice is whether we are committed enough to achieving excellence to be marked as a master in a field or whether we will be content to be a journeyman or even a novice. For many, being "good enough" is sufficient as they work for mastery of a set of skills. The excitement of the young athletes who participate in the Special Olympics makes us realize that transcending personal limits is often as satisfying as being recognized as the very best in a given arena for the proverbial fifteen minutes of fame.

Much personal satisfaction comes with noticing where we are on the leading edge of our own practice as we define our

CASE STUDY: RULES OF PRACTICE

❖ As to the customers, the products must be as advertised, safe within the guidelines of the Food and Drug Administration (FDA), and fairly priced for the value given.

❖ As to the company, the sales campaign must be as effective as possible to generate the largest feasible portion of market share.

CASE STUDY: INTERNAL GOODS

❖ The leadership team is in this business to develop and sell products that they believe will genuinely benefit others, whether through enhanced physical abilities (as with this product) or even to increase someone's quality of life through humor or health.

❖ The leadership team also wants to provide employment for those who work for the company and to treat them fairly.

❖ Finally, business is a game. As CEO, I want to demonstrate and improve my skills of growing a company within the constraints of the market and the rules of the game.

personal trajectory of excellence. Thus, being able to confront our fear and make a set of cold calls to launch a career in sales may seem to a veteran marketer like a baby step, where for a new person the achievement is monumental. Our mentors and coaches can help us see where we need to fine tune our work to become even better at what we do.

EXTERNAL GOODS: WHAT ARE THE EXTERNAL GOODS—TITLE, PRESTIGE, FINANCIAL REWARDS—THAT ARE IMPORTANT AND NEED TO BE SOUGHT AND PROTECTED?

Those who excel at a practice are in demand. Those who are very good in highly valued practices can command a high salary and get status. In the process of choosing that practice to pursue, each of us has to carefully critique our own talents and abilities to determine what will bring sufficient external goods so that we can support ourselves and meet our own ego needs. Again, we may engage in practices that we thoroughly enjoy that do not have enough value in the community to provide us with an appropriate standard of living. For example, we may need to carefully explore whether our need for security is too high to make us willing to risk all in order to possibly become a very successful entrepreneur. We may need to acknowledge when our need for status through title or education is important enough to make us forego other opportunities as we seek our certifications and diplomas. As we each make these decisions, we have to know ourselves very well.

CASE STUDY: EXTERNAL GOODS

❖ *I am responsible for making the financial numbers as approved by the Board of Directors, both in terms of product sold and management of expenses.*

❖ *The leadership team wants a company that has brand recognition so that the products are desired and thus purchased.*

One effective manager stated that he was able to foster excellence in his employees by giving them the external rewards that they wanted rather than trying to give everyone the same thing. A young father valued salary more than perks, so he received bonuses for his work. A widow valued traveling more than money, so the manager rewarded her work by sending her to every conference and appropriate training so she could see the United States. Another person wanted to move ahead in his profession, so he was allowed to do *pro bono* work for local charities in order to strengthen his professional networks and raise his profile in the local community. Attending to the internal and external goods that are important to employees can contribute to an excellent organization.

People always ask whether excellence can be taught. Experience seems to indicate that one who has a modicum of talent can become a good "B+" practitioner but may not be able to bridge the gap to become a good "A" practitioner. Those who through innate talent are good "A" practitioners, with practice and work, can become an "A+." Clearly, we all have different talents and gifts that we can honor and hone. At the same time, we need to recognize the bittersweet truth that by choosing to pursue excellence in one practice we may need to forgo excellence in others for which we have equal aptitude. Many of us are confronted with the challenge of the proverb "be not a Jack-of-all-trades, but a master of one."

COMMUNITY EXPECTATIONS: *WHAT DOES EACH MEMBER OF THE COMMUNITY CONSIDER TO BE THE COMPETENCIES OF THE ETHICAL DECISION MAKER?*

For this step, we join in conversation with others to ascertain whether our determination of the core competencies match those held by other members of the community, particularly those who are acknowledged as masters in the field. To complete this phase, we consider the expectations that each constituent has for a competent ethical decision maker. In determining what makes a good person in this role, we need to not focus on what makes us happy but what kind of person we want to become. A good teacher is fair yet demanding, stretching the minds of students. Sometimes students say that they would be happier in a class that is not hard. However, often those teachers who give easy classes are also not seen as good in their profession—either by their students or their peers.

As we consider the concerns of the stakeholders, we need to remember that they don't get to veto the option. The goal is to assure that the competencies as we have defined them and the considered opinions of the stakeholders are met. This is where a conversation about the requirements of the practice might help. As we talk with others to define excellence in a role, we begin by meeting current professional expectations. Perhaps with time we can participate in raising the bar, both as we sharpen our own sense of excellence as well as clarify the expectations others have for people in this role.

Often, we have vague ideas about what a good professional is but don't really know how to evaluate them or sort through our own conflicting desires. A skilled decision maker will listen to what the stakeholders want, modify the practice where appropriate, and educate the stakeholders in the

CASE STUDY: STAKEHOLDERS

❖ *Me, the CEO of the Company, who is the decision-maker*

❖ *The VP of Sales and Marketing, responsible for creating and implementing the ad campaign, expects to be supported by the CEO so he is able to effectively do his job and sell the product.*

❖ *Shareholders of the Company, whose stock value depends on the financial success of the company, expect that the CEO will meet the legal requirements of running a company and do what is required to responsibly manage the top line (expenses) and bottom line (profits for the company).*

❖ *Employees of the Company, who depend on a fiscally sound company for employment, expect that the CEO will manage the company effectively to minimize their anxiety about job security.*

❖ *Customers expect that the product will be as advertised and give the results promised.*

❖ *Kids who are bullied because your company appears to advocate bad behavior, if they thought about it, would want you to not advocate behavior that might cause them more grief.*

❖ *Members of the community, who are not aware of bullying and who watch the commercials, want a commercial that is engaging and amusing.*

trade-offs and requirements of the practice where needed. At this point, we make a preliminary determination as to the proper ethical action. As we review our choices, we evaluate the options against our own stated competencies and standards. If the option does not meet our own threshold expectations of competency, then the option is not ethical. Only options that meet the core requirements of the practice are considered in the next three steps. Thus, if an option does not meet the threshold requirement of demonstrating competency in the field as determined by the individual practitioner, others in the field, and the key stakeholders, the option is, by definition, unethical.

Evaluate each option that meets the requirements of the competencies against the core virtues: integrity, courage, justice, and civility. Include a working definition of the content of those virtues so that points of agreement and disagreement can be determined.

Once an act meets the requirements of the core competencies, it is judged against the virtues. MacIntyre chooses the core virtues of courage, honesty, and justice. However, he does not claim that his list is exhaustive, and so I have added the virtue of civility as instances of workplace bullying and uncivil discourse have escalated in the past two decades. As he defines a virtue, MacIntyre is very clear that pursuit of the virtues is essential for the good life. Thus, a key critique of our culture is that we have abandoned the quest for virtue and thus find the good life illusory.

A virtue is an acquired human quality, the possession and exercise of which tends to enable us to achieve those goods that are internal to practices and the lack of which effectively prevents us from achieving any such goods.[18] According to MacIntyre, while we may receive all of the external goods of a practice, unless we attend to the virtues, we will not have any of the internal goods such as satisfaction, joy, and peace in our work. Whether from our own experience or as we watch the media clips of executives in handcuffs doing the "perp walk" as they go to trial or to prison, we see that achieving the brass ring of financial success alone will not guarantee long-term satisfaction.

A critique of MacIntyre is that he doesn't describe the ethical content of the virtues nor tell us how to clarify what elements are critical parts of each

CASE STUDY: EVALUATE AGAINST THE COMPETENCIES

OPTION 1: RUN THE ADVERTISING CAMPAIGN

❖ *This option overwhelmingly meets the requirements of most of the constituents. Only one small segment of the community has any particular problem with running the ad.*

OPTION 2: DO NOT RUN THE ADVERTISING CAMPAIGN

❖ *If a reasonably priced advertising campaign to substitute for the proposed ad campaign cannot be found, not running the ad will not meet the competencies of the majority of the stakeholders. The market share will not increase, employees might get nervous, the VP of Sales will not feel supported, and the shareholders will not believe I am doing my job well. For the purposes of this exercise, we'll assume that a reasonably priced alternative is available, otherwise analysis would stop here.*

EVERYDAY ETHICS: *Making Wise Choices in a Complex World*

virtue. For example, while MacIntyre is clear that truth-telling is essential both for our own sense of well-being and the preservation of practices, he neither tells us what constitutes a life of integrity nor how to get there. Thus, to begin to understand the content of the virtues as extolled in our chosen tradition, we draw upon the wisdom and learning of the other theorists as we determine what behaviors and attitudes are essential marks of the virtues we choose to embrace.

INTEGRITY IS THE TRUTH THAT NEEDS TO BE TOLD SO WE ARE TRUE TO OURSELVES AND THE PRACTICE CAN RETAIN ITS INTEGRITY IN THE FACE OF THE CORRUPTING INFLUENCE OF INSTITUTIONS

As we consider how to be true to ourselves and as we work to assure that other people have the information they need to make good choices, the Responsibilities Lens might be useful in helping us remember what commitments we have made. Whether looking at the broad agreements that are part of our social contract or the specific agreements that are part of our particular relationships, the questions posed by Kant help us explore our motives and our obligations that shape the virtue of truth-telling. Attending to integrity will also help us remember to treat each person with dignity and inherent respect.

The Relationship Lens helps us remember to step back from the situation and ask what information we would want if we didn't know who we were in a particular situation. We can borrow the veil of ignorance concept from Rawls to help us determine what is essential for a well-functioning system and move away from only considering our small part in the puzzle. We can then attend to instituting and refining processes that assure that the practice is true to itself.

MacIntyre departs from Kant by asserting that the codes of ethics may change from culture to culture. Thus, MacIntyre repudiates the notion of universal principles that Kant posited and moves rather to the notion of universal virtues. MacIntyre states that while the norms of the community, especially their application in specific circumstances, may change from time to time, every community must value certain core virtues if the community is to flourish.[19] Again, as we see the call to a return to ethics in our business community, the argument can be made that rather than attending to the core virtue of integrity, we began to tolerate deception and chicanery in our business leaders, as long as our bottom line—our salaries and our stock portfolios—became fat.

COURAGE IS THE CAPACITY TO RISK HARM OR DANGER TO ONESELF. THIS VIRTUE HAS A ROLE IN HUMAN LIFE BECAUSE OF ITS CONNECTION WITH CARE AND CONCERN[20]

In today's business climate, courage is required not only for individual acts but also to hold those who are responsible for our institutions accountable. The exercise of personal courage involves engaging in the hard work of learning about ourselves and holding ourselves accountable, even when it is not convenient. As we have gone through each of the lenses, the hubris attached to each lens has been articulated. Hubris is that quality that allows us to avoid accountability for meeting the norms of the community either through arrogance, pride, or passion.

As discussed in Chapter 6, failing to face our own tendencies to hubris, the places where we don't want to be accountable to ourselves and our communities, causes a deep tear in the fabric of our community. Many who study history assert that when a community that has achieved excellence loses its moral fiber, that society begins a decline and risks losing all it has accomplished. In our business community, the ultimate act of courage is whistle-blowing. Even after being extolled in the press for extraordinary courage, those who hold their leaders accountable often find that they are unemployed and blackballed. Thus, while we say we value the courage it takes to confront the system and expect that individuals will hold the organizations accountable, those who actually speak up may find their careers derailed.

JUSTICE REQUIRES THAT WE TREAT OTHERS ACCORDING TO UNIFORM AND IMPERSONAL STANDARDS [21]

Justice is a more complex conversation. At its core, justice is the study of appropriate relationships in the community. At the edge, the legal system mediates among people when relationships are broken. The question becomes how one looks at the right treatment of people, the right use of private and public property, and the proper exercise of power. Different ethical traditions have varying understandings of the way that individuals and the community should use their power and property. Examining a traditional way of organizing the themes of justice may be useful. Four categories of justice help us understand the conversation.

❖ *Contributive Justice:* How do we assure that people get a measure of the goods and services in the community based on what they have contributed? People who take very high risks and have high exposure in the community tend to get more financial reward than those who live more conservative lives and make measured choices.

❖ *Retributive Justice:* This conversation assures that people are appropriately punished for violating the rules of the community. Paul Tillich, a 20th century theologian, asserts that if we err too far on the side of mercy, not holding people accountable for their actions, we in fact keep them as children and deny them the opportunity to be adults who are responsible for themselves—the greatest

EVERYDAY ETHICS: *Making Wise Choices in a Complex World*

gift we have in this life.[22] Thus, in the business community we have to assure that people who engage in fraud, theft, and dishonesty are held appropriately accountable for the effects their actions have upon our economic life.

- ❖ *Distributive Justice:* The process of determining who should get what goods and services in the community forms the content of the conversation about distributive justice. One problem is that we have different criteria for distribution of goods based on what goods are being distributed.[23] The primary categories are merit, what we earn through our work and effort; need, the threshold necessities, such as food, housing, and education, that we deserve because we are part of a community; and market, what we can buy because we have the resources. In conversation, members of the community make decisions about who gets what and how those goods should be distributed.

- ❖ *Restorative Justice:* An emerging conversation about justice invites us to consider how we restore community when someone has violated our trust. Begun as a way to help juveniles who had engaged in petty crime see that their acts impacted people's lives, the concept of restorative justice has merit for businesses. As we learn to rebuild relationships that have been frayed by technology and mobility, principles of restorative justice can help businesses, individuals, and the communities that they share find ways to work together for common goals.

Each lens has a different slant on what is considered a just act. Because the claim of members of the community is so strong, each theory has addressed the various components of justice, as the use of power and impact of influence profoundly shapes our choices. In each case, the claim of justice requires that we subordinate our interests to those of the other people who also lay claim to an opportunity for the good life. As we look at the particular focus of each lens, we see that as we are called to justice, we begin to limit the prerogatives of individuals and institutions while working to avoid the vices that beset us as human beings in a contingent, flawed society.

For the individual focused lenses, we are asked to limit personal power so that the community can flourish. For the community focused

CORE JUSTICE FRAMEWORKS

A just act is where I only claim rights I'm willing to grant to others.	*A just act is where the community limits power so individuals can flourish.*
RESPONSIBILITIES LENS	RELATIONSHIP LENS
RESULTS LENS	REPUTATION LENS
A just act is where I limit my choices for the well-being of all.	*A just act is where I honor and respect the integrity and courage of all.*

lenses, we are asked to limit collective power so individuals can thrive. Again, through careful balance of the interests of all, justice can be achieved. Many businesses find that they want to give back to their communities, and so, within the constraints of their fiduciary responsibility to their shareholders, subordinate their financial interests to build the common good. Employees volunteer to help in myriad ways and companies support the efforts.

By working with others in the community, the people who otherwise would be faceless statistics become real human beings with lives and dreams. As we work with the people whose lives our business decisions impact, we become aware of the ripple effect that our decisions have in our communities. Many businesses also find that they want to nurture individuals in their organizations, assuring that each is treated with justice and dignity. True leadership emerges as one skillfully balances between the needs of the individual, the organization, and the community at large.

CIVILITY REQUIRES THAT WE TREAT OTHERS WITH RESPECT AND DIGNITY

While MacIntyre did not include civility in his list of virtues, in a world where shouting at each other has become the norm and road rage is commonplace, considering the contours of civility is important.

First, civility embraces the notion of ordinary good manners—please and thank you. These seemingly tiny acts of civility provide the social glue that helps us remember that the persons with whom we interact are humans who are to be treated with dignity and respect. Actually seeing those who work with us and serve us in varying capacities reminds us that all work is useful and that none of us make it in this world alone. Many times we don't even see those whom we consider unimportant, thus rendering them invisible.

Secondly, civility embraces the notion of treating those with whom we disagree or are in conflict with respect and dignity. In an age where being right is more important than being thoughtful, we polarize every conversation and insist on portraying people, their motives, and their actions as the purist of white or the darkest of black. While finding middle positions is often derogatorily condemned as playing in the murkiness of shades of grey, we need to remember that, to the artist working with pigments, white is the absence of all color and black is the presence of all color. All of the hues of the rainbow are possible only because of differences. As we track political conversations, we notice the tendency to demonize each other rather than listen for points of convergence and search for a meaningful resolution that satisfies both.

Shouting, rather than listening, becomes the norm. Pulling data out of context and magnifying tiny parts of the puzzle rather than seeing the whole substitutes for careful thought and analysis. In an age where change and insecurity has seemingly caused us to lose our center, whole new career fields are emerging to help us manage our conflict and resolve our differences.

Finally, civility includes the notion of building trust and reciprocity that are needed for healthy communities. Robert D. Putnam, in *Bowling Alone*, charts the reduction of social trust in the United States as he reports sociological data tracking the decline of reciprocity and civility.[24] Putnam interprets the data to show that, as we have become more anonymous, as we don't think that we will see each other again, and as we don't have a face to put on our actions, the need to be kind to one another diminishes. The social cost for a loss of civility is an increase in preventive lawyering and litigation. When businesspeople knew that they would see each other not only in boardrooms but also in church and in civic organizations, their need to maintain civil relationships was much higher. With larger and more complex communities, we never know when or if we will be in relationship with a particular person again, so it doesn't matter how we treat them. Thus, having a reputation for integrity and courage doesn't matter—because no one knows anyone well enough to know the other's reputation.

As we no longer have webs of relationships where we see each other in multiple settings, many believe that they have no good reasons to develop social trust and social capital through cooperation. Rather than sealing deals with handshakes, to protect ourselves we resort to putting everything in writing. Rather than being kind to a stranger, trusting that a stranger will at some point be kind to us, we eye everyone suspiciously and turn our backs. In the process, we forget that embracing the virtue of civility not only makes the world a better place, but also enables us to have strong webs of relationships, even with strangers, relationships that enhance our businesses, strengthen our community, and lower our legal bills. However, to accomplish this goal, we must be willing to embrace the virtue of civility for the sake of the virtue itself, not to gain any ulterior reward. In the process, the thin trust that we bestow upon strangers can nourish a rich community that is ultimately not only more safe but also more enjoyable.

For each option that meets the requirements of the virtues, determine the one that will best support the actor's requirements of unity of life.

After an act is judged against the virtues, it is measured against our unity of life, that which gives meaning and purpose to our life and supports us becoming a moral person rather than one who

CASE STUDY: EVALUATION AGAINST THE VIRTUES

OPTION 1: RUN THE ADVERTISING CAMPAIGN
❖ *This option meets the virtue of integrity because the ad campaign is accurate. Running the campaign is not particularly courageous in that I know that the campaign will be successful. It is fair because people are treated with uniform standards. However, an argument can be made that the ad campaign does not meet the test of civility because the story line does not treat others with respect and dignity, given that taunting and physical retribution is glorified.*

OPTION 2: DO NOT RUN THE ADVERTISING CAMPAIGN
❖ *Assuming the alternate campaign also tells the truth, the test for integrity is met. Not running the ad campaign is courageous because I am taking a stand for the least advantaged in the community. Not running the campaign is fair because I am treating people alike. Finally, by substituting a campaign that treats people with respect and dignity, I am promoting civility.*

OPTION 1: RUN THE ADVERTISING CAMPAIGN

❖ *This option does not meet our unity of life, the goal of having a company that is financially successful, sustainable, and a good member of the community. Even though the short-term goal of a good revenue stream may be met, framing the conversation within the role of not only being a good CEO but also running a socially respected company means that this option fails the test.*

OPTION 2: DO NOT RUN THE ADVERTISING CAMPAIGN

❖ *Having the courage to not run the campaign means that over the long haul, the reputation of the company will be enhanced. Depending on how the second campaign is designed, I might even be able to demonstrate how, through the sale of its products, the company enhances civility and justice while respecting others.*

does a series of ethical acts but who may not have a coherent worldview. As we rank the options from the most preferred to the least preferred, we remember that this step invites us to consider the ultimate newspaper test: Would we want this decision on the front page of the local news? As we consider our own mortality, the end of life, it is helpful to focus on what has come to be called the "bucket list," what we want be, do, and have by the end of our life.[25]

Each of us has particular virtues we want to cultivate. We have certain things that we want to do. We also have goals we want to achieve, which may include staying in business. As each of us strives to find meaning in life, we also shape our own life's story. A useful exercise might be to consider what we would want written in the company's annual report or what the comments at our retirement party would reveal.

The unity of life question invites us to consider our lives as a whole, not just as a set of separate, unconnected actions.

Evaluate from the vantage point of empathy

The vantage point of empathy demands that we carefully assess not only our intellectual strengths but also our emotional health. Thus, the final step in the analysis is determining which of the remaining options best meets the requirements of our conscience and our core beliefs. As discussed earlier, a core belief is a notion or idea that is held with affection that results in passion or action. Actions that are consistent with our core beliefs are marked by a commitment that defines us and has the potential to energize and transform both us and the community. Thus, each of us needs to see what kinds of commitments have emotional energy behind them —a passion that makes our heart race or our voice become strident. Hopefully each one of us has a commitment that causes us to get on a soapbox to persuade the whole world of the value of that commitment.

MacIntyre asserts that as we begin cultivating the core virtues, we will be able to shape an ethical life for ourselves. His final provisional definition of a virtue is

> those dispositions which will not only sustain practices and enable us to achieve the goods internal to practices, but which will also sustain us in the relevant kind

of quest for the good, by enabling us to overcome the harms, dangers, temptations and distractions which we encounter, and which will furnish us with increasing self-knowledge and increasing knowledge of the good.[26]

While this definition begins to move us from the notion of seeing ourselves as ethical if we accomplish a set of discrete moral acts to striving to have the habits of thought and action of a moral person, MacIntyre doesn't ever directly address the issue of emotions and the human spirit. To fill this gap, other authors investigate the role of our emotions and the life of the spirit in the shaping of the human person. To provide a perspective on this facet of our lives, we turn to the work of Charles Shelton, a psychologist who studies the formation of conscience. As he explores the contours of conscience, Shelton begins with the core teleological assumption that we as humans strive to be good in the roles we embrace.

Like MacIntyre, Shelton finds that each of us must take responsibility for placing our self in a life history, or a narrative, that shapes and gives meaning to our life. As we determine how we fit into the history of our particular world and find for ourselves the meaning of our lives, Shelton asserts that we need to explore who we are, who we are becoming, and who we desire to be. One useful tool may be to ask questions that help us clarify the requirements of our conscience and help us develop a good conscience. Shelton poses these questions as "exercises for the conscience" to help us become a good person.[27]

CASE STUDY: ACT WITH AWARENESS OF MIND/EMOTION INTERPLAY

OPTION 1: RUN THE ADVERTISING CAMPAIGN

❖ *This option does not meet the test of a conscience that is softened by gratitude for opportunities given, a concern for personal safety, or empathy for others.*

OPTION 2: DO NOT RUN THE ADVERTISING CAMPAIGN

❖ *Not running the ad campaign meets the test of an act done with gratitude that serves others. By assuring that my campaign provides positive role models for all members of the community, I can reflect back my gratitude for a community that is safe for me and those about whom I care.*

HOW DOES THIS OPTION

❖ *Support* our moral beliefs and commitments?

❖ *Support* our own notions of self-respect, respect for others, and a realistic look at who we are and others?

❖ *Support* our ideals, our moral vision, and hope for the community?

❖ *Assure* that we do not think of ourselves as better than we are or appropriate for ourselves prerogatives that we should not have?

❖ *Meet* the criteria of empathy, compassion, and love?

- ❖ *Mitigate* against our personal defenses that allow us to cope in this world and function?

- ❖ *Support* our emotional health and acknowledge the complexity of our lives?

Each of these questions provides a lodestar for helping us determine a virtuous course of action. As we learn to habitually ask these or similar questions while making both simple and complex decisions, we cultivate the habits of the heart that, according to Robert Bellah and others who write in what is known as a communitarian tradition, are essential for a healthy community.

Our sense of who we are as businesspeople absolutely determines how we will behave in our work community. A person who is disgruntled and sees herself exploited by her employer will behave very differently than one who sees himself as an integral part of the community. The ability to correctly assess our skills and talents, our strengths and weaknesses, is critical for identifying who we are. Who we are becoming is decided by the myriad of choices we make. A person who chooses to go to law school and practice law becomes a very different person than one who chooses to get a Ph.D. in English and specialize in the novels of Charles Dickens. Each of our career choices, as well as the way we choose to deal with the specific incidents in our lives, shapes us as a person and contributes to the narrative of our life.

"Who we desire to be" is an essential component of our life story. Our mentors, our guides, our heroes help to determine the trajectory of our lives. As we begin to see possibilities for our futures and choose not only actions but habits of thought and being, we can participate in our own transformation. For example, Shelton asserts that those who cultivate habits of gratitude are healthier and happier than those who see the world through a dark, misty fog of resentment.

Daniel Goleman, in *Primal Leadership*, asserts that one must have both self-awareness, knowledge of one's emotions, as well as one's reason, and self-management, where one is able to keep disruptive emotions under control, and display a full array of virtues in order to be an effective leader. As one tends to both the emotional and rational sides of the person, one can be and become a virtuous person, a leader and mentor in the business community.

Evaluate from the vantage point of integration

The vantage point of integration is the place where we make peace with ourselves—our best self and our worst self. Each person has places of fear, anxiety, meanness, and perversity. As we become ethically mature, we embrace and befriend what Carl Jung called our "shadow self." Often, our shadow self has the intention to protect us, and if we listen to that voice too closely we wind up in self-sabotage.

BLIND SPOT

The Reputation Lens allows us to cultivate our personal virtues within a coherent personal narrative while we are an integral part of the community. However, if we use this lens without the balance of other viewpoints, we become self-righteous. As those of us who are especially privileged cultivate the virtues, we somehow believe that we are entitled to the blessings of our lives. We forget that others have sacrificed to allow us to be who we are. A colleague once quipped about a politician born into privilege who seemed blind to the needs of the less advantaged that "he was born on third base but thinks he hit a triple."

From the vantage point of empathy, if we fail to look clearly at the benefits we receive because of our role, we might think that the perks are deserved because of who we are as a person. As a military spouse, I saw high-ranking officers forget that they were human beings who happened to have a particular rank. In matters of their personal life, they would demand to be treated according to their professional rank instead of remembering that their rank should not have made any difference in the benefits they received.

Finally, as we take our identity from our role rather than our authenticity as a person, we become afraid that someone will discover who we really are— a charlatan and a fraud. The TV show *Undercover Boss* has helped CEOs remember that they really aren't any better than their employees. As the execs take on the different responsibilities in the organization, they learn that they may not be as talented or special as they think. The greatest gift that someone from this lens can give themselves is to periodically step out as a human being, without rank or title.

CASE STUDY: ACT FROM YOUR INTEGRATED CORE

OPTION 1: RUN THE ADVERTISING CAMPAIGN

❖ *This option does not help me live into your role as servant leader. Running a campaign that demeans others, even in a humorous way, does not serve those who cannot defend themselves. In fact, running the campaign may in a small way contribute to an unsafe community.*

OPTION 2: DO NOT RUN THE ADVERTISING CAMPAIGN

❖ *Not running the ad campaign helps me live into my role as servant leader. By assuring that my campaign model the best of community behavior, I can subtly shape the conversation about what is acceptable behavior for members of the community.*

VICES AND RISKS

The opposite of virtues are vices, which emerge as we take ethical risks and do not diligently work to assure that we are being ethical. From the vantage point of intention, a misuse of reason leads to carelessness of thought. This trait expresses itself in the Reputation Lens as a tendency to become hard of heart as we believe we are entitled to the prerogatives of our positions. In the process, we fail to notice how our abuse of personal power is impacting others, reducing them to pawns in our personal game rather than individuals entitled to dignity and respect.

From the vantage point of empathy, as we fail to manage our own emotions, we begin to believe the press-releases of those who fawn over us. We fail to reflect and don't consider that people may just be brown-nosing rather than remembering the responsibilities that come with the role. Many people who have been put on pedestals depend on good friends to tell them the truth so they don't develop feet of clay and topple because of an ethical breach.

Finally, we run the risk of being overwhelmed with the responsibilities of the role and even more isolated from those who would support us. We fail to follow through on commitments, greatly diminishing our effectiveness. We would benefit at looking at the world from the vantage point of the Responsibilities Lens, as we clarify our duties while balancing our excess sensibility with rationality and our fretting over the community with genuine care for ourselves.

HUBRIS

Hubris, excessive pride and arrogance, moves us from unintentional ethical wrongdoing to intentional wrongdoing. Those who act with hubris have a deliberate disregard for the ethical requirements of the community as they work to further their own agenda. For the Reputation Lens, from the vantage point of intention, hubris shows up as entitlement—because of our privileged status, in particular situations we claim benefits that aren't available to others. As people question our integrity, our leadership suffers as we feel misunderstood.

The entitlement can come both on the personal front or whole industries. The newspapers have a perpetual parade of people who don't understand that with position comes responsibility. Examples can be found in the business community, such as Jack Abramoff, a former powerful lobbyist who in 2006 pleaded guilty to fraud, tax evasion, and conspiracy to bribe public officials.

He came to national attention as we found out that he received more than $82 million from Indian tribes with casinos on their property. He then revealed that he defrauded the clients out of millions of dollars.[28] On August 9, 2010, Rod Blagojevich was found guilty of one count of making false statements to the FBI, and the jury was hung on 23 other counts, including of racketeering and extortion.[29] However, the greatest act of hubris was refusing to resign from his position as Governor of Illinois. Staunchly maintaining his innocence, Blagojevich became the first governor in the history of the state of Illinois to be impeached. In the face of a lack of confidence in his ability to govern given the Federal charges, Blagojevich refused to resign, preferring to go through the ordeal of impeachment.[30]

We see the same kind of hubris for professions as a whole. As the dust was settling after the economic meltdown of 2009, Yves Smith, a well-respected commentator on financial and economic matters, noted that rather than holding the financial industries responsible for gambling with our money, "we have institutionalized a dangerous arrangement, that of socialized losses and

EVERYDAY ETHICS: *Making Wise Choices in a Complex World*

privatized gains, a 'heads I win, tails you lose' setup."[31] Smith continues that the financiers are not being held to any accountability. In fact, in the aftermath, the regulation of the financial market is even less than it was before the meltdown because the regulators "genuinely believe that what is best for the financier class is best for the economy, and by extension, society. With extortion, the authorities might actually recognize the industry needs to be curbed, but are daunted by the task. And the fear of doing much leaves the perpetrators effectively in charge."[32]

From the vantage point of empathy, we fluff ourselves up, suffering from unrealistic self-esteem. As we become enamored with our role, we believe that we are our position. In the process, we lose our personal authenticity and become a shell of who we can be. Believing that we are special, we demand prerogatives from others and lose the center of meaning that comes from being a servant leader.

As we work to become "all that we can be," we need to remember that we are special—just like everyone else. As we look at ourselves with clear eyes and engage with others from a position of compassion and emotional maturity, we avoid the hubris that comes from a sense of entitlement and unrealistic self-esteem. As we make our final choice, we should assure ourselves that our action comes from our commitment to be a whole person who considers the implications of our actions from all of our varied roles—employers, employees, consumers, and citizens. As we resist the temptation to view our choices from only one narrow perspective, we become people of virtue and choose that which meets both short-term needs and long-term goals.

Consider the critiques of the lens

Much emphasis has been placed on the virtues lens from Aristotle forward based on the belief that by exercising and intentionally embracing the virtues, one will develop an ethical character. Virtues, habits of ethical action, create tendencies for people to behave in a predictable way based on "distinctive patterns of emotional response, deliberation, and decision as well as more overt behavior."[33] Those in the virtue ethics tradition claim that a person with an ethical character has the three following characteristics.

First, the person will behave *consistently* in different situations. Thus, one who has developed the virtue of compassion would be expected to behave compassionately in a variety of situations as they arise in life. Second, the person would show *stability* of behavior, exhibiting behavior flowing from the virtues in similar situations. Thus, one who has developed the virtue of truth-telling would be expected to tell the truth in recurring similar situations. Third, as people develop an *integrated personality* through habitually embracing the virtues, they would demonstrate related virtues in various situations. Thus, a person who is compassionate would also be expected to be kind and civil, virtues related to compassion.[34]

While the theories concerning character have been developed by philosophers and ethicists, an emerging field of moral psychology brings the tools of that discipline to the question of whether or not people in fact develop "character" based on intentionally embracing the virtues as envisioned by the virtue theorists. John M. Doris, a leading moral psychologist, compiled the research to test the claim that the three characteristics of behavior that mark people of good character exist. Doris suggests that the answer is "no." Instead, Doris puts forward a complementary theory called situationism that he asserts better accounts for the reality we see: good people doing bad things in different situations.

To explore whether or not people demonstrated *consistency of behavior* when faced with external pressure to behave unethically, Doris turned to the very famous Milgram study. Stanley Milgram, a professor at Yale University found that ordinary people would inflict pain on others if they believed that an authority figure required or condoned the pain.[35] Milgram wanted to study the relationship between people's conscience and their respect for authority. The study was inspired by the defense put forward by many German citizens during the Nuremberg Trials that they were merely following orders. Many studies that replicated the work of Milgram would suggest that rather than the ethical dispositions determining whether or not we behave properly in a particular situation, people will behave according to the population norm.

Another body of research demonstrates that people do not in fact show *stability of behavior* in similar situations. Another famous study is the Stanford Prison Experiment, where a group of stable, ethically mature students were selected to participate in a prison simulation. The experiment was terminated after six days rather than the full two weeks because those given the "role" of guards behaved completely out of character and those given the "role" of prisoners were unable to cope.[36] The Stanford Experiment helped us understand the scandal concerning prisoner abuse at Abu Ghraib: the problem was not the proverbial "bad apple," but a culture that condoned the behavior, a "bad barrel."[37] Thus, the culture of an organization is much more important than previously thought in shaping the behavior of people. Those who worked at Enron and contributed to the financial implosion or those who worked for the mortgage and banking companies who contributed to the banking crises were probably caring friends, thoughtful citizens, and basically good people. Yet, they participated in highly unethical activities as expected and condoned by the corrupt culture.

The final characteristic, a *well-integrated personality*, also does not hold under research scrutiny or anecdotal observation. Many of us have had the experience of behaving one way in one situation and completely differently in another. Those who study character and moral formation find that decisions made about ourselves as children carry forward in life, popping up unbidden and causing us to behave in ways that do not represent our "best self."[38] As anyone who has been

EVERYDAY ETHICS: *Making Wise Choices in a Complex World*

through a twelve-step program to break the tie of addiction or who has been through a program of therapy will attest, change is hard.

Does this mean that we should give up on virtue ethics? MacIntyre recognizes the importance of culture as he underscores the importance of continuing conversations, people continually reiterating what specific behaviors count as ethical action in their particular community. Also, as part of the teleological tradition, virtue ethics is aspirational, helping us define what we *should* become. While behaving consistently in accordance with stated values is hard, with mindfulness we can be more successful than if we ignore the challenge. While having stable values that show up as predictable behavior in different situations is difficult, as we pay attention to our various contexts we can choose behaviors that correspond with our core values and commitments. And finally, the task of having an integrated personality is a lifetime challenge. As we journey through life, we are tested in the fire to determine our mettle. Thus, moving our ethical commitments from implicit to explicit becomes an important process to help us become a responsible, ethical member of a community.

STEP 4: BE RESPONSIBLE
Rank the options from least preferred to most preferred

Having determined the elements of the practice and then evaluated each option against the criteria of the ethical decision maker's understanding of the core competencies, the stakeholders' understanding of the core competencies, the virtues, the ethical decision maker's dreams for unity of life, and the whisperings of conscience, the next step is to rank the options from least preferred to most preferred. As the options are ranked, we can summarize why the ranking of options was made and demonstrate the primacy given to the virtues, the character of the ethical decision maker.

As we rank the options, we summarize why we chose this ranking of options and demonstrate the primacy given to the core values. First we must show how we privileged community—helping ourselves and others become self-actualized, reaching our desired goals because of equality of opportunity and result, as we bring the needs and concerns of the least advantaged into clear focus and champion their cause. Then, we show how we privileged rationality—as we logically assessed the system of justice, we identified ways to assure that all are

CASE STUDY: RANK THE OPTIONS

OPTION 2: DO NOT RUN THE ADVERTISING CAMPAIGN

❖ *This option will meet the requirements of a courageous act that promotes civility. This act also reflects the best of a servant leader who cares not only about customers but also about the community as a whole.*

OPTION 1: RUN THE ADVERTISING CAMPAIGN

❖ *This option does not meet the tests of the lens. If I run the ad, I will not be supporting the virtue of civility. By running an ad that does not promote respect among people, I am in a small way contributing to the increase of uncivil actions in the community.*

included in the community and those without power have access to the goods of life needed to thrive.

Strive for ethical maturity

The final stage before acting is much like going through a checklist one more time—have we corrected for any unintended bias that might have appeared? For this stage, a final look at the tools for analysis is useful. With the final check, we can make sure that the option we choose is the most ethically mature choice available to us.

CASE STUDY: STRIVE FOR ETHICAL MATURITY

❖ *By not running the ad, I am establishing yourself as a leader who lives in a community comprised of people who are working to be healthy and safe. With even this seemingly small step, I am participating in the ongoing conversation about what it means to be a person-in-community, one who respects others and is concerned with their well-being. Having the conversation is not easy as different people have divergent notions about what being a good member of the community means. However, by taking a stand, I am forwarding the conversation.*

As we strive for ethical maturity, we begin to question what Rosemary Haughton calls the "taken-for-granted separation between the material and spiritual, between physical and mental, [as] we struggle to express in that language the disintegrating conclusions of quantum physics, and 'field' theory, in which there are no 'things' at all, but only relationship, information, movement."[39]

All of us who work in business need to explore what our professional ethics will look like in a world not defined by individual action, facts, and stability, but by the fluid situation Haughton describes where our only lodestar is what we believe responsible human beings should do to build a community in which all can thrive. As we begin to see ourselves as whole humans, we can resist taking only our "useful" self to work. If we only come to work with a skill set that will enhance the bottom line and guarantee the well-being and success of the organization, we will deny whole segments of who we are as people and breed "passivity, submissiveness, and dependence."[40] The emerging academic and popular inquiry into spirituality at work addresses the question of how we can take our whole selves to work and contribute to the life of the economic community.

From the vantage point of intention, we analyze our own course of action. For the Reputation Lens, the interplay of reflection and community conversation allows us to discern the ethical qualities and resulting behaviors needed to excel in our role. For those of us living through these changing times, freedom comes from our ability to imagine what we would like to become and what we want our businesses to be, and then to deliberately choose a particular direction while we work to make that dream a reality. To act from a thoughtful consideration of the specific situation rather than mindlessly responding to a determined world, we must be willing to take responsibility for ourselves and our community, including the community that manufactures goods and provides services—the world of business.

The vantage point of empathy allows us to view our lives with gratitude. Being thankful allows us to hold our power lightly, so we do not become overbearing. We develop self-efficacy, the belief that we can take on new challenges and master them. Gratitude also allows us to deal with the inevitable vicissitudes of life with equanimity and poise. We know we have weathered storms before; soon whatever challenges are present will pass and we will have developed even more resilience.

Finally, we use the vantage point of integration to weave our story, our personal, coherent narrative about what we do and why we do it. Speaking from our center of authenticity, we have a powerful voice for building consensus. Our actions fit within the long view of our life as we test options against our understanding of who we are and what we want to accomplish.

Act with courage

After we make our choice, we should be able to communicate our decision to others. Creating a short statement that could be placed in a memo to others in the company or a press release helps us learn to articulate our ethical decisions so that we answer the core questions of the Relationship Lens.

Be true to the perspective of the ethical lens

Remembering that this vantage point is like framing a picture through a camera lens, we can assure that we are living into the best of our roles. Another notion is that we each frame and name what we see in our lives. As we fashion the statement, we know that we have a specific role in the community and we make our decision mindful of those obligations. The expectations of others as well as our own understanding of the role requirements are considered.

Looking forward in time, we seek to make choices that will strengthen the legacy of the role and develop a strong individual character. We should remember to allude to the virtues that are important as well as the unity of life of the organization. Remember that these announcements become part of the narrative of the organization. As such they are instrumental in demonstrating which traditions are important to the organization and assure that a tradition of excellence is continually reiterated.

We write the statement in such a way that the core questions are answered: 1) what respected human qualities and virtues are demonstrated by this decision (e.g., courage, moderation, justice); 2) how does this decision demonstrate the qualities and virtues that a person who is respected in this role has (e.g., competence, loyalty, diligence, fairness); 3) how does this decision demonstrate the qualities of a person in this profession (e.g., commitment to public service, self-regulation, trust, integrity)?

FOLLOW CHECKLIST FOR ACTION

As we move to action, using the perspective of the Reputation Lens, we will:

❖ *Consider* the role of individuals and the company. The goal is to assure that each person's role is respected, their mandate for action is clear, and they are equipped to fulfill their role.

❖ *Seek* excellence in everything. Expedience is the enemy of ethical action. By consistently working to improve, excellence becomes the hallmark of our action.

❖ *Consider* the end of life questions. When our retirement notice is written, what do we want to have done, to have, and to be? By keeping our eyes on our personal goals, we will develop the habits of action and character that will become our signature in this life.

Because most of the work in ethics is persuasion, we should be able to articulate clearly what choice we have made and why. After giving a bit of background information to set the stage for the problem, we can frame the statement so that we answer the core questions of this particular lens. Who am I? What virtues do I need to cultivate? What guidance does my conscience give in this situation? And who is my neighbor? How can I move into a place of servant leadership, expanding my vision to include my relationship with the whole community?

STEP 5: RETURN TO AWARENESS

After we describe our resolution of the problem, we next consider whether the ethical analysis made sense. Did we like the result? What were the problems with the process? What are the sticking points with the process? How was the process enhanced or modified by adding the world of emotion and attending to the virtues that are essential for all of us to be effective in our world?

Reflect on results

As we reflect on the results that come from our actions, we can put strategies in place to become ever more ethically mature. Ethical maturity occurs as we move from only thinking of ourselves to noticing how our choices impact others as well as the institutions of our community. As we grow in ethical maturity, we seek solutions that are systemic and will improve life for as many as possible.

From the vantage point of intention, personal growth and maturity is defined as identifying and cultivating the virtues that support your roles in the community. As we become familiar with our own emotions and those of others, from the vantage point of empathy, we will be able to integrate your emotion and intellect in order to support the community as a whole. Finally, as our vantage point of integration matures, we will learn to live from a deep knowledge that we are a representation of that which infuses all of life. We will know that we are one with all who inhabit and cherish this planet.

Seek continuous improvement

The process of continuous improvement involves developing strategies to assure accurate self-assessment. In many spiritual traditions, the process of self-assessment involves thinking neither better nor worse of ourselves than we should as we learn to be content no matter what our situation. We hear inspiring stories of people who were incarcerated in the German concentration camps and were able to be gentle and thrive. Viktor Frankl recounts that part of his secret was to see the guards as human beings. The German guards knew how to interact with people who gave up their humanity, but were thrown off balance by those who retained their humanity and saw their captors as fully human as well.[41]

As we attend to developing the virtues essential for our varying roles, we are cautioned to watch for intended and unintended results. We also need to attend to new questions or answers that were not complete. The trajectory for maturity is not necessarily smooth, but as we attend to our character while supporting others in their journey, we can get there. As we take responsibility for our own self-development while respecting the path of others, we will learn to live with gentleness, grace, and maybe even a dollop of frivolity. In the process, we will learn how to live from our center while we find meaning for our lives.

Finally, as we are called to balance, we need to address whether we are being overly attached to our own sense of entitlement and self-righteousness in our need to be "special," or whether we are detached from our situation enough to begin to develop compassion and empathy for those with whom we live and work. As we become aware of being part of a larger community and celebrate the amazing diversity of choice and experience, we begin to take the long view and, with gratitude, celebrate our lives. We will become aware of those places where our fear overwhelms us so that we are not able to notice the gifts of others. We will also be aware of our tendencies toward unrealistic self-esteem, not accurately seeing both our gifts and our challenges, that keeps us from being effective while walking gently in this world. If we do not attend to our spirit as we do our work, we risk losing our center, the core of our being that allows us to act from certainty and authenticity. We will also notice where we have power to help others judge members of their community by their character rather than external characteristics. In the process, we will become aware of our own sacred identity.

CONCLUSION

The Reputation Lens invites us to consider how to attend to our character and embrace the virtues that allow us to become effective leaders in our community. Beginning with the ethical key phrase, "What is a good character?" we learn to develop the habits of personal reflection as we seek the counsel of others in the community who will help us become virtuous while becoming an integral part of the community. To avoid becoming overwhelmed with either self-righteousness or fear, we learn to continually attend to developing a *healthy, functioning conscience*. As we embrace the spiritual focus, we can turn from attending only to ourselves as we ask, "Who is my neighbor?" With detachment, seeking to see the spark of the divine in each person, we can seek excellence rather than expedience in all that we do and in the process become effective leaders.

CONTINUING THE CONVERSATION

1. Using either the fourth problem in the simulation or another fact pattern, analyze the situation using the Reputation lens. Was the problem easy to do, indicating that this might by your preferred method of working ethical problems? Was the process difficult, indicating that this may not be your ethical home?

2. Read an op-ed piece in your local paper or a national paper and find examples of virtue ethics thinking. In what ways did the author appeal to the competencies of the practice? What virtues were described as important for this particular practice?

3. Review the chart that opened this chapter, paying special attention to the gifts of this tradition. Considering both your own life as well as others who make decisions using the vantage of this tradition, what are the strengths of the Reputation Lens? Give examples of situations in which you have seen excellent results as someone used the viewpoints and processes of this lens to make a decision.

4. What strategies can you put in place to help you begin to strengthen your own mastery of this lens? How can you help the organizations in which you work, either paid or volunteer, ask the core questions to help them make better ethical decisions?

5. Review the chart that opened this chapter, this time attending to the weaknesses of the tradition. Considering both your own life as well as that of others who make decisions using the vantage of this tradition, what are the weaknesses of the Reputation Lens? Give examples of situations in which you have seen problematic results as someone used the viewpoints and processes of this lens to make a decision.

6. What strategies can you put in place to help you recognize and attend to the imbalance that comes from an inappropriate appropriation of the Reputation Lens, whether concerning abuse of power or hubris in your personal and professional life? How do you know when you are improperly using the tools of this lens? How can you help the organizations in which you work ask the core questions to help them avoid imbalance or hubris?

USING THE BAIRD METHOD

As explored in this text, two elements are required to make an effective ethical decision: a *process* for making the decision and *criteria*, or guidelines, by which to judge whether or not an option is ethical. As you learn to consistently practice these two elements, you become more ethically mature.

The following exercise uses the five decision steps known as the Baird Decision Model. The ethical criteria will be value priorities for The Four Ethical Lenses. Using the decision model with the ethical lenses is known as the Baird Method—a logical way to work through an ethical decision step by step.

❖ STEP ONE: *Be Attentive*

1. Choose an ethical dilemma or scenario for resolution.
2. Gather information from the scenario and figure out what is going on—the context of the problem.

   ❖ *Who is making the decision? What is the role of that person in the situation?*

   ❖ *What facts are important to resolve the situation?*

   ❖ *What are the perceptions and beliefs of people who are involved that might impact the decision?*

   ❖ *What assumptions are you making about this situation that might impact the decision?*

   ❖ *What is the issue that has to be resolved (a short statement of the problem)?*

❖ STEP TWO: *Be Intelligent*

1. Explore the values in tension and pinpoint the concerns and criteria for action for each lens.

   RESPONSIBILITIES LENS: ❖ *What are the rules/principles involved? What are the reasons for those rules?*

   RESULTS LENS: ❖ *What is the goal? What will make you happy? What will create the greatest good for as many people as possible?*

   RELATIONSHIP LENS: ❖ *What result is fair? Who has power? Who needs to be protected? What processes—order of decision making—are needed to get a fair result?*

   REPUTATION LENS: ❖ *What actions are required because of our role? What virtues are important in this situation?*

❖ STEP THREE: *Be Reasonable*

1. Identify options for action that would resolve the ethical dilemma.
2. Choose one option for action that would meet the criterion for an ethical action for each lens.

❖ STEP FOUR: *Be Responsible*

1. Put together an action plan for resolution of this dilemma. Would you have an order for trying the interventions—the various options or just use one?
2. If you were going to use more than one option, what would the order be? What would be the criteria for moving to the next step of the intervention?

❖ STEP FIVE: *Be Reflective*

1. Reflect on your selected option. What would you expect to be the fallout from your action plan? Who would find your plan ethical? Who would criticize your plan and why?

The highest good is like water.
Water gives life to the ten thousand things and does not strive.
It flows in places men reject and so is like the Tao.
In dwelling, be close to the land.
In meditation, go deep in the heart.
In dealing with others, be just and kind. In speech, be true.
In business, be competent. In action, watch the timing.
No fight; no blame.

From the Tao Te Ching—8[1]

CHAPTER 11

Life with Integrity, Grace — and a Dollop of Frivolity

"GREED IS GOOD!" SO DECLARES GORDON GEKKO, the hero/villain of *Wall Street*, the 1987 block-buster movie that reviewer Jeff Stone notes "perfectly embodies the Reagan-era credo" of unbridled ambition as Gekko entices the young Bud Fox into his lair with promises of power and privilege. Stone comments that the movie "grabs your attention while questioning the corrupted values of a system that worships profit at the cost of one's soul."[2]

At the end of the 90s and then again at the end of the first decade of the 21st century, with almost monthly exposés of companies and their readers who clearly violated the law as well as societal norms, people at cocktail parties and journalists asked whether those who were hauled before grand juries and then trundled off to prison were a few bad apples who needed to be plucked from the barrel of commerce before all the contents were spoiled or whether they represented the whole crop, signaling that something was deeply wrong with our community. The answer is probably "yes" to both.

Many of those corrupt executives who became household names pushed the envelope of accepted behavior. As long as stock prices kept going up, no one asked too many questions, because we had a matrix of expectations and practices that allowed the behavior to be both tolerated and celebrated. Lester Thurow reminds us that crony capit~li~.. e~ ~sts ev. ~wh ~re. Examine the .~ ~ ~any financial boom in American histo~~ ~nd ~~e f ~~~ ~~ ~da1~, The En~ ~~s, Worldcoms, and Mercks are no~ ab~ ~malit~ ~s in a basi~ ~y sour~ ~ystem. ... At ~he end of a boom the pressure to ~eep ~~ ~ go~d time~ going ju~~ a l~~tle longer is enormous.[3]

After watching *Wall Street*, the question was asked how Gekko knew that Fox would be a good candidate to be drawn into his web of greed and destruction. Fox sent the first signal: he brought Gekko a box of smuggled cigars for his birthday. Through that first act, Gekko intuited that Fox's desire to advance was greater than his commitment to the community norms and law. Faced with a set of desires and goals that were complex and conflicting, the young stock-broker found that his drive to succeed according to Wall Street's definition was greater than his willingness to live by the values and norms that would lead to personal satisfaction and allow the community as a whole to thrive.

CAN'T WE JUST RETURN TO THE "GOOD OLD DAYS?"

Evaluating the status of business ethics at the beginning of the 21st century, one is tempted to longingly yearn for a return to some mythological Camelot where community ethics were strong and individuals and businesses were able to thrive. However, those days probably never existed. Each era has both challenges and celebrations as it plays out its act on the grand stage of history.

As we take a long view back, determining that other periods of time were more or less ethical becomes difficult. Different periods of time have varied expectations and definitions of the right use of people, property, and power. Thus, whether observers accept the overall set of practices that define the business climate of a community as ethical depends on how congruent business ethics are with community ethics.[4] When the personal values of community members are mirrored in the corporate behaviors, businesses are touted as ethical partners in the community. However, when the shadow side of business comes to the fore and expectations for financial transparency and fair dealings change, we claim a crisis in ethics and scramble to find ways to regulate behavior and shame the practitioners into addressing the new problems. Looking at the three broad areas where we evaluate our ethics helps us put our history in some sort of perspective.

RIGHT TREATMENT OF PEOPLE

In one sense, our businesses are more ethical than they have ever been because we have an ever-increasing commitment to human dignity and respect. Our founding fathers boldly proclaimed in The Declaration of Independence that

We hold these truths to be self evident, that all men are created equal, that they are endowed by their Creator with certain unalienable Rights, that among these are Life, Liberty, and the pursuit of Happiness.

Over the past 250 years of our existence, members of the community have worked relentlessly to make that dream a reality.

In terms of relationships between employer and employee, at this time in American history, men and women, both minorities and those in the majority, have a greater opportunity for access to positions and privilege than ever before. Those with physical and mental handicaps are given more opportunity for participation in the wider community than ever.

In terms of the relationship between producer and consumer, our products are safer than they have ever been. We have an ever-increasing number of mandates for safety (with some asking when a product should be considered safe enough). We also have pushes for quality improvement in organizational processes as seen in the Baldrige Initiative and Sigma 6. The transparency between producer and consumer is also greater than ever, with information about products and services available to all—from nutritional information on the packaging of products to magazines and websites that give the vitals for equipment, cars, and machinery.

At the same time, we have seen an erosion in personal privacy and choice in the name of security and safety. Alcohol abuse and drug use are not tolerated as random drug and alcohol screening is accepted as *de rigueur*. During the 60s and 70s, sexual harassment was named and then not tolerated. The treatment of women that was accepted even 30 years ago is no longer welcome in the workplace. Monitoring one's use of computers at work is expected. Finally, the use of global positioning devices to keep track of employees is gaining in popularity. Some companies are even putting GPS devices in their employees' badges so their every move can be tracked. While knowing where one's employees are in the event of disaster might be useful, most people find "Big Brother watching" a bit unnerving.

RIGHT USE OF PROPERTY

The hallmark of American capitalism is the right to private property, including the right to use our own resources in the way that we choose. Traditional property law provides that within the boundaries that mark our land, we own rights to the core of the earth and the dome of the sky. However, those property laws have historically not addressed what happens when toxins leave one property and enter another. Those laws also did not address what happens when resources become scarce.

One of the most amazing shifts in the past fifty years is the commitment to cleaning up the environment. No longer are companies allowed to transfer the cost of environmental degradation caused by pollution. Public land is expected to be preserved for the use of the whole rather than parceled out for the use of a few. Citizens are demanding that the Securities and Exchange Commission require public companies to include in their reports some analysis of the risk posed by global warming and potential effects on our "carbon footprint." While finding the proper balance between the unregulated use of one's private property and protection of the environment as a whole is difficult, the conversation has moved to the forefront of public discourse. Thus, in our treatment of the land, air, and water, our ethical benchmark has been raised.

Technology also challenges our traditional understanding of property. While ownership of a coat or a book is clear-cut, ownership of electronically transmitted data is more problematic. One of the ironies of the day is that young Republican students, while aligning themselves with the party that historically has defended property right by asserting the primacy of negative rights, vigorously defend their right to download music and make copies of movies without the permission of copyright holders.

While staunchly maintaining the right to use their physical property as they see fit, they don't seem to believe that taking someone else's cyber-property is illegal. The proliferation of these practices made possible by the internet continues to prompt questions about whether traditional copyrights and patents are the best way to protect and foster innovation. A related question is the right protection of copyrights and patents that protect innovation. As the cost of pharmaceuticals increases, those who need the drugs question whether a company has a right to set prices so high in one market (e.g., the United States) that those who need the medications cannot afford them while the cost is less in other national markets (e.g., Canada). As the costs for payment are shifted to third parties in the form of insurance, the traditional regulators of the market don't work. We have yet to effectively deal with these questions in an expanding global market.

Right Use of Power

Finally, we must be ever vigilant to assure that the quest for power and greed doesn't corrupt individuals and organizations. While a market economy appears to be the best economic model for maximizing the wealth of individuals and can also assist in increasing the well-being of an overall society, unregulated capitalism also has the power to economically destroy many individuals while benefitting a few. A key critique of the ethical theory of Mill and the corresponding economic model of Adam Smith is that issues of distribution of resources are not considered.

Thus, ethics and public policy constrain the individual acquisition of wealth and power to assure that the community can thrive. Further, as we work to maintain the proper calibration between individual initiative and socially imposed restraints, we need to remember that American capitalism is just one expression of this economic model. As public policy experts work to find the best way to harness the benefit of capitalism while moderating for its excesses, we can learn from the other economic models that are tailored to assure that cultural differences are acknowledged while the various economies flourish.[6]

However even in light of the different versions of capitalism, Alice Rivlin, former vice chair of the Board of Governors of the Federal Reserve System and director of the White House Office of Management and Budget, notes that three tensions make public policy in a capitalistic economy difficult: 1) if markets are to work, agreed-upon rules must be in place to govern the right use of people, property, and power, 2) social, environmental, and other public policies must be in place to keep people and companies from shifting the cost of business from themselves to others, and 3) we have public goods such as "armies and navies, police, roads, parks, and public health services—that private investors operating on their own will not provide."[7]

Rivlin reminds us that we must constantly tinker with our policies as conditions change. To effectively manage the process, as individuals in community we must attend to the overarching goal of our community: working to assure that individuals can thrive while the community remains strong. Rivlin notes that at this particular time in history we have three dilemmas:

> First, how do we make capitalism work better for people in the bottom quarter or third of the distribution of skill, education, income, and luck? .... Second, irresponsible behavior and corporate excesses abuse trust in egregious ways—not just trust in one company, but trust in the whole system .... If [people working hard for low wages] come to believe that the system is corrupt, that the bosses lie and cheat and make out like bandits at the expense of hard-working folks, something very fundamental is lost .... Third, [how do we assure that] our commitment to private decisions and the profit motive [doesn't get] in the way of recognizing that there are things we need government to do or at least to organize.[8]

Thus, depending on where we are in the boom-bust economic cycle, one of these three perennial dilemmas will move to center stage while the others might be in the shadows.

Mirroring Rivlin's concerns, when asked whether companies are more ethical or less ethical than they were 50 years ago, many find the imbalance of salaries and benefits between those at the top of the corporate ladder and those in the middle and the bottom the prime indicator of a lack of ethics. During the 1970s, the difference in salaries between the top and the bottom of organizations was the narrowest that it has ever been. Interestingly, that period is the high-water mark of unionization.

While in the 70s, inequities existed between salaries of women and minorities, for white males, the difference between the top and bottom was often a variable of 30 or less. Thus, the CEO of an organization would not make more than 30 times the salary of the lowest paid person in the organization. Currently, for many companies the variable has increased exponentially.[9] Thus, even though the gap between men's and women's salaries is shrinking, that overall reduction in differential is caused by men's salaries being reduced rather than women's income being increased.

Yet, the issue is not simple. When we look at only the economy of the United States we have concerns about eroding salaries and soft jobs as employment opportunities are moved overseas. When we look at global resource distribution, we realize that by comparison, most of us in the United States are very wealthy. The conundrum of appropriate balance between individual initiative and equality of opportunity and result becomes even more difficult to solve.

INCREASING COMPLEXITY AS WE MOVE TO A GLOBAL ECONOMY

At the beginning of the industrial revolution (prior to the 1850s), organizations were small and thus easy to manage. Because family-based businesses are not complex, having congruity between individual and community values and business practices was simple. Further, because the communities were also small and mobility was low, people knew each other and thus the social relationships provided constraints on unethical business practices. While we had international trade, the scale was relatively tame and information about different markets was very limited.

By the beginning of the 20th century, corporations became more complex as they began to reap economic gain from realizing economies of scale. The number of employees grew and the financial structures became complex. In order to manage the changes, the discipline of scientific management grew, which increased efficiency but had the unintended result of depersonalizing workers. As the economic well-being of the United States began to increase, given our comparatively unregulated market, we continued to outpace other national markets in terms of overall economic growth. Two landmark pieces of legislation kept the power relationships in balance: the antitrust legislation of the 1890s and the legislation legitimizing and regulating unionization of the 1930s.

Equilibrium was reached in the 50s and 60s as the power relationships between employers and employees was balanced because of unionization and industrialization had matured. World War II had given us an opportunity for unprecedented economic growth. With the industrial decimation of our primary competitor Europe, the U.S. had two decades of near global monopoly power. However, several interrelated events threw the U.S. out of balance. We found ourselves mirroring the events and the disquiet of the emergence of the full blown Industrial Revolution, that period called the Gilded Age and populated with Robber Barons and huddled masses of very poor wage earners.

First, in the early 1990s, the technological revolution emerged. Whole new industries came to the fore that were not anticipated and thus not regulated. With wireless telephones, the ability to stay connected to far comers of the world and markets increased. With video equipment, news and images moved in matters of seconds across the globe. With computers, the speed and transparency with which information was communicated across the globe greatly influenced prices on Wall Street and market fluctuations in different comers of the world. Advances in medicine meant that we were able to fight against disease and death in ways that were absolutely unforeseen. The expectations and policies that were in place for an industrial economy did not meet the needs of the "wired" community.

Second, our monopoly status was challenged by the growth of the manufacturing capacity of other countries. After World War II, Japan provided a strong challenge as it embraced technology and a commitment to quality. As other Asian countries began developing their manufacturing and technical capabilities, jobs began moving off-shore to take advantage of the lower wage scales. The tension is palpable: as consumers we love keeping prices low; as employees we hate the personal insecurity of participating in a global workforce.

The fluidity of information provided by technology exponentially increases the availability of both a global workforce and global marketplace. When x-rays can be digitally sent to India to be read overnight by technicians and then sent back to the United States before the next business day, defining the norms of health care ethics and accountability for error becomes challenging. Again, as patients we love having good information available for our doctors; if we are the workers who have been displaced, we are not as sanguine about the innovations.

Finally, access to the stock market became democratized. Where in 1952 only 4% of Americans owned stock, either directly or through mutual or pension funds, by 2000, 48.8% of all families owned corporate stock.[10] Further, even those in who made less than $10,000 per year increased their ownership from 5.4% in 1995 to 7.7% in 1998.[11] In addition, stock ownership for African-Americans continued to grow from 26% in 1998 to 37% in 2001 while ownership for white Americans remained relatively flat at 51%. Even though African-Americans are still less likely to invest than white Americans, clearly the trend indicates an increased interest in investments.[12]

Unfortunately, this trend reversed itself with an increase in stock ownership, much of it in pension funds. By 2008, more than three quarters of the stock in play in the market was owned by institutions, who did not as aggressively track the performance of the companies as individuals.[13] Thus, the need for financial transparency became even greater. Of course, when the stock market crashes, the wealth of a vast number of people in the community evaporates. Thus, a privatized and highly accessible market is a proverbial double-edged sword.

At the end of the 20th century, burgeoning technology created new sources of wealth, mirroring the increase of wealth that came as steel mills, the Model T, and electricity burst upon the scene. At the same time that we began playing with our new technology, science changed our understanding of the physical as well as our social world. Our worldview, expanded by quantum physics, quarks, gluons, and the string theory, opens for us a world that is more complex than the simple mechanical model of our world embraced by our great-grandparents. Thus, we must rearticulate the norms and traditions of the past into the narrative of the present to learn to live effectively. Like learning to see a fractal emerge from a random data set, we must learn to see the beauty of complexity in the seemingly random chaos that surrounds us.

EMBRACING COMPLEXITY AND MOVING TOWARD WISDOM

Those who are uncomfortable with the ambiguity of complexity want to return to the certainty of the principles by which our fathers and mothers lived, the perceived glory days of America. However, as seen above, even a cursory review of history reveals that the "good old days" weren't quite as good as we would like to believe.

One proffered solution is to reduce everything to rules—when we have a perceived breach of ethics, we just enact more rules and regulations to tell us what to do. However, as explored in earlier chapters, the law and its enforcement mechanisms are not designed to answer every question. In addition, we also know that because the world and its values are pluralistic, no one set of rules or norms will be acceptable to all. The other extreme, letting everyone do what he or she believes is best is also not the answer. Both individuals and organizations need to know the size of the proverbial sandbox—what actions are acceptable and what is not acceptable. As we have seen in our exploration of the Four Ethical Lenses, the size of the sandbox is established in ongoing conversations about how we should balance among the four core value sets.

Our current conversation thus becomes a variation on an old theme, a conversation introduced into Western thought by Plato and Aristotle. One set of folks believes that we just need to find the ideals, those timeless principles which endure for all people at all times. Another set believes that we have to use our reason and skill to solve the concrete problems of this life. Both conversations are useful as we are deciding what to do with the difficult employee who manages to fight with everyone or the cantankerous consumer who buys a prom dress on Friday and returns it soiled on Monday claiming that "it just doesn't fit."

Most of us need both principles to give us ethical touchstones for our lives and prudential judgment to help us move our core values and commitments into action within an ever-changing kaleidoscope of circumstances. As we learn to exercise sound ethical discretion, we take the best of our ideals and testing them against the situations in which we find ourselves. In the process, we learn the habits of thinking and patterns of acting that help us live out our dreams for ourselves, our organizations, and our world.

The goal of ethical maturity is the ability to know when to absolutely follow the rules and when to bend them a tad and exercise mercy. Reviewing the tensions implicit in our core value sets, we note that the wise leaders of our community are those who know how to appropriately and effectively balance between *autonomy*, the needs of individuals, and *equality*, the needs of the group. Those who are deemed wise use the resources of *rationality*, their minds, as well as *sensibility*, their emotions, when making decisions.

PRINCIPLES AND PRUDENTIAL JUDGMENT

Beginning with the law as the threshold, our society has stated that these rules cannot be violated without substantial penalty. We have one set of laws which articulate seemingly universal principles, e.g., thou shalt not murder, thou shalt not steal. For these laws, the question is when violating these norms might (in limited circumstances) be excused or justified. We have another set of laws that define the rules of the game—what taxes have to be paid, what requirements for not polluting might be, what structure for organizations is permissible. For this set of rules, often businesspeople effectively play the edges between acceptable and inacceptable behavior. Drawing on basketball, one of our central metaphors for business, many believe the adage, "No harm, no foul." At the public policy level, society acting through its representatives, determines which laws represent the non-negotiable norms of the community and which ones are rules of the game that can be tweaked to meet the needs and challenges of new circumstances.

The second level of decision making is the range of legal activities that have different ethical weight. The most difficult ethical choices are between two or more options, all of which are legal. In these cases, which have been the focal point of this book, the core values and commitments need to be carefully weighed as choices are prudently made.

For these decisions, business ethicist Robert Spitzer distinguishes between the silver rule—the ethical minimum—and the golden rule—the ethical maximum. The silver rule defines our ethical boundary and often mirrors our legal requirements. This set of ethical rules is proscriptive—"Thou shalt not …." By following these rules, we work to minimize the harm we do to others. The formula for the silver rule is "Do not do unto others as you would not have them do unto you." The golden rule is the ethical maximum. This set of rules are prescriptive— "Thou shall …." By following these rules, we seek to maximize the good we can do. The formula for the golden rule is "Do the good to others that you would want them to do to you."[14]

In exercising prudential judgment, the first step is to know the parameters between the silver and golden rules. The logical requirements of each set the boundaries for appropriate ethical options. Then, depending on the circumstances and the resources available, we can choose an action that is appropriately placed between the two ends of the continuum. Depending on the problem before us and the constraints of an organization, we may opt for the silver rule as a way to assure that the needs of the majority of the stakeholders are met. At other times, we may find that the golden rule is more appropriate as we are able to be generous and proactive to meet the needs of the community. In the process, we use both the ideals and intuitions of the deontological tradition and the reality and insights of the teleological tradition in making a prudential judgment about which of the available ethical options we will choose.

The Interplay of Intuition and Insight

A persistent conversation in ethics is whether our intuition is useful in making our ethical decisions. This conversation was first begun by Plato, who asserted that through human intuition we can know the ideal forms that then provide guidance for ethical decision making. The counterpoint was provided by Aristotle, who asserted that empiricism and logic were the fountainhead of knowledge for ethical decisions. Aristotle asserted that our minds "alone gave man the intuitive capacity to grasp final and universal truths."[15] As this conversation has evolved over the ensuing 2000 years, no resolution is in sight. However, for purposes of applied business ethics, both schools of thought are useful.

The first role of intuition is sensing that something just isn't right. While all of us have different thresholds of ethical sensibility, we need to assure that our antennae are always tuned to the ethical implications of an act. As our community continues to mature, behaviors that were acceptable yesterday may not meet ethical muster tomorrow. Part of having a well-trained sense of ethics is noticing what is on the horizon, where are the norms about to change. A commentator noted that at the time that Ken Lay and other Enron executives engaged in their creative financing, close to 95% of what they did was perfectly legal. As the implications of the edge of the law became manifest, the edge moved and under the legal requirements of Sarbanes-Oxley, the behavior that allowed them to soar is no longer acceptable.

　　　　　　　　　　　Everyday Ethics: *Making Wise Choices in a Complex World*

Once we sense that something is not right, we can use the tools of our reason to sort out whether or not our instincts are in fact accurate. Using the spiral of the *Baird Decision Model*, we can work through what we know and begin to inventory that information and ask good questions. At the point that our mind no longer has answers, if we wait quietly, we get what Lonergan calls insight—in a sense, informed intuition. We see connections that we didn't see before; we understand the world in a way that we could not before.

Once we have the insight, the cycle begins again. Our intuition is now informed by the experience, and we see new data and have other pieces of information that don't fit. We have a novel situation that requires a different approach. Nothing is lost, but the next layer of wisdom and understanding is added.

As we thoughtfully and intentionally move back and forth between intuition and insight, we learn to live with integrity and grace. We are able to have a sense of our core identity and know both the principles that we will follow and the goals that are important to us. We are able to see that we sometimes do the right thing and sometimes we miss the mark. Hopefully, in the middle we learn to laugh at ourselves and at the wonder of life, learning to live with a dollop of frivolity.

The world of business is the place where we buy and sell and provide services to each other. In the marketplace our gifts are recognized and we contribute to the well-being of the planet while we grow in wisdom and understanding. In our scurrying for wealth, power, and prestige, many of us take ourselves much too seriously and forget to live our lives with joy. One of my favorite definitions of vocation is that place where our heart's desire meets the world's greatest need. As we move from seeing our work as just a job to embracing it as vocation, we find great joy and the world can become just a tad bit better.

CONCLUSION — *THE WISDOM OF THE TAO*

As we bring our journey to a close, Number 8 of the *Tao Te Ching* provides a marvelous metaphor for the world of business and summarizes nicely the paths we have walked.

> *The highest good is like water.*
>
> *Water gives life to the ten thousand things and does not strive.*
>
> *It flows in places men reject and so is like the* Tao.

As we look at the history of business, we see that civilization grew along the trade routes. In the process of buying and selling, people flowed through wonderful new lands and encountered different ways of living and contextualizing the world. The world of business is not the world of conflict; it is the world of friendship. Business does not particularly care about national borders;

it goes where the money is found and people have needs that can be met. Business thrives on friendly competition and networks of relationships, not asking about religion or politics if the deal would be jeopardized. Yet, business, like water shaping the land, powerfully molds our culture. We enjoy the products, revel in the technology, and our lives are never again quite the same.

In dwelling, be close to the land.

One of the observations about Ken Lay and his leadership team is that they forgot that they were selling energy. Rather than focusing on their core competencies, they got excited about moving money around and seeing if they could sell the proverbial "blue sky." Many a company has failed because they forgot to attend to their customers: they moved away from "the land." The tension is staying tuned to the present while anticipating the future. The *Tao* reminds us to live in the present as we attend to our business and stay connected with both our product and our community.

In meditation, go deep in the heart.

One of the critiques of business is that we have made each other objects rather than people. As we go deep into our hearts, we notice the essential humanity of each other and cannot treat either ourselves or those with whom we work as invisible cogs in a machine. Psychologists have opined that the heart attacks of executives that seem to plague those who are in their 50s and 60s are caused as much by the shutting down of the emotions as by physical stress. Denied the connection to our deeper self and the rest of the community, the heart seizes as it breaks. As we learn to go deep within our hearts, we can find the balance that keeps us sane in the frenzy of the business world.

In dealing with others, be just and kind. In speech, be true.

These admonitions of the *Tao* provide the foundation for every ethical theory. While our situations are complex, a handful of key questions provide the necessary lodestars. When Robert Spitzer is invited to consult with corporations about ethics, he works through a process where the organization and individuals reduce their principles to four or five core questions that they ask in every difficult situation. These questions often deal with justice, kindness, and integrity. Each of us should have a concrete sense of when we would rather be unemployed than do something that goes against our core ethical values.

In business, be competent.

In action, watch the timing.

No fight: no blame.

The first step towards becoming an effective ethical decision maker is to continuously become better at what we do. As we exercise prudential judgment, we will begin to notice when to act and when to become silent. Aikido is one of the most effective forms of martial arts because its practitioners are trained to go with the force of the attack, letting the force expend itself and then turning it back on itself, instead of meeting opposing force directly with counter-force. By watching the opponent and then moving to throw him off balance, the athlete both conserves energy and is victorious.

In the world of business as we learn to know ourselves, be clear about our principles, and move intentionally toward the greater good, we become masters of ourselves and leaders in our communities. In the process we learn that ethics is about how we live every day. We then are able to make wise choices in a complex world with integrity, grace, and a dollop of frivolity.

CONTINUING THE CONVERSATION

1. Do you think that business as a whole is more or less ethical than it was 50 years ago? What do you see as evidence that it is more ethical than it was in the mid-50s? What do you see as evidence that it is less ethical than it was in the mid-50s?

2. How do you see the balance between the "silver rule" and the "golden rule" of business? Find an example in contemporary business where choices were made within the parameters of the two ethical choices? Does the balance chosen by the company make sense to you?

3. Do the words of the *Tao Te Ching* resonate with you? How do you see your own journey either mirroring or contradicting the wisdom of the *Tao*?

APPENDICES

Appendix A

From Ethics to Law:
Responsibility and Accountability

SIX LEVELS OF RESPONSIBILITY

Personal ethical beliefs and actions

The first level of responsibility and accountability springs from the personal beliefs and values that we have about what kind of a person we want to be and what we will do. While these beliefs are formed in community, in the final analysis we each have a set of commitments and values that we embrace and that determine how we as an individual will choose to live in community.

Community ethical beliefs and values

The second level of responsibility and accountability flows from the expectations that the community has about us, both as a person and as a professional. These are shared values that can come from the family, religious communities, ethnic and cultural communities, or professional communities.

Organizational codes of ethics

The third level of responsibility and accountability arises from the rules created by a business or non-profit organization for members of that group. These are often developed by those who are part of the organization and provide the norms that guide the behavior of all members.

Administrative Law

The regulations that are passed by a local community, state legislature, or Congress or their administrative agencies, rules that all people must follow, form the fourth level of responsibility and accountability. These regulations, enforced by the judicial system, tell people what standards they must follow and work to provide a level playing field for people in the community. These rules have the impact of law but may not exceed the authority of the law passed by the legislative body that gives the administrative agency permission to develop the rules.

Civil law

The fifth level of accountability and responsibility is found in laws that are passed by a local community, state legislature, or Congress that all people must follow. The Civil law also includes the "common law," derived over hundreds of years by custom and precedent rather than written laws passed by the legislature (e.g., libel, slander, malpractice).

Criminal law

The final level of accountability is those ordinances and statutes enacted by a local government, state legislature, or Congress that are enforced by a prosecutor or other governmental official. The difference between civil law and criminal law hinges on who can file an action (a citizen vs. a prosecutor) and the potential penalty (a fine vs. a jail sentence).

CONTENT OF THE RULES

The rules and expectations of each of these diverse groups have different content—the specific behavior that is allowed or prohibited takes different forms. For persons-in-community, the perennial tension is harmonizing among individual values and the various restraints imposed by community values. If the dissonance between the individual values of the majority and the rules of the community is too great, the community risks unrest or revolution.

PERSONAL CODE	❖ Rules, both written and unwritten
	❖ Results we want to accomplish
	❖ Relationships we want to nurture
	❖ Virtues and character we wish to develop
COMMUNITY VALUES	❖ Informal or unwritten rules that all are expected to follow
	❖ Results we want to accomplish as a community
	❖ Relationships that are important to maintain
	❖ Reputation that matches group self-understanding
ORGANIZATIONAL CODE	❖ Mission and vision statements
	❖ Organizational and individual law
	❖ Employee handbook that states all of the norms and rules of the organization
ADMINISTRATIVE LAW	❖ Laws about property: safety requirements (OSHA), labeling (FDA), proper landuse (zoning)
	❖ Laws about people: equal access (ADA) and treatment (minimum wage laws)
	❖ Laws limiting use of power: price (utilities) and advertising (FDA) requirements
CIVIL LAW	❖ Laws about property: theft, embezzlement
	❖ Laws about people: harassment, assault, malpractice
	❖ Laws limiting use of power: sexual harassment, intimidation, monopolies
CRIMINAL LAW	❖ Laws about property: theft, embezzlement
	❖ Laws about people: harassment, assault, murder
	❖ Laws limiting use of power: conflict of interest, fraud, misrepresentation

EVERYDAY ETHICS: *Making Wise Choices in a Complex World*

CONUNDRUMS

As we each determine how best to work and play in various communities, we need to learn how to work with and harmonize the differences. In the process we have some core decisions we must make.

PERSONAL CODE
- ❖ Deciding which action matches our moral beliefs and will meet our obligations while achieving our goals
- ❖ Choosing among conflicting goals and commitments
- ❖ Deciding what to do when my ethical values conflict with those of the community or employer
- ❖ Deciding what to do when personal virtues/character conflict with the community or employer

COMMUNITY VALUES
- ❖ Deciding what action meets predominate community ethical beliefs and values
- ❖ Deciding how to resolve differences between ideas about what is ethical
- ❖ Deciding how to negotiate individual ethics and community values
- ❖ Deciding when to renegotiate public norms when the reputation of the community doesn't match internal image or self-understanding (e.g., racist, sexist)

ORGANIZATIONAL CODE
- ❖ Deciding whether we must follow the code of ethics in a particular situation
- ❖ Deciding whether any particular rule applies to the specific action that one is going to take
- ❖ Deciding what the rules require in the particular situation
- ❖ Deciding what to do if our employer or a constituent requests or requires us to violate the code of conduct

ADMINISTRATIVE LAW
- ❖ Knowing the content of the administrative rules
- ❖ Knowing what specific behavior will violate the regulation
- ❖ Deciding what to do if our employer or a constituent requests or requires us to violate the law

CIVIL LAW
- ❖ Knowing what the laws are that will result in civil liability—money damages
- ❖ Knowing what specific behavior will violate the law
- ❖ Deciding what to do if our employer or a constituent requests or requires us to violate the law

CRIMINAL LAW
- ❖ Knowing what the laws are that will result in criminal liability—a fine or jail sentence
- ❖ Knowing what specific behavior will violate the law
- ❖ Deciding what to do if our employer or a constituent requests or requires us to violate the law

ENFORCERS

Each set of rules is enforced by various entities. One clear trajectory is that violations of personal codes of ethics are very private whereas the greater the violation of the community norm, the more public and protracted the enforcement. Because the consequences are increasingly severe, the procedural safeguards for each level of enforcement increase.

PERSONAL CODE
- ❖ Individuals have a personal set of ethical criteria and norms they will not violate
- ❖ Our conscience is the primary source of accountability
- ❖ We also have friends and colleagues who have permission to hold us accountable for our core commitments

COMMUNITY VALUES
- ❖ The community, through such actions as shunning or shaming, punishes one who violates community norms
- ❖ Different communities have appointed people as the guardians of the norms, whether formally or informally

ORGANIZATIONAL CODE
- ❖ The board or committee given the responsibility for enforcing the ethical conduct of the members of the community conducts an investigation to determine whether the code was violated
- ❖ In companies, the HR department is often responsible for the procedural enforcement of the handbook or organizational codes

ADMINISTRATIVE LAW
- ❖ The charge is filed by an individual or a state agency that believes an administrative regulation has been breached or a law has been violated
- ❖ The claim is adjudicated in an administrative hearing or judicial proceeding that determines the validity of the claim

CIVIL LAW
- ❖ The charge is filed by an individual who believes a contract has been breached or a law has been violated
- ❖ The judicial system determines the validity of claims made in a civil lawsuit and the appropriate penalty
- ❖ In some cases the person charged is entitled to a hearing before a six-member jury

CRIMINAL LAW
- ❖ The charge is filed by the state (through an attorney general, district attorney, or county attorney) after a complaint is filed by an individual or after a grand jury proceeding
- ❖ The charge is adjudicated by the judicial system in a criminal proceeding
- ❖ In some cases the person charged is entitled to a hearing before a twelve-member jury

PENALTIES

The penalty for each level of violation is increasingly severe. While people may hypothesize that people have died (or chosen to commit suicide) because of a guilty conscience, the community itself determines the severity of the penalty. Research into patterns of compliance indicates that to assure that we follow the law, laws must either be frequently enforced with mild penalties or infrequently enforced with high penalties—big fines or imprisonment. If community norms are infrequently enforced with low penalties, people who don't embrace the norms and are not self-regulating and law-abiding will take the risk of being caught and count on low penalties.

PERSONAL CODE
- Personal sense of failure or guilt
- Commitments broken because of short-term expedience
- Relationships broken because of lack of consistent, ethical behavior
- Reputation that does not match what we think is important

COMMUNITY VALUES
- Demoralization of members of the organization
- Criticism in the press or among other groups for being "unethical"
- Relationships broken because of lack of consistent, ethical behavior
- Tarnished reputation

ORGANIZATIONAL CODE
- Having disciplinary action taken if the Code of Ethics is violated, including termination
- Loss of professional accreditation
- Loss of ability to have a contract with the organization

ADMINISTRATIVE LAW
- Money judgment and/or fine
- Loss of license or professional accreditation

CIVIL LAW
- Money judgment
- Injunction (order not to do something)

CRIMINAL LAW
- Fines or jail sentence
- Loss of right to vote and participate in the community
- Deportation (if not a citizen)

Appendix B

Distinctions between rational and relational ethics

Lawrence Kohlberg delineated a widely-accepted schema for tracking ethical development based on reason—using one's mind to determine the right way to behave in community. Kohlberg's theory was criticized for suggesting that men were more ethically developed than women. Norma Haan, building on the work of Carol Gilligan and others, used a different measure for ethical growth and developed a schema for tracking ethical development based on relationship—using one's emotion as a lodestar for how to behave in community. Interestingly, Kohlberg's theories fit nicely with the core assumptions of the deontological theories; Haan's theories fit nicely with the core assumptions of the teleological theories. A comparison of the two theories tends to support a key claim of this text: that the effective ethical decision maker uses both skill sets while moving toward ethical maturity.

EVERYDAY ETHICS: *Making Wise Choices in a Complex World*

CONTENT OF THE STAGES OF MORAL JUDGMENT

The first comparison is the specific content of the two theories. Kohlberg defines the levels by how we respond to the rules of the community; Haan defines the levels by how we maintain social balance between ourselves and others, both individuals and groups.

	KOHLBERG—RULES	HAAN—RELATIONSHIP
LEVEL 1	*Punishment and obedience* Right is literal obedience to rules and authority, avoiding punishment, and not doing physical harm.	*A versus B* Vacillates between compliance with others and thwarting others. Balance occurs when self is indifferent to situations, unequal exchanges of good and bad; momentary compromises.
LEVEL 2	*Individual instrumental purpose and exchange* Right is serving one's own or others' needs and making fair deals in terms of concrete exchange.	*Prudential compromises by A & B* Trade to get what self wants; sometimes others must get what they want. Balances of coexistence (equal exchanges of good and bad in kind and amount).
LEVEL 3	*Mutual interpersonal expectations, relationships and conformity* The right is playing a good (nice) role, being concerned about other people and their feelings, keeping loyalty and trust with partners, and being motivated to follow rules and expectations.	*A compromises to "good" B's; bad B's rejected* Emphasis on exchanges is based on sustaining good faith (and excluding bad). Self-interest thought to be identical with others' interests).
LEVEL 4	*Social system and conscience maintenance* The right is doing one's duty in society, upholding the social order, and maintaining the welfare of society or the group.	*A and B = A B common* Systematized, structured exchanges based on understanding that all of us can fall from grace. Thus balances are conscious compromises made by all people including the self (common interests protect the self's interest).
LEVEL 5	*Prior rights and social contract or utility* The right is upholding the basic rights, values, and legal contracts of a society, even when they conflict with the concrete rules of the group.	*A = B* Integration of self-interest with other's mutual interests to achieve mutual, personally and situationally specific balances. (Balances are preferably based on mutual interests or if necessary, compromises, or the lesser of two evils.)

SOCIAL PERSPECTIVE OF THE STAGES OF MORAL JUDGMENT

The next comparison focuses on the different ways that the two theories contextualize the social perspective of the person making the decision. Again, for Kohlberg the focus is on the individual figuring out how to negotiate the community while for Haan the focus is on the individual fitting into the community.

	KOHLBERG—*RULES*	HAAN—*RELATIONSHIP*
LEVEL 1	This stage takes an egocentric point of view. A person at this stage doesn't consider the interests of others or recognize they differ from their own, and doesn't relate two differing points of view. Actions are judged in terms of physical consequences rather than in terms of psychological interests of others. Authority's perspective is confused with one's own.	People at this stage assimilate their experiences to the self's interest. No sustained view of other's interest; no view of mutual interest. The person believes that they have unqualified rights to secure their own good. Others are objects who compel or thwart self or who can be compelled by self.
LEVEL 2	This stage takes a concrete individualistic perspective. A person at this stage separates their own interests and points of view from those of authorities and others. He or she is aware that everybody has individual interests to pursue and these conflict, so right is relative (in the concrete individualistic sense). People integrate or relate conflicting individual interests to one another through instrumental exchange of services, through instrumental need for the other and the other's good will, or through fairness giving each person the same amount.	People at this stage accommodate to others' interest when forced. They differentiate others' interests from the interests of the self but have no view of mutual interests. This person believes that they have a right to secure their own good as others do. Others are subjects who want their own "good" as I want my own "good."
LEVEL 3	This stage takes the perspective of the individual in relationship to other individuals. A person at this stage is aware of shared feelings, agreements, and expectations, which take primacy over individual interests. People relate points of view through the "concrete Golden Rule" putting themselves in the other person's shoes. They do not consider the generalized "system" perspective.	Emphasis on exchanges is based on sustaining good faith (and excluding bad). Self-interest thought to be identical with others' interests).

	KOHLBERG—*RULES*	HAAN—*RELATIONSHIP*
LEVEL 4	This stage differentiates the societal point of view from interpersonal agreement or motives. A person at this stage takes the viewpoint of the system, which defines roles and rules. He or she considers individual relations in terms of place in the system.	People at this stage accommodate self interests to common interests. They assimilate common interest with self-interest (seeing self as an object among objects). All persons fall from grace. Thus, a person at this stage subscribes to the common regulation to promote their own interests as well as others'. (Some private self-interests are not subject to negotiation.)
LEVEL 5	The stage takes a prior-to-society perspective— that of a rational individual aware of values and rights prior to social attachments and contracts. The person integrates perspectives by formal mechanisms of agreement, contract, objective impartiality, and due process. They consider the moral point of view and the legal point of view, recognize the conflict between those two views, and find it difficult to integrate them.	People at this stage assimilate their self interests, the interests of others, and mutual interests. Self, other, and mutual interests are differentiated and coordinated. These people know that they have human vulnerability, weaknesses, and strengths as a moral agent, but also have a responsibility to their own self, others, and that mutual interests require that we treat each other as a moral being. Because they recognize that others also have strengths and weaknesses, they require others to collaborate in achieving and sustaining moral balance. They see the need to sometimes forgive others for their impositions, given the complexity of situations and the individuality of all.

OBSERVATIONS ABOUT MORAL DEVELOPMENT

The third comparison focuses on the different ways that the two theorists see ethical development. Again, for Kohlberg, one can develop by considering higher levels of thinking, thus reinforcing the cognitive foundations for his theory. Haan asserts that as one experiences moral imbalance one develops ethically, thus reinforcing the interactional or relational foundations for her theory.

As we study the implications of the two theories, we note that for maximum moral growth, we need a combination of theory and practice—we have to know both the various lenses that have been used over time to find the right behavior and we need experience, either through life or through case studies and simulations to get a sense of how we would really react to real-life situations and practice our decision-making skills.

ASPECTS OF DEVELOPMENT	KOHLBERG—COGNITIVE THEORY	HAAN—INTERACTIONAL THEORY
STARTING STATUS OF THE YOUNG	Blind obedience, then egoistically self-serving	Morally naïve but immediately induced to participate reciprocally
GENERAL DESCRIPTION OF MOVEMENT	Invariant stage sequence recapitulates the history of moral philosophy	Gradual progression toward more complex, discriminating dialogical skills
NECESSARY CONDITION	Logical development	Social-emotional experience
MOTIVATION FOR DEVELOPMENT	Comparison with others' higher-stage thinking and preference for more differentiated moral thought	Practical realization that more differentiated exchanges and solutions work better, the need to regard oneself as moral
VEHICLE OF CHANGE	Cognitive-moral disequilibrium	Social/intersubjective disequilibrium
USE OF MORAL TRADITION	Rediscovery of historical moral principles; deductively using these to make decisions	Uses historic moral principles in own constructions; reinterpreted, creative use of tradition
SOCIAL INTERCHANGE	A *sufficient* but not necessary element of development and action	The *necessary* but not sufficient element of development and action
LIMITING CONDITION	Lack of exposure to organizationally complex societies	Human interchanges that prevent participation whether in simple or complex societies
RECOMMENDED EDUCATIONAL INTERVENTION	Exposure to higher-stage moral thought, which produces cognitive disequilibrium	Opportunity to participate in actual and important moral experience

EVERYDAY ETHICS: *Making Wise Choices in a Complex World*

DIFFERENCES IN VIEWS OF ACTION BETWEEN THE TWO THEORIES

The final comparison examines the differences between how the two theories describe the decision-making process. Leaders who are working on their own ethical development as well as trying to create environments where their employees can make good ethical decisions should attend to both sets of information. The research would indicate that to create ethical environments, one should attend both to the individual's ethical maturity as well as the relationships in the organization that foster good decisions making. Thus, our current conversation about whether the problem is a few bad apples or bad systems may need to move to the next level where the answer is both-and—we need people who are equipped to make good decisions and organizational systems that help them make those decisions.

	KOHLBERG—COGNITIVE THEORY	HAAN—INTERACTIONAL THEORY
CONTEXT	Cognitive choices of separate persons drawn from the general rules or principles of their attained stages of development	Dialogue between persons that considers the particularities of the situation
PROCESS	Deduction of proper action from previously acquired generalized rules or principles	Participants' inductive clarification of everyone's self-interests and claims through full and free participation in dialogues
CRITICAL DETERMINER OF ACTION CHOICE	Determination of which general class of rules or principles apply to a specific situation	Essential conditions that facilitate or deter equalizing moral action
EFFECTS OF NONMORAL CONCERNS, E.G., EMOTIONS OR PECULIAR SITUATIONS	Comparison with others' higher-stage thinking and preference for more differentiated moral thought	Practical realization that more differentiated exchanges and solutions work better, the need to regard oneself as moral
CAPACITY FOR ENACTMENT	Persons' achievement of the principled stages or B-substage thinking, or judgment that self is responsible	Persons' level of moral skill, the public nature of dialogues, participants' mutual expectancies, the inductive discovery of solutions that match situations and ought therefore "to work"
DETERRENTS TO ACTION	Development only to lower stage	Persons' experience of stress and the situation's potential for moral oppressiveness
REASONS (MOTIVE) FOR ACTING	Judgment that self is responsible	To maintain a view of self as moral along with maintaining enhancing relations with others
SOCIAL STIPULATIONS THAT INSURE CITIZEN'S MORAL ACTION	Promote higher-stage development in individual persons	Provide opportunities for full participation

APPENDIX C

Excellence and efficiency

DISTINCTION BETWEEN EXCELLENCE AND EFFICIENCY

AS WE LOOK AT ETHICAL ACTION and our character as ethical decision makers, we are often evaluated against the primary touchstone of a market economy—economic efficiency. While efficiency is valuable, it needs to be moderated with a commitment to excellence. Without that tempering, the virtue of efficiency may morph into the vice of expediency. Below is a chart that summarizes the observations of Alasdair MacIntyre in the second edition of *After Virtue*, which helps us identify the distinctions between the moral content and effects of excellence and efficiency.

	EXCELLENCE	EFFICIENCY
DEFINITION	*EXCELLENCE* is a virtue that is definable independent of and before the establishment of enforceable rules of justice.	*EFFICIENCY* is a virtue that is defined as following the rules of justice until the rules change and thus has no independent ethical content.
GOAL	*EXCELLENCE* inherently strives for progress in achieving those qualities that mark excellence and also or progress in identifying our ideas and recognition of the highest perfection.	*EFFICIENCY* inherently strives to identify those means that will be effective in securing the goods and becoming effective insuring those means to secure the goods.

	EXCELLENCE	EFFICIENCY
REASON FOR ACTING	EXCELLENCE has a reason for acting, the goals of achieving excellence and being subject to the virtue of justice.	EFFICIENCY finds the reason for acting to maximize the satisfaction of its own wants and needs.
EVALUATION OF THE VIRTUE	EXCELLENCE is judged in terms of standards established within and for some specific form of systematic activity and is best thought of in terms of role in community.	EFFICIENCY judges people in terms of their acquisition of riches, power, status, and prestige.
EVALUATION OF PEOPLE	EXCELLENCE judges people in terms of their achievement of community values such as awareness, maturity, and competence.	EFFICIENCY judges people in terms of their acquisition of riches, power, status, and prestige.
ETHICAL REQUIREMENT	EXCELLENCE requires that a person seek goals in light of the virtues embodied by the community.	EFFICIENCY requires only that a person act to maximize satisfaction of his own wants and needs.
ETHICAL MATURITY	EXCELLENCE requires that a person continue to progress in reaching the ideals of the community and recognize what is the highest perfection.	EFFICIENCY requires that a person identify the strategies to acquire goods and become skilled in using those strategies to "get ahead."
PERSONAL MORAL STANDARDS	EXCELLENCE requires that people have personal moral standards that are harmonized with those of the community at large.	EFFICIENCY requires only that people follow the rules of justice until the rules change. Thus, people who are efficient may not have any personal moral standards.
DEFINITION OF JUSTICE	EXCELLENCE defines justice in terms of merit and what we deserve, using the same standards for all.	EFFICIENCY defines justice in terms of reciprocity of effective cooperation with the other person.
EFFECT OF BREAKING THE RULES	EXCELLENCE recognizes that someone who breaks rules generally hurts himself.	EFFICIENCY believes that someone who breaks rules generally hurts other people.

ENDNOTES

CHAPTER 1

1   James Burke, *The Day the Universe Changed* (Boston: Back Bay Books, 1995), 7.

2   Herman E. Daly and John B. Cobb, Jr., *For the Common Good* (Boston: Beacon Press, 1995). Daly and Cobb hyphenate the term person-in-community to emphasize the integral relationship that we have as individuals who cannot live without community. The ongoing conversation between individuals and the community significantly shapes our behavior and our expectations about how we and others are to be treated.

3   Christopher K. Germer, Ronald D. Siegel, and Paul R. Fulton, eds., *Mindfulness and Psychotherapy* (New York: Guilford Press, 2005), 25.

4   Joseph A. Petrick and John F. Quinn, *Management Ethics: Integrity at Work* (Thousand Oaks: Sage Publications, 1997). Petrick and Quinn provide the central insight for the organization of the four frameworks model. They developed a method for determining which of the primary frames one uses in management settings. A significant difference between their model and mine is that I place the justice theories of John Rawls and others opposite of Immanuel Kant and other deontologists. Petrick and Quinn posit a "systems development ethics," which includes contemporary system theorists (45-55). I believe that Rawls fits within that general construct. The other difference is that I renamed the ends of the continua. In particular, I see "fidelity" and "charity" as being ethical categories that also relate to economic systems. I believe that the essential conversation for ethics is considering and balancing the competing claims of the individual and the community.

EVERYDAY ETHICS: *Making Wise Choices in a Complex World*

5   Manuel Velasquez, et al., "Consistency and Ethics," *Issues in Ethics*, v1 n4 (Summer 1988). Daniel Goleman, Richard E. Boyatzis, and Annie McKee, *Primal Leadership: Recognizing the Power of Emotional Intelligence* (Boston: Harvard Business Press, 2002).

6   Alfred T. Hennelly, S.J., *Liberation Theologies: The Global Pursuit of Justice* (Mystic: Twenty-Third Publications, 1995), 209-211. The same conversations happen within the Eastern tradition as the balance among the four core values is sought. As leading teachings in Hinduism and Buddhism are charted over history, the same tendency to correct for over identification with one core value over another is seen.

7   Edward O. Wilson, *Consilience: The Unity of Knowledge* (New York: Vintage Books, 1998). Wilson asserts that the Enlightenment Project had three characteristics. First, was the unity of knowledge, the notion that through the use of reason one could understand the world. Second was progress, the notion that civilization as a whole will continue to improve. Finally, the project includes a method for learning which holds that all of nature is organized by universal laws of physics. See "The Enlightenment Project Lecture Supplement," Bruce W. Hauptli, last modified September 18, 2006, http://fiu.edu/~hauptli/TheEnlightenmentProjectLectureSupplement.html.

8   Peter R. Berger and Thomas Luckman, *The Social Construction of Reality: A Treatise in the Sociology of Knowledge* (Garden City: Anchor Books, 1967).

9   Ibid.

10 Karl Marx, *Das Kapital*, ed. Frederich Engles and Serge L. Levitsky (Washington, DC: Regnery, 2000).

11 Alasdair MacIntyre, *After Virtue: A Study in Moral Theory*, 2nd ed. (Notre Dame: University of Notre Dame Press, 2007).

12 For many years the United States Army had the slogan "Be All You Can Be," which aptly describes the plea of developmental psychologists, theologians, and philosophers who all enjoin us to become responsible, fully "self-actualized" adults. "Be All You Can Be" was created in 1980 by E.N.J. Carter for the advertising firm N.W. Ayer & Son.

13 See Catherine Keller, *From a Broken Web: Separation, Sexism and Self* (Boston: Beacon Press, 1988) and John Shotter, *Conversational Realities: Constructing Life through Language* (Thousand Oaks: Sage Publications, 1994).

14 Hans Jonas, *The Imperative of Responsibility: In Search of an Ethics for the Technology Age* (Chicago: University of Chicago Press,1985).

15 Daly and Cobb, *Common Good*.

16   Norma Haan, et al., *On Moral Grounds: The Search for Practical Reality* (New York: New York University Press, 1980).

17   Victoria Neufeldt and David Bernard Guralnik, eds., *Webster's New World Dictionary of American English, Third College Edition,* (Macmillan General Reference, 1990), s.vv. "morality," "ethics."

18   See Lisa Sovie Cahill, "Christian Character, Biblical Community, and Human Values," in *Character and Scripture: Moral Formation, Community, and Biblical Interpretation,* ed. William P. Brown (Grand Rapids: Wm. B. Eerdmans Publishing Company, 2002). Cahill distinguishes between ethical acts and moral character. The question becomes whether the ethical person is one who in fact does ethical acts or one whose character has been formed to be predisposed to act ethically, even if from time to time they may miss the mark and act unethically. Perhaps the difference is that those of us who are born predisposed to be ethical resonate with the teleological tradition while those who are born ethically challenged resonate with the deontological tradition.

19   Nel Noddings, *Caring: A Feminine Approach to Ethics and Moral Education,* 2nd ed. (Berkeley: University of California Press, 2003).

20   Charles Shelton, *Achieving Moral Health: An Exercise Plan for Your Conscience* (New York: Crossroad, 2000).

21   Daniel Goleman, Richard Boyatzis, and Annie McKee, *Primal Leadership: Recognizing the Power of Emotional Intelligence* (Boston: Harvard Business School Press, 2000).

22   Bernard J.F. Lonergan, *Method in Theology* (Toronto: University of Toronto Press, 1973).

23   Germer, et al., *Mindfulness and Psychology.*

24   Mark Clayton, "BP Report on Cause of Gulf Oil Spill Spreads the Blame," *Christian Science Monitor,* September 8, 2010, http://csmonitor.com. Marc Kaufman, " BP Points to Innovations Arising from Gulf Oil Spill," *Washington Post,* September 2, 2010, http://washingtonpost.com. For BP's response to the oil spill, see "Gulf of Mexico Response," BP.com, accessed November 11, 2010, http:// BP.com/ GulfOfMexicoResponse.

25   This model was developed from the work of Jacques Maritain, a Christian existentialist philosopher. See Lewis Galantiere and Gerald B. Phelan, *Existence and the Existent: An Essay on Christian Existentialism* (Garden City: Image Books, 1956). Parallels are also seen in Eastern Philosophy. For the same work from a Buddhist worldview, see Ken Wilber, *Sex, Ecology, Spirituality: the Spirit of Evolution,* 2nd ed., (Boston: Shambhala, 2000).

26   Andrew Newberg, Eugene d'Aquili, and Vince Rause, *Why God Won't Go Away: Brain Science and the Biology of Belief* (New York: Ballantine Books, 2002), 24-26.

27 Daniel Goleman, *Emotional Intelligence: Why It Can Matter More Than IQ* (New York: Bantam Books, 1995).

28 Edward S. Golub, *The Limits of Medicine: How Science Shapes Our Hope for a Cure* (Chicago: University of Chicago Press,1997), 90.

29 Ibid., 53.

30 Christine Hauser and Anahad O'Connor, "Virginia Tech Shooting Leaves 33 Dead," *The New York Times*, April 16, 2007, http://nytimes.com/2007/04/16/us/16cnd-shooting.html.

31 Alex Johnson, Pete Williams, Chris Jansing, and Alison Stewart, "Worst U.S. Shooting Ever Kills 33 on Va. Campus," April 17, 2007, MSNBC.com, http://msnbc.msn.com/id/18134671/#.

32 Goleman, *Emotional Intelligence*, xii.

33 Gen. 2:18-20 (New International Version).

34 "Name Power," FactMonster.com, accessed November 11, 2010, http://www.factmonster.com/ipka/A0768229.html.

35 Matt Ridley, *Nature via Nurture: Genes, Experience and What Makes Us Human* (New York: HarperCollins, 2003), 92.

36 Ibid.

37 Ibid.

38 Ibid., 96.

39 "Culture Clash Daunts Hispanic Women in College," The NSHP Network, May 10, 2004, http://network.nshp.org/profiles/blogs/culture-clash-daunts-hispanic.

40 Diane Vaughan, *The Challenger Launch Decision: Risky Technology, Culture, and Deviance at NASA* (Chicago: University of Chicago Press, 1997).

41 "Reason" begins in the upper left corner because it is the question for "individual-reflection." The questions spiral around the center counter-clockwise, in a way that tends to parallel our own quest for self-knowledge. The placement corresponds to Ken Wilbur's model of consciousness, which will be explored in Chapter 5.

42 The United States has a bias toward individualism, so everything we do tends to be evaluated against the question of whether or not we should limit the rights of individuals. Other cultures, particularly

Asian cultures, have a bias toward the community. Thus, when they balance ethical considerations, they tend to consider whether they should encroach upon the prerogatives of the community. This difference leads to much misunderstanding in international business transactions.

43   Those who believe in one God, such as the Jewish, Christian, and Islamic traditions, are part of what is called the Theistic traditions. Those who believe in the Sacred but not one God, such as the Buddhist, Hindu, and Wiccan traditions, are part of what is called the non-theistic traditions. Those who believe in human reason and spirit to shape our existence together are part of what is called the humanistic tradition (or pejoratively secular humanism).

44   "Living into" is a phrase used to describe our aspirations, values that we have but may imperfectly express in our day to day actions. This phrase reminds us that becoming ethically mature is a life-long process.

45   Immanuel Kant, *Groundwork for Metaphysics of Morals*, trans. Allen W. Wood (New Haven: Yale University Press, 2002).

46   One of the defining points of the Enlightenment was the "mind/body" split that emerged from René Descartes' notions of consciousness: "I think, therefore I am." This idea, called dualism, led philosophers to explore the reality of the observer and the "external" reality of the physical. As the physical world was subjected to scientific rigor, that which could not be seen, measured, or tasted was perceived as not as "real," and by implication, not as valuable, as that which could be verified scientifically. Thus, because the Spirit could not be seen, "God" was relegated to wholly transcendent, outside of the affairs of humans. Because emotions were chimeric, they were suspect. Monism has been reclaimed by feminist philosophers and those who claim that we have inappropriately narrowed Descartes' teachings. Thus, monists claim that we are complex persons, comprised of body and spirit, mind and emotion—all of which is valid and valuable. See Richard Tarnas, *The Passion of the Western Mind* (New York: Harmony Books, 1991), 278-279, and Nancy Rule Goldberger, et al., *Knowledge, Difference and Power: Essays Inspired by Women's Ways of Knowing*, 96-102.

47   This text is an example of meta-ethics, as I present the similarities and differences among the ethical theories that are part of the human tradition and harmonize all the various approaches to ethics through the Four Ethical Lenses detailed in Chapters 6-10. I believe that as the gifts of all the ethical lenses are used, we can be more effective ethical decision makers in this world.

48   Bernard Lonergan, *Insight: A Study of Human Understanding*, Vol. 3 of *The Collected Works of Bernard Lonergan* (Toronto: University of Toronto Press, 1957), 90-92.

49   Burke, *The Day the Universe Changed*, 7.

CHAPTER 2

1   Lonergan, *Insight*, 311.

2   "Cambodian Genocide Program," Yale Center for International and Area Studies, 2010, http://www.yale.edu/cgp/.

3   Daly and Cobb, *Common Good*.

4   Ibid.

5   Gen., 1:27, 2:21-23 (NIV).

6   Ibid.

7   Ibid.

8   For an example, see Marie-Luise von Franz, *Creation Myths* (Boston: Shambhala 2001).

9   Daniel J. Siegel, The Developing Mind (New York: Guilford Press, 2001), 63.

10 See Daly and Cobb, *Common Good*.

11 Frank G. Kirkpatrick, *The Ethics of Community* (Oxford: Blackwell Publishers, 2001), 91.

12 See Daly and Cobb, *Common Good*.

13 One of the tasks of philosophy is to put concepts into categories. Ethical and moral qualities are those personal or communal virtues that are embraced and desired. Political qualities, those kinds of things that one can expect in a community, flow from moral qualities. Thus, if autonomy—the ability to choose for oneself how to live—is a desired moral quality, political freedom should follow. Because our popular culture does not separate the two carefully, this text will refer to both traditional moral qualities as well as the political ramifications of those attributes.

14 Kirkpatrick, *Ethics of Community*, 92.

15 Ibid.

16 Joan C. Tronto, *Moral Boundaries: A Political Argument for an Ethics Care* (New York: Routledge, 1993), 28-30.

17 Dr. Seuss [Theodor Geisel], *Horton Hatches the Egg* (New York: Random House, 1940).

18   The "rule of law" provides the legal underpinning of the United States Constitution. The agreement that we each have made with the rest of our community is that we will follow the laws of the land whether or not we agree with them, they benefit us, or we will get caught breaking the law. The social contract we have with each other is based on enlightened self-interest, which says that I have a better shot of getting the good things of life if we all follow the same rules.

19   The first edition of this book was published in 2005. As the second edition was being prepared, President Obama was launching his initiative to help mend the breach between the Israelis and Palestinians, the eighth U.S. President to take on the task. As one looks for solutions to seemingly intractable problems, taking the long view and celebrating incremental improvements keeps one from total discouragement. See Chris McGreal, "Obama Warns Middle East Leaders 'Chance May Not Come Again Soon,' *Guardian*, September 2, 2010, http://guardian.co.uk/world/2010/sep/02/middle-east-peace-talks-israel-palestine.

20   Tronto, *Moral Boundaries*, 35-39.

21   MacIntyre, *After Virtue*, 242.

22   Ibid., 12, 32-33.

23   Todd Wilkenson, "Bridges to 'Nowhere,'" *Christian Science Monitor*, June 15, 2004.

24   Neufeldt, *Webster's Dictionary*, s.v. "economics."

25   Marica Baron, *Kantian Ethics Almost Without Apology* (Ithaca: Cornell University Press, 1999).

26   A key question concerning justice is whether fairness requires only that we use the gifts and privileges we inherit appropriately or if, somehow, these gifts themselves must be subject to distribution. Michael Nozick, a theorist in the line of Kant, asserts that a just distribution only requires fundamental fairness from the birth starting position—no matter how unequal our family wealth or genetic inheritance may be. Rawls asserts that our natural talents should be considered a common asset and thus subject to the claim of the community. (Michael J. Sandel, *Liberalism and the Limits of Justice* [Cambridge: Cambridge University Press, 1992], 78-80). This conversation becomes increasingly important as biological research shows that the gap between "haves" and "have-nots" is growing wider in the United States, not just because of systemic injustice but because people of comparable wealth and aptitude for academic and financial success are intermarrying. These families give their children incredible advantage because they have both access to the resources for maximum self-development but also the appetite for self-development, which tends to guarantee success in our community. (Ridley, *Nature via Nurture*, 90-95).

27   Stephen M. Johnson, *Character Styles* (New York: W. W. Norton and Company, 1994), 4-5.

28   Michael Walzer, *Spheres of Justice: A Defense of Pluralism and Equality*, (New York: Basic Books, 1984), 21-26.

29   Jack Weatherford, *The History of Money* (New York: Three Rivers Press, 1998), 106-107.

30   Rose Marie Berger and Brian Bolton, "Between the Lines: Coca-Cola or Clean Water?" *Sojourners Magazine*, April 2004.

31   Stephen Mihm, "Is Madoff Wall Street's Biggest Villain?" *Room for Debate* (blog), *New York Times*, March 12, 2009, http://roomfordebate.blogs.nytimes.com/2009/03/12/is-madoff-wall-streets-greatest-villain.

32   Yves Smith, *Econned: How Unenlightened Self Interest Undermined Democracy and Corrupted Capitalism* (New York: St. Martins' Press, 2010), 134-135.

33   William Greider, *The Soul of Capitalism: Opening Paths to a Moral Economy* (New York: Simon & Schuster, 2003), 57.

34   In the world of business ethics, robust conversations have discussed whether organizations can be "ethical" or whether responsibility always falls on individuals. To the degree that those employed by the organization are committed to carrying out the firm's values, the organization itself can be seen as an ethical decision maker. One must ever be mindful, however, that individuals within the firm, particularly those in positions of power, shape both the stated values of the organization and how those values translate into action. Enron boasted a thorough and salutary code of ethics that was handed out to each employee. Those in Enron's C-suites from Ken Lay on down systematically undermined the values of the organization by the policies and practices they pursued.

35   Neufeldt, *Webster's Dictionary*, s.v. "efficiency."

36   Deborah Stone, *Policy Paradox: The Art of Political Decision Making* (New York: W.W. Norton, 1997).

37   Jared Bernstein, "The Wal-Mart Debate: A False Choice Between Prices and Wages," Economic Policy Institute, Issue Brief #223, June 15, 2006, http://www.epi.org/publications/entry/ib223/; Kari Lydersen, "Target: Wal-Mart Lite," CorpWatch, April 20, 2006, http://www.corpwatch.org/article.php?id=13508&printsafe=1.

38   Dr. Amy K. Glasmeier, Living Wage Calculator, accessed November 11, 2010, http://livingwage.geog.psu.edu/.

39   Roger E. Backhouse, *The Ordinary Business of Life: A History of Economics from the Ancient World to the Twenty-First Century* (New Jersey: Princeton University Press, 2004), 128-129.

40 Robert Greenleaf, *Servant Leadership* (New York: Paulist Press, 1977). See also Henry Blackaby and Richard Blackaby, *Spiritual Leadership* (Nashville: Broadman & Holman, 2001).

41 Manuel Velasquez, *Business Ethics: Concepts and Cases*, 5th ed. (Englewood Cliff: Prentice Hall, 2002).

42 The notion of stakeholder theory was first introduced by Edward R. Freeman in *Strategic Management: A Stakeholder Approach* (Boston: Pitman, 1984). Since then, the concept has been the subject of vigorous academic debate. For two competing views see Aneel Karnani, "The Case Against Corporate Social Responsibility," *Wall Street Journal*, August 23, 2010, http://online.wsj.com/article/NA_WSJ_PUB:SB10001424052748703338004575230112664504890.html and David Martel, "The Case for Corporate Social Responsibility," DevlopmentCrossing.com, http://developmentcrossing.com/profiles/blogs/the-case-for-corporate-social.

43 William C. Frederick, *Values, Nature, and Culture in the American Corporation* (New York: Oxford University Press, 1995).

44 Ibid., 25.

45 Ibid., 136.

46 As the full economic impact of the Industrial Revolution emerged in the late 18th century, a persistent question was what to do with unemployment and poverty. One school of thought, advanced by Adam Smith and others, was to just leave the problem alone, subject to the vagaries of the "invisible hand" and moderated by individual acts of charity, almsgiving (See Backhouse, *Ordinary Business of Life*, 123-126). The desolation caused by those policies provided much grist for Charles Dickens and other novelists of the time. In the United States, after 150 years of laissez-faire, when faced with the economic devastation of the Depression, the government stepped in and over a fifty year period initiated a wide array of federally and state funded programs to provide the poor with a needed "leg-up" on the economic ladder. The wheel turned again at the end of the 20th century when a shift was made back to "faith-based initiatives" that were believed to be more effective at eradicating poverty and unemployment than government funded opportunities. Each approach provides its own set of problems and opportunities for abuse—which is why the conversation never seems to be resolved and people cynically echo the words of Christ (although somewhat out of context) "The poor you will always have with you." (Matthew 26:11, NIV).

47 Gabriel Madway, Reuters, "Lessons from the Dot-Com Crash," March 10, 2010, http://www.canada.com/business/fp/Lessons+from+crash/2667255/story.html; Tom Regan, "After the Dot-Com Crash," *Christian Science Monitor*, December 27, 2001, http://csmonitor.com/2001/1227/p13s1-stin.html.

48 "Those (Expletive) Enron Tapes," *San Francisco Chronicle*, June 16, 2004.

49   Scott Turow, "Cry No Tears for Martha Stewart," *New York Times*, May 27, 2004.

50   Smith, *Econned*, 134-135.

51   Amartya Sen, *On Ethics and Economics* (Berlin: Blackwell, 1987), 78-79.

52   Lynn Sharp Paine, *Value Shift: Why Companies Must Merge Social and Financial Imperatives to Achieve Superior Performance* (New York: McGraw Hill, 2002).

53   Robert Gilpin, *The Political Economy of International Relations* (Princeton: Princeton University Press, 1987).

54   Ibid., 28.

55   Velasquez, *Business Ethics*, 230-231.

56   Peck, "Mapping a Geographical Strategy," *Rocky Mountain News*, June 7, 2004.

57   Velasquez, *Business Ethics*, 231.

58   Gwladys Fouche, "Where Tax Goes up to 60 Per Cent, and Everybody's Happy Paying It," *Guardian*, November 16, 2008, http://guardian.co.uk/money/2008/nov/16/sweden-tax-burden-welfare/print.

59   "China's Export Dominance Must Force U.S. Rethink," *The Great Debate* (blog), Reuters, March 23, 2010, http://blogs.reuters.com/great-debate/2010/03/23/chinas-export-dominance-must-force-u-s-rethink; Martin C. McGuire and Hiroshi Ohta, "Implicit Mercantilism, Oligopoly, and Trade," *Review of International Economics*, 13(1), 165-184, 2005, http://sipec-square.net/~ohta/download/roie_497.pdf.

60   Federal Spending, National Priorities Project, http://www.nationalpriorities.org/print/5851.

61   Ibid.

62   See Donald C. Clark, "The Chinese Legal System," University of Washington School of Law, July 4, 2005, http://docs.law.gwu.edu/facweb/dclarke/public/ChineseLegalSystem.html.

63   Paul Spicker, "An Introduction to Social Policy: The Welfare State," http://www2.rgu.ac.uk/publicpolicy/introduction/wstate.htm.

64   Albert Bandura, *Self-Efficacy: The Exercise of Control* (New York: W.H. Freeman, 1997).

65   Adapted from William McCarty and John Bagby, *Irwin's Legal and Ethical Environment of Business*, 3rd ed. (Chicago: Irwin, 1996).

66 On September 9, 2010, "Don't ask, don't tell" was ruled unconstitutional by Virginia Phillips, a federal judge in California, in the case *Log Cabin Republicans v. The United States* (Case 2:04-cv-08425). On September 21, 2010, Congress refused to move ahead on a bill that would have repealed the DADT policy (http://voices.washingtonpost.com/federal-eye/2010/09/dont_ask_dont_tell_vote_set_fo_1.html?hpid=topnews).

67 The caps in the official name of the Patriot Act (The USA PATRIOT Act) are intentional, as the act's name is an acronym for "Uniting and Strengthening America by Providing Appropriate Tools Required to Intercept and Obstruct Terrorism."

CHAPTER 3

1 Tarnas, *Passion*, 278 (see chap. 1, n. 46).

2 Ibid, 279.

3 Nelson identified the deontological school of thought with the Protestant tradition and the teleological school of thought with the Roman Catholic tradition. He did so to point to the theological roots of these secular traditions and then noted that at some point what are now called liberal or mainstream Protestants in America rejected their theological roots and adopted the teachings of the Roman tradition. Those in the Evangelical tradition tend to maintain the traditional deontological heritage. I have chosen to remain with the philosophical designations while noting that many times our philosophy is deeply informed by our theology. Further, even though the rhetoric of the Calvinist tradition may be softened where each person is responsible for their own "salvation" and one's position in life indicates how well one is doing, the tendency towards marginalizing the poor and moving toward a powerful central government reemerged at the end of the twentieth century. See Robert Nelson, *Reaching for Heaven on Earth: The Theological Meaning of Economics* (Lanham: Rowman & Littlefield, 1991), 16-23.

4 Appendix C contains a chart that summarizes this section of text.

5 Adapted from Nelson, *Reaching for Heaven*, 54.

6 See Padmasiri de Silva, "Buddhist ethics," in *A Companion to Ethics*, ed. Peter Singer (Oxford: Blackwell Publishers Ltd., 1991).

7 Robert Audi, ed., *The Cambridge Dictionary of Philosophy*, 2nd ed., 396.

8 Nicole Oresme, *Livre du ciel et du monde* (1377).

9   Thomas Hobbes, *Leviathan or The Matter, Forme and Power of a Common Wealth Ecclesiasticall and Civil* (1651).

10 The inspiration for this line comes from Guy Noir, Private Eye, the ultimate existentialist, who was created by Garrison Keillor and whose escapades can be followed on the radio program *Prairie Home Companion*.

11 *The Journals of Søren Kierkegaard: A Selection, no. 1395*, ed. and trans. Alexander Dru (London: Oxford University Press, 1938).

12 Nelson, *Reaching for Heaven*, 54-55.

13 Ibid, 54.

14 The founding of the United States gets its legitimacy from the principles of natural law, which come from "the laws of nature and Nature's God," which lead to "these truths [that are] self-evident" and give us the right to be self-governing.

15 Max Weber, *The Protestant Ethic and the Spirit of Capitalism* (New York: Routledge, 1992).

16 Robert Greenstein and Scott Barancik, "Drifting Apart," Center on Budget and Policy, July 1990. "The growth in the incomes of the richest one percent of Americans," observes the Center on Budget and Policy Priorities, "has been so large that just the increase between 1980 and 1990 in the after-tax income of this group equals the total income the poorest 20 percent of the population will receive in 1990." The gap between the wealthy and the middle class has widened such that "in 1980, the total amount of after-tax income going to the 60 percent of households in the middle of the income spectrum … was 12 percent greater than the income going to the wealthiest fifth of households. By 1990, however, the income going to the middle three-fifths will be seven percent less than that received by the top fifth … Census data indicate that the gaps between both the rich and the poor and the rich and the middle class are wider now than at any other time since the end of World War II."

17 Weber, *Protestant Ethic*.

18 Charles Dickens, *A Christmas Carol*, first published in 1843.

19 Mark Clayton, "Environmental Peacemaking," *Christian Science Monitor*, March 4, 2004.

20 Ibid.

21 Michael Smith, "Realism," in Singer, *Companion to Ethics*, 402-405.

22 See Stanley J. Grenz, and John R. Franke, *Beyond Foundationalism: Shaping Theology in a Postmodern Context* (Louisville: Westminster John Knox Press, 2001). Grenz and Franke give a very coherent des-

cription of postmodernism and then assert that assuming the foundations hold is the best way to proceed.

23   Fred Lawrence, "Lonergan, the Integral Postmodern?" *Method: Journal of Lonergan Studies* 18:2 (Fall 2002).

24   Wilber, *Sex, Ecology, Spirituality*, 525 (see chap. 1, n. 25).

25   Tronto, *Moral Boundaries*, 2-3.

26   Robert Wuthnow, *After Heaven: Spirituality in America Since the 1950s* (Berkeley: University of California Press, 1998), 162.

27   Ibid.

28   Lonergan, *Insight*, 619.

CHAPTER 4

1   Fred Post of the University of Toledo named the five step process "The Baird Decision Model." Dr. Post was part of a full day seminar on teaching ethics that I presented. He went back to his university, rewrote his syllabus, and at the following year's Academy of Legal Studies in Business was one of the four featured Master Teacher's with his presentation on The Baird Decision Model. The name stuck.

2   Lewis Carroll, *Alice's Adventures in Wonderland* (London: MacMillan, 1865).

3   Ps 85:10 (The New English Bible).

4   Gordon D. Kaufman, *In Face of Mystery: A Constructive Theology* (Cambridge: Harvard University Press, 1993), 179.

5   Ibid, 178.

6   Daniel Indiviglio, "Does Hurd's New Oracle Gig Prove Business Ethics Don't Matter?" *The Atlantic*, September 12, 2010, http:// theatlantic.com/business/archive/2010/09/does-hurds-new-oracle-gig-prove-business-ethics-dont-matter/62559/.

7   Lonergan, *Method in Theology*, 9.

8   Reuters, "Dissidents Scoff at Move Stripping Eisner as Chairman," Business with CBNBC, March 5, 2004, http://msnbc.msn.com/id/4455951.

9   Paine, *Value Shift*.

10 Ibid.

11 *2009 National Business Ethics Survey*, 41.

12 Craig Mindrum, "Creating a Community of Character," *Talent Management Magazine*, August 2010, 28.

13 Patrick J. Kiger, "Truth and Consequences." *Working Woman*, May 2001, 56. The lead story features Judith Neal, who was a manager at Honeywell in Illinois. She was sent to identify a problem at one of the plants. She discovered that supervisors were falsifying test data, which led to an internal investigation and fines. Neal was eventually marginalized by her employers and her life was threatened. She sued under the False Claims Act and ten years later received back pay and damages.

14 Steven L.Winter, *A Clearing in the Forest: Law, Life and the Mind* (Chicago: University of Chicago Press, 2001), 76-85.

15 See Frederick, *Values, Nature, and Culture*.

16 Conversation with Mark Schlander, employee at IBM, Boulder, CO.

17 Anne Wilson Schaef, *Women's Reality: An Emerging Female System in a White Male Society* (San Francisco: Harper Row, 1985).

CHAPTER 5

1   Robert Frost, "The Road Not Taken" in *Perrine's Literature: Structure, Sound, and Sense*, 11th ed., Thomas R. Arp and Greg Johnson (Connecticut: Wadsworth Publishing, 2011).

2   Lonergan, *Insight*, 619.

3   Albert Bandura, *Self-Efficacy: The Exercise of Control* (New York: W.H. Freeman, 1997), 21.

4   Ibid, 20.

5   Greider, *Soul of Capitalism*, 53-56.

6   Hilberg, "The Nazi Holocaust," in *Corporate and Governmental Deviance: Problems of Organizational Behavior in Contemporary Society*, eds. M. David Ermann and Richard J. Lundman (New York: Oxford University Press, 2002), 169-172.

7   Velasquez, *Business Ethics*, 35-37.

8   Test this assertion by asking whether people watch Fox News, known for conservative viewpoints, or MSNBC, known for liberal viewpoints. Another test is the newspapers that people read: for example, the *Wall Street Journal*, known for conservative editorial positions, or the *Washington Post*, known for more liberal editorial positions.

9   Patricia Gorman Berry, *How to be BrainWise* (New York: Oxford University Press, 2006).

10 Goleman et. al., *Primal Leadership*, 39.

11 Wuthnow, *After Heaven*, VIII.

12 Daniel A. Helminiak, *Spiritual Development: An Interdisciplinary Study* (Chicago: Loyola Press, 1987).

13 Lonergan, *Method*, 9.

14 Don Edward Beck and Christopher C. Cowan, *Spiral Dynamics: Mastering Values, Leadership and Change* (Malden: Blackwell Publishing, 2006).

15 Ermann and Lundman, *Deviance*.

16 Richard H. Thaler and Cass R. Sunstein, *Nudge* (New York:Penguin Books, 2009).

17 Lawrence Kohlberg, "Moral Stages and Moralization: The Cognitive-Developmental Approach," in *Moral Development and Behavior: Theory, Research, and Social Issues* (New York: Holt, Rinehart and Winston, 1976), 31-53.

18 Elizabeth Liebert, *Changing Life Patterns: Adult Development in Spiritual Direction* (St. Louis: Chalice Press, 2000).

19 Janet Hagberg, *Real Power: Stages of Personal Power in Organizations*, rev. ed. (Salem: Sheffield, 1984).

20 Haan et al., *Moral Grounds*.

21 Jane Loevenger, *Ego Development* (San Francisco: Jossey-Bass, 1977).

22 Leonard Shlain, *The Alphabet Versus the Goddess: The Conflict Between Word and Image* (New York: Penguin, 1988).

23 Jonas, *Imperative of Responsibility*.

24 "About Us," SustainAbility, http://sustainability.com/philosophy.

25 Telis Demos, "Beyond the Bottom Line," *Fortune*, October 23, 2006, http://money.cnn.com/magazines/fortune/fortune_archive/2006/10/30/8391850/index.htm; Michelle Nichols, "Banks Value Social Responsibility More after Crisis," Reuters, September 22, 2010, http://reuters.com/article/idUSTRE68L4SH20100922.

26 Reported by Arja Adair, Executive Director of Colorado Foundation for Medical Care.

CHAPTER 6

1 Kierkegaard, *Journals*.

2 Philosophy seeks to identify the principles underlying conduct, thought, and human behavior using the tools of the mind. Theology seeks to identify the same through studying God and the relationships between God and humans. Many philosophers have a deep theological faith but confine their arguments to those that can be supported through reason and logic.

3 For a more detailed description of these theorists, please see Appendix B.

4 Nelson, *Reaching for Heaven*, 20-21.

5 Wilber, *Sex, Ecology, Spirituality*.

6 As Plato was exploring the notion of Ideals, he said that we were like the person chained to the cave with his back to the light. The person could see the shadows on the wall and mistook the shadows for reality. The task of becoming self aware is to remove the chains and turn around to see life in the light, embracing and realizing the ideals that are in fact reality. As Richard Parnas states, "The Platonic perspective thus asks the philosopher to go through the particular to the universal, and beyond the appearance to the essence .... The true structure of the world is revealed not by the senses, but by the intellect, which in its highest state has direct access to the Ideas governing reality." Parnas, Passion, 8, 12.

7 Wilber, *Sex, Ecology, Spirituality*, 25.

8 Daly and Cobb, *Common Good*, 125.

9 Ibid., 127.

10 "Firefighters Watch as Home Burns to Ground," Jason Hibbs, WPSDLocal6.com, September 29, 2010, http://wpsdlocal6.com/news/local/Firefighters-watch-as-home-burns-to-the-ground-104052668.html; "For-Pay Fire Department Lets Man's House Burn," Alex Pareene, *The War*

Room (blog), *Salon*, October 4, 2010, http://www.salon.com/news/politics/war_room/2010/10/04/libertarian_fire_department.

11   Wilber, *Sex, Ecology, Spirituality*, 239.

12   Petrick and Quinn, *Management Ethics*, 48.

13   Ibid. 98.

14   Wuthnow, *After Heaven*.

15   John Donne, *Devotions Upon Emergent Occasions*, "Meditation xvii" (1634).

16   Wuthnow, *After Heaven*.

17   Personal interview with William C. Convery, iii, State Historian for the state of Colorado. Convery states that in almost every conversation, someone inquired about elk and deer—no matter how bizarre we might consider the question.

18   For a discussion of the different regulatory needs of government and commerce, see Jane Jacobs, *Systems of Survival: A Dialogue on the Moral Foundations of Commerce and Politics* (New York: Vintage Books, 1992). See also Joel Bakan, *The Corporation: The Pathological Pursuit of Profit and Power* (Toronto: Viking Canada, 2004).

19   Personal interview with Fr. Michael Sheeran, S.J., President of Regis University.

20   Martin Luther King, "I Have a Dream," (speech, Washington DC, August 28, 1963).

21   Gutenberg is widely credited with inventing the printing press, but similar devices, which used woodblock printing, appeared in China as early as 593 AD. The first known movable type was also Chinese—invented by Bi Sheng c. 1040. Gutenberg's press was considered more influential because Europe did not share China's isolationism and because he used an alloy of lead, tin, and antimony, rather than the porcelain of Sheng's type, which made his press more suitable to large-scale printing.

22   Tarnas, *Passion*, 225.

23   The early colonies in the United States had the same policy of giving privileges to those who were part of the established faith, usually the faith tradition of the settlers who established the colony. Each of the colonies came to be free from established religion and persecution and then promptly established their own faith and persecuted others from different faith traditions. The First Amendment to the United States Constitution was intended to bring an end to the practice of seizing the property of those churches who lost the political leadership battle.

24 Members of the Jewish community had a precarious position in feudal Europe. Because of the commonality of language, members of the community could communicate across national boundaries; thus, trusted members of the community were available to carry messages for those in power. Also, because of the Christian prohibition against usury, the Jewish community became the money lenders, facilitating commerce and war across Europe. However, the Jewish community was vilified as the ones who "killed Christ." Sir Walter Scott's novel Ivanhoe has as a central theme the love/hate relationship between the Jewish and Christian communities during this period of time.

25 Robert C. Greer, *Mapping Postmodernism: A Survey of Christian Options* (Downers Grove: Intervarsity Press, 2003), 31.

26 See Kant, *Groundwork*, 9-12.

27 Ibid., 13-21.

28 Sandel, *Liberalism*, 2-3.

29 Carol Gilligan, *In a Different Voice: Psychological Theory and Women's Development* (Cambridge: Harvard University Press, 2003), 21-22.

30 Ermann and Lundman, *Deviance*.

31 Linda J. Kerber, *No Constitutional Right to Be Ladies: Women and the Obligation of Citizenship* (New York: Hill and Wang, 1998), 217-18. Kerber records one such chronicle of the suppression of women as full participants in the political and economic structure of America. For example, the perceived tendencies of women to be overly emotional were used as a reason to exclude them from juries. Of course, in the words of one jurist, women were also needed to assure that the fabric of our society was kept intact by being home to cook dinner.

32 John Gray, *Men Are from Mars, Women Are from Venus: The Classic Guide to Understanding the Opposite Sex* (New York: HarperCollins, 1992).

33 As cited in Velasquez, et al., "Consistency and Ethics."

34 Haan, et al., *Moral Grounds*.

35 Appendix C compares the findings of Kohlberg and Haan. One of the most interesting comparisons is what is required for change. Again, both approaches used together get a better result than either individually.

36 Bandura, *Self-Efficacy*, 114-115.

37 Gilligan, *Different Voice*, 129.

38 Nel Noddings, *Caring: A Feminine Approach to Ethics and Moral Education*, (Berkeley: University of California Press, 1984).

39 Haan, et al., *Moral Grounds*, 61-62.

40 Lonergan, *Insight*, pp. 618-624.

41 Frederick, *Values, Nature, and Culture*.

42 Shelton, *Moral Health*.

43 Thaler, *Nudge*.

44 Wuthnow, *After Heaven*, 2.

45 Ibid., 184.

46 "As Slow As Possible" is a composition by John Cage, intended as an avant-garde commentary on the passage of time. He stated that his piece should be played "as slow as possible," but omitted the detail of just how slow. One performance ran 29 minutes; another took 71; others were 9, 12, or 15 hours. The longest performance to date is a 639-year performance in Halberstat, the life-span of a particular pipe organ. The performance is ongoing, and it will end in September of 2640. "First Notes for 639-Year Composition," BBC News, February 5, 2003, http://news.bbc.co.uk/2/hi/entertainment/2728595.stm.

47 Wuthnow, *After Heaven*, 185.

48 This phrase has been used in many different contexts. Its exact beginning is not known.

49 Mark McIntosh, *Mystical Theology: The Integrity of Spirituality and Theology* (Malden: Blackwell, 1998), 6.

50 Christopher Bryant, *Jung and the Christian Way* (San Francisco: Harper & Row, 1983), 73-75. Bryant notes that "Jung calls the rejected elements of the personality the shadow...This shadow element is by no means wholly passive. It makes its influence felt in disconcerting ways, like a child who ignored by grown-ups makes a nuisance of himself in order to attract attention."

51 "Lea Fastow, Wife of Former Enron CFO, Begins Jail Term," *Yahoo! News*, July 26, 2004, http://story.news.yahoo.com.

52 William F. Lynch, *Images of Hope: Imagination as Healer of the Hopeless*, (Notre Dame: University of Notre Dame Press, 1984), 224.

53 Bandura, *Self-efficacy*, 45-60.

CHAPTER 7

1   Steven Mitchell, trans. *Tao Te Ching: A New English Version* (New York: Harper Row, 1988), 33.

2   The end of the modern era and the beginning of the postmodern era is placed, for convenience, at 1950. The twin images of Hiroshima and the view of the earth from space provided visceral support for the notion that we are connected. In science, the Heisenberg principle provided the final nail in the coffin for the assertion of the modern era that through science we would be able to determine ultimate truth.

3   John Witte, *Law and Protestantism: The Legal Teachings of the Lutheran Reformation* (New York: Cambridge University Press, 2002).

4   John Calvin is known as the father of Calvinism, which informed traditions such as the Presbyterians and then the movement known as the Anabaptists (because they didn't baptize infants), which was the precursor of the various Baptist and Holiness denominations. Richard Hooker is the father of the Anglican tradition as he systemized the reform teaching of Calvin with the liturgical understandings of the Catholic tradition. The legacy of the Anglican Tradition in the United States is the Episcopal and the Methodist church. St. Ignatius of Loyola is the founder of the Jesuit Order. Ignatius also focused on the individual's relationship with God as seen in the *Spiritual Exercises* that provides the cornerstone of Jesuit spirituality. See Nelson, *Reaching for Heaven*.

5   Kerber, *No Constitutional Right to be Ladies*.

6   Rights for women and minorities are pretty well established in the United States. However, members of the gay/lesbian/bi-sexual/transgendered community are still not given full membership, for example in the realm of marriage (which is authorized by the state) or service in the military. A rash of high school bullying also targets members of the GLBT community, resulting in a series of suicides as teens were unable to deal with their tormentors. John Cloud, "Bullied to Death?", *Time*, vol. 176, no. 16, 2010.

7   Noddings, *Caring*, 80.

8   Ibid, 84-85.

9   Jonas, *Imperative of Responsibility*, 12.

10   Laura Nash and Scotty McLennan, *Church on Sunday, Work on Monday: The Challenge of Fusing Christian Values with Business Life* (San Francisco: Jossey-Bass, 2001), 34.

11   John Eldredge, *The Journey of Desire: Searching for the Life We've Only Dreamed Of* (Nashville: Thomas Nelson, 2000), 13.

12 Ronald Rolheiser, *The Holy Longing: The Search for Christian Spirituality* (New York: Doubleday, 1999), 5.

13 David Whyte, *The Heart Aroused: Poetry and the Preservation of the Soul in Corporate America* (New York: Currency Doubleday, 1994), 168.

14 Ibid, 177.

15 Rolheiser, *Holy Longing*, 32.

16 Ibid , 27.

17 Kant, *Groundwork*.

18 Theodore Denise, Sheldon Peterfreund, and Nicholas White, *Great Traditions in Ethics*, 9th ed (Belmont: Wadsworth, 1999), 207.

19 Sandel, *Liberalism*, 9.

20 Ibid., 8.

21 Kant, *Groundwork*, 30-31.

22 The conversation about the virtues and vices of flame retardant baby clothes has been going on since the mid-70s. The following two references give two interesting perspectives on the issue. As the science is contested, figuring out what Kant would do is problematic—which is why this work is interesting. See Julia Wasson, "Take Action—Remove Toxic Flame Retardants from Kids' Products," *Blue Planet, Green Living* (blog), July 30, 2009, http://organicgreenandnatural.com/2009/07/30/take-action-remove-toxic-flame-retardants-from-kids-products.

23 Sandel, *Liberalism*, 18.

24 Velasquez, *Business Ethics*, 98.

25 Associated Press, "EchoStar, Viacom Resolve Programming Fee Dispute, Restore Channels to DISH Network," chron.com, March 11, 2004. http://chron.com/disp/story.mpl/business/2444172.html.

26 Velasquez, *Business Ethics*, 98.

27 Ibid., 99.

28 Lynch, *Images of Hope*, 224.

29 Ibid, 225.

30   "The Tuskegee Timeline," Centers for Disease Control and Prevention, last modified February 12, 2009, http://cdc.gov/tuskegee/timeline.htm; " The Tuskegee Syphilis Experiment," infoplease.com, accessed November 16, 2010, http://www.infoplease.com/ipa/A0762136.html.

31   Ronald Munson, *Intervention and Reflection: Basic Issues in Medical Ethics*, 6th ed, (Belmont: Wadsworth/Thomson Learning, 2000), 19.

32   David Lazarus, "Bankruptcy Has Its Rewards for PG&E Execs," *San Francisco Chronicle*, July 23, 2004.

33   "Mel Gibson Making a Cameo Comeback," *New York Post*, October 18, 2010, http://www.nypost.com/p/pagesix/cameo_comeback_for_gibson_Peu6uwUDgzCvcnPvKzvp1K.

34   Robert Nozick, *Anarchy, State, and Utopia* (New York: Basic Books, 1974), 151.

35   Karen Lebacqz, *Perspectives from Philosophical and Theological Ethics: Six Theories of Justice* (Minneapolis: Augsburg, 1986), 56.

36   Ibid, 56.

37   Nozick, *Anarchy*, 160.

CHAPTER 8

1   Langston Hughes, "Harlem," in *The Collected Poems of Langston Hughes*, ed. Arnold Rampersad (New York: Vintage Books, 1995), 426.

2   For a careful exploration of the critiques of utilitarianism relative to distributive justice, see Lebacqz, *Perspectives*, 22-32.

3   Hedonism is the philosophy that the primary motive for acting is individuals seeking their own pleasure. Often, people who embrace this philosophy are considered selfish as they live for the pleasures of today and give little concern to the worries of tomorrow. *New World Encyclopedia*, s.v. "hedonism," last modified April 3, 2008, http://newworldencyclopedia.org/entry/Hedonism.

4   Broader in scope than utilitarianism, consequentialism asserts that the rightness of an action should be determined by the outcomes, the consequences, of the action. Ibid., s.v. "teleological ethics," last modified July 6, 2008, http://newworldencyclopedia.org/entry/Teleological_ethics.

5   Kerber, *No Constitutional Right to be Ladies*, 218, citing 112 Cong. Rec. 17,769 (1966).

6   Ibid., 359. In a footnote, Kerber discusses *Taylor v. Louisiana*, 419 U.S. 522, 537 (1975), which found systems where women had to "opt in" for jury service rather than automatically be included in the pool unconstitutional. "The decision in *Taylor* would be reinforced when, in *Duren v. Missouri*, 439 U.S. 357 (1979), Ruth Bader Ginsburg argued the case of a black man charged with crime in a state in which women had multiple opportunities to claim exemption from jury service on the grounds of sex. *Taylor* overturned "opt in" systems; *Duren* overturned "opt out" systems."

7   Adam Smith, *The Theory of Moral Sentiments* (1759), 350 and *The Wealth of Nations* (1776).

8   Market equilibrium is defined as that state where the demand for a product is in balance with the supply of the product, a state that results in stability of price.

9   Gilpin, *Political Economy*, 28-29.

10 Lonergan, *Method*, 50.

11 Frederick Ferré, *Living and Value: Toward a Constructive Postmodern Ethics* (Albany: State University of New York Press, 2001), 221.

12 Goleman, et al., *Primal Leadership*, 61.

13 Lonergan, *Insight*, 619-620.

14 Lonergan defines terminal values as "the values that are chosen; true instances of the particular good, a true good of order, a true scale of preferences regarding values and satisfaction." The notion is that one should choose to pursue long-term goals rather than be satisfied with short term, temporary achievements. Lonergan, *Method*, 50.

15 Ibid., p. 35.

16 Taylor Branch, *Parting the Waters: America in the King Years 1954-1963* (New York: Simon and Schuster, 1988).

17 Lonergan, *Method*, 53.

18 Ibid., 50.

19 Rosemary Haughton, *Images for Change: The Transformation of Society* (New York: Paulist Press, 1997), 104.

20 Lebacqz, *Perspectives*, 16.

21 John Stuart Mill, *Utilitarianism*, quoted in *Great Traditions in Ethics*, 9th ed., ed. Theodore Denise (Belmont: Wadsworth, 1999), 180.

22 This particular feature of utilitarianism causes some confusion. If I am making a choice about where to live or what career to follow, and I am single with no family obligations, the data set is a point of one—me. If I have family obligations, I now need to consider them in the decision process—very quickly getting us from creating my personal good to creating the greatest good for the greatest number of people. Now, I may choose to ignore their happiness—and they may choose to not be part of my family. So, with this lens, we always begin with what will make me happy and then move to harmonizing happiness among the various members of the community in which we live and work.

23 *Star Trek II: The Wrath of Kahn*, directed by Nicholas Meyer (1982).

24 U.S. Population as of October 2010. "U.S. and World Population Clock," U.S. Census Bureau, http://census.gov/main/www/popclock.html.

25 Jennifer Rosenberg, "Oklahoma City Bombing," About.com, accessed November 16, 2010, http://history1900s.about.com/cs/crimedisaster/p/okcitybombing.htm.

26 Mill, *Great Traditions in Ethics*, 174.

27 "Maslow's Hierarchy of Needs," Abraham-Maslow.com, http://abraham-maslow.com/m_motivation/Hierarchy_of_Needs.asp.

28 "The most popular form of this saying—'You can't have your cake and eat it too'—confuses many people because they mistakenly suppose the word 'have' means 'eat,' as in 'Have a piece of cake for dessert.' A more logical version of this saying is 'You can't eat your cake and have it too,' meaning that if you eat your cake you won't have it any more. The point is that if you eat your cake right now you won't have it to eat later. 'Have' means 'possess' in this context, not 'eat.'" Paul Brians, Common Errors in English Usage, 2nd ed., (Sherwood: Franklin, Beedle & Associates, 2008).

29 *Wikipedia*, s.v. "tipping point," last modified October 9, 2010, http://en.wikipedia.org/wiki/Tipping_point.

30 Although the roots of this metaphor have been traced back to an Arab proverb, one of the earliest published instances comes from Charles Dickens, who wrote: "As the last straw breaks the laden camel's back, this piece of underground information crushed the sinking spirits of Mr. Dombey." Charles Dickens, *Dombey & Son* (London 1846-48).

31 Mark Frankel, "When the Tulip Bubble Burst," review of *Tulipomania: The Story of the World's Most Coveted Flower*, by Mike Dash, *Bloomberg Businessweek*, April 24, 2000, http://businessweek.com/2000/00_17/b3678084.htm.

32 Greg Griffin, "Nacchio Hit with 42 Insider-Trading Counts," *Denver Post*, December 21, 2005, http://denverpost.com/nacchio/ci_5341259.

33 MSNBC News Services, "Lay, Skilling Guilty on Nearly All Counts. MSNBC.com, May 25, 2006, http://msnbc.msn.com/id/12968481/.

34 Mike Whitney, "The United States of Foreclosure," The Market Oracle, March 20, 2007, http://marketoracle.co.uk/Article566.html.

35 Douglas G. Jacobs, "Suicide and Male Workers," *The Journal of Employee Assistance*, April 2003, http://findarticles.com/p/articles/mi_m0PLP/is_1_33/ai_n18616193.

36 Giles Wilson, "J.D. Salinger: A Glimpse inside of the Life of a Recluse," BBC News, March 23, 1999, http://news.bbc.co.uk/2/hi/uk_news/301077.stm.

37 Kevin Carey, "Education Funding and Low Income Children," Center on Budget and Policy Priorities, November 5, 2002, http://cbpp.org/cms/index.cfm?fa=view&id=1428; Dan Lips, Shanea Watkins, and John Fleming, "Does Spending More on Education Improve Academic Achievement," American Heritage Foundation, September 8, 2008, http://heritage.org/Research/Reports/2008/09/Does-Spending-More-on-Education-Improve-Academic-Achievement.

38 Carol S. Park, "Student Attendance and Mobility and the Effects on Student Achievement in Mathematics and Reading," December 2006, http://aplusschools.org/pdf/Park_PPS_student_attendance_and_mobility_12_06.pdf.

39 Nanci Hellmich, "Food Fright: Black Neighborhoods in LA Have Poor Choice," USA Today, August 5, 2003, http://usatoday.com/news/health/2003-08-04-food-usat_x.htm; "Mississippi State University Study: Rural, Poor at Disadvantage in Grocery Access," Mississippi State University, August 13, 2003, http://msstate.edu/web/media/detail.php?id=2189.

40 John F. Henry. "'Bad' Decisions, Poverty, and Economic Theory: The Individualist and Social Perspectives in Light of 'The American Myth'," *Social Economics* (2007) 36:17–2; Steven Malanga, "In America, The Poor Don't Work," Manhattan Institute for Policy Research, September 10, 2008, http://manhattan-institute.org/html/miarticle.htm?id=2963.

CHAPTER 9

1 Amos 5:24 (NIV).

2 Denise, et al., *Great Traditions*, 332.

3 Neufeldt, ed. *Webster's*, s.v. "ecology," 429.

4   Robert N. Bellah, et al., *The Good Society*, (New York: Vintage Books, 1992).

5   Frederick, *Values, Nature, and Culture*, 136.

6   Acts 5 (NIV) tells the story of Ananias and Sapphira, who came to Peter and represented that they were giving all they had from the sale of a piece of property to the church when in fact they were holding a portion back. Acts recounts that God struck them dead for the misrepresentation—harsh punishment indeed for lying. The issue was not that they hadn't given all to Peter; the issue was that they lied.

7   Karl Marx, *Critique of the Gotha Program* (Moscow 1875). One of Marx's most famous quotes is "From each according to his abilities, to each according to his needs." This particular quote is the subject of much angst and upset as people debate redistribution of wealth in a community.

8   John A. Rawls, *A Theory of Justice* (Cambridge: Belknap Press, 1971), 144.

9   Ibid., 143. Interestingly, behavioral economists are starting to question exactly how rational we are. For an exploration of how the theory of the rational, efficient market is flawed, see Justin Fox, *The Myth of the Rational Market: a History of Risk, Reward, and Delusion on Wall Street* (New York: HarperCollins, 2009). For an argument that we are humans, not economic machines, see Thaler and Sunstein, *Nudge*. Rawls did not go to the extreme of the economists; rather, he claimed that many of us thought carefully about our choices and worked to make good, useful choices instead of destructive choices.

10   Rawls, *Theory of Justice*, 143, 148-149.

11   Nozick, *Anarchy*, 239.

12   Catherine Jack Deavel and David Paul Deavel, "Choosing Love: The Redemption of Severus Snape," in *The Ultimate Harry Potter and Philosophy* (Hoboken: John Wiley & Sons, 2010), 53.

13   Bellah, *The Good Society*, 83.

14   Rawls, *Theory of Justice*, 48ff.

15   Ibid, 20.

16   Ibid, 302.

17   Ibid.

18   David E. Kromm, WaterEncyclopedia.com, s.v. "Ogallala Aquifer," accessed November 16, 2010, http://waterencyclopedia.com/Oc-Po/Ogallala-Aquifer.html.

19   Rawls, *Theory of Justice*.

20   When the law was passed, "gender" was added as a floor amendment. Thus, the legislative history focuses on the discrimination against African-Americans. It turns out that women were anxious to be rid of their systemic barriers to success as well. Jo Freeman, "How 'Sex' Got Into Title VII: Persistent Opportunism as a Maker of Public Policy," chap. 12 in *We Will Be Heard: Women's Struggles for Political Power in the United States* (Lanham: Rowman & Littlefield, 2008).

21   Rawls, *Theory of Justice*.

22   Frederick, *Values, Nature, and Culture*, 136-139.

23   Ibid., 139-142.

24   Tom Peters and Robert Waterman, *In Search of Excellence: Lessons from America's Best Run Companies* (New York: Harper & Row, 1982).

25   Frederick, *Values, Nature, and Culture*, 142-145.

26   Ibid, 145-148.

27   Joel Bresler, "Follow the Drinking Gourd: A Cultural History, http://followthedrinkinggourd.org; "Follow the Drinking Gourd," Owen Sound's Black History, http://osblackhistory.com/drinking-gourd.php.

28   Timothy R. Clark, "Leadership and the Geo-Ethical Shock," *Leadership Lessons* (blog), October 29, 2010, http://trclark.wordpress.com/2010/10/29/leadership-and-the-geo-ethical-shock.

29   Peter Fedynsky, "US Income Disparity Highest Ever," October 25, 2010, OANews.com, http://www.voanews.com/english/news/usa/US-Income-Disparity-Highest-Ever-105708773.html.

30   "Conspicuous Consumptions," *Time*, November 2, 2007, http://time.com/time/printout/0,8816,1680158,00.html.

31   Fedynsky, "US Income."

32   "Lessons from Ben and Jerry," *The Cape Cod Critic* (blog), January 29, 2009, http://thecapecodcritic.blogspot.com/2009/01/lessons-from-ben-and-jerry.html.

33   D.H. Lawrence, "The Rocking-Horse Winner," in *Harper's Bazaar*, July 1926.

34   Hanna Rosin, "The Evil Empire: The Scoop on Ben & Jerry's Crunchy Capitalism," *The New Republic*, September 1995, http://jonentine.com/articles/evil_empire.htm.

35 Charles Westin, "Sweden: Restrictive Immigration Policies and Multiculturalism," Migration Information Source, June 2006, http://migrationinformation.org/USFocus/display.cfm?ID=406.

36 Wikipedia, s.v. "Swedish Social Democratic Party," last modified November 14, 2010, http://en.wikipedia.org/wiki/Swedish_Social_Democratic_Party.

37 "Sweden Tax Rates," Taxrates.cc, accessed November 16, 2010, http://taxrates.cc/html/sweden-tax-rates.html.

38 Kiflemarium Hande, "The Current Debate on Cultural Diversity in Sweden," *Journal of Cultural Diversity*, 2008.

39 "Defense Spending by Country," *Rickety* (blog), accessed November 16, 2010, http://rickety.us/2009/06/defense-spending-by-country.

40 "United State Tax Rates," Taxrates.cc, accessed November 16, 2010, http://taxrates.cc/html/us-tax-rates.html.

41 "Tax Data: State and Local Burdens," Tax Foundation, August 7, 2008, http://taxfoundation.org/taxdata/show/336.html.

42 Anup Shah, "World Military Spending," Global Issues, last modified July 7, 2010, http://globalissues.org/article/75/world-military-spending.

CHAPTER 10

1 King, "I Have a Dream."

2 Roger Crisp and Michael Slote, eds., *Virtue Ethics* (New York: Oxford University Press, 1988), 3.

3 Charles Shelton, *Achieving Moral Health*, 48.

4 Goleman, et al., *Primal Leadership*, p. 39.

5 Bandura, *Self-efficacy: The Exercise of Control*, p. 43.

6 Shelton, *Moral Health*, 48.

7 A quick search of the internet reveals different lists of virtues. The Virtues Project has 52 core virtues listed (http://virtuesproject.com/virtues.html). Benjamin Franklin has a list of 13, eight personal virtues and five social virtues (http://school-for-champions.com/character/franklin_virtues.htm).

A group called Real American Heroes lists more than 100 virtues that heroes embody (http://www.heroesfacts.us/virtues/hero). The task is for each of us to determine which virtues are important for us to embody—and, just like the values, when the virtues need to be highlighted.

8 MacIntyre, *After Virtue*.

9 Shelton, *Moral Health*, 37-38.

10 MacIntyre, *After Virtue*, 187.

11 Mary Bateson, *Composing a Life* (New York: Grove Press, 1989).

12 Kate Chenery. *Tweedy, Secretariat's Meadow: The Land, The Family, The Legend*, (Manakin-Sabat: Dementi Milestone, 2010), 90.

13 Howard Shultz and Dori Yang, *Pour Your Heart Into It: Building a Company One Cup at a Time* (New York: Hyperion, 1997).

14 These support groups (as they have come to be called) have traditionally been our churches, synagogues, mosques, and ashrams. While for the past 200 years the continued secularization of ethics has philosophically separated us from our theological roots, for many Americans, our religious teaching provides the conceptual foundation for our ethical beliefs. Thus, our church and other social communities are often the ones who hold us accountable and provide crucibles for growth.

15 Michael W. Austin, "Why Harry and Socrates Decide to Die: Virtue and the Common Good," in *The Ultimate Harry Potter and Philosophy*, 266.

16 MacIntyre, *After Virtue*, 187.

17 Alasdair MacIntyre, *Whose Justice? Which Rationality?*, (Notre Dame: University of Notre Dame Press, 1988), 35-40.

18 MacIntyre, *After Virtue*, 191.

19 Ibid, 193.

20 Ibid, 192.

21 Ibid.

22 Paul Tillich, *Love, Power, and Justice: Ontological Analysis and Ethical Applications* (New York: Oxford University Press, 1960).

23   Walzer, *Spheres of Justice.*

24   Robert Putnam, *Bowling Alone: The Collapse and Revival of American Community* (New York: Simon & Schuster, 2000), 42-147.

25   *The Bucket List,* a film written by Justin Zackham, directed by Rob Reiner, and released by Warner Bros. in 2008, traces the last days of two terminally ill men who have a list of things they want to do before they "kick the bucket."

26   MacIntyre, *After Virtue,* 219.

27   Shelton, *Moral Health.* 38.

28   Susan Schmidt and James V. Grimaldi, "Abramoff Pleads Guilty to 3 Counts," *Washington Post,* January 4, 2006.

29   "Blagojevich Found Guilty on Single Count in Corruption Trial," CNN.com, August 17, 2010, http://www.cnn.com/2010/CRIME/08/17/blagojevich.trial/index.html.

30   Ray Long and Rick Pearson "Impeached Gov. Rod Blagojevich Has Been Removed from Office," *Chicago Tribune,* January 30, 2009.

31   Smith, *Econned,* 277.

32   Ibid, 284.

33   John M. Doris, *Lack of Character: Personality and Moral Behavior,* (New York: Cambridge University Press, 2002), 17.

34   Ibid, 22.

35   See Stanley Milgram, *Obedience to Authority: An Experimental View* (New York: Harper and Row, 1974).

36   Phillip G. Zimbardo, "The Stanford Prison Experiment," http://www.prisonexp.org/.

37   "Researcher: It's not bad apples, it's the barrel," CNN.com, May 21, 2004, http://cnn.com/2004/US/05/21/zimbarbo.access.

38   Johnson, *Character Styles.*

39   Haughton, *Images for Change,* 43.

40 Lynch, *Images of Hope*, 225.

41 Viktor Frankel, *Man's Search for Meaning* (Boston: Beacon Press, 2006).

CHAPTER 11

1 Mitchell, trans., *Tao Te Ching*.

2 Jeff Shannon, from *Widescreen Review*, http://www.amazon.com/Wall-Street-VHS-Charlie-Sheen/dp/6301016289.

3 Lester Thurow, "Business Scandals," Commonwealth Magazine, July 2002.

4 The difficulty with trying to decide whether businesses were more ethical 50 or so years ago is that the community expectations have changed. Fifty years ago, what we now claim is discrimination against African-Americans and women was just the way that business was done. Before the work of Ralph Nader and others, customers had no expectation of either transparency about the descriptions or safety in the products they bought. Before the work of Rachel Carson in her seminal work Silent Spring, the effects of corporate pollution were not even noticed. Thus, as the bar is raised, the temptation is to assert that business is less ethical than before. However, taking the long view, we notice ever-greater expectations for how people are treated and the transparency with which financial transactions are reported.

5 The Declaration of Independence of the Thirteen Colonies, http://www.ushistory.org/Declaration/document/index.htm.

6 See Charles Hampden-Turner and Fon Trompenaars, *The Seven Cultures of Capitalism: Value Systems for Creating Wealth in the United States, Britain, Japan, Germany, France, Sweden, and the Netherlands* (London: Piatkus, 1993) and *Building Cross-Cultural Competence: How to Create Wealth from Conflicting Values* (New Haven: Yale University Press, 2000).

7 Alice M. Rivlin, "Challenges of Modern Capitalism," *Regional Review*, Quarter 3, 2002, Federal Reserve Bank of Boston.

8 Rivlin, 4-5.

9 Robert Greenstein and Scott Barancik, *Drifting Apart: New Findings on Growing Income Disparities between the Rich and the Poor, and the Middle Class*, (Washington, DC: Center on Budget and Policy Priorities, 1990); Holly Sklar, "Let Them Eat Cake," *Z Magazine*, November 1998, 29-32. A current push is to narrow the gap between those at the top and those at the bottom. The problem is complex

because one of the primary incentives for performance was issuing stock. One proposal is to not allow companies to consider any income to executives over a certain amount—say $1,000,000 per year—as a deductible expense for companies. The thought is that such a proposal will provide a strong incentive for companies to reduce the compensation of the top brass.

10 A. Srikanth, "Stock Market Crashes and Bubbles - Why Do Investors Never Learn?" *Investment World*, April 23, 2000, http:// blonnet.com/iw/2000/04/23/stories/0823h011.htm. See also the New York Stock Exchange Report, *Shareownership* 2000, http://nyse.com/pdfs/shareho.pdf, as well was the "New York Stock Exchange's Historical Perspective," http://nyse.com/about/TodayIn-NYSE.html. See also "The Roots of Broadened Stock Ownership," http:// house.gov/jec/tax/stock/stock.htm.

11 Bruce Bartlett, "Stock Ownership is Becoming Widespread," *National Center for Policy Analysis Idea House*, January 24, 2000, http://ncpa.org/sub/dpd/index.php?Article_ID=10647.

12 Mark Thomsen, "Stock Ownership Increasingly Black and White," SocialFunds.com, June 11, 2001, http://socialfunds.com/news/article.cgi/article596/html.

13 "Institutional Ownership Multiplies," NACD Directorship, September 2, 2008, http://www.directorship.com/institutional-ownership-multiplies/; "Historic Stock Market Volatility and the Concentration of Ownership in Stocks," *Trader Feed* (blog), October 30, 2008, http://traderfeed.blogspot.com/2008/10/historic-stock-market-volatility-and.html; Marshall E. Blume and Donald B. Keim, "Trends In Institutional Stock Ownership and Some Implications," March 12, 2008, http://finance.wharton.upenn.edu/~keim/research/InstitutionalOwnership_12Mar2008.pdf.

14 Robert J. Spitzer, *The Spirit of Leadership: Optimizing Creativity and Change in Organizations* (Provo: Executive Excellence, 2000), 215-230.

15 Tarnas, *Passion*, 60.

16 Whyte, *The Heart Aroused*.

Bibliography

AUDI, Robert, ed. *The Cambridge Dictionary of Philosophy*. 2nd ed. Cambridge, MA: University of Harvard Press, 1999.

AUSTIN, Michael W. "Why Harry and Socrates Decide to Die: Virtue and the Common Good." In *The Ultimate Harry Potter and Philosophy*. Hoboken, NJ: John Wiley & Sons, 2010.

BACKHOUSE, Roger E. *The Ordinary Business of Life: A History of Economics from the Ancient World to the Twenty-First Century*. Princeton, NJ: Princeton University Press, 2002.

BAKAN, Joel. *The Corporation: The Pathological Pursuit of Profit and Power*. Toronto: Viking Canada, 2004.

BANDURA, Albert. *Self-Efficacy: The Exercise of Control*. New York: W.H. Freeman and Company, 1997.

BARON, Marcia W. *Kantian Ethics Almost Without Apology*. Ithaca, NY: Cornell University Press, 1999.

BATESON, Mary. *Composing a Life*. New York: Grove Press, 1989.

BECK, Don Edward, and Christopher C. Cowan. *Spiral Dynamics: Mastering Values, Leadership and Change*. Malden, MA: Blackwell Publishing, 2006.

BELLAH, Robert N., Richard Madsen, William M. Sullivan, Ann Swidler, and Steven M. Tipton. *The Good Society*. New York: Vintage Books, 1992. First published 1991 by Knopf. Page references are to the 1992 edition.

BERGER, Peter and Thomas Luckman. *The Social Construction of Reality: A Treatise in the Sociology of Knowledge*. Garden City, NY: Anchor Books, 1967.

BERRY, Patricia Gorman. *How to be BrainWise*. New York: Oxford University Press, 2006.

BIRKLAND, Thomas A. *An Introduction to the Policy Process: Theories, Concepts, and Models of Public Policy Making*. Armonk, New York: M.E. Sharpe, 2001.

BLACKABY, Henry, and Richard Blackaby. *Spiritual Leadership*. Nashville, TN: Broadman & Holman Publishers, 2001.

BOK, Derek. *The Trouble with Government*. Cambridge, MA: Harvard University Press, 2001.

BRANCH, Taylor. *Parting the Waters: America in the King Years 1954-63*. New York: Simon and Schuster, 1988.

BRIANS, Paul. *Common Errors in English Usage*. 2nd ed., Sherwood, OR: Franklin, Beedle & Associates, 2008.

BROWN, William P., ed. *Character & Scripture: Moral Formation, Community, and Biblical Interpretation*. Grand Rapids, MI: William B. Eerdmans Publishing Company, 2002.

BRYANT, Christopher. *Jung and the Christian Way*. San Francisco: Harper & Row, 1983.

BURKE, James. *The Day the Universe Changed*. Boston: Back Bay Books, 1995.

CAHILL, Lisa Sowle. *Christian Character, Biblical Community, and Human Values*. In *Character and Scripture: Moral Formation, Community, and Biblical Interpretation*. Edited by William P. Brown. Grand Rapids, MI: Wm. B. Eerdmans Publishing Company, 2002.

CARR, Nicholas. *The Shallows: What the internet is doing to our brains*. New York: Wm. B. W. W. Norton & Company, Inc., 2010.

CARROLL, Lewis. "Alice's Adventures in Wonderland." *The Junior Classics, Vol 5*. NP: P.F. Collier and Son Corporation, 1938, 1948. Originally published by the Macmillan Company, ND. Page references are to the 1948 edition.

CRISP, Roger, and Michael Slote. *Virtue Ethics*. New York: Oxford University Press, 1998. First printed 1997 by Oxford University Press. Page references are to the 1998 edition.

DALY, Herman E., and John B. Cobb, Jr. *For the Common Good*. Boston: Beacon Press, 1995.

DEAVEL, Catherine Jack, and David Paul Deavel. "Choosing Love: The Redemption of Severus Snape," in *The Ultimate Harry Potter and Philosophy*. Hoboken, NJ: John Wiley & Sons, 2010.

DECLARATION of Independence of the Thirteen Colonies in Congress. July 4, 1776.

DENISE, Theodore C., Sheldon P. Peterfreund, and Nicholas P. White. *Great Traditions in Ethics*. 9th edition. Belmont, CA: Wadsworth Publishing Company, 1999.

DICKENS, Charles. *A Christmas Carol*. New York: Signet Classic, 1984.

——. *Dombey & Son*. London 1846-48.

DORIS, John M. *Lack of Character: Personality and Moral Behavior*. New York: Cambridge University Press, 2002.

ELDREDGE, John. *The Journey of Desire: Searching for the Life We've Only Dreamed Of*. Nashville, TN: Thomas Nelson, Inc., 2000.

ERMANN, M. David, and Richard J. Lundman. *Corporate and Governmental Deviance: Problems of Organizational Behavior in Contemporary Society*. 5th ed. New York: Oxford University Press, 1996.

ETZIONI, Amitai. *The Spirit of Community: Rights, Responsibilities, and the Communitarian*. New York: Crown Publishers, Inc., 1993.

FAURE, Bernard. *Double Exposure: Cutting across Buddhist and Eastern Discourses*. Translated by Janet Lloyd. Stanford, CA: Stanford University Press, 2004.

FERRÉ, Frederick. *Living and Value: Toward a Constructive Postmodern Ethics*. Albany, NY: State University of New York Press, 2001.

FOX, Justin. *The Myth of the Rational Market: A History of Risk, Reward, and Delusion on Wall Street*. New York: HarperCollins, 2009.

FRANKL, Viktor. *Man's Search for Meaning*. Boston: Beacon Press, 2006.

VON FRANZ, Marie-Louise. *Creation Myths*. Boston: Shambhala 2001.

FREDERICK, William C. Values, *Nature, and Culture in the American Corporation*. New York: Oxford University Press, 1995.

FREEMAN, Jo. "How 'Sex' Got Into Title VII: Persistent Opportunism as a Maker of Public Policy." In *We Will Be Heard: Women's Struggles for Political Power in the United States*. Lanham, MD: Rowman & Littlefield, 2008.

FROST, Robert. "The Road Not Travelled." In *Perrine's Literature: Structure, Sound, and Sense*. Edited by Thomas R. Arp and Greg Johnson. 3rd ed. New York: Houghton Mifflin Harcourt, 1978.

FULLER, Robert C. *Ecology of Care: An Interdisciplinary Analysis of the Self and Moral Obligation*. Louisville, KY: Westminster/John Knox Press, 1992.

GERMER, Christopher K., Ronald D. Siegel, and Paul R. Fulton, eds. *Mindfulness and Psychotherapy*. New York: Guilford Press, 2005.

GILLIGAN, Carol. *In a Different Voice: Psychological Theory and Women's Development*. Cambridge, MA: Harvard University Press, 2003.

GILPIN, Robert. *The Political Economy of International Relations*. With the assistance of Jean M. Gilpin. Princeton, NJ: Princeton University Press, 1987.

GOLDBERGER, Nancy Rule, Jill MattuckTarule, Blythe McVicker Clinchy, and Mary Field Belenky, eds. *Knowledge, Difference, and Power: Essays Inspired by Women's Ways of Knowing*. New York: BasicBooks, 1996.

GOLEMAN, Daniel. *Emotional Intelligence: Why It Can Matter More Than IQ*. New York: Bantam Books, 1997.

GOLEMAN, Daniel, Richard Boyatzis, and Annie McKee. *Primal Leadership: Recognizing the Power of Emotional Intelligence*. Boston: Harvard Business School Press, 2000.

GOLUB, Edward S. *The Limits of Medicine: How Science Shapes Our Hope for a Cure*. Chicago: University of Chicago Press, 1997.

GRAY, John. *Men Are from Mars, Women Are from Venus: The Classic Guide to Understanding the Opposite Sex*. New York: HarperCollins, 1992.

GREENLEAF, Robert. *Servant Leadership*. New York: Paulist Press, 1977.

GREER, Robert C. *Mapping Postmodernism: A Survey of Christian Options*. Downers Grove, IL: Intervarsity Press, 2003.

GREIDER, William. *The Soul of Capitalism: Opening Paths to a Moral Economy*. New York: Simon & Schuster, 2003.

GRENZ, Stanley J., and John R. Franke. *Beyond Foundationalism: Shaping Theology in a Postmodern Context*. Louisville, KY: Westminster John Knox Press, 2001.

HAAN, Norma, Eliane Aerts, and Bruce A. B. Cooper. *On Moral Grounds: The Search for Practical Morality*. New York: New York University Press, 1980.

HAGBERG, Janet. *Real Power: Stages of Personal Power in Organizations*. Revised edition. Salem, WI: Sheffield Publishing Company, 1984.

HAMPDEN-TURNER, Charles M., and Alfons Trompenaars. *Building Cross-Cultural Competence: How to Create Wealth from Conflicting Values*. New Haven, CT: Yale University Press, 2000.

————. *The Seven Cultures of Capitalism: Value Systems for Creating Wealth.* New York: Bantam Doubleday Dell, 1993.

HAUGHTON, Rosemary Luling. *Images for Change: The Transformation of Society.* New York: Paulist Press, 1997.

HELMINIAK, Daniel A. *Spiritual Development: An Interdisciplinary Study.* Chicago: Loyola Press, 1987.

HENNELLY, Alfred T., S.J. *Liberation Theologies: The Global Pursuit of Justice.* Mystic, CT: Twenty-Third Publications, 1995.

HILBERG, Raul. "The Nazi Holocaust." In *Corporate and Governmental Deviance: Problems of Organizational Behavior in Contemporary Society.* Edited by M. David Ermann and Richard J. Lundman. New York: Oxford University Press, 2002.

HOBBES, Thomas. *Leviathan; or, The Matter, Forme and Power of a Common Wealth Ecclesiasticall and Civil.* 1651.

HUGHES, Langston. "Harlem." In *The Collected Poems of Langston Hughes.* Edited by Arnold Rampersad. New York: Vintage Books, 1995.

JACOBS, Jane. *Systems of Survival: A Dialogue on the Moral Foundations of Commerce and Politics.* New York: Vintage Books, 1992.

————. *The Natures of Economies.* New York: The Modern Library, 2000.

JOHNSON, Stephen M. *Character Styles.* New York: W. W. Norton and Company, 1994.

JONAS, Hans. *The Imperative of Responsibility: In Search of an Ethics for the Technology Age.* Chicago: University of Chicago Press,1985.

KANT, Immanuel. *Groundwork for Metaphysics of Morals.* Translated by Allen W. Wood. New Haven, CT: Yale University Press, 2002.

KAUFMAN, Gordon D. *In Face of Mystery: A Constructive Theology.* Cambridge, MA: Harvard University Press, 1993.

KELLER, Catherine. *From a Broken Web: Separation, Sexism and Self.* Boston, MA: Beacon Press, 1988.

KERBER, Linda K. *No Constitutional Right to be Ladies: Women and the Obligations of Citizenship.* New York: Hill and Wang, 1998.

KIERKEGAARD, Søren. *The Journals of Søren Kierkegaard: A Selection, no. 1395.* Edited and translated by Alexander Dru. London: Oxford University Press, 1938.

Kirkpatrick, Frank G. *The Ethics of Community*. Malden, MA: Blackwell Publishers, 2001.

Kohlberg, Lawrence. "Moral Stages and Moralization: The Cognitive-Developmental Approach," in *Moral Development and Behavior: Theory, Research, and Social Issues*. New York: Holt, Rinehart and Winston, 1976.

Lao-tzu. *Tao Te Ching: A New English Version*. Translated by Steven Mitchell. New York: Harper & Row, Publishers, 1988.

Lebacqz, Karen. *Perspectives from Philosophical and Theological Ethics: Six Theories of Justice*. Minneapolis, MN: Augsburg Publishing House, 1986.

Leher, Jonah. *How We Decide*. New York: Houghton Mifflin Harcourt, 2009.

Liebert, Elizabeth. *Changing Life Patterns: Adult Development in Spiritual Direction*. St. Louis, MO: Chalice Press, 2000.

Loeb, Paul Rogat. *Soul of a Citizen: Living with Conviction in a Cynical Time*. New York: St. Martin's Griffin, 1999.

Loevenger, Jane. *Ego Development*. San Francisco: Jossey-Bass Publishers, 1977.

Lonergan, Bernard. *Insight: A Study of Human Understanding*. Vol. 3 of *The Collected Works of Bernard Lonergan*. Toronto: University of Toronto Press, 1957.

—————. *Method in Theology*. Toronto: University of Toronto Press, 1973.

Lynch, William F. *Images of Hope: Imagination as Healer of the Hopeless*. Notre Dame, IN: University of Notre Dame Press, 1974.

MacIntyre, Alasdair. *After Virtue: A Study in Moral Theory*. 2nd edition. Notre Dame, IN: University of Notre Dame Press, 1984. First printed 1981 by University of Notre Dame Press. Page references are to the 1981 edition.

—————. *Three Rival Versions of Moral Enquiry: Encyclopadeia, Genealogy, and Tradition*. Notre Dame, IN: University of Notre Dame Press, 1990.

—————. *Whose Justice? Which Rationality?* Notre Dame, IN: University of Notre Dame Press, 1988.

Marion, Jim. *Putting on the Mind of Christ: The Inner Work of Christian Spirituality*. Charlottesville, VA: Hampton Roads Publishing Company. 2000.

Maritain, Jacques. *Existence and the Existent: An Essay on Christian Existentialism*. Translated by Lewis Galantiere and Gerald B. Phelan. Garden City, NY: Image Books, 1956. First printed 1948 by Pantheon Books. Page references are to the 1956 edition.

MARX, Karl. *Critique of the Gotha Program*. Moscow 1875.

————, *Das Kapital*. Edited by Frederich Engles and Serge L. Levitsky. Washington, DC: Regnery, 2000.

McCARTY, William, and John Bagby. *Irwin's Legal and Ethical Environment of Business*. 3rd edition. Chicago: Irwin, 1996.

McCRACKEN, Grant. *Chief Culture Officer: How to create a living, breathing corporation*. New York: Basic Books, 2009.

McDOWELL, Banks. *Ethics and Excuses: The Crisis in Professional Responsibility*. Westport, CN: Quorum Books, 2000.

McINTOSH, Mark A. *Mystical Theology: The Integrity of Spirituality and Theology*. Malden, MA: Blackwell Publishers, 1998.

MILGRAM, Stanley. *Obedience to Authority: An Experimental View*. New York: Harper and Row, 1974.

MILL, John Stuart. *Utilitarianism*. Quoted in *Great Traditions in Ethics*. Edited by Theodore Denise. 9th ed. Belmont, CA: Wadsworth, 1999.

MUNSON, Ronald. *Intervention and Reflection: Basic Issues in Medical Ethics*. 6th ed. Belmont, CA: Wadsworth/Thomson Learning, 2000.

NASH, Laura, and Scotty McLennan. *Church on Sunday, Work on Monday: The Challenge of Fusing Christian Values with Business Life*. San Francisco: Jossey-Bass, 2001.

NELSON, Robert. *Reaching for Heaven on Earth: The Theological Meaning of Economics*. Lanham, MD: Rowman & Littlefield, 1991.

NEUFELDT, Victoria, and David Bernard Guralnik, eds., *Webster's New World Dictionary of American English*. Third College Edition. Macmillan General Reference, 1990.

NEWBERG, Andrew, Eugene d'Aquili, and Vince Rause. *Why God Won't Go Away: Brain Science and the Biology of Belief*. New York: Ballantine Books, 2002.

NODDINGS, Nel. *Caring: A Feminine Approach to Ethics and Moral Education*. 2nd ed. Berkeley, CA: University of California Press, 2003. Page references are from the 1984 edition.

NOZICK, Robert. *Anarchy, State, and Utopia*. New York: Basic Books, Inc., 1974.

ORESME, Nicole. *Livre du ciel et du monde*. 1377.

EVERYDAY ETHICS: *Making Wise Choices in a Complex World*

Paine, Lynn Sharp. *Value Shift: Why Companies Must Merge Social and Financial Imperatives to Achieve Superior Performance*. New York: McGraw Hill, 2002.

Palmer, Parker J. *Let Your Life Speak: Listening for the Voice of Vocation*. San Francisco: Jossey-Bass, 2000.

Pearson, Christine and Christine Porath. *The Cost of Bad Behavior: How incivility is damaging your business and what to do about it*. New York: Portfolio, 2009.

Peck, M. Scott. *People of the Lie: The Hope for Healing Human Evil*. New York: A Touchstone Book, 1983.

Peters, Tom, and Robert Waterman. *In Search of Excellence: Lessons from America's Best Run Companies*. New York: Harper & Row, 1982.

Petrick, Joseph A., and John F. Quinn. *Management Ethics: Integrity at Work*. Thousand Oaks, CA: Sage Publications, 1997.

Putnam, Robert D. *Bowling Alone: The Collapse and Revival of American Community*. New York: Simon & Schuster, 2000.

Rawls, John. *A Theory of Justice*. Cambridge, MA: Belknap Press of Harvard University Press, 1971.

Ridley, Matt. *Nature via Nurture: Genes, Experience and What Makes Us Human*. New York: HarperCollins, 2003.

Rolheiser, Ronald. *The Holy Longing: The Search for Christian Spirituality*. New York: Doubleday, 1999.

Sandel, Michael J. *Liberalism and the Limits of Justice*. Cambridge, MA: Cambridge University Press, 1992.

Schaef, Anne Wilson. *Women's Reality: An Emerging Female System in a White Male Society*. San Francisco: Harper & Row, Publishers. 1985.

Schultz, Howard, and Dori Jones Yang. *Pour Your Heart into It: How Starbucks Built a Company One Cup at a Time*. New York: Hyperion, 1997.

Sen, Amartya. *On Ethics and Economics*. Berlin: Blackwell, 1987.

Seuss, Dr. [Theodor Geisel]. *Horton Hatches the Egg*. New York: Random House, 1940.

Shelton, Charles. *Achieving Moral Health: An Exercise Plan for Your Conscience*. New York: Crossroad Publishing Company, 2000.

Shlain, Leonard. *The Alphabet Versus the Goddess: The Conflict Between Word and Image*. New York: Viking Penguin, 1988.

SHOTTER, John. *Conversational Realities: Constructing Life through Language.* Thousand Oaks, CA: Sage Publications, 2002. First printed 1993 by Sage Publications. Page references are to the 2002 edition.

SIEGEL, Daniel J. *The Developing Mind.* New York: Guilford Press, 2001.

DE SILVA, Padmasiri. "Buddhist Ethics." In *A Companion to Ethics.* Edited by Peter Singer. Oxford: Blackwell Publishers Ltd., 1991.

SMITH, Yves. *Econned: How Unenlightened Self Interest Undermined Democracy and Corrupted Capitalism.* New York: St Martin's Press, 2010.

SPITZER, Robert J. *The Spirit of Leadership: Optimizing Creativity and Change in Organizations.* Provo, UT: Executive Excellence, 2000.

STONE, Deborah. *Policy Paradox: The Art of Political Decision Making.* New York: W. W. Norton, 1997.

SWINDALL, Clint. *Engaged Leadership: Building a culture to overcome employee disengagement.* Hoboken, NJ: Prentice Hall, 2002.

TARNAS, Richard. *The Passion of the Western Mind.* New York: Harmony Books, 1991.

THALER, Richard, and Cass R. Sunstein. *Nudge.* New York: Penguin Books, 2009.

TILLICH, Paul. *Love, Power, and Justice: Ontological Analysis and Ethical Applications.* New York: Oxford University Press, 1960. First printed 1954 by Oxford University Press. Page references are to the 1960 edition.

TRONTO, Joan C. *Moral Boundaries: A Political Argument for an Ethic of Care.* New York: Routledge, 1993.

TWEEDY, Kate Chenery. *Secretariat's Meadow: The Land, the Family, the Legend.* Manakin-Sabot, VA: Dementi Milestone, 2010.

VAUGHAN, Diane. *The Challenger Launch Decision: Risky Technology, Culture, and Deviance at NASA.* Chicago: University of Chicago Press, 1997.

VELASQUEZ, Manuel. *Business Ethics: Concepts and Cases.* 5th ed. Englewood Cliff, NJ: Prentice Hall, 2002.

WALZER, Michael. *Spheres of Justice: A Defense of Pluralism and Equality.* New York: Basic Books, 1984.

WEATHERFORD, Jack. *The History of Money.* New York: Three Rivers Press, 1998.

WEBER, Max. *The Protestant Ethic and the Spirit of Capitalism.* New York: Routledge, 1992.

WHYTE, David. *The Heart Aroused: Poetry and the Preservation of the Soul in Corporate America*. New York: Currency Doubleday, 1994.

WILBER, Ken. *Sex, Ecology, Spirituality: The Spirit of Evolution*. 2nd ed. Boston: Shambhala, 2000.

WILSON, Edward O. *Consilience: The Unity of Knowledge*. New York: Vintage Books, 1998.

WINTER, Steven L. *A Clearing in the Forest: Law, Life and the Mind*. Chicago: University of Chicago Press, 2001.

WITTE, John Jr. *Law and Protestantism: The Legal Teachings of the Lutheran Reformation*. New York: Cambridge University Press, 2002.

WUTHNOW, Robert. *After Heaven: Spirituality in America Since the 1950s*. Berkeley, CA: University of California Press, 1998.

Index

A

Absolute
  immanent 75
  transcendent 75

Abramoff, Jack 298

accountability
  Responsibilities Lens 176

Adam and Eve 20, 41

adult
  dignity 111
  emotions 126
  fully functioning   *See* fully functioning
  independent responsible 26, 41, 45, 95
  young 132

Affirmative action 33, 35

African-American
  discrimination 7
  economic life 224, 251
  education 251
  investing 315

Age of Enlightenment 6, 72, 150, 155, 171

Age of Reason 6

agreements
  identification of 70, 83, 87
  implied 181
  explicit/implicit 190

"Allegory of the Cave" 76, 147

anarchy
  abuse of autonomy 44

anecdotes 122

apathy
  abuse of equality 45
  elections 55
  work 118

Aquinas, Saint Thomas
  Relationship Lens 150
  Reputation Lens 269
  Results Lens 203
  teleological tradition 72

Aristotle
  Reputation Lens 262, 269
  Results Lens 150, 203
  teleological tradition 72
  theoretical evolution 149
  virtue ethics 8, 318

assumptions
  core 79, 121, 155
  factual 121
  flawed 121
  inherited 121
  shared 73
  underlying 167

Augustine, Saint
  deontological tradition 72
  Relationship Lens 150, 235
  Responsibilities Lens 171

authority
  component of belief systems 99
  contested 30
  ethical agent 211

evidence 122
leadership 184
religious 72, 172
role of 24
vice 194
author's expertise 122

autonomy
abuse of 44
common good 42
economics and 51, 55, 58, 172
equality, and 2, 11, 40, 42, 67, 72
Kant commitment to 188
lack of 245
market 110
merit 54
political 70, 173
Relationship Lens 125, 176
Responsibilities Lens 125, 176
secondary values 44
values in tension 104, 181

B

bailouts 54, 225

Baird Decision Model™
SEE Be Attentive, Be Intelligent, Be Reasonable,
Be Responsible, Be Reflective

balance
Responsibilities Lens 176

Bandura, Albert 118, 159

basic liberties 248, 261

Bateson, Mary Catherine
Composing a Life 275

Be Attentive
defined 12
decision step 94-102
Relationship Lens 242-244
Reputation Lens 274-278
Responsibilities Lens 178-180
Results Lens 210-212

Be Intelligent 13, 102
defined 12
decision step 94-102
Relationship Lens 244-247
Reputation Lens 278-279
Responsibilities Lens 180-182
Results Lens 212-216

Be Reasonable 13, 120
defined 12
decision step 94-102
Relationship Lens 247-261
Reputation Lens 279-301
Responsibilities Lens 182-196
Results Lens 210-212

Be Responsible 14, 130
defined 12
decision step 94-102
Relationship Lens 261-264
Reputation Lens 301-304
Responsibilities Lens 178-180
Results Lens 210-212

Be Reflective 15, 139
defined 12
decision step 94-102
Relationship Lens 264-266
Reputation Lens 304-306
Responsibilities Lens 178-180
Results Lens Lens 210-212

belief system(s)
authority
natural sciences 31
philosophical and religious 28
social sciences 31
anecdotes 122
core values 73
definition 15
experience 25
formation of 15
of others 36
reason 25
Results Lens 211

EVERYDAY ETHICS: *Making Wise Choices in a Complex World*

duties
  delight in 163
  fiduciary 108
  higher 111
  human 71, 127, 171
  imperfect 181
  perfect 181
  personal 128, 151, 156, 160
  prima facie 181
  traditional 191

E

EchoStar 185

Ecologizing 57, 113, 254

ecology
  biology 96, 138
  moral 236
  of care 253
  sociological 236

economic justice
  consumer worldview 52
  producer worldview 55
  ecological worldview 57

economic(s)
  assumption 121
  balance with ethics 6, 51, 57
  core beliefs and 73
  core values and 51
  defined 51
  growth 57
  law and 81
  neuro- 161
  macro 261
  self-interest 84
  social democracy 61, 86
  social science 31, 72
  technology and 68
  triple bottom line 60
  value-free vs. normative 60

economizing 57, 113

economy
  controlled 63
  deregulated 68
  feudal 51, 260
  general 15, 54, 56, 117, 122, 205, 313
  global 87, 138, 154, 225, 314
  industrial 7, 315
  market   *See* market economy
  mixed 61, 63
  neo-mercantile 63
  new 153
  political position 74
  political organization and 61
  pure 72
  regulated 73, 153
  rural 260
  stable 40
  sustainable 64, 138
  United States 314

Ecuador 88

Edsel, Ford 214

efficiency
  contrast with excellence 336-337
  defined 56
  economic 61, 195
  goal of 102
  growth 55, 57, 314
  value 108, 208

egoism 149

Einstein, Albert
  relativity, theory of 7

Eisner, Michael 103

Eldredge, John 175

emotional intelligence 5, 19, 206

emotivism 49

empathy, vantage point of
  blind spot 128, 193, 223, 256, 297

EVERYDAY ETHICS: *Making Wise Choices in a Complex World*

J

K

L

EVERYDAY ETHICS: *Making Wise Choices in a Complex World*

EVERYDAY ETHICS: *Making Wise Choices in a Complex World*

military 63
security 70
taxation policy 61

neutral event
  naming of 15, 19
  noticing 17
  responding to 23

Newton, Isaac
  Newtonian physics 32
  teleological tradition 72

nihilism
  defined 88
  Lonergan 90

Nirvana 75, 77, 78

Noddings, Nel
  Caring 173
  ethic of care 11, 160
  feminist philosopher 126
  Responsibilities Lens 170
  universal ideal 174

notice, right to 249

Nozick, Robert 196

O

option(s)
  Be Intelligent 92, 102, 119
  detailed exploration 114
  neutral event 23-24
  Relationship Lens 247, 261
  Reputation Lens 279, 301
  Responsibilities Lens 182, 197
  Results Lens 216, 228
  values-in-tension 113, 171

Oresme, Nicole 75

original position
  birth position 236
  discrepancy in wealth 196

inheritance 53
reflective equilibrium 248

original sin 77

P

Paine, Lynn Sharp
  stakeholders 103
  Value Shift 60, 103

Palmer, Parker
  Reputation Lens 268

PATRIOT Act, USA 67

people   SEE person(s)

pension funds
  CalSTRS 103
  Disney Corporation 103
  stock market 315
  value of 225

perfect duties 180-181

person
  ethical,   SEE ethical person
  moral,   SEE moral person
  self-regulating 14

physics
  Newtonian 32
  quantum 32

Plato
  "Allegory of the Cave" 76, 147
  deontological tradition 72
  individual tradition 74
  Relationship Lens 235
  Responsibilities Lens 171
  theoretical evolution 5, 149

pluralism
  ethical 151
  moral 149
  religious 168

plurality
    religious 28

Ponzi scheme 54

postmodern
    constructive 89, 90, 147, 206
    conversation 8-9
    era 6
    ethics 189, 236
    dualism 31
    movement 6, 80, 163
    theorists 88, 211, 235

postmodernism
    cafeteria believers 89
    conversation 8-9

poverty
    barriers 228
    charity and 84
    cycle of 227
    ignore 227
    increasing 83
    response to 261
    view of 26
    wages 57

privacy
    employee 110, 220
    personal 29, 280, 311
    right of 67
    Responsibilities Lens 176

Protestant
    Catholicism and 30, 155
    Reformation 6, 52, 72, 155, 172
    conception of the human 76-77
    racism 7
    tradition 72, 73, 172
    work ethic 82
    world view 28

prudential judgment 316-318

Puritan 78, 82

Q

quota 251-252

R

rationalism 89, 140

rationality
    abuse of 47
    common good 42
    secondary values 46

Rawls, John
    A Theory of Justice 8
    balance of power 157
    Bellah and 238
    claims of justice 160
    community tradition 74
    deontological tradition 8, 72, 146
    just savings principle 250
    Nozick and 196
    procedural justice 75, 150
    Relationship Lens 234ff
    theoretical evolution 149

reflection
    aesthetic 121
    in decision process expedient 100
    moral 121

reflective equilibrium 242, 248

reflective process 139, 173 203

regulations
    relationship to ethics 64

Relationship Lens
    blind spots 128
    compared to Reputation Lens 269, 289
    compared to Results Lens 228
    conceptual map 234
    core ethical framework 5-6
    core heuristic questions 15, 153
    core justice frameworks 291

EVERYDAY ETHICS: *Making Wise Choices in a Complex World*

tipping point
  Results Lens 218
  Relationship Lens 238

triple bottom line 60, 115, 138

truth
  absolute 36
  assess 13
  ethical 8
  integrity and 181, 289
  theory of 25
  "truth" 17, 72, 90
  universal 9, 32, 173, 318

truthfulness
  Reputation Lens 273
  Responsibilities Lens 176
  loyalty, in tension with 181

U

uncertainty principle 7

United States, The
  central narrative 50
  charity as value 49
  Civil Rights Movement 35
  civility as value 293
  Congress 66
  economy 52, 61, 63, 312, 314
  education 227
  equality of opportunity 50, 221
  health care 124
  immigration policy 86, 153, 260
  individual power 172, 225
  justice as value 239
  living wage 57
  public policy 246
  Puritan heritage 78
  religious diversity 28, 89
  radical individualism 8, 40, 237
  security as value 67, 214, 261
  separation of church and state 28
  simplicity as value 78, 82

slavery 159, 237, 261
tax policy 59, 86, 261
whistleblowers as valued 106
world view 16

unity of life
  criteria for action 310
  defined 293
  Reputation Lens 293-294

universalizability
  criteria for action 197
  defined 184
  Responsibilities Lens 184-185

utilitarianism
  cost-benefit 283
  critique of 216
  definition 157
  hedonistic 211
  ideal 211
  Mill, John Stuart 152
  Modern Period 212
  Reputation Lens 283
  Results Lens 202, 203, 205
  teleology 71

utils of happiness
  criteria for action 228
  defined 219
  Results Lens 219-222

V

values in tension
  Baird Decision Model 104
  critical thinking skills 120
  Relationship Lens 246
  Reputation Lens 278
  Responsibility Lens 181
  Results Lens 215
  stakeholder 13

vantage point
  of empathy SEE empathy

EVERYDAY ETHICS: *Making Wise Choices in a Complex World*

EVERYDAY ETHICS: *Making Wise Choices in a Complex World*